OTHER A TO Z GUIDES FROM
THE SCARECROW PRESS, INC.

120. *The A to Z of Middle Eastern Intelligence* by Ephraim Kahana and Muhammad Suwaed, 2009.
121. *The A to Z of the Baptists* William H. Brackney, 2009.
122. *The A to Z of Homosexuality* by Brent L. Pickett, 2009.
123. *The A to Z of Islam, Second Edition* by Ludwig W. Adamec, 2009.
124. *The A to Z of Buddhism* by Carl Olson, 2009.
125. *The A to Z of United States–Russian/Soviet Relations* by Norman E. Saul, 2010.
126. *The A to Z of United States–Africa Relations* by Robert Anthony Waters Jr., 2010.
127. *The A to Z of United States–China Relations* by Robert Sutter, 2010.
128. *The A to Z of U.S. Diplomacy since the Cold War* by Tom Lansford, 2010.
129. *The A to Z of United States–Japan Relations* by John Van Sant, Peter Mauch, and Yoneyuki Sugita, 2010.
130. *The A to Z of United States–Latin American Relations* by Joseph Smith, 2010.
131. *The A to Z of United States–Middle East Relations* by Peter L. Hahn, 2010.
132. *The A to Z of United States–Southeast Asia Relations* by Donald E. Weatherbee, 2010.
133. *The A to Z of U.S. Diplomacy from the Civil War to World War I* by Kenneth J. Blume, 2010.
134. *The A to Z of International Law* by Boleslaw A. Boczek, 2010.
135. *The A to Z of the Gypsies (Romanies)* by Donald Kenrick, 2010.
136. *The A to Z of the Tamils* by Vijaya Ramaswamy, 2010.
137. *The A to Z of Women in Sub-Saharan Africa* by Kathleen Sheldon, 2010.
138. *The A to Z of Ancient and Medieval Nubia* by Richard A. Lobban Jr., 2010.
139. *The A to Z of Ancient Israel* by Niels Peter Lemche, 2010.
140. *The A to Z of Ancient Mesoamerica* by Joel W. Palka, 2010.
141. *The A to Z of Ancient Southeast Asia* by John N. Miksic, 2010.
142. *The A to Z of the Hittites* by Charles Burney, 2010.
143. *The A to Z of Medieval Russia* by Lawrence N. Langer, 2010.
144. *The A to Z of the Napoleonic Era* by George F. Nafziger, 2010.
145. *The A to Z of Ancient Egypt* by Morris L. Bierbrier, 2010.
146. *The A to Z of Ancient India* by Kumkum Roy, 2010.
147. *The A to Z of Ancient South America* by Martin Giesso, 2010.
148. *The A to Z of Medieval China* by Victor Cunrui Xiong, 2010.
149. *The A to Z of Medieval India* by Iqtidar Alam Khan, 2010.
150. *The A to Z of Mesopotamia* by Gwendolyn Leick, 2010.
151. *The A to Z of the Mongol World Empire* by Paul D. Buell, 2010.
152. *The A to Z of the Ottoman Empire* by Selcuk Aksin Somel, 2010.
153. *The A to Z of Pre-Colonial Africa* by Robert O. Collins, 2010.
154. *The A to Z of Aesthetics* by Dabney Townsend, 2010.
155. *The A to Z of Descartes and Cartesian Philosophy* by Roger Ariew, Dennis Des Chene, Douglas M. Jesseph, Tad M. Schmaltz, and Theo Verbeek, 2010.
156. *The A to Z of Heidegger's Philosophy* by Alfred Denker, 2010.
157. *The A to Z of Kierkegaard's Philosophy* by Julia Watkin, 2010.
158. *The A to Z of Ancient Greek Philosophy* by Anthony Preus, 2010.
159. *The A to Z of Bertrand Russell's Philosophy* by Rosalind Carey and John Ongley, 2010.
160. *The A to Z of Epistemology* by Ralph Baergen, 2010.
161. *The A to Z of Ethics* by Harry J. Gensler and Earl W. Spurgin, 2010.

The A to Z of the Gypsies (Romanies)

Donald Kenrick

The A to Z Guide Series, No. 135

THE SCARECROW PRESS, INC.
Lanham • Toronto • Plymouth, UK
2010

Published by Scarecrow Press, Inc.
A wholly owned subsidary of
The Rowman & Littlefield Publishing Group, Inc.
4501 Forbes Boulevard, Suite 200, Lanham, Maryland 20706
http://www.scarecrowpress.com

Estover Road, Plymouth PL6 7PY, United Kingdom

British Library Cataloguing in Publication Information Available

Library of Congress Cataloging-in-Publication Data

The hardback version of this book was cataloged by the Library of Congress as
follows:

Kenrick, Donald.
  Historical dictionary of the Gypsies (Romanies) / Donald Kenrick. — 2nd ed.
    p. cm. — (Historical dictionaries of peoples and cultures ; no. 7)
    Includes bibliographical references.
    1. Romanies—History—Dictionaries. 2. Romanies—Biography—
Dictionaries. I. Title.
DX115.K46 2007
909'.0491497003—dc22   2007002232

ISBN 978-0-8108-7561-6 (pbk. : alk. paper)

☉™ The paper used in this publication meets the minimum requirements of
American National Standard for Information Sciences—Permanence of Paper
for Printed Library Materials, ANSI/NISO Z39.48-1992.
Printed in the United States of America

Contents

Editor's Foreword

This volume, which was previously in the Europe country series, is now where it belongs, in a special series of Historical Dictionaries of Peoples. Like many other peoples, the Gypsies, or Romanies, or whatever other names they are known by, cannot be defined simply by the country they live in, and this far-flung community inhabits several dozen countries. Indeed, while many of them have settled down voluntarily or through official persuasion, large numbers still move about within and among countries, being genuine Travelers, another alternative name. But while they do live in different places and have different characteristics depending on where they live, which language they speak, and which clans they belong to, they nevertheless recognize one another and themselves as part of a special people, and they have increasingly created organizations and engaged in cultural and other activities to express this solidarity. There is also no doubt that outsiders regard them as a different group no matter what their passports may say.

Thus, *Historical Dictionary of the Gypsies (Romanies): Second Edition* has to cover a very broad field, providing information of a fairly general nature, so we can learn more about this people, but also specific entries on the different countries they live in, where the situation may differ substantially from place to place and also one period to another. Other entries present important figures, traditional leaders, politicians and civil rights workers, writers, artists, and musicians—persons in different walks of life who have contributed to the community. There are also entries on various publications and organizations. This comprises most of the dictionary section. The introduction describes the overall situation and how it has been evolving, while the chronology traces the major events from year to year. Of particular interest is the bibliography, which helps readers track down books and articles on multiple aspects of the Gypsies, their history, and their culture that are not easily found by the general public.

It must be obvious that writing a reference work on such a dispersed population, and especially one that has not been sufficiently researched and where much of what is written is not necessarily reliable, is a particularly arduous task. It requires someone who is familiar with many facets and has a passion for detail—someone like Donald Kenrick, who wrote the first edition as well. He has been involved with Gypsy studies for nearly four decades now. Academically, he studied linguistics with special emphasis on Romani dialect. Dr. Kenrick not only has lectured and written extensively on the Gypsies but has also been involved in the Gypsy civil rights movement as secretary of the Gypsy Council and the National Gypsy Education Council in Great Britain. More practically, he served as an interpreter at four World Romany Congresses. The result is an expanded and updated second edition that tells us considerably more than before.

Jon Woronoff
Series Editor

Preface

This publication is designed to be a tool for all those working in civil rights, culture, education, immigration, and politics who need more information concerning a name, date, or event related to the past and current history of the Romany and other Gypsy people. But it will also be of interest for the general reader.

For reasons of space alone, this handbook cannot fulfill the role of a complete who's who, discography, or directory of organizations. The Internet sites listed will be the best way to trace the current contact details for the latter. There are entries for those Gypsies who have become historically significant in their field, many of whom have excelled in music and entertainment, and the representatives of international bodies. Regrettably few scientists appear, as professional people have often hidden their Gypsy origin. Conversely, entertainers proclaim their Romany grandmother with enthusiasm.

This was originally a volume in a series devoted to Europe. Additional entries have been added for several countries on the road the Romanies took from India to the west. I have also included important social topics such as "marriage," and more dates of birth have been traced.

What I hope the reader will find is a concise, yet informative, companion that is accessible and promotes an understanding of the history of the Romany people and other Gypsy groups. Major organizations and museums have been listed as an entry into the subject for those who wish to go deeper. Finally, there is a small selection of current addresses of the main journals and websites (at the end of the bibliography) to help readers get in touch with the vast network available to them.

As the Romani proverb says: It is easy to begin but hard to finish. I welcome corrections and suggestions for inclusion in any future edition.

Acknowledgments

I have drawn heavily on the knowledge of experts in different fields, the published literature, and websites listed in the bibliography. The following experts have been particularly helpful for this new edition: Antonio Gomez Alfaro, Milena Hübschmannová, Valdemar Kalinin, Elena Marushiakova, and Veselin Popov.

Amy Lewin, Emanuelle de la Lubie, and Sunny La Valle assisted in the research for the A–Z entries. The final form of the entries remains, however, the responsibility of the author.

Reader's Note

For typographical reasons, Romani words cited are spelled in accordance with general international usage, not in the standard alphabet adopted by the fourth World Romany Congress for writing the language.

- *č* = *ch*, pronounced as in *church*
- *š* = *sh*, as in *ship*
- *ž* = *zh*, as in *leisure*
- *x* as in *loch* or German *doch*
- *rr* is a guttural or retroflex *r* (as opposed to trilled or flapped *r*), depending on the dialect

It has regrettably not been possible to reproduce in one font all the accents used in all the languages of Europe.

Gypsy and *Traveler* have been capitalized and spelled thus—except in citations, names of organizations, and book titles. This volume uses the term *Romani* for the Gypsy language and *Romany* (Roma) for the people. *Gypsy* and *Romany* are used as synonyms throughout the text except in entries referring to Asia; here the term *Gypsy* implies an industrial or commercial nomad (a so-called peripatetic) not necessarily of Indian origin.

The definition of who is a Gypsy varies. This dictionary includes as Gypsies those who are accepted as such by the community or who proclaim themselves to be Gypsies. A number of non-Gypsy organizations and non-Gypsies whose life or works are relevant to Gypsy history have also been included in the dictionary. They are identified by the name in the entry header being in italics, for example, *SHAKESPEARE, WILLIAM*.

Cross-references in the text are in bold type. The terms *Gypsy, Rom, Roma, Romani,* and *Romany* on their own are, however, never printed in bold.

Acronyms and Abbreviations

ACERT	Advisory Committee for the Education of Romanies and other Travellers
AGO	Association of Gypsy Organisations
BBC	British Broadcasting Corporation
c.	circa; about
CDCC	Conseil de Coopération Culturelle
CDMG	European Committee on Migration
CEDIME-SE	Center for Documentation and Information on Minorities in Europe–Southeast
CMERI	Centre Missionaire Evangelique Rom International
CMG	Communauté Mondiale Gitane
CIR	Comité International Rom
CIS	Commonwealth of Independent States
CIT	Comité International Tzigane
CJPO	Criminal Justice and Public Order Act
CLRAE	Congress of Local and Regional Authorities of Europe
CPRSI	Contact Point for Roma and Sinti Issues
CRT	Centre de Recherches Tsiganes
CSCE	Conference on Security and Cooperation in Europe
ECOSOC	Economic and Social Council (of the United Nations)
ECRE	European Committee on Romani Emancipation
ERRC	European Roma Rights Center
Est.	Established
EU	European Union
fl.	floreat; active
GIRCA	Gypsy International Recognition, Compensation, and Action
GLS	Gypsy Lore Society
hCa	Helsinki Citizens Assembly

IRU	International Romani Union
IRWN	International Roma Women's Network
ITM	Irish Traveller Movement
JGLS	*Journal of the Gypsy Lore Society*
Kolhoz	*Kollektivnoe hozyaistvo* (collective farm)
MBE	Member of the (Order of the) British Empire
MG-S-ROM	Specialist Group on Roma/Gypsies (of the Council of Europe)
MP	Member of Parliament
MRG	Minority Rights Group
NATT	National Association of Teachers of Travellers (UK)
NGO	Nongovernmental organization
OB	Officer of the (Order of the) British Empire
ODIHR	Office for Democratic Institutions and Human Rights
OSCE	Organization for Security and Cooperation in Europe
PER	Project on Ethnic Relations
RRS	Council of Slovak Roma (Slovakia)
SS	*Schutzstaffel* (Storm Troopers)
UK	United Kingdom
UN	United Nations
UNESCO	United Nations Economic and Social Organization
UNICEF	United Nations Children's Fund
UNITE	Unified Nomadic and Independent Transnational Education
USSR	Union of Soviet Socialist Republics
WRC	World Romany Congress

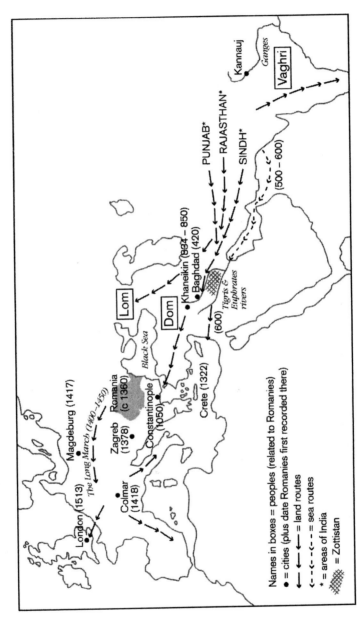

The Romanies' Route from India to Europe

Names in boxes = peoples (related to Romanies)
● = cities (plus date Romanies first recorded there)
→ = land routes
–‹– –‹– = sea routes
* = areas of India
▨ = Zottistan

Vaghri

Kannauj

Ganges

PUNJAB*
RAJASTHAN*
SINDH*

(500 – 600)

Khaneikin (834 – 850)
Baghdad (420)

Tigris & Euphrates rivers

Lom

Dom

(600)

Crete (1322)

Black Sea

Romania (c 1360)

Zagreb (1378)

Constantinople (1050)

Magdeburg (1417)

The Long March (1400–1450)

London (1513)

Colmar (1418)

Chronology of Gypsy History

224–241 Persia: In the reign of Shah Ardashir, Gypsies first come from India to work.

420–438 Persia: Bahram Gur, Shah of Persia, brings Gypsy musicians from India.

661 Arab Empire: Indians (*Zott*) brought from India to Mesopotamia.

669/670 Arab Empire: Caliph Muawiya deports Gypsies from Basra to Antioch on the Mediterranean coast.

c. 710 Arab Empire: Caliph Walid resettles Zott from Mesopotamia to Antioch.

720 Arab Empire: Caliph Yazid II sends still more Zott to Antioch.

820 Arab Empire: Independent Zott state established in Mesopotamia.

834 Arab Empire: Zott defeated by Arabs and many of them resettled in border town of Ainzarba.

855 Arab Empire: Battle of Ainzarba fought. Greeks defeat the Arabs and take Zott soldiers and their families as prisoners to Byzantium.

c. 1050 Byzantium: Acrobats and animal doctors active (called *athingani*) in Constantinople.

1192 India: Battle of Terain fought. Last Gypsies leave for the west.

1290 Greece: Gypsy shoemakers appear on Mount Athos.

1322 Crete: Nomads reported on the island.

1347 Byzantium: Black Death reaches Constantinople. Gypsies move west again.

1348 **Serbia:** Gypsies reported in Prizren.

1362 **Croatia:** Gypsies reported in Dubrovnik.

1373 **Corfu:** Gypsies reported on the island.

1378 **Bulgaria:** Gypsies living in villages near Rila Monastery.

1384 **Greece:** Gypsy shoemakers reported in Modon.

1385 **Romania:** First transaction recorded of Gypsy slaves.

1399 **Bohemia:** The first Gypsy is mentioned in a chronicle.

1407 **Germany:** Gypsies visit Hildesheim.

1416 **Germany:** Gypsies expelled from Meissen region.

1417 **Holy Roman Empire:** King Sigismund issues safe conduct to Gypsies at Lindau.

1418 **France:** First Gypsies reported in Colmar. **Switzerland:** First Gypsies arrive.

1419 **Belgium:** First Gypsies reported in Antwerp.

1420 **Holland:** First Gypsies reported in Deventer.

1422 **Italy:** Gypsies come to Bologna.

1423 **Italy:** Andrew, Duke of Little Egypt, and his followers set off to visit Pope Martin V in Rome. **Slovakia:** Gypsies reported in Spissky.

1425 **Spain:** Gypsies reported in Zaragoza.

1447 **Catalonia:** Gypsies first reported.

1453 **Byzantium:** Turks capture Constantinople. Some Gypsies flee westward. **Slovenia:** A Gypsy smith is reported in the country.

1468 **Cyprus:** Gypsies first reported.

1471 **Switzerland:** Parliament meeting in Lucerne banishes Gypsies.

1472 **Rhine Palatinate:** Duke Friedrich asks his people to help the Gypsy pilgrims.

1485 **Sicily:** Gypsies first reported.

1489 **Hungary:** Gypsy musicians play on Czepel Island.

1492 **Spain:** First draft of the forthcoming law of 1499 drawn up.

1493 **Italy:** Gypsies expelled from Milan.

1498 **Germany (Holy Roman Empire):** Expulsion of Gypsies ordered.

1499 **Spain:** Expulsion of the Gypsies ordered (Pragmatica of the Catholic Kings).

1500 **Russia:** Gypsies first reported.

1504 **France:** Expulsion of Gypsies ordered.

1505 **Denmark:** Two groups of Gypsies enter the country. **Scotland:** Gypsy pilgrims arrive, probably from Spain.

1510 **Switzerland:** Death penalty introduced for Gypsies found in the country.

1512 **Catalonia:** Gypsies expelled. **Sweden:** First Gypsies arrive.

1514 **England:** Gypsies first mentioned in the country.

1515 **Germany:** Bavaria closes its borders to Gypsies.

1516 **Portugal:** Gypsies mentioned in literature.

1525 **Portugal:** Gypsies banned from the country. **Sweden:** Gypsies ordered to leave the country.

1526 **Holland:** Transit of Gypsies across country banned.

1530 **England and Wales:** Expulsion of Gypsies ordered.

1534 **Slovakia:** Gypsies executed in Levoca.

1536 **Denmark:** Gypsies ordered to leave the country.

1538 **Portugal:** Deportation of Gypsies to colonies begins.

1539 **Spain:** Any males found nomadizing to be sent to galleys.

1540 **Scotland:** Gypsies allowed to live under own laws.

1541 **Czech lands:** Gypsies accused of starting a fire in Prague.

1544 **England:** Gypsies deported to Norway.

1547   **England:** Boorde publishes specimens of Romani.

1549   **Bohema:** Gypsies declared outlaws and to be expelled.

1553   **Estonia:** First Gypsies appear in the country.

1554   **England:** The death penalty is imposed for any Gypsies not leaving the country within a month.

1557   **Poland and Lithuania:** Expulsion of Gypsies ordered.

1559   **Finland:** Gypsies appear on the island of Åland.

1562   **England:** Provisions of previous acts widened to include people who live and travel like Gypsies.

1563   **Italy:** Council of Trent affirms that Gypsies cannot be priests.

1573   **Scotland:** Gypsies to either settle down or leave the country.

1574   **Ottoman Empire:** Gypsy miners working in Bosnia.

1579   **Portugal:** Wearing of Gypsy dress banned. **Wales:** Gypsies first reported.

1580   **Finland:** First Gypsies reported on the mainland.

1584   **Denmark and Norway:** Expulsion of Gypsies ordered.

1586   **Belarus:** Nomadic Gypsies expelled.

1589   **Denmark:** Death penalty imposed for Gypsies not leaving the country.

1595   **Romania:** Stefan Razvan, the son of a slave, becomes ruler of Moldavia.

1611   **Scotland:** Three Gypsies hanged (under 1554 law).

1633   **Spain:** Pragmatica of Felipe IV takes effect. Gypsies expelled.

1637   **Sweden:** Death penalty introduced for Gypsies not leaving the country.

1692   **Austria:** Gypsies reported in Villach.

1714   **Scotland:** Two female Gypsies executed.

1715 **Scotland:** Ten Gypsies deported to Virginia.

1728 **Holland:** Last hunt clears out Gypsies.

1746 **Spain:** Gypsies to live in named towns.

1748 **Sweden:** Foreign Gypsies expelled.

1749 **Spain:** Round-up and imprisonment of all Gypsies ordered.

1758 **Austro-Hungarian Empire:** Maria Theresa begins assimilation program.

1759 **Russia:** Gypsies banned from St. Petersburg.

1765 **Austro-Hungarian Empire:** Joseph II continues assimilation program.

1776 **Austria:** First article published on the Indian origin of the Romani language.

1782 **Hungary:** Two hundred Gypsies charged with cannibalism.

1783 **Russia:** Settlement of nomads encouraged. **Spain:** Gypsy language and dress banned. **United Kingdom:** Most racial legislation against Gypsies repealed.

1791 **Poland:** Settlement Law introduced.

1802 **France:** Gypsies in Basque provinces rounded up and imprisoned.

1812 **Finland:** Order confines nomadic Gypsies in workhouses.

1822 **United Kingdom:** Turnpike Act introduced: Gypsies camping on the roadside to be fined.

1830 **Germany:** Authorities in Nordhausen remove children from their families for fostering with non-Gypsies.

1835 **Denmark:** Hunt for Travelers in Jutland. **United Kingdom:** Highways Act strengthens the provisions of the 1822 Turnpike Act.

1837 **Spain:** George Borrow translates St. Luke's Gospel into Romani.

1848 **Transylvania:** Serfs (including Gypsies) emancipated.

1849 **Denmark:** Gypsies allowed into the country again.

1855 **Romania:** Gypsy slaves in Moldavia emancipated.

1856 **Romania:** Gypsy slaves in Wallachia emancipated.

1860 **Sweden:** Immigration restrictions eased.

1865 **Scotland:** Trespass (Scotland) Act introduced.

1868 **Holland:** New immigration of Gypsies reported.

1872 **Belgium:** Foreign Gypsies expelled.

1874 **Ottoman Empire:** Muslim Gypsies given equal rights with other Muslims.

1875 **Denmark:** Gypsies barred from the country once more.

1876 **Bulgaria:** In a pogrom, villagers massacre the Muslim Gypsies in Koprivshtitsa.

1879 **Hungary:** National conference of Gypsies held in Kisfalu. **Serbia:** Nomadism banned.

1886 **Bulgaria:** Nomadism banned. **Germany:** Bismarck recommends expulsion of foreign Gypsies.

1888 **United Kingdom:** Gypsy Lore Society established.

1899 **Germany:** Police Gypsy Information Service set up in Munich by Alfred Dillmann.

1904 **Germany:** Prussian Parliament unanimously adopts proposal to regulate Gypsy movement and work.

1905 **Bulgaria:** Sofia conference held, demanding voting rights for Gypsies. **Germany:** A census of all Gypsies in Bavaria is taken.

1906 **Finland:** Mission to the Gypsies set up. **France:** Identity card introduced for nomads. **Germany:** Prussian minister issues special instructions to police to "combat the Gypsy nuisance."

1914 **Norway:** Some 30 Gypsies are given Norwegian nationality. **Sweden:** Deportation Act also makes new immigration of Gypsies difficult.

1918 **Holland:** Caravan and House Boat Law introduces controls.

1919 **Bulgaria:** Istiqbal organization founded.

1922 Germany: In Baden, all Gypsies are to be photographed and fingerprinted.

1923 Bulgaria: Journal *Istiqbal* [Future] starts publication.

1924 Slovakia: A group of Gypsies is tried for cannibalism; they are found innocent.

1925 USSR: All-Russian Union of Gypsies established.

1926 Germany: Bavarian state parliament brings in a new law "to combat Gypsy nomads and idlers." **Switzerland:** Pro Juventute starts a program of forced removal of Gypsy children from their families for fostering. **USSR:** First moves to settle nomadic Gypsies.

1927 Germany: Legislation requiring the photographing and finger-printing of Gypsies instituted in Prussia. Bavaria institutes laws forbidding Gypsies to travel in large groups or to own firearms. **Norway:** The Aliens Act bars foreign Gypsies from the country. **USSR:** Journal *Romani Zorya* (Romany Dawn) starts publication.

1928 Germany: Nomadic Gypsies in Germany are to be placed under permanent police surveillance. Prof. Hans F. Günther writes that it was the Gypsies who introduced foreign blood into Europe. **Slovakia:** Pogrom takes place in Pobedim.

1929 USSR: Nikolai Pankov's Romani book *Buti i Džinaiben* [Work and Knowledge] published.

1930 Norway: A doctor recommends that all Travelers be sterilized. **USSR:** First issue of the journal *Nevo Drom* [New Way] appears.

1931 USSR: Teatr Romen opens in Moscow.

1933 Austria: Officials in Burgenland call for the withdrawal of all civil rights for Gypsies. **Bulgaria:** Journal *Terbie* [Education] starts publication. **Germany:** The National Socialist (Nazi) Party comes to power, and measures against Jews and Gypsies begin. Gypsy musicians barred from the State Cultural Chamber. Sinto boxer Johann Trollmann stripped of his title as light-heavyweight champion for "racial reasons." Act for the Prevention of Hereditarily Ill Offspring, also known as the Sterilization Act, instituted. During "Beggars' Week," many Gypsies arrested.

Latvia: St. John's Gospel translated into Romani. **Romania:** General Association of the Gypsies of Romania founded. National conference held. Journals *Neamul Tiganesc* [Gypsy Nation] and *Timpul* [Time] start publication. **USSR:** Teatr Romen performs the opera *Carmen*.

1934 **Germany**: Gypsies who cannot prove German nationality expelled. **Romania:** Bucharest "international" Congress.

1935 **Germany:** Marriages between Gypsies and Germans banned. **Yugoslavia:** Journal *Romano Lil* starts publication.

1936 **Germany:** The right to vote removed from Gypsies. **June**—Internment camp at Marzahn opened. General Decree for Fighting the Gypsy Menace instituted. **November**—Racial Hygiene and Population Biological Research Unit of the Health Office begins its work. The minister of war orders that Gypsies should not be called up for active military service.

1937 **Poland:** Janusz Kwiek elected king of the Gypsies.

1938 **Germany:** **April**—Decree on the Preventative Fight against Crime: All Gypsies classed as antisocial. Many Gypsies arrested to be forced labor for the building of concentration camps. **June**—Second wave of arrests to provide labor to build the camps. **Autumn**—Racial Hygiene Research Center begins to set up an archive of Gypsy tribes. **October**—National Center for Fighting the Gypsy Menace established. **December**—"Fight against the Gypsy Menace" ordered. **USSR:** Government bans Romani language and culture.

1939 **Germany:** **September**—Deportation of 30,000 Gypsies planned. **October**—Settlement Decree: Gypsies not allowed to travel. **November**—Gypsy fortune-tellers arrested and sent to Ravensbrück concentration camp.**German-occupied Czech lands:** Nomadism forbidden. **German-occupied Poland:** Special identity cards issued for Gypsies.

1940 **Austria: August**—Internment camp built in Salzburg. **October**—Internment of the Gypsies in Burgenland ordered. **November**—Internment camp for Gypsies set up in Lackenbach. **Czech lands: August**—Labor camps set up in Lety and Hodonín. **France: April**—Government opens internment camps for nomads. **Germany:** Heinrich Himmler orders the resettlement of Gypsies in western Poland.

1941 Baltic States: December—Governor Hinrich Lohse orders that Gypsies should "be given the same treatment as Jews." **Croatia:** Jasenovac concentration camp opened. **Czech lands: October**—Decision that Gypsies from the so-called Protectorate are to be sent to a concentration camp. **Germany: March**—Exclusion of Gypsy children from school begins. **July**—Reinhard Heydrich, Heinrich Himmler's deputy, brings the Gypsies into the plans for a Final Solution to the "Jewish problem." **Latvia: December**—All 101 Gypsies in the town of Libau are executed. **Poland: October**—A Gypsy camp is set up in the Jewish ghetto of Lodz for 5,000 inmates. **Serbia: May**—German military commander states that Gypsies will be treated as Jews. **November**—German military command orders the immediate arrest of all Jews and Gypsies, to be held as hostages. **Slovakia: April**—Decree separating the Gypsies from the majority population. **USSR: June**—*Schutzstaffel* (Storm Troopers) Task Forces move into the occupied areas and systematically kill Jews and Romanies. **September**—Task forces carry out mass executions of Jews and Romanies in the Babi Yar valley. **December**—Task Force C murders 824 Gypsies in Simferopol. **Yugoslavia: October**—German army executes 2,100 Jewish and Gypsy hostages (as reprisal for soldiers killed by partisans).

1942 Bulgaria: August—6,500 Gypsies registered by the police on one day. **Croatia: May**—The government and the Ustasha order the arrest of all Gypsies and their deportation to the extermination camp in Jasenovac. **Germany: March**—A special additional income tax is levied on Gypsies. **July**—A decree of the army general staff again orders that Gypsies not be taken for active military service. **September**—Himmler and Justice Minister Otto Thierack agree to transfer any Gypsies in prison to concentration camps. **December**—Himmler issues the order to deport the Gypsies in Greater Germany to the concentration camp of Auschwitz-Birkenau. **Poland: January**—All Sinti and Romanies from the Lodz ghetto are transported and gassed at Chelmno. **April**—Romanies are brought into the Warsaw ghetto and kept in the prison in Gesia Street. **May**—All Gypsies in the Warsaw district to be interned in Jewish ghettoes. **July**—Several hundred Polish Romanies killed at Treblinka extermination camp. **Romania: Spring and Summer**—Some 20,000 Romanies are deported to Transnistria. **Serbia: August**—Harald Turner, head of the German military administration, announces that "the Gypsy question has been fully solved."

1943 Poland: January—Gypsies from Warsaw ghetto transferred to the extermination camp at Treblinka. **February**—First transports of Sinti and Romanies from Germany are delivered to the new Gypsy Section in Auschwitz-Birkenau concentration camp. **March**—At Auschwitz, the *Schutzstaffel* (Storm Troopers) (SS) gasses some 1,700 men, women, and children. **May**—A further 1,030 men, women, and children gassed by the SS at Auschwitz. SS major Dr. Josef Mengele transferred at his own request to Auschwitz. **July**—Himmler visits the Gypsy Section in Auschwitz and orders the Gypsies killed. **USSR: November**—Minister for the Occupied Eastern Territories orders all nomadic Gypsies in the territories are to be treated as Jews.

1944 Belgium: January—A transport of 351 Romanies and Sinti from Belgium dispatched to Auschwitz. **Holland: May**—A transport of 245 Romanies and Sinti sent to Auschwitz. **Poland: 2 August**—1,400 Gypsy prisoners are sent from Auschwitz to Buchenwald concentration camp. The remaining 2,900 Gypsies are killed in the gas chamber. **Slovakia: Autumn**—Romanies join the fight of partisans in the National Uprising.

1945 27 January—At 3:00 P.M., the first Soviet soldiers reach the main camp at Auschwitz and find one Romany among the survivors. **May**—World War II ends in Europe. All surviving Gypsies freed from camps. **Bulgaria:** Gypsy Organization for the Fight against Fascism and Racism set up. **Germany:** Nuremburg Trials of Nazi leaders begin. Crimes against Gypsies are included in the charges.

1946 France: Mateo Maximoff's novel *The Ursitory* published. **Poland:** Roma Ensemble founded.

1947 Bulgaria: Teatr Roma established in Sofia.

1951 Bulgaria: Teatr Roma in Sofia closed.

1952 France: The Pentecostal movement among Gypsies starts.

1953 Denmark: Gypsies readmitted to the country.

1958 Bulgaria: Nomadism banned. **Czechoslovakia**: Nomadism banned. **Hungary:** National Gypsy organization established.

1960 England and Wales: Caravan Sites Act reduces provision of caravan sites. **France:** Communauté Mondiale Gitane established.

1962 German Federal Republic: Courts rule that Gypsies were persecuted for racial reasons. **Norway:** Government Gypsy Committee established.

1963 Ireland: Report of the Commission on Itinerancy published. **Italy:** Opera Nomadi education scheme set up. **Yugoslavia:** Gypsies move to Shuto Orizari after Skopje earthquake.

1964 Ireland: Itinerant Action Group set up.

1965 France: Communauté Mondiale Gitane banned. Comité International Tzigane set up. **Italy:** Pope Paul VI addresses some 2,000 Gypsies at Pomezia.

1966 United Kingdom: Gypsy Council set up.

1967 Finland: National Gypsy Association established.

1968 England and Wales: Caravan Sites Act: Councils to build sites. **Holland:** All districts must build caravan sites.

1969 Bulgaria: Segregated schools are set up for Gypsies. **Europe:** Council of Europe Assembly passes a positive resolution on Gypsies. **Yugoslavia, Macedonia:** Abdi Faik elected a member of Parliament.

1970 Norway: Report published on proposed work with the Gypsies. **United Kingdom:** National Gypsy Education Council established.

1971 United Kingdom: First World Romany Congress held near London. Advisory Committee on the Travelling People starts work in Scotland.

1972 Czechoslovakia: Sterilization program for Gypsies begins. **France:** Band known as Los Reyes (later the Gypsy Kings) founded. **Sweden:** Stockholm's Finska Zigenarförening founded. **United Kingdom:** Romany Guild founded.

1973 German Federal Republic: Three Gypsies shot by farmer in Pfaffenhofen. **Scandinavia:** Nordiska Zigenarrådet set up to link organizations. **Yugoslavia, Macedonia:** Radio broadcasts in Romani start from Tetovo.

1975 Europe: Council of Europe Committee of Ministers adopts a positive resolution on nomads. **Hungary:** The first issues of the magazine *Rom som* [I Am a Romany] appear.

1977 Netherlands: Legalization of 500 "illegal" Gypsy immigrants. **United Kingdom:** Cripps Report on Gypsies published. **United Nations:** Subcommission passes resolution on protection of Gypsies.

1978 Switzerland: Second World Romany Congress held in Geneva.

1979 Hungary: National Gypsy Council formed. First national exhibition of self-taught Gypsy artists held. **Norway:** ABC Romani primer produced for mother-tongue teaching. **Romania:** St. John's Gospel published underground in Romani. **United Nations:** International Romani Union recognized by the United Nations Economic and Social Council.

1980 Yugoslavia: Romani grammar in Romani published in Skopje.

1981 Europe: Congress of Local and Regional Authorities of Europe resolution on helping nomads held. **German Federal Republic:** Third World Romany Congress in Göttingen held. **Poland:** Pogrom instigated in Oswiecim. **Yugoslavia:** Gypsies granted national status on an equal footing with other minorities.

1982 France: New François Mitterrand government promises to help nomads.

1983 Europe: Council of Ministers passes a resolution on stateless nomads. **Italy:** Gypsy caravans removed from Rome at the start of the Annus Sanctus. **United Kingdom:** First national Pentecostal convention held. Belfast Traveller Education Development Group established in Northern Ireland. **Yugoslavia, Kosovo:** Romani teaching begins in one school.

1984 Europe: European Parliament passes a resolution on aiding Gypsies. **India:** Chandigarh Festival held.

1985 France: First International Exhibition (Mondiale) of Gypsy Art held in Paris. **Ireland:** Report of the Travelling People Review Body published. **Sweden:** Gypsy family attacked in Kumla with stones and a firebomb.

1986 France: International Gypsy conference held in Paris. **Spain:** Gypsy houses set on fire in Martos. **Yugoslavia, Sarajevo:** International Romany seminar held.

1988 **Hungary:** Organization Phralipe founded.

1989 **Europe:** Council of the Europe resolution on promoting school provision for Gypsy and Traveler children held. **Germany:** Government initiates the deportation of several thousand foreign Gypsies from the country. Gypsies demonstrate at the site of the concentration camp at Neuengamme against the deportation of asylum seekers. **Hungary:** Roma Parliament set up. **Poland:** First Romane Divesa Festival held. **Romania:** Border guards shoot party of Gypsies. **Spain:** Gypsy houses attacked in Andalusia.

1990 **Poland:** Permanent exhibition on Romanies opens in Tarnow. Fourth World Romany Congress held near Warsaw; standard alphabet for Romani adopted by the Congress. Journal *Rrom p-o Drom* [Romanies on the Road] starts publication. **Romania:** Miners attack Romany quarter in Bucharest. **Yugoslavia:** Egyptian Associations formed in Kosovo and Macedonia.

1991 **Czech Republic:** Romani teaching starts at Prague University. **Italy:** Ostia international conference held. **Macedonia:** Romanies have equal rights in new republic. **Poland:** Pogrom instigated in Mlawa. **Slovakia:** Government gives Romanies nationality status and equal rights. **Ukraine:** Police attack settlement of Velikie Beryezni.

1992 **Hungary:** Arson attack occurs on Gypsies in Kétegyháza. **Poland:** Attack occurs on remaining Gypsies in Oswiecim. **Slovakia:** Romathan Theater established in Košice. **Ukraine:** Mob attacks Gypsy houses in Tatarbunary. **United Nations:** Commission on Human Rights passes resolution on protection of Gypsies. Gypsies recognized as an ethnic group.

1993 **Bulgaria:** A crowd of Bulgarians attacks the Gypsy quarter in Malorad, killing one Romany man. **Czech Republic:** Tibor Danihel drowns running away from skinhead gang. Seven Romanies deported from Ustí nad Labem to Slovakia. **Europe:** Congress of Local and Regional Authorities of Europe Resolution on Gypsies held. **Germany:** First International Conference on Romani Linguistics held in Hamburg. **Hungary:** Gypsies recognized as a national minority. International Conference held in Budapest. **Macedonia:** Romani language officially introduced in schools. **Romania:** Three Gypsies killed in pogrom in Hadareni. **Slovakia:** Cyril Dunka beaten up by police after a parking incident. **United Kingdom:** Scottish Gypsy/Traveller Association set up. **United Nations:** Romany Union upgraded to Category II consultative status.

1994   France: Standing Conference of Romany Associations formed in Strasbourg. **Hungary:** Organization for Security and Cooperation in Europe meeting sets up Contact Point for Roma and Sinti Issues in Budapest, based initially in Warsaw. Gypsies vote for their local Romany councils. **Poland:** Office for Democratic Institutions and Human Rights organizes Warsaw seminar on Romanies. Gypsy boy beaten up and houses inhabited by Romanies attacked in Debica. **Spain:** European Congress held in Seville. **United Kingdom:** Criminal Justice Act: Nomadism criminalized.

1995   Austria: Four Roma killed by a bomb in Oberwart, Burgenland. **Bulgaria:** One Gypsy dies following an arson attack on a block of flats in Sofia. Angel Angelov shot by police in Nova Zagora. **Czech Republic:** Tibor Berki killed by skinheads in Zdár nad Sázavou. **Europe:** Council of Europe sets up specialist advice group on Romanies. **Hungary:** Second International Exhibition (Mondiale) of Gypsy Art held. International Romani Union organizes "Sarajevo" Peace Conference in Budapest. Gypsies attacked and injured in Kalocsa. **Poland:** Gypsy couple murdered in Pabianice. Grota Bridge settlement of Romanian Gypsies in Warsaw dispersed by police. Residents deported across the border to Ukraine. **Slovakia:** Mario Goral burned to death by skinheads in Ziar nad Hronom. **Turkey:** Zehala Baysal dies in police custody in Istanbul.

1996   Albania: Fatmir Haxhiu dies of burns after a racist attack. **Bulgaria:** Kuncho Anguelov and Kiril Perkov, deserters from the army, shot and killed by military police. Three Romanies beaten by skinheads in Samokov. **Czech Republic:** Romany children banned from swimming pool in Kladno. **Europe:** European Court of Human Rights rejects the appeal by Mrs. Buckland against the refusal of planning permission in England for her caravan. First meeting of the Committee of Experts of the Council of Europe held. **France:** Second meeting of the Standing Committee of Gypsy Organizations in Strasbourg held. **Greece:** Police raid camp in Attica. Police officer shoots Anastasios Mouratis in Boetia. **Hun-**

gary: European Roma Rights Center set up in Budapest. **Ireland:** National Strategy on Traveller Accommodation proposed. **Poland:** Houses occupied by Romanies attacked in Wiebodzice. **Romania:** Twenty-one Romany houses burned down in Curtea de Arges. Mircea-Muresul Mosor shot and killed by chief of police in Valcele. **Serbia:** Gypsies attacked in Kraljevo. **Slovakia:** Eighteen-year-old Romany youth beaten to death by skinheads in Poprad. Jozef Miklos dies when his house is set on fire in Zalistie. **Spain:** Romany Union's second "Sarajevo" Peace Conference, in Gasteiz (Vittoria). **Turkey:** Five thousand evicted from Selamsiz quarter of Istanbul. **Ukraine:** "Mrs. H" raped by police in Mukacevo. Two brothers shot by police in Velikie Beryezni.

1997 Bulgaria: February—Killing of three Gypsies by police reported. Police attack the Gypsy quarter in Pazardjik. **November**—International conference on Gypsy children and their education held. **Czech Republic: February**—Appeals court in Pilsen quashes acquittal of inn owner Ivo Blahout on a charge of discrimination. **March**—Four skinheads sentenced to prison in connection with the 1993 death of Tibor Danihel. **August**—Several hundred Romanies fly to Canada to seek asylum. Monument erected at Hodonin to concentration camp victims. **France: March**—Jose Ménager and Manolito Meuche shot dead by police in Nantes. **Greece: April**—One hundred families evicted from Ano Liosia. Partially resettled in a guarded camp. **Hungary: February**—Gypsies beaten up in Szombathely police station and in a police car in Mandatany in separate incidents. **May**—Fifth annual International Conference on Culture held in Budapest. **Norway: November**—In Bergen, Ian Hancock receives Thorolf Rafto Prize on behalf of the Romany people. **Poland: June**—Romanies attacked in Wiebodzice. **Romania: January**—Mob attacks Gypsy houses in Tanganu village. **Spain: November**—European Congress of Gypsy Youth held in Barcelona. **Turkey: January**—Mob attacks Gypsies in Sulukule district of Istanbul. **Ukraine: January**—Gypsies beaten by police in four separate incidents in Uzhorod. **United Kingdom: November**—National Front demonstrates in Dover against asylum seekers from the Czech and Slovak republics.

1998 Bulgaria: November—Prince Charles of Britain visits Stolipino, Romany quarter of Plovdiv. **Czech Republic: 4–6 September**—International Romany cultural festival RESPECT held in Prague.

December—International Conference on the Roma at Castle Stirin. **United Kingdom: 16 May**—Music festival in London with Czech and Polish Gypsy bands composed of asylum seekers. **October**—Home Secretary Jack Straw introduces visas for Slovak citizens to keep out asylum seekers. **19 October**—In Wales, Cardiff County Council organizes a Gypsy and Traveller Awareness Day. **United States:** New Jersey governor Christine Whitman signs Assembly Bill 2654, which rescinds the last anti-Gypsy law of any U.S. state. **December**—International Romani Union delegation, led by Rajko Djurić, attends Nazi Gold Conference on Holocaust assets in Washington.

1999 Bulgaria: June—Sofia Conference on Peace and Security held for Roma in the Balkans. **Czech Republic: January**—More than 100 prominent persons sign protest to government over locating of pig farm on concentration camp site. **France:** Loi Besson encourages the provision of council-run caravan sites. **Greece: February**—Local authority sets fire to five Roma houses in Aspropyrgos to construct Olympic sports facilities. **Macedonia: September**—Government admits 500 Roma refugees from Kosovo held for a week at the border. **Romania: December**—International Conference on Public Policies and Romany Women held in Bucharest. **Turkey: November**—Organization for Security and Cooperation in Europe Istanbul Conference welcomes the development of the Romany civil rights movement.

2000 Romania: January—Doctors of the World colloquium on Gypsies in Europe held in Bucharest. **Czech Republic: July**—Fifth World Romany Congress held in Prague. **Finland:** Publication of St. Luke's Gospel in Romani. **Germany: May**—Conference on "Die unerwünschte Deutschen" ("The Unwanted Germans") held in Stuttgart. **Poland:** International Romani Union and Romany National Congress sign joint declaration in Warsaw. **Vatican: March**—Pope John Paul II asks forgiveness for the mistreatment of Gypsies by Catholics. **United Kingdom: September**—A thousand police block access to the traditional Horsmonden Fair.

2001 Germany: November—Romany writers meet in Cologne and agree to set up an international association. **India: April**—International Romani Union leaders visit the Romano Kher (Nehru House) in Chandigarh. **Italy: November**—Two hundred members of the National

Alliance march to protest new Roma housing in Rome. **Macedonia: January**—Magazine *Roma Times* begins publication. **Poland: August**—Permanent Romany Holocaust exhibition opened at Auschwitz. **Russia: July**—Thirty skinheads attack a Gypsy camp in Volgograd, killing two adults. **Serbia: July**—Anti-Roma graffiti appear in Panchevo and Surdulica. **South Africa:** Roma attend the World Conference against Racism, held in Durban.

2002 Croatia: September—One hundred Croat parents prevent Roma children from entering a newly integrated school in the village of Drzimurec-Strelec. **Finland:** *Drabibosko liin*, the first ABC reader for Gypsies in Finland, published. **July:** International Romani Writers Association founded in Helsinki. **France: October**—Delegation representing a dozen Gypsy organizations meets minister of the interior to discuss slow process of caravan site provision. **Hungary: June**—A Rom—Laszlo Teleki—appointed as the state secretary for Roma affairs. **Ireland: March**—Housing Act criminalizes trespass by caravans. **July**—Traveller Movement pickets the Dail (Parliament) opposing the new Housing Act. **Poland: May**—Romany National Congress organizes an alternative International Romany Congress in Lodz. **United Kingdom: November**—Exhibition held of Gypsy children's photos at the Victoria and Albert Museum, London.

2003 Croatia: October—Ms. Mukic, deputy ombudsman, criticized for condemning segregation in schools. **Hungary: June**—World Bank sponsors international conference on Roma in eastern Europe in Budapest. **Ireland:** Internal Security Bill proposes fines of 3,750 euros for Travelers who trespass. **Switzerland: August**—British Gypsies protest against UK policy at a UN conference in Geneva. **United Kingdom:** Fifteen-year old Irish Traveler Johnny Delaney killed in a racist attack in Liverpool. **5 November**—Villagers in Sussex burn caravan and effigies of Gypsies.

2004 France: 16 December—Council of Europe and the European Roma and Travellers Forum sign a partnership agreement in Strasbourg. **Greece:** More Gypsy settlements are cleared away near the Olympic Games venues in Athens. **Spain: November**—Gypsy organizations hire Saatchi and Saatchi to mount a campaign to change public attitudes toward Gypsies. **United States: 8 November**—Sen. Hillary Clinton presents the keynote address at the conference Plight of the Roma, held at Columbia University.

2005 Austria: 4 February—President Heinz Fischer attends a memorial ceremony for the four Roma killed in 1995. **Bulgaria: 31 August**—Authorities destroy 25 Roma houses in the Hristo Botev district of Sofia. **Europe: 28 April**—European Parliament adopts a resolution on Roma rights. **17 May**—European Court of Human Rights opens the case against discrimination in the city of Ostrava, Slovakia. **Finland: September**—International Romany Music Festival held in Porvoo. **German: 12 September**—International Antiziganismus Conference held in Hamburg. **Norway: 27 April**—Gypsies take part in demonstration outside the Parliament in Oslo stressing need for education. **Russia: January**—Four hundred Roma leave the town of Iskitim after a pogrom. **Slovakia: 17 March**—United Nations Committee on the Elimination of Racial Discrimination rules that Slovakia's housing policies violate international law. **Spain: 13 September**—The flamenco musical *Los Tarantos* (based on *Romeo and Juliet*) opens in Madrid. **United Kingdom: May**—Sylvia Dunn stands for Parliament from Folkestone against Conservative Party leader Michael Howard. **25 July**—Government announces £8 million fund for new and refurbished caravan sites. **October**—A Scottish parliamentary committee criticizes the government for not improving the quality of life of Gypsy and Traveler families.

Introduction

Describing the early history of the Gypsies is like putting together a jigsaw puzzle when some of the pieces are missing and parts of another puzzle have been put into the box. The Gypsies suddenly appeared in Europe speaking an Indian language, yet there is no sure trace of their passage across the Middle East. But their language is the key to the route of their travels as they borrowed words from the various peoples they met as they journeyed west.

The Gypsies, or Romanies, are an ethnic group that arrived in Europe around the 14th century. Scholars argue about when and how they left India, but it is generally accepted that they did emigrate from northern India sometime between the 6th and 11th centuries, then crossed the Middle East and came into Europe. Some stayed in the Middle East. The Nawwar in particular are mentioned in the dictionary. Their language (closely related to European Romani) also belongs to the North Indian group, alongside Hindi and Punjabi.

The word *Gypsy* is an abbreviation of "Egyptian," the name by which the Romany immigrants were first called in western Europe because it was believed they came from Egypt. The French word *gitan* and Spanish *gitano* also come from this etymology. The German word *Zigeuner* and Slav *tsigan* or *cigan* have a different source. They come from the Greek word *athinganos*, meaning "heathen." This term was originally used of a heretical sect in Byzantium and, because the Gypsies who arrived in Europe were not Christians, they were given the name of this sect.

The Gypsies' name for themselves is *Rom* (with the plural *Roma* in most dialects). This is generally considered to be cognate with the Indian word *dom*, whose original meaning was "man." Even groups (such as the Sinti) that do not call themselves *Rom* still preserve this word in their dialect in the sense of "husband."

Some six million Gypsies or Romanies live in Europe, and they form a substantial minority in many countries. The vast majority have been settled for generations. Most still speak the Romani language. As the Romanies are an ethnic group and not a class, individuals pursue various professions; some are rich and others poor. It is only in western Europe that Gypsies are seen as a nomadic people and that the term *Gypsy* is loosely used for industrial nomads who are not of Indian origin.

EARLY HISTORY

The ancestors of the Gypsies of Europe began to leave India from the sixth century onward. Some left voluntarily to serve the rich courts of the Persian and later Arab dynasties in the Middle East. Others were brought as captives. A third, smaller group, who were nomadic, found that their way back to India had been cut off by conflict and instead moved westward.

The first Gypsy migration into Europe during the 14th and 15th centuries included farmworkers, blacksmiths, and mercenary soldiers, as well as musicians, fortune-tellers, and entertainers. They were generally welcome at first as an interesting diversion in the dull everyday life of that period. Soon, however, they attracted the antagonism of the three powers of the time: the state, the church, and the guilds. The civil authorities wanted everyone to settle legally at a permanent address, to have a fixed name, and to pay taxes. The church was worried about the heresy of fortune-telling, while the guilds did not like to see their prices undercut by these newcomers who worked all hours of the day and night, with wives and children helping, trading from tents or carts.

Other factors also led to feelings of mistrust toward the newcomers. They were dark-skinned, itself a negative feature in Europe, and were suspected in some countries of being spies for the Turks because they had come from the east. Some problems were also caused by small groups of Gypsies who claimed—with some justification—to be Christians fleeing from Muslim invaders from Turkey and lived mainly by asking for alms.

It was not long before these feelings of antagonism and mistrust led to a reaction. As early as 1482, the assembly of the Holy Roman Empire passed laws to banish the Gypsies from its territory. Spain introduced similar legislation 10 years later, and other countries soon followed. The punishment for remaining was often death. There was some migration to Poland, mirroring that of the Jews. The policy of expulsion failed in most cases, however, as the countries to which they were deported often returned them quietly over the borders. Only the Scandinavian countries and the Netherlands managed to efface all visible trace of Gypsies for over two centuries. Most governments finally had to try a new policy—enforced integration or assimilation.

In Spain in 1499 and in Hungary in 1758, new laws required Gypsies to settle down or leave the country. They had to become land workers or be apprenticed to learn a craft. But they also had to be assimilated into the native population. Everywhere laws forbade Gypsies to wear their distinctive colorful clothes, to speak their language, to marry other Gypsies, or to ply their traditional trades. As a result of these policies, today large populations of long-settled Gypsies can be found in Spain and Hungary, while in Romania Gypsy land workers and craftspeople were reduced to a status below that of serfs, to virtual slavery.

The latter part of the 19th century saw a new migration westward as Romania released its Gypsies from bondage. Many thousands emigrated, some as far as America, Australia, or South Africa. Well over a million Gypsies live in North and South America today, with the Kalderash clan forming the majority.

The nomadic Gypsies, however, have survived as a distinctive group until the present day. The reason for this was partly the inefficiency of local constabularies but also that the Gypsies developed as a fine art the practice of living on the border of two countries or districts and slipping over the border when the forces of law and order approached. Also, the nobility and large landowners throughout Europe protected the Gypsies. They encouraged seminomadic families to stay on their land and were able to employ the men as seasonal laborers. The women could serve in the house or sing and dance when guests came.

In the 19th and 20th centuries in western Europe, Gypsies encountered problems finding stopping places. Camping on the side of the main roads was made difficult by laws such as the UK Highways Act of 1835. Large shantytown settlements developed on wasteland, but then the authorities stepped in and evicted the families. Such incidents occurred in England, starting with the Epping Forest eviction of 1894 and continuing until the 1960s. In this way, many families who would have settled down were forced back into nomadism.

Discriminatory laws (on language and dress) fell into abeyance, but laws against nomadism remained a threat, in both western and eastern Europe, to those Gypsies practicing traditional crafts. Studies from all over the world have shown that sedentary peoples have an inherent fear of the nomad, even when the latter performs useful services. The policy of banning nomadism without helping the nomads to settle proved a failure throughout Europe, and Gypsy nomadism continued unchecked until World War II.

THE HOLOCAUST

When the Nationalist Socialist Party came to power in Germany in 1933, the nomadic Gypsies were already subject to restrictions. But the Nazis regarded Gypsies as a race and made both nomads and sedentaries subject to the Nuremberg Laws of 1935. These forbade marriages between Gypsies and "Aryan" Germans. Adolf Hitler's Germany saw the Gypsies as no less a danger to the purity of the German race than the Jews and set about their isolation and eventually their destruction.

This policy of exclusion was a contrast to the assimilationist policies practiced in the past. Gypsies were now not allowed to practice music as a profession, and boxers were similarly barred from competition. Next, Gypsy children were excluded from school. Camps were set up for nomads on the edge of towns. They were guarded, and the inmates were not allowed to practice their traditional trades but were put into labor gangs. Even sedentary Gypsies were removed from their houses and placed in these internment camps.

In 1939 it was decided to send all 30,000 Gypsies from Germany and Austria to Poland. In May 1940 the first steps in this program were taken with the expulsion of more than 3,000. The deportations were stopped largely because of a shortage of transport. In 1942 Heinrich Himmler, the head of the *Schutzstaffel* (Storm Troopers) (SS), signed the so-called Auschwitz Decree, and in the following year some 10,000 German Gypsies were sent to the Auschwitz concentration camp. A sterilization campaign was undertaken both within and outside the camps. The slave labor of the Gypsies was needed, for example, in the underground factories where the V1 and V2 rockets were made, but they were not to be permitted to reproduce.

In the occupied countries of eastern Europe, the *Einsatzgruppen* task forces massacred Gypsies in the woods outside the towns where they lived. Then extermination camps were opened, the four largest being Belzec, Chelmno, Sobibor, and Treblinka. Gypsies were brought to these camps—sometimes in their own caravans—and shot or gassed, alongside Jews. It is estimated that between a quarter million and a half million Gypsies were killed during the Nazi period.

AFTER 1945

In the first years following the end of the Nazi domination of Europe, the Gypsy community was in disarray. The small educational and cultural organizations that had existed before 1939 had been destroyed. The family structure was broken with the death of the older people, the guardians of tradition. While in the camps, the Gypsies had been unable to keep up their customs—the *Romanía*—concerning the preparation of food and the washing of clothes. They solved the psychological problems this presented by not speaking about the time in the camps. Only a small number of Gypsies could read or write, so they could not tell their own story. But also they were unwilling to tell their stories to others, and few non-Gypsies were interested anyway. In the many books written describing the Nazi period and the persecution of the Jews, Gypsies usually appear as a footnote or an appendix.

It was hard for the Gypsies to come to terms with the Holocaust, for a persecution on this scale had never occurred before. There had been executions of smaller numbers, but nothing like this. A group of survivors in Munich began collecting evidence of the Gypsy genocide, but it was not until 20 years after the downfall of Hitler that Jewish writers such as Miriam Novitch, Ben Sijes, and Sylvia Steinmetz made available to the public a documentation of the fate of the Gypsies under the Nazis. No global reparations were made, and not many individuals received restitution. Eventually those Gypsies who held German citizenship did receive compensation for their suffering. In recent years, Swiss banks and other international funds have helped individual aging survivors.

After 1945 in both eastern and western Europe, a return to nomadism was discouraged, if not suppressed, though many Yugoslav Romanies came west as migrant workers. In western Europe, the supply of empty land for caravans has diminished. The increasing speed of motor traffic makes living on the side of the road, whether in a horse-drawn wagon or a truck-drawn caravan, too dangerous. Gypsies were largely seen as a social problem to be integrated into the wider community. A term often used was "resettlement," although most of the nomads concerned had never been settled in the first place. Pressure from central governments to set up camp sites was largely ignored by the local authorities, the Netherlands being an exception.

In the east, they were one more minority likely to cause trouble to the monocultural states created by communism. Here, where several million Gypsies lived under totalitarian rule, they were not allowed to form organizations, and their language was again suppressed. In most countries of eastern Europe, the Gypsy population was very large, and policies were evolved to meet the challenge of this large unassimilated minority. In the case of the Soviet Union, Josef Stalin had decided that the Gypsies had no land base and therefore could not be a nation, and their earlier status as a nationality was abolished. Assimilated Gypsies were encouraged to change the "nationality" in their passports to that of the majority and answer the census questions, for example, as Serbs or Russians. The few activists were sent into internal exile or imprisoned, such as the parliamentarian Shakir Pashov in Bulgaria.

In eastern Europe, too, the small numbers of nomads were forcibly prevented from traveling by laws and by measures such as shooting or confiscating their horses and removing the wheels from their caravans. Here and there, however, Gypsy national sentiment was still alive. In Czechoslovakia, organizations were formed and began to demand their rights—a demand temporarily quashed after Soviet troops entered Prague in 1968.

In the west after the end of World War II, the communities were smaller in number and largely continued or returned to being nomadic. But it was in the west that the foundations of an international Gypsy organization could be formed. The real beginning was the committee known as the Comité International Tzigane, set up in Paris by Vanko Rouda. This body organized the first World Romany Congress, and since then further international congresses have been held by the In-

ternational Romani Union. The fourth Congress in Warsaw in 1990—
as the political changes in eastern Europe began—saw the attendance
for the first time of delegations or individuals from Romania, the Soviet Union, and even Albania. The fifth Congress was held in Prague
with considerable support from the Czech government and international organizations. The emergence of the rival Romani National Congress has, however, not helped the Gypsies to present a united front for
their aspirations.

The idea of Romanestan, a homeland for the Gypsies, emerged in
Poland in the 1930s, clearly influenced by the Zionist movement. Since
1945 this has not been seriously considered, though many intellectuals
are fostering the link with the "Motherland" of India. Two festivals have
been held in Chandigarh (Punjab) to which Gypsy intellectuals and musicians were invited from Europe. Some Gypsy writers have introduced
Hindi and Sanskrit words into their poetry.

RECENT POLITICAL CHANGES IN EASTERN EUROPE

With the fall of the totalitarian regimes in Eastern Europe came a new
freedom to form organizations. The new opportunities for travel both
from and to Eastern Europe have enabled the holding of international
Gypsy festivals such as those in Bratislava and Gorzow, in addition to
formal conferences. Newspapers opened as fast as pavement cafés. The
Gypsies who had never completely forgotten how to trade privately
were the first to set up small businesses. Their ability to survive the
changes better than their compatriots led to jealousy and an outbreak of
anti-Gypsy violence in Poland. The road to capitalism was not as
smooth as had been expected, and with no Jews to act as scapegoats,
the population of Eastern Europe in general turned to the Gypsies as the
reason for their real or imagined troubles.

Freedom also meant freedom for right-wing racists to organize, and
this movement was facilitated by a falling away of the control previously exercised by the police. As early as January 1990, a crowd of 700
Romanians and ethnic Hungarians attacked the Gypsy quarter in Turu
Lung, Romania. Thirty-six of the 42 houses belonging to Romanies
were set on fire and destroyed. Two similar incidents took place that
year in Romania, resulting in the death of four Gypsies. In September

1990, skinheads attacked Romany houses in Eger and Miskolc, Hungary. The following year saw a pogrom in Mlawa, Poland, where nine houses were destroyed, and Bohemia (Czechoslovakia), where a Gypsy was killed during an attack by skinheads on a Romany club. Between January 1990 and August 1991 there were 88 racist attacks reported in Eastern Europe, during which 20 Romanies were killed. Police have often stood by during these attacks and are sometimes themselves aggressive toward the Gypsies. In Rostock in the former East Germany, a refugee center inhabited by Romanies among others was burned down by right-wing rioters. These attacks have continued to the present day, though they are now less common; a selection is listed under each country entry and in the chronology. It is estimated that more than 220 Romanies have been killed in racial incidents in eastern Europe.

In the former Czechoslovakia, Hungary, Macedonia, and Romania, Gypsy political parties have stood in the elections, alone or alongside established parties, and Romanies have been elected to Parliament partly by the votes of their own people. In Bulgaria, "ethnic" parties are theoretically banned, while the surviving population in Poland is too small to have any political influence, though there are musical groups and cultural centers.

Many Romanies, particularly those from Poland and Romania, have sought asylum in the west since 1990 because of the harassment they were suffering, but very few were granted refugee status. At the end of 1996, the German government announced plans to repatriate 30,000 Gypsies to Romania, from where they had fled to avoid racist attacks during which many houses had been burned. Less has been heard about an earlier repatriation program from Germany to the former Yugoslav republic of Macedonia, while individual families have been less publicly returned from Great Britain and France.

The comparatively smaller Gypsy populations in most western countries saw a revival of national feeling as they came into contact with the Romani-speaking communities of the east. These had retained their traditions and under the new regimes found it easier to travel and to invite other Gypsies to their festivals and competitions. The Romani language is being revived in the west by the influx of immigrant and refugee families for whom it is still the dominant community language.

The European Union and the Council of Europe began to take an interest in the Gypsies by inviting their organizations to send representatives to meetings, with the aim of creating a unified voice, while passing resolutions calling on national governments to work toward improving the living conditions of Gypsies. The overall effect was that Gypsy people have been recognized by cross-national bodies as a minority in their own right and measures have been introduced, if not implemented, in most countries toward improving their situation. The pages of the dictionary will reveal a plethora of meetings and ad hoc organizations that have been trying to exert pressure on national governments to ameliorate the living conditions of the Romanies of eastern Europe in particular. As activist Nicolae Gheorghe recently said, "There is a growing gap between an almost restless activism on the international stage and the situation on the ground, where we are not seeing as much tangible progress as we would like."

The sedentary Gypsies of eastern Europe have quite different needs from the nomadic Gypsies of many western countries. The former's children had not managed to acquire many new skills or paper qualifications, as the years of compulsory education had often been spent in segregated schools or classes. They were the first to go in the new capitalist climate in the East when factories began to downsize and shed surplus labor. They have found it the hardest to obtain new jobs because of discrimination. The nomads of the west are self-employed and primarily seek secure stopping places for their caravans.

Several eastern European countries, including Poland, entered the European Union in May 2004. This has not yet led to the predicted massive new migration to the west. It is noteworthy that the large Spanish Gypsy population has not felt any great desire to migrate—at least no farther than the south of France. Under Gen. Francisco Franco, they were treated as second-class citizens, and the end of official discrimination merely brought a new unofficial discrimination. The Spanish Gypsies or *gitanos* are still at the bottom of the ladder for housing and jobs, while their children are not easily accepted into schools.

In the west, some young Gypsies are coming out of houses and taking to the caravan life again. In eastern Europe, the Romani language is beginning to be taught in schools, and intellectuals of Gypsy origin are finding their roots and reaffirming their identity. Writers have been, pessimistically or optimistically, predicting the disappearance of the Gypsies each generation since they came to Europe at the beginning of the second millennium, but they have survived as an ethnic group and will do so into the foreseeable future.

THE DICTIONARY

– A –

ABAD, MARINA (LA CANILLAS). Spain. Contemporary singer who follows in the Gypsy tradition of flamenco. She stars with the flamenco-rock band Ojos de Brujo.

ABDI, FAIK. Macedonia. Contemporary political activist. In 1948, he was a founding member of **Phralipe**. This was the first Romany cultural association permitted by the postwar Communist authorities in **Macedonia** and acted as a covert forum of Romany national aspirations. Son of a blacksmith, Abdi was one of only a handful of Roma of his generation in the former Yugoslavia to obtain a university degree. He attended the first **World Romany Congress** in London while serving as an MP in the Macedonian Parliament (1969–1974). He later formed the Roma Emancipation Party but suffered from a campaign by the government to undermine his authority through various allegations. He was deprived of his passport for four years to prevent his participation in international meetings.

ACKOVIC, DRAGOLJUB (1952–). Yugoslavia (Serbia). Journalist and broadcaster. He studied at Belgrade University. From his youth, he took part in the drive for the advancement of the Gypsies and participated in international gatherings. He has published many articles and two books—one on the history of the Gypsies in **Yugoslavia** and the other on the **Jasenovac** concentration camp. Ackovic currently works as a journalist and has been responsible for broadcasts in Romani. He is also president of the Romano Kulturako Klubi in Belgrade.

ACTON, THOMAS (1948–). England. Sociologist and author. Professor of Romany Studies at Greenwich University. He has been active in the **Gypsy Council**, **National Gypsy Education Council**, and other bodies.

ADAM, GEJZA. Slovakia. Contemporary teacher and political activist. The president of the Únia Rómskej Obcanskej Iniciatívy (Romany Union Citizens' Initiative). He is currently teaching music in **Košice**.

ADELSBURGER, SIDONIE (1933–1943). Austria. Schoolgirl who died in **Auschwitz** and whose story was retold as fiction by Erich Hackl in his book *Abschied von Sidonie* [Farewell to Sidonie].

ADJAM, TIKNO. France. A mythical resistance fighter and **poet** during World War II. He was apparently invented by a French priest as a vehicle for poems (later printed in 1955 in *Études Tsiganes*) to raise the spirits of Gypsies in the internment camps.

ADVISORY COMMITTEE ON TRAVELLERS. Scotland. Est. 1971. A committee set up to advise the secretary of state for Scotland mainly on the provision of camping sites for **Travelers**. Members include the Traveler **Charles Douglas**. It has published a series of reports with recommendations.

ADVISORY COUNCIL (originally Committee) FOR THE EDUCATION OF ROMANIES AND OTHER TRAVELLERS (ACERT). United Kingdom. Chair: David Cannon. In 1988 the National Gypsy Education Council split, with some of the committee forming ACERT. The council has widened its work with Gypsies from mere **education**.

AFGHANISTAN. Estimated Gypsy population: 7,000. Afghanistan is the first country to the west of **India** and **Pakistan** where we can identify industrial nomads who do not speak any of the local languages but a dialect from North India, in this case, Inku. Aparna Rao has identified four **clans**—Jalali, Pikraj, Shadibaz, and Vangawala—who fall into this definition of "Gypsies." The locals call them "Jat," which is used in a pejorative way: They will say of a child or a teenage girl of whose behavior they do not approve, *"Misle Jat asti"* (They Are Like a Jat).

The Jalali have performing monkeys, sell fruit, and are professional musicians, while the Pikraj trade in donkeys and horses. The Shadibaz also train monkeys, and the Vangawala, as their name indicates, sell bangles. They live on the edge of Afghan society.

ALBAICÍN, JOAQUÍN (1966–). Spain. Author. He has written a history of the Romany people as well as short stories and the novel *La serpiente terrenal*.

ALBAICÍN, MARIA. Spain. 20th-century actress. She was a **film** star in **Spain** in the 1920s whose films included *La fuente mágica*, *Los pianos mecánicos*, and *Café de Chinitas*.

ALBAICÍN, MIGUEL (1949–). Spain. Actor. He appeared in the **film** *El amor brujo*, directed by Antonio Roman.

ALBAICÍN, RAFAEL. Spain. 20th-century bullfighter and actor. He appeared in several **films**, including *La fiesta sigue*, *Maria Antonia*, and *La Caramba*.

ALBANIA. Estimated Gypsy population: 100,000, in addition to a small number of so-called **Egyptians**. The first Gypsies probably arrived in Albania during the 14th century, though the first record is from 1523. From 1468 to 1912, the country was part of the **Ottoman Empire**. **Music** and craftwork were common **occupations** of the Romanies in the area. Around 1920, a law stopped Gypsies from **dancing** in public for money. From 1934—the previous regulation having failed to stop the practice—dancers had to pay a special fee to license their performances. During World War II, the **Italians** who were mainly in control seem to have ignored the Gypsy population, as did the postwar Communist government. Music reemerged as an important occupation.

The fall of Communism, as elsewhere in Eastern Europe, led to the emergence of latent anti-Gypsy sentiments. Early in 1996 stories appeared in the Albanian press of Gypsies killing their own children to sell their organs for transplants. These reports seem to have followed a court case in which some Romanies in Durres were accused of selling their children for adoption. In July 1996 Fatir Haxhiu, a 15-year-old boy, died as a result of being burned during a racist attack. The Gypsies of Albania are mainly Muslim and speak Balkan **dialects** of Romani. A branch of the cultural association **Romani Baxt** has been formed and Albanians have taken part in Romani **summer schools**.

ALIEV, MUSTAFA (MANUSH ROMANO) (1928–2004). Bulgaria. Playwright and politician. He was director of the **Teatr Roma** in Sofia until 1951 when it was closed, after which he worked in a Turkish **theater**. Aliev became an MP on the list of the Union of Democratic Forces in the first post-Communist parliament in 1990. However, at the next election he was not reelected. A booklet has been published in Poland containing some of the songs he collected.

ALL-PARTY PARLIAMENTARY GROUP ON ROMA AFFAIRS. United Kingdom. Est. 2003. Spokesperson: Paul Stinchcombe, MP. The group was set up in 2003 to alert the British government to the Third World living conditions of Roma Gypsies in the **European Union** accession countries of central and eastern Europe. Its report *Roma Rights in Stage One Accession Countries* outlines the situation of Roma in four such nations: **Hungary**, the **Czech Republic**, **Poland**, and **Slovakia**. The group was a joint initiative of **European Dialogue** and Stinchcombe, the Labour Party MP for Wellingborough and Rushden. Its stated purpose is "to raise the profile of Roma human rights issues within the states of central and eastern Europe that are acceding to the EU." All-party groups by definition have to have at least one member from three or more parties.

ALL-PARTY PARLIAMENTARY GROUP ON TRAVELLER LAW REFORM. United Kingdom. Est. 2001. Chairperson: Kevin McNamara, MP. The group, in accordance with House of Commons rules, is composed of MPs from the Labour, Conservative, and Liberal parties. Its stated purpose is to effect the social inclusion of the Gypsy and **Traveler** community and improve relations between the settled and Traveler communities. The Group have been active in debates in Parliament.

ALPHABET. It seems probable that the Gypsies did not bring any writing system with them when they came to Europe. The alphabet given in Jean-Paul Clébert's book *The Gypsies* is spurious. Publications in Romani in the 20th century have used the Latin or Cyrillic alphabets. The first **World Romany Congress** recommended a broad phonetic alphabet based on Latin letters, and most literature produced since then has been in the Latin alphabet.

The alphabet of the first World Romany Congress was as follows:

a b č čh d e f g h ȟ i j k kh l m n o p p ph r s š t th u v z ž

At the second Congress, ȟ was replaced by x. At the fourth World Romany Congress in Warsaw in 1990, a writing system elaborated by linguist **Marcel Cortiade** was adopted. Its purpose was to enable speakers of different **dialects** to use the same spelling system to represent different dialect pronunciations. The presidium of the **International Romani Union** approved the alphabet on 7 April 1990. Later, a meeting of the Language Commission of the Union, held during the Helsinki **Summer School**, recommended that no change be made in the alphabet for a period of 10 years. It has been adopted in the **Netherlands** and **Romania** for **educational** purposes and has been used in a number of publications.

The alphabet accepted at the fourth Congress was as follows:

a b č c ç ćh d e f g h i j k kh l m n o p p ph r rr s š t th θ u v x z ž 3

The letters ç and Ø are used morphophonemically, that is, they always represent the same grammatical form but are pronounced differently. So, in *raklesØe* (to the boy) and *raklenØe* (to the boys), Ø is pronounced as *t* in the former word and *d* in the latter. The letters *ch* and *3* are pronounced differently according to the dialect. Most speakers of **Vlah** dialects would read them as *shy* and *zhy* (approximately the sound in English *treasure*), while speakers of Balkan dialects would read them as aspirated *tch* and (English) *j*.

AMADOR, RAIMUNDO (1959–). Spain. **Flamenco** guitarist. In the 1980s, together with his brother Rafael, he fused flamenco with blues to produce "a fast witty sound" (*The Guardian*). He has recorded with B. B. King. CD: *Isla menor*.

AMALA (FRIENDS) SUMMER SCHOOL. Serbia. The **Summer School**, held in Valkjevo, is a learning center for Roma culture and **art**.

AMARO DROM ("OUR ROAD"). (1) *See* INTERNATIONAL UNION OF THE ROMA OF THE BALTIC STATES AND THE COMMONWEALTH OF INDEPENDENT STATES. (2) A name used for their periodicals by several organizations, including the **Roma Parliament (Hungary)**.

AMAYA, CARMEN (1913–1963). Spain. **Dancer**. She emigrated to the United States at the time of the Spanish Civil War. Her metallic, harsh voice and powerful dancing gained her success in the New York nightclub scene. She appeared in more than 30 **films**. A biography, *A Gypsy Dancer*, was published in 1942.

AMAYA, LORENZA FLORES (LA CHUNGUITA). Spain. Contemporary **dancer**. A **flamenco** performer whose career started in 1965, she is the younger sister of **Micaela Amaya**.

AMAYA, MICAELA (LA CHUNGA) (1937–). Born in Marseilles, **France**, but raised in **Spain**. **Flamenco dancer**. She is the elder sister of **Lorenza Flores Amaya**.

AMAYA, PEPE. Spain. **Flamenco dancer**. He took part in the Paris Exhibition of 1900.

AMENZA KETANE ("WE TOGETHER"). **Music** group from **Austria** whose latest music contains traditional **Lovari** songs together with more modern songs from the pen of Hojda and **Ceija Stojka**.

AMERICA. *See* UNITED STATES.

AMICO ROM. *See* CIOABA, LUMINITA MIHAI; THEM ROMANO.

ANDO DROM. Hungarian band, founded by **Jeno Zsigo**, that plays **Vlah music** in a popular style. They are currently one of the most successful of **Hungary**'s professional Romany ensembles. CDs: *Kaj phirel o Del* [Where God Walks] and *Phari Mamo* [It's Hard, Mother].

ANGOLA. In spite of a ban introduced in 1720, a number of Gypsy families arrived in the country during the time when it was a Portuguese colony. It is unlikely the community survived to the present day.

ANTHEM. *See* "GELEM, GELEM"; NATIONAL ANTHEM.

ANTI-SOCIAL BEHAVIOUR ACT OF 2003. United Kingdom. This Act introduced stronger powers against unauthorized **caravan** sites than the **Criminal Justice and Public Order Act of 1994**.

APPLEBY FAIR. Traditional horse fair in the north of **England** dating back to 1685, attended nowadays mainly by Gypsies and tourists. Attempts were made by local people to ban it in the 1960s and the Boswells—a respected Romani family—set up a defense committee to save the fair. In 2001 the fair was suspended because of foot and mouth disease. It takes place from the second Wednesday in June. Moving the popular **Derby** horse race from midweek to the same weekend to suit **television** audiences has produced a clash of interests. Most Gypsies seem to have opted for Appleby, and in 2003 some 10,000 Gypsies and other **Travelers** attended.

ARCADE FOUNDATION. Sweden. An internationally run Roma organization dedicated to developing and supporting Roma-related projects around the world.

ARGENTINA. *See* BERNAL, JORGE; SOUTH AND CENTRAL AMERICA.

ARLIA. *See* ERLIA.

ARMENIA. Estimated Gypsy population: 10,000. The Romanies came into contact with Armenian speakers on their way from **India** to

Europe as they passed through the Caucasus and what is now northeastern **Turkey**. A number of Armenian words were borrowed by Romani at this time, such as *bokoli* (a type of cake or bread). Some Gypsies remained in Armenia and other parts of what was the **Soviet Union** as well as **Turkey**. They are known as Bosha or **Lom**.

ARPAD, TONI (1929–). Hungary. A **cimbalom** player, he has played with Muszikas and other folk bands, including the Klezmer group Di Naye Kapele.

ART. Since 1945 a number of Gypsy artists have emerged. In **Austria**, **Karl Stojka** and his sister, **Ceija Stojka**, have become well known. Karl's paintings have been exhibited widely outside Austria. In the **Czech Republic**, Rudolf Djurko paints on glass. Another painter in the Czech Republic is Mirka Preussova. Unschooled artists have emerged, particularly in **Hungary** where there have been two national exhibitions of work by self-taught Gypsy artists, the first held in 1979 and the second in 1989. Seventeen artists showed their work at the second exhibition, including **János Balázs**. Artists in **England** include the couple Damian and Delaine LeBas and Daniel Baker. *See also* KOCI, FERDINANT; MONDIALE OF GYPSY ART.

ASHKALI. The Ashkali are an ethnic group in **Kosovo** who are related to the Romanies but do not speak the language. It is likely that they did once speak it. They could alternatively be the descendants of a **nomadic** group of local origin such as the many **Travelers** in Europe who are not of **Indian origin**. Similar groups in **Albania** and **Macedonia** are called *evgit* or *gupt* (as opposed to the Romani Gypsies who are in Albanian called *medjup*) to the extent that the majority population distinguishes between the groups. All three names appear to be derived from the term *Egyptian*.

The largest number of Ashkali live in Ferizaj. Many are educated and have professional qualifications. They have taken the lead in wanting to be called Egyptians, rather than Ashkali, and claim descent from Egyptians who came to the Balkans many centuries ago. There have also been Ashkali political associations, some of which survived the recent conflict. The pro-Albanian Democratic Party of the Ashkali of Kosovo was set up in Ferizaj in 2000.

During the hostilities, Ashkali were attacked first by **Serbs** and then by Albanians, and many fled to neighboring Macedonia and **Montenegro**. The situation at the time of writing is that it is still not safe for Ashkali in many parts of Kosovo.

ASOCIACIÓN SECRETARIADO GENERAL GITANA. Spain. A Catholic-oriented organization operating from Madrid. It works for improvements in the **educational** and employment prospects of Gypsies. The association publishes the bulletin *La Senda* devoted to training and employment.

ASSOCIATION OF GYPSIES/ROMANI INTERNATIONAL. United States. Est. 1995. President: Harold Lush. A Christian nonprofit association set up with the intention of assisting the Gypsy population.

ASSOCIATION OF GYPSY ORGANISATIONS (AGO). United Kingdom. Est. 1977. Secretary: Roy Wells. Formed by ex-members of the **Gypsy Council**, it linked a number of Gypsy and Gypsy-support organizations. Its activities ceased around 1981, except for a small number of projects now run by the independent Gypsy Sites Management and Welfare Committees.

ASSOCIATION OF ROMA COMMUNITIES OF THE BALTIC COUNTRIES AND THE COMMONWEALTH OF INDEPENDENT STATES (ARBCIS). *See* INTERNATIONAL UNION OF THE ROMA OF THE BALTIC STATES AND THE COMMONWEALTH OF INDEPENDENT STATES.

AŠUNEN ROMALEN ("LISTEN, ROMANIES"). A **radio** program broadcast from Belgrade (1981–1987).

ATHINGANI. Czech Republic. An organization for the **education** of Romani youth. *See also* ATSINGANI.

ATKINS REPORT. United Kingdom. The report on the working of the **Caravan Sites Act of 1968** prepared for the British government in 1991 by a firm of private consultants, W. S. Atkins Planning and Management Consultancy. The researchers were G. Clark and

D. Todd. The report accepts that the Caravan Sites Act was intended to enable Gypsies to continue their traditional way of life while using official **caravan** sites and criticizes local councils for not carrying out the provisions of the Act (which has since been repealed). The report also accepted the idea of "designation," by which Gypsies were barred from certain areas of **England** and **Wales**.

ATSINGANI (ATHINGANI) ("UNGODLY"). Heretical Christian sect that flourished in the **Byzantine Empire** during the eighth and ninth centuries. The term was used pejoratively and two Byzantine emperors (Michael II and Nikephorus I) were referred to by their enemies as *athingani*. When the Gypsies arrived from the east, they did not practice Christianity but were probably still following Hinduism or Zoroastrianism. As a result, they, too, were called *athingani*. The Atsingani who settled in Thrace (near the modern town of Plovdiv in **Bulgaria**) from 803 may well have been Gypsies. The term has survived in the names given to the Gypsies in many countries, including *cingene* in **Turkey**, *tsigan* in most Slav-speaking countries, and the **German** *Zigeuner*, **Italian** *zingari*, and **French** *tsigane*.

AUSCHWITZ. Nazi concentration camp in **Poland**. Auschwitz (**Oswiecim**) was opened in 1940, and Gypsies were among its first prisoners. Several transports of **Czech** Gypsies arrived in the camp in 1942. A satellite camp was opened nearby at Auschwitz-Birkenau, and in March 1943 a Gypsy Family Section was created within the barbed-wire fences of the larger camp. Between March 1943 and August 1944, more than 20,000 Romanies were brought to Auschwitz and held in poor conditions. The death rate from disease and malnutrition was high, especially among the children. On 16 May 1944 the *Schutzstaffel* (Storm Troopers) (SS) attempted to take the Gypsies to the gas chambers but were frustrated by resistance with improvised weapons. Following this, all the able adult internees were sent to other camps to work, and the remaining prisoners, some 2,900 **women**, children, and elderly men, were gassed on the night of 2/3 August 1944. The memorial to the several million people killed in Auschwitz has an inscription in Romani. *See also* AUSCHWITZ DECREE; GERMANY; HOLOCAUST.

AUSCHWITZ DECREE (AUSCHWITZ-ERLASS). In December 1942 Heinrich Himmler, head of the Nazi police, issued an order that Gypsies from **Germany** and a number of other, mainly western European, countries should be sent to the new **Auschwitz**-Birkenau camp. Certain categories of Gypsies were to be exempted—for example, those who had served in the armed forces of Germany and any **Sinti** who were considered to be of pure Gypsy blood and capable of forming a small company of nomads that would be preserved as a form of living museum. When the instructions to the police were published early in 1943, these exemptions were mostly ignored, so that when the time finally came to arrest the Gypsies and deport them to the concentration camp, few exceptions were made. *See also* HOLOCAUST.

AUSTRALIA. Size of Gypsy population unknown; estimates range from 500 to 20,000. Many Gypsies were deported to Australia from **England** as petty criminals when this penalty was introduced in 1787. The first was probably Lazarus Scamp, who arrived on the *Scarborough* in 1790. He had been sentenced in Hampshire in 1788 for stealing a sheep. The main **clans** to be found today are English Romanies (descendants of the earlier deportees and newer voluntary emigrants), **Kalderash** (who came from 1898 on), and Roma from Eastern Europe after 1945. Organizations include the Romani Association of Australia (founded 1990) and Romani International Australia. There is an annual gathering, now held at Byron Bay. Notables among the Romani community include university lecturer Kenneth Lee, writer Yvonne Slee, **poets** Lee Fuhler and Henry Lawson, and musician and playwright Brian Hungerford.

AUSTRIA. Estimated Gypsy population: 25,000. Gypsies probably first reached Austria in the 15th century. From 1758 **Maria Theresa** began a policy of settling nomads and assimilating them. She prohibited Gypsies from living in tents, wandering, dealing in horses, speaking in Romani, and marrying other Gypsies. All of these decrees were ignored by the Gypsies, or "New Hungarians" as she wished them to be called. By the 20th century, however, the majority of the Gypsies were at least semisettled, traveling only in the summer.

In 1924 a Gypsy primary school opened in Stegensbach, **Burgenland**, and seems to have operated successfully after a difficult start. No provision was made in the school program for classes in Romani, German being the only language used, but it did include special subjects like the violin and Gypsy history, as well as a topic entitled "Die Zigeuner als Landplage" [The Gypsies as a National Plague]. The Nazis closed the school in 1938.

Austria was annexed to Adolf Hitler's **Germany** in 1938, and the measures already operating against Gypsies in Germany were applied to Austria. Gypsies were fingerprinted and forbidden to leave the country. In June 1938, sporadic arrests began of Romany men, who were sent to the Dachau concentration camp. In autumn 1939 several hundred **women** were arrested and sent to Ravensbrück camp. An internment camp was then set up at Salzburg (Maxglan) to hold Gypsies in readiness for a planned deportation to **Poland** that did not happen until much later. In November 1940 a forced labor camp was opened at Lackenbach. The families were permitted to live together, but conditions in many ways resembled a concentration camp. The highest total of inmates was 2,300 in November 1941. Many died in the early years from the poor conditions and were buried in the nearby **Jewish** cemetery. In 1941, transports containing 2,000 persons were sent from Lackenbach to the Jewish **Lodz Ghetto**, mainly women and children. Few survived. A further 2,600 Gypsies were sent from Austria to **Auschwitz**, including many from the Salzburg camp, which was closed.

One bright chapter in this sad story was the action of Baron Rochunozy, who was determined that none of the families who worked for him should fall into the Nazis' hands. He helped them to escape across the frontier to **Hungary** and was later forced to flee himself. Toward the end of the war, conditions were improved in Lackenbach camp as the prisoners were put to work helping the German war effort and many were able to survive. Two-thirds of the approximately 11,000 Austrian Romanies and **Sinti** are estimated to have perished during the Nazi period.

After 1945, those Gypsies who had been imprisoned in Lackenbach or Salzburg did not get any compensation until 1961. It was not until 1988 that they were put on the same basis as those who had been in the concentration camp at Auschwitz. In 1948 the minister of the interior issued a circular warning, using Nazi terminology, against the "Gypsy plague" and Gypsies passing themselves off as ex-concentration camp prisoners.

The small number of Austrian Romanies and Sinti surviving the **Holocaust** has been augmented by immigrants coming to work, in particular from **Yugoslavia**, and more recently by refugees from Eastern Europe. Considerable anti-Gypsy feeling persists among the Austrian population at large. This sentiment surfaced in 1995 when a sign appeared near the Romani settlement of Oberwart in Burgenland reading (in German) "Romanies back to **India**." When four Gypsies tried to remove it, a bomb blew up, killing all four. The Austrian playwright Elfrieda Jeleneck wrote a play on the subject but, because of the racist attacks on her, decided the play should have its performances in Hamburg and not in Vienna. The probable perpetrator was to commit suicide in prison.

The first Gypsy organization in Austria, Verein Roma, was founded in 1989 in Oberwart and was followed by other groups. In 1993 some Gypsies were given recognition as a *Volksgruppe* (ethnic group)—a status shared, for example, by the Hungarians and Croats. The 5,000 or so Gypsies recognized as the ethnic group are those who belong to families who have been in Austria for three generations. They have some legal rights as a result of this status. There is now a Romani advisory council (which includes non-Romani representatives) that advises the prime minister. A fund (Roma-Fonds) has been set up to provide after-school help for Gypsy children.

The unrecognized Gypsies are in a precarious situation, as they are affected by a number of laws for aliens (e.g., the Asylum Law of 1992 and the Aliens and Residence Laws of 1993). Neither the police nor the authorities have been particularly helpful to these Gypsies. In 1996, Nicola Jevremović and his wife were beaten by police after a traffic incident. Their complaint ended up with their being given suspended prison sentences for "resisting arrest."

The **Romano Centro**, Vienna, acts as a cultural and advice center for many Romanies. Other associations, including the Kulturverein Österreichischer Roma (Cultural Association of Austrian Roma), are also based in Vienna. A Documentation and Information Center was set up in 1996 in the capital with government support. Recently workers at the University of Graz have developed an extensive collection of reading materials in the Burgenland **dialect** of Romani. *See also* CARINTHIA.

AUTONOMIA FOUNDATION. Hungary. Est. 1990. Founder: Andras Biro. A voluntary organization that includes work with Romanies among its activities. In the past it has supported income-generating projects in cooperation with registered local Romani groups.

AVEN AMENTZA FOUNDATION ("COME WITH US"). Romania. Est. 1990. Also known as Romanathon. President: Vasile Ionescu. The main aim of Aven Amentza is to aid the institutional building and development of Roma communities. This is achieved through policies for asserting ethnic identity such as multicultural **education**.

– B –

BAGLAENKO, VALENTIN (1938–1988). Crimea, Union of Soviet Socialist Republics. Singer. He first performed with a Gypsy Circus and finally in 1967 joined the **Teatr Romen**. He has toured in Europe with the Kharkov Operetta and performed as a horse rider and **dancer**, as well as making several recordings.

BAIRD, JOHN (1799–1861). Scotland. Cleric. The leader of a mission to reform Gypsies and **Travelers** in **Scotland** in the 19th century.

BAJRAMOVIĆ, ŠABAN (1936–). Serbia. Singer and composer. He has performed in the **films** of Emir Kusturica and has often sung on **radio**. He has also recorded his songs.

BAKO, MARIA. Hungary. Contemporary actress. She was the star of the **Italian film** *Un'anima divisa in due* directed by Silvio Soldini. She was invited to the Venice Film Festival of 1993 but was refused entry by the immigration authorities at Milan airport, who suspected her of being an illegal immigrant.

BALÁZS, GUSTAV. Hungary. Contemporary musicologist and **dance** instructor. He has studied the Gypsy form of the **csardas** in **Hungary**

and Transylvania and teaches a dance **summer school** each year in Hungary. He is currently resident in the **Netherlands**.

BALÁZS, JÁNOS (1905–1977). Hungary. Artist. Self-taught, he began to draw as a child but was discouraged by his parents. He took up painting again in 1968. His first solo show was in 1977 at Salgotarjan, and his work has been exhibited since then in **Hungary** and abroad. Balázs said that his paintings show distorted figures because their basic source stems from our own distorted world.

BALIARDO, MANERO (1940–). France. Singer. Born in Montpellier, where he still lives. He is a cousin of **Ricardo Baliardo**. He works as a builder and sings largely for his own entertainment.

BALIARDO, RICARDO (MANITAS DE PLATA) (1921–). France. **Musician.** His stage name literally means "Little Hands of Silver." Born in Arles, he learned to play the guitar from his father, who was a horse dealer. Baliardo has made many recordings and has toured widely. He is father to three of the **Gypsy Kings** and uncle to the other four.

BALIĆ, SAIT (1938–1998). Serbia. Engineer and political activist. He was a member of the Parliament of **Serbia** and was elected president at the third **World Romany Congress**.

BALKANROM. Sofia. A Romany federation founded in Sofia on 28 January 2000 with representatives from 10 Balkan countries.

BALOGH, ATTILA (1956–). Hungary. Writer. His **poems** and essays are mainly written in Hungarian. He is director of the From the Danube to the Ganges Foundation, which aims at reconstructing the origins of Europe's Gypsies.

BALOGH, KÁLMÁN (1959–). Hungary. **Musician.** A **cimbalom** player from Miskolc, he was taught by his uncle Elemér, also famous in his time, and then studied classical music at the Ferenc Liszt Academy of Music in Budapest. Possessing a wide repertoire, he has played with many bands such as Teka and Muszikas and has recorded as a soloist. He has made a number of tours throughout the world, including three in North America. Balogh also teaches the cimbalom. CD: *Gypsy Music from the Hungarian Villages.*

BALTIC STATES. *See* ESTONIA; LATVIA; LITHUANIA.

BALT-SLAVIC ROMANI. A name given by some scholars to a cluster of Romani **dialects** spoken in **Belarus, Lithuania, Poland,** and **Russia** by more than 800,000 persons.

BALTZAR, VEIJO (1942–). Finland. Author. As a child he shared a tiny cottage with his horse-dealer father, mother, and nine sisters and brothers. He describes Gypsy life and culture from inside his own group in his first novel *Polttava tie* [Burning Road], published in 1968. This work was translated into Swedish. The second novel *Verikihlat* [The Blood Engagement], published the following year, describes the consequences of a vendetta, while the third, *Mari* (1973), is the story of a **woman**'s role in Gypsy society. His latest book is *Phuro* [Old Man, 2000]. He is also a talented painter. Baltzar was the prime mover in the setting up of the **International Romani Writers Association** in 2002.

BAMBERGER, JAKOB. Germany. 20th-century boxer. A runner-up in the national flyweight championships of **Germany**. He was a member of the Olympic team in 1936. In 1940 he was arrested in Prague and sent to the Flossenburg and later Dachau concentration camps.

BANAT. Province in the Balkans bordering **Romania** that has at different times been under **Hungarian** (c. 850–c. 1550), **Ottoman** (c. 1550–1718), and **Austrian** (1718–1920) rule. Records exist of Gypsies in the 18th century engaged in charcoal burning, gold washing, bear leading, horse trading, and coppersmithing. They performed services for the villagers, the value of which was recognized in an edict of 1757 to stop tax collectors from driving Gypsies out of the villages by extortionate taxation. In 1763 a census recorded some 5,000 Gypsies. Historian Angus Fraser has suggested, on linguistic grounds, that the **Kalderash** coming into western Europe in the 19th century had emigrated from the Banat and not from **Wallachia** and **Moldavia**, as others maintain. In 1920 the Banat was divided between Hungary and **Yugoslavia**. During World War II, the Yugoslav Banat was under direct German military rule, and persecution of the Gypsy minority began toward the end of the war.

BANGA, DEZIDER (1939–). Slovakia. **Poet.** He writes in both Slovak and Romani. A collection of his works in Slovak—*Piesen nad vetrom* [Song of the Wind]—was published in 1964. He has also collected and published folktales and songs. Banga set up the organization Romani Kultura.

BANJARA. A tribe found throughout **India** who live a similar life to that of the **nomadic** Gypsies of Europe. They are also known as Lambadi or Gor. Their language—which belongs to the northwestern family of Indian languages—is called Gor-Boli. In 1953 the first congress was held of the All-India Banjara Seva-Sangh. A Banjara delegation attended the second **World Romany Congress**. Dr. Shyamala Devi was one of the first of the tribe to go through university. She has visited Europe many times and made a video about the Banjara–Romany connection.

BARGOENS. A variety of Dutch spoken by **Travelers** in **Belgium** and **Holland** (the *Woonwagenbewoners*). Some of the vocabulary is of Romani origin, for example, *lobie* (money).

BARI, KÁROLY (1952–). Hungary. **Poet** and dramatist. He was imprisoned in 1970 because of his "political" poems. He spent 16 years collecting and publishing Gypsy tales and songs from **Hungary**, where he lives, and Transylvania, *Cigány Folklór*. Nevertheless, Bari writes mainly in Hungarian and regards himself as a Hungarian rather than a Gypsy author. He edited an anthology of poetry and tales and also has many books of poetry of his own.

BARRETT, FRANK (FRANCIE) (1977–). Ireland. Boxer. An **Irish Traveler** and the amateur light welterweight champion of **Ireland**. He carried the Irish flag and took part in the 1996 Olympic Games. This did not stop him being refused entry as a **Traveler** to a Galway nightclub in 1999.

BAXT ("GOOD FORTUNE"). Cultural festival held in Trondheim, **Norway**, in April 2000.

BAYASH (BEYASH; BOYASH). Gypsy **clan** living in eastern **Hungary** and Transylvania. They do not speak Romani but an archaic form of **Romanian**. A start has been made on developing a written language.

BELARUS. Estimated Gypsy population: 17,500; the census in 2000 counted 11,500. The main groups are Belarussian Roma and **Haladitka**. The first document referring to Gypsies on the territory of present-day Belarus dates from 1501 when Earl Alexander of **Lithuania** gave the Gypsies a certain autonomy under their chief Vasil, in Belarus, Lithuania, and **Poland**. In 1586, however, the Parliament of Lithuania-Poland issued a decree expelling all Gypsies who refused to settle down. This applied to Belarus as well. There was still some measure of self-government, as in 1778 when Jan Marcinkiewicz was appointed the chief of the Gypsies in the area around Mir, and he continued in this role until 1790. At that time there was a famous academy where bear trainers were educated at Smorjan. In 1780 the Polish king Stanislaw II authorized a non-Gypsy, Jakob Zniemarowski, to be **king** over the Romany people in Belarus (as well as Lithuania, **Ukraine**, and Poland). He continued to rule until 1795, when Belarus was annexed by the **Russian** Empire. From then until 1991, the history of Gypsies in Belarus followed that of Russia and the **Soviet Union**.

During the occupation by **Germany** (1941–1944), half of all the Gypsies in Belarus were killed by the **Einsatzgruppen** and army units in concentration camps, such as Polask and Trastiniets, as well as in the woods near their homes. Others, including Admiral Kotslowski, served in the Soviet armed forces or the partisans.

After the end of World War II in 1945, little cultural activity took place, though from 1987 to 1989 **Valdemar Kalinin** ran the folk group Belvelitko (Evening Party). The major **dialect (Balt-Slavic)** is similar to that of northern Russia and had been used during the 1930s for literacy purposes. Since the breakup of the Soviet Union, there have been some isolated racist incidents, including a pogrom at Sitlagorsk. Nevertheless there has been a new wave of emigration from the Baltic countries following nationalist attacks there.

The Belarussian Association of Gypsies campaigns against discrimination, in particular in the fields of housing and **education**. Oleg Kozlovski is the chairperson of the Cultural Association of Roma. There is also a cultural group in Mogilev headed by A. Kasimirov. *See also* BELARUSSIAN ASSOCIATION OF GYPSIES.

BELARUSSIAN ASSOCIATION OF GYPSIES. Belarus. President: Vladimir Mateev. The main activities of the association are campaigning against discrimination, in particular in the fields of housing and **education**, and for **reparations** for the **Holocaust**. *See also* BELARUS.

BELGIUM. Estimated Gypsy population: 30,000 (excluding **Travelers**). The territory of present-day Belgium saw its first Gypsies possibly as early as 1400, but certainly in 1419 in Antwerp and again in 1420, with the arrival in Brussels of Duke Andrew of **Little Egypt**. In 1421 they came to Bruges. Duke Andrew said he and his followers had been expelled from their homes by the **Turks**, and he was given money and food. Later opinion turned against these "pilgrims." In 1504 the bailiff of Rouen was told by King Louis XII of **France** to chase any "**Egyptians**" across the frontiers and out of the country. A period likely followed when very few Gypsies were in the country. Decrees in 1856 and 1900 said that foreign nomads should not be included in the population registers. In 1872 they were to be stopped from entering the country and those already there, expelled. In 1933 the Foreigners Police was set up, and one of its tasks was to issue special passes for nomads. In 1941 the occupying **German** forces withdrew these passes and introduced the nomad's card (*zigeunerkaart*), which was not abolished until 1975.

At the outbreak of World War II perhaps only 20 extended families were living permanently in Belgium, together with others who had been trapped there by the outbreak of war. **Nomadic** Gypsies were arrested under the orders of the Germans from October 1943 in both Belgium and northern France, which was administered from Brussels. The encampments were surrounded and everyone taken. No serious effort was made to seek out house-dwelling Gypsies. The nomads were held in local prisons and gradually transferred to Malines. On 15 January 1944, a party of 351 Romanies of mixed nationality was handed one piece of bread and loaded into cattle trucks for the journey to **Auschwitz**. Some 300 died or were killed in that camp. The remainder were transferred to other camps, and 12 of these survived until the end of the war. There are four groups:

1. **Manouche** and **Sinti** who have traveled for several centuries in Belgium, France, and Germany
2. **Vlah** Roma who came to western Europe from **Romania** in the 19th century and the beginning of the 20th
3. Roma who came from eastern Europe (especially **Yugoslavia**) after 1945
4. Some 7,000 non-Romany Travelers (known as *Woonwagenbewoners* or *Voyageurs*), some of whom speak **Bargoens**

Many Romanies of the second and third groups still travel, whereas the Manouche, Sinti, and Travelers mostly live on **caravan** sites. Many are moving into houses. In Flanders and Brussels, some 30 official camping sites are available for about 400 families. It is estimated that 50 more permanent or transit sites are needed for a similar number who park their caravans on private sites, usually without planning permission. In Wallonia, a few illegal sites are tolerated; only one could be regarded as more or less official. Most of the nomads live from recycling or house-to-house sales of craftwork.

There has been no long-term Gypsy organization in Belgium, although individual lawyers and others have helped with casework. The Vlaams Centrum Woonwagenwerk was founded in 1977 but the Association des Roms de Belgique no longer functions. Romano Dzuvdipe and Opre Roma are two recently established Romany organizations, representing more than 70 percent of the Gypsy community in Belgium, with more than 20,000 members. Ijmer Kajtazi Wolf Bruggen is the chair of both organizations. In February 2004 the central government recognized the existence of house-dwelling Roma for the first time, inviting their representatives to the inaugural meeting of Belgian Intercultural Dialogue.

BELUGINS, ALEKSANDR ALEDZUNZ (LEKSA MANUŠ) (1941–1997). Latvia. Librarian, **poet**, and translator. A graduate of the Latvian State University, he was later research librarian at the Institute of Scientific Information in Moscow. Following his long military service in Kazakhstan, he wrote the story "Where Are You, Roma?" His writings include a translation (published in the journal *Roma*) of the **Indian** classic the *Ramayana*. He was competent in many Romani **dialects**, and several of his poems have been published in *Roma* and—in translation—in various other periodicals. He was also the editor of an anthology of Gypsy poetry and of a Romani children's ABC primer for both **Russian** and **Latvian** Romani.

BENG. The Romani word for the Devil. It is likely that it was already used by the Romanies for reptiles inhabiting the Hindu version of Hell and was transferred to the dragonlike Devil they saw being killed by St. George in **Byzantine** icons.

BENTINCK, RUTH (née ST MAUR) (1867–1953). Tangier. Socialist and suffragette, campaigning for the vote for women in the United Kingdom. She was the daughter of Rosina Swan, a Gypsy from Higham in Kent and Edward St Maur, a relation of the Earl of Somerset.

BERBERSKI, SLOBODAN (1919–1989). Belgrade. **Poet**. He was elected president of the **World Romany Congress** at the first congress in 1971, serving until the second. In 1972 he became the editor of the Romani newspaper *Krlo e Rromengo* ([Voice of the Roma]; nine issues in the Romani and **Serbian** languages from 1972 to 1973). His poetry was inspired by Romany symbols, traditions, and images of everyday life.

BERGITKA ROMA. The so-called mountain Gypsies of **Poland**. They are later arrivals and speak a different **dialect** from the lowland Gypsies.

BERNAL, JORGE (LOLO) (1968–). Argentina. Political activist who has attended many international conferences. A **Kalderash** Rom from Buenos Aires, he is president of the Romany Organization for Latin America and is actively involved in collecting Romani folktales from his homeland.

BESSARABIA. This territory belonged to **Russia** from 1812 to 1917. In 1818 the status of the Gypsies there was changed from "slave" (as it had been when the area was part of **Moldova/Romania**) to "serf."

Romania regained the territory in 1917 but after 1945 it was retaken by the **Soviet Union** and divided between the Moldavian and **Ukrainian** republics.

BETTER FUTURE. Croatia. Secretary: Ramiza Mehmedi. A Romany **women**'s organization based in Zagreb. It aims to raise the status of Roma women in **Croatia** and improve their health and literacy.

***BEWLEY, VICTOR* (1914–1999).** Ireland. Social reformer and philanthropist. Bewley was an energetic man who aided **Irish Travelers** in the 1960s and 1970s by raising the issue of their needs. He founded the Dublin Committee for Travelling People, which pressed for accommodation in housing and "halting sites" for the city and country Travelers. He advised the minister for local government on a program of settlement and was the chairperson of the National Council for Travelling People.

BIBLE TRANSLATIONS. The first time a complete gospel was translated into Romani was in 1837, by **George Borrow**. Chapter 10, verses 30–37, of the Gospel of Luke had been translated into **Czech** Romani by Anton Puchmayer in 1821 and published in his book *Romani Chib*. Details of many post-1945 translations can be found in the bibliography (in the section Literature in Romani).

BIELENBERG, RAYA. Union of Soviet Socialist Republics. Contemporary singer. It is recounted that when the Moscow Romany Theatre came to play in her town, she jumped on the stage and joined in the singing. The director was so impressed, he hired her on the spot. Later, she married a Norwegian journalist and since then has lived in **Norway** and Paris. She has made several records of traditional songs. Currently she plays in the group Raya and her Gypsy Legacy with members of her family.

BIENNALE KLEINERE SPRACHEN. *See* ZIGEUNERLEBEN.

BIHARI, JANOS (1764–1827). Hungary. **Musician**. He composed **Verbunkos** music and led his own band. In 1808 he wrote the piece

"Krönungs-Nota" for the coronation of Empress Maria Louisa and collaborated in the composition of the "Rakoczy March," later to become the Hungarian national anthem. He was one of the Gypsy musicians who influenced **Franz Liszt**.

BILA, VERA (1954–). Czechoslovakia. Singer. From **Rokycany**, Bila's repertoire includes songs with contemporary themes. With her group Kale, she has made two recordings and toured much of Europe and the **United States**. She was also the main focus of the documentary *Ziganska Musica* (1988), made by Joachin Kreck in **Germany**. CD: *Kale Kaloré*.

BIRTH. The birth of a child, whether male or female, is a matter of joy for the whole family. For the **Kalderash**, the name is traditionally given by the **Ursitory**.

BISMARCK, OTTO VON (1815–1898). Germany. Politician. In 1886, as newly appointed chancellor of the Second German Empire, Bismarck sent a letter to all the states comprising the empire to unify, at least in practice, the various valid decrees against Gypsies. Bismarck recommended the expulsion of all foreign Gypsies to free the territory of the country completely and permanently from this "plague."

BITTEL, MAY (1953–). Switzerland. **Sinto** pastor and civil rights activist. Founder of the GIRCA (Gypsy International Recognition, Compensation, and Action) Association. He has for more than 25 years been an activist for the Gypsy cause, in **Switzerland** as well as abroad, and is the symbol of the fight for recognition of the Swiss Gypsies' rights. Bittel is a member of the Swiss foundation Assurer l'avenir des Gens du Voyage and the Swiss Commission against Racism.

BITTOVA, IVA (1958–). Slovakia. **Musician** and composer. A violinist and composer who comes from a musical family, including her sister **Ida Kelarova**. She creates pieces merging Gypsy, folk, and jazz idioms. CDs: *Iva Bittova with the Skampa Quartet* and *Bilé Inferno*.

BLACK VIRGIN. A number of churches where there is a statue of the Black Virgin have been the object of pilgrimages by Gypsies. In 1471 a Gypsy chief, Duke Paul of **Egypt**, went to visit the statue of the Black Virgin of Guadalupe at Santiago de Compostela in **Spain**. Some scholars believe that the Gypsies see in the Black Virgin a reminder of the **Indian** goddess Kali.

BLAIRGOWRIE. Village in **Scotland** famous for its berries and **music**. In season, many **Travelers** and townspeople come to help in the picking, and informal music-making sessions take place in the evenings after the picking is over. An annual music festival is also held. **Belle Stewart** and her family are closely associated with Blairgowrie, and she wrote the song "The Berryfields o' Blair" in the 1920s.

BLOCH, JULES (1880–1953). France. Academic and author. He was an expert on **Indian** studies. In 1953 his book *Les Tsiganes* was published in the French series Que Sais-je? The current edition has been radically rewritten.

BLOCK, MARTIN (1891–?). Germany. Academic and author. A professor of linguistics at Marburg University, he wrote in 1936 the book *Die Zigeuner: Ihr Leben und ihre Seele* [The Gypsies: Their Life and Their Soul], which summarized what knowledge there was at the time among outsiders of the Gypsies' life and beliefs. He disappeared shortly afterward, and it is believed he died in a concentration camp.

BLYTHE, JAMES. Scotland. Historical figure. Ancestor of a **clan** of **Travelers** in the south of **Scotland**.

BODY SHOP HUMAN RIGHTS AWARDS. Launched in 2000, these awards demonstrate a continuing commitment to ethical consumerism by the Body Shop global cosmetics brand. In 2002 the focus of the awards was the right to housing, and the **Romani Baxt Foundation** in Sofia, **Bulgaria**, was selected as a winner from 50 nominees.

BOGDAN, JANOS (1963–1998). Hungary. Teacher. A **Bayash** Romani, he studied at the universities of Szeged and Budapest before starting a teaching career. He helped to set up and became the first headmaster in 1994 of the **Gandhi School** in Pecs. He was killed in a car crash.

BOJAXHIU, AGNES (BLESSED MOTHER TERESA) (1910–1997). Born in Skopje, Macedonia. An **Ashkali**, she became a Catholic and immigrated to **India**, where she ran an order based in Calcutta to help the poor.

BOORDE, ANDREW (1490–1549). England. Author. He compiled an encyclopedia entitled *The Fyrst Boke of the Introduction of Knowledge* (1547). It had a chapter on Romani, which includes some of the earliest specimens of the language, probably collected in Calais.

BORROW, GEORGE (1803–1881). England. Author and linguist. He lived with Gypsies in **England** and visited **Spain** to learn the language of the Gypsies there. He then translated St. Luke's Gospel into Spanish **Caló**. Borrow also wrote several works on the Gypsies, in particular *The Bible in Spain* (1843), *Lavengro* (1851), and *The Romani Rye* (1857).

BOSHA (POSHA). *See* LOM.

BOSNIA-HERZEGOVINA. The 1991 census recorded 8,000 Romanies, but the estimated Gypsy population then was 80,000. An unknown number of Bosnian Romanies sought refuge in other countries during and after the 1992–1995 war. Official estimates of the current population range between 30,000 and 60,000.

Before 1428, the Gypsy population of Bosnia probably consisted of only a handful of families, but no records from that time exist. Then in the period 1428–1875, Bosnia was under the rule of the Turkish **Ottoman Empire,** and Gypsies followed the conquerors into the area. Under Turkish rule, the Gypsies were treated as any other minority ethnic group, with some discouragement of **nomadism,** largely because of the difficulty of collecting taxes from nomads. In 1574 Sultan Salim II decreed that the Gypsies who worked in the Bosnian mines were to be exempted from certain taxes and had to choose a headman for each group of 50 adults.

From 1875 to 1918 the country was under the rule of the Austro-Hungarian Empire. In 1918 it became part of the newly established **Yugoslavia** and then in 1941 was incorporated into the puppet fascist state of **Croatia**.

In the federal state of Yugoslavia that was reestablished after 1945, the Romanies were recognized as a national minority in the Republic of Bosnia and Herzegovina. They were allowed to run their own organizations and use the **Romani language**. In 1986 the **Sarajevo Conference** was held, which was a landmark in the development of Romani culture for the whole of Europe. Delegates came from many countries—though not from the local community—and Romani was used by many of the speakers as well as in the final conference report.

During the armed conflict in Bosnia in 1992–1995, Gypsy men were conscripted for military service by all three warring parties (Bosnians, Croats, and Serbs). Men from Zavidovici formed an all-Romany unit called Garavi Vod that fought alongside the Bosnian government forces. It is thought that some 80 Romanies were killed in the **Serbian**-run concentration camp at Manjaca. At least 500 were killed during the fighting in Bihac, **Sarajevo**, and Zvornik. There was no functioning Romany organization in Bosnia during the war period except in Sarajevo. At the end of hostilities in 1995, there were still sizable Romany populations in Tuzla, Sarajevo, and other towns, although many had fled to western Europe.

Some 300–400 Gypsies are living in what was the Serbian district of Ilidza in Sarajevo, and others are in Gorica. The Gypsy population of all Sarajevo is between 1,000 and 2,000, with a high proportion of children. Some six active organizations operate in Bosnia. Braca Romi (Romani Brethren) functions locally in Sarajevo, as do other bodies in Kiseljak, Visoko, and Zenica. The German-based **Gesellschaft für Bedrohte Völker** helped set up the All-Bosnian Romany Union, which held its first conference in 1997. A "Council of Roma" was set up by the **Organization for Security and Cooperation in Europe** mission in Bosnia.

At the time of writing, several thousand Romany refugees from Bosnia are still in **Germany** and smaller numbers in other western countries. Some are being sent back to Bosnia, though the new constitution does not allow all the Gypsies who once lived in Bosnia to become citizens of the new federation, as they may not all be able to establish residence. A fact-finding mission under the auspices of the **Council of Europe** visited Bosnia in May 1996. It recommended that both parts of the Republic (Bosnia-Croatia and **Republika Srpska**) recognize Romanies as a nationality. The granting of equal rights to other minorities—Bosnian Muslims, Serbs, and Croats—has meant squeezing the Roma out from participation in politics at the higher levels.

Many examples have been reported of police abuse and racist attacks by Bosnians and Serbs. In 2000 the Bosnian villagers of Meskovici verbally abused Roma passing along the main road on their way to their own nearby settlement and for a short time set up barricades. In 2002 a Mr. Mehic from Sapna was accused of robbery and beaten with sticks in the police station. He was then thrown out of a police car near his house, sustaining severe injuries.

Several deputations visiting Tuzla and other towns found that the Romanies are at the bottom of the list for receiving humanitarian help from outside agencies. Roma returning to their hometowns and villages have found difficulty in establishing their right to live on the land they previously occupied.

BOSWELL, SYLVESTER GORDON (fl. 19th–20th centuries). England. Soldier and author. He was born in the large Gypsy camp on the North Shore in Blackpool, the 11th son of Trafalgar Boswell. He served in World War I in the Royal Veterinary Corps. He then married and traveled across the British Isles, later settling in Lincolnshire, near Spalding. Boswell was a close friend of members of the **Gypsy Lore Society**. He succeeded in saving and expanding the threatened **Appleby Fair**. In 1970 *The Book of Boswell*, his autobiography, was published from a transcript of a tape recording made by him. It contains a lively account of his life in the army and on the roads.

BOSWELL MUSEUM. A privately run **museum** of **caravans** and other traditional items in Lincolnshire, **England**.

BRATINKA REPORT. In October 1997 the **Czech Republic** government adopted the report by Pavel Bratinka, minister without portfolio, entitled *On the Situation of the Romani Community in the Czech Republic*. It addressed a number of issues including discrimination and **education**. In particular it proposed amending the Citizenship Law of 1992 to enable more Gypsies of **Slovak** origin living in the Czech Republic to obtain Czech citizenship.

BRATSCH. France. Founded in 1979, a popular non-Gypsy band that sings in Romani as well as Yiddish, Kurdish, and other languages. Their CD, somewhat misleadingly entitled *Gypsy Music from the Heart of Europe*, contains three Gypsy songs.

BRAZIL. Estimated Gypsy population: over 600,000. The first to arrive were deportees in the time when the country was a Portuguese colony. Maria Fernandes (whose presence was recorded in 1591) had been **transported** from **Portugal** for stealing donkeys. The Association for the Preservation of Gypsy Culture believes there are some one million Gypsies in the country, 300,000 being **nomadic**. Few have birth certificates, and this limits their access to public services. Claudio Iovanovitchi represents the Gypsies on the National Council for the Protection of Racial Equality, while they took part in the First National Conference to Promote Racial Equality in 2005.

BREGOVIĆ, GORAN (1950–). Yugoslavia. Composer and performer. He wrote the **music** for the **film** *The Time of the Gypsies*. In his live performances, he incorporates Romany musicians.

BRIAVAL, COCO. France. Contemporary **musician**. He is a musician in the **Django Reinhardt** style. His music has been recorded with the title *Musique Manouche*.

BRITISH COMMITTEE ON ROMANI EMANCIPATION. *See* EUROPEAN COMMITTEE ON ROMANI EMANCIPATION (ECRE).

BRITISH ROMMANI UNION. United Kingdom. Est. 1990s. President: **poet** Tom Odley. It has had a strong Romany nationalist position.

BRNO MUSEUM. The town of Brno in the **Czech Republic** is the home of the Museum of Romani Culture, founded in 1991. The **mu-**

seum now has its own building. It publishes a journal and books as well as offering public lectures. The director is Jana Horvathova.

BROTHERTON COLLECTION. Part of the Leeds University Library, Leeds, **England**. It is one of the largest collections of books on Gypsy subjects. The original collection was donated by Mrs. McGrigor Phillips in 1950, and an endowment enables its continued progress.

BRUSSELS DECLARATION (1996). A roundtable on the Roma/Gypsies was held in the European Parliament in Brussels on 12 July 1996, attended by representatives from the major Romany organizations and those working with Gypsies. The declaration adopted by the participants called for recognition of the **Romani language** and way of life in the school system. It also asked for special attention to be paid to creating employment possibilities for Gypsies, as well as health care. The Gypsy organizations said they needed support and asked for the international bodies in Europe to each appoint someone as an official representative of the Romany people.

BRYNNER, YUL (1920–1985). Born on Sakhalin Island, Japan. Actor and **film** star whose trademark was his shaved head. He played the King of Siam in the Broadway (1951) and film (1956) versions of Richard Rodgers and Oscar Hammerstein's *The King and I*. He also gained critical acclaim for his role as leader of the Magnificent Seven in the film of the same name in 1956. In a June 1978 *New York Times* interview, he said it was uplifting to hear the call *"Upre, Roma!"* (Arise, Romanies!) at the second **World Romany Congress**, of which he was a patron, and announced that he intended to go to the forthcoming **Chandigarh Festival**. However, his claim to have Romany ancestry is thrown into doubt by his son Rock's biography (*The Man Who Would Be King*), which states that his father was brought up with Gypsies but was not one himself. He appears on a Mantitor LP, produced in New York, singing in Russian and Romani with Aliosha Dimitrievitch.

BUCHAREST CONFERENCE (1934). This conference was organized by **Lazarescu Lazurica** and the Uniunea Generala a Romilor din Romania (General Union of the Gypsies of **Romania**). There were a number of invitees from abroad, though it is uncertain whether any attended. A number of resolutions were passed, and the final declaration asked for equal civil rights for Gypsies and help with **education** and employment. However, it brought little if any change. It has been considered as the first international meeting of Gypsies.

BUCOVINA CLUB. Previously an all-night club in Frankfurt with Gypsy music. DJ Stefan Hantel (Shantel) has compiled a remix of the kind of music that might have been heard in the Club on the CD *Bucovina Club/Shantel*.

BUFFALO (*BUBALUS BUBALIS*). The Asian buffalo played an important part in the migration of the Romanies from **India** to Europe. Many Romanies were brought by the Arabs as captives from India to serve as herdsmen in Mesopotamia and from there to the coast of the Mediterranean. Gypsies were photographed and painted with buffalo in the 19th century in Rumelia and Transylvania. It is likely that they had accompanied herds of buffalo from **Turkey** into the Balkans under the **Ottoman Empire**.

BULGARIA. Estimated Gypsy population: 700,000; the 2001 census gave the revised number as 365,797. Many Roma tended to identify themselves to the authorities as ethnic **Turks** or Bulgarians. The town of Sliven has a Gypsy population of around 20,000.

The **Atsingani** who came to Bulgaria in the ninth century may well have been the first Roma in the country. By 1396 Bulgaria had become part of the **Ottoman Empire**, and the empire's tax records in 1430 mention Gypsies (*Cingene*) for the first time. The Gypsies were treated generally as other ethnic minorities by the Ottomans, provided they paid their taxes. There were many craftsmen and farm workers. Some of the Bulgarian Gypsies converted to Islam, while other Muslim Gypsies arrived with the Turkish conquerors.

In 1878 Bulgaria was liberated from the Ottoman Empire. In 1886 the new government instituted a decree forbidding **nomadism**, and the Frontier Law could be used to prevent the immigration of Gypsies. Neither of these measures was enforced, however. As a result of economic (rather than legal) pressure, many Gypsies took jobs in the newly opened factories—in textile factories in Sliven, for example. Others continued to nomadize until well after World War II.

The central government wished to prevent nomadic and Muslim Gypsies from voting under the new constitution. A conference of Gypsies in Sofia in 1905 was organized to protest this law, and Bulgarian lawyer Marko Markoff helped the Gypsies in their campaign. A committee was formed and a manifesto drawn up. In 1919 voting was extended and made compulsory for the whole population.

Between the two world wars, Christian missionaries were active among the Gypsies in Bulgaria. In the 1930s the Scripture Gift Mission published brochures in two **dialects** of Romani, and A. Atanasakiev translated two of the gospels. In Sliven, however, the Gypsies were working in factories and turning toward socialism. Romany trade unionists in Sliven were to take a lead in 1927 in organizing a petition to the U.S. government against the execution of anarchists Nicola Sacco and Bartolomeo Vanzetti. Gypsies had also taken part in the largely peasant uprisings against the government in 1923. The Gypsy periodical *Terbie* [Education], which was the organ of the Muslim National Cultural Organization, appeared in 1933 but closed in 1934 when opposition political parties were banned.

During World War II, some Gypsies from the towns were rounded up and sent to work in labor camps. Others, however, served in the army, and still others joined the partisans. Dimiter Nemtsov from Sliven, who was serving with the Bulgarian army of occupation in **Yugoslavia**, deserted and joined the local resistance movement. In May 1942 a decree was issued providing for Gypsies to be directed to compulsory employment. A year later, some Gypsies from Sofia had been sent to labor camps in Dupnitsa and elsewhere. Those who remained had only limited access to the center of town and the trams.

After 1944 the Gypsies were at first encouraged by the Communist government to develop their own ethnicity. A newspaper was set up under the aegis of the Communist Party, and a theater **Teatr Roma** was established in Sofia in 1947. The newspaper was at first given the Romani name *Romano Esi* [Romany Voice], but the name was changed three times and finally given a Bulgarian title *Nov Put* [New Way]. The first editor was **Shakir Pashov**. It proclaimed integration into socialist society as the desirable aim for the Gypsies and was to cease publication with the fall of the Communist regime. In 1945 the Gypsy-led organization Ekhipe (Unity) was founded with the aim of raising the cultural and **educational** level of the Gypsies. Pashov was its head. It was soon closed and absorbed into the Otechestven Front (Fatherland Front), a mass organization allied to the Communist Party. The Romany theater in Sofia was closed in 1951 and its director, **Mustafa Aliev** (Manush Romanov), left to work in a Turkish theater. Pashov himself was interned in a labor camp on the island of Belen.

The government was determined to end nomadism, which was banned in 1958. A circular in the following year referred to 14,000 traveling Gypsies and also stressed the need to get the Gypsies to integrate to the Bulgarian majority and not align themselves with the Turkish minority. The government opened many boarding schools for Gypsy children from poor families and seasonal workers. From the 1950s Muslim Gypsies alongside ethnic Turks were pressurized to adopt Bulgarian names. Gypsies accused of nationalist deviation during this period were sent into internal exile.

When the Communist Party fell from power in 1989, Gypsies were allowed once more to have their own journals and organizations. Four acknowledged Gypsies were elected to the first democratic Parliament.

The collapse of the Communist regime, on the other hand, led to a rise in anti-Gypsy articles in the press and racist attacks. Skinheads attacked Gypsies in Pleven at the end of 1995. Others attacked homeless children who slept in the Sofia railway station. In March 1995 one Rom died when a block of apartments was set on fire in Sofia. Two fatal attacks on Roma were carried out by private security guards. In May 2002, 19-year-old Miroslav Zankov was killed at the abandoned military airport in Gabrovnitsa, near Montana, and in August of the same year, a 21-year-old named Pavel was shot and killed in Sofia.

Serious violence against Roma in Bulgaria continues: Three Romany men sustained gunshot wounds and several others were brutally beaten by 10 police officers and rangers while collecting wood for heating in the forest near Lukovit in northern Bulgaria in March 2003. That May, 13-year-old Assen Todorov was beaten by his teacher while studying at a Romany school in the northern Bulgarian village of Bukovlak.

There have been other reports of police brutality. Five Romanies, including Angel Angelov, died in custody during 1995 and 1996; no action has been taken against the police regarding these deaths. In March 1996 police officers from Pleven were given a suspended sentence of eight months in prison for beating two boys in Vidin. In 2001 a police sergeant was sentenced to pay compensation to Mitko Naidenov after he had beaten him so badly that the victim was hospitalized for 12 days. Heavy-handed police raids took place in March 1996 in Russe and in April in Barkach.

Prejudice and discrimination exists at all levels of society. In 2004 Sevda Nanova was awarded 300 euros damages against a clothing store in Sofia that refused to serve her. In the same year, lawsuits were started against two restaurants in Blagoevrad that barred Roma from their premises. In November 2005 the Sofia District Court found that Metody Assenov had been discriminated against two years previously when a food production company refused to employ him because he was a Romany. He was awarded damages of approximately $300. Housing is a serious issue, as well. Roma have been evicted from housing in many towns, including in August 2005 from the Hristo Botev neighborhood in Sofia.

In 2002, the Ministry of the Interior initiated programs to improve its relations with the Roma and formed a special group to attract them to work in the ministry, using the **Romani language** in training. Already from the end of 2001, the ministry had reserved places in the Police Academy for minority candidates, to address their underrepresentation in the police. The government reported that the number of Romany police officers rose from 59 to 158 during the year, including 4 officers, 89 sergeants, and 55 constables. A special Officer for Roma Training Programs was appointed, and bilingual training manuals were published.

The Framework Program was created by the **Human Rights Project** in 1998 and supported by more than 75 organizations throughout the country. In April 1999 it was approved by the government. Much of the money allocated for the implementation of the Action Plan was not exclusively earmarked for Roma, but for disadvantaged groups, including the Roma, and many of the proposals contained in earlier drafts of the Action Plan were missing from the final version; for example, the plan to create a fund to help in the process of desegregation of the

Roma schools. In October 2003 the Bulgarian government approved the Action Plan for Implementation of the Framework Program for Equal Integration of Roma.

There have been a number of projects that have attempted to improve economic opportunities for Roma, including the Ethnic Integration and Conflict Resolution project launched in Lom in 2000. That project includes providing limited funds to small enterprises that employ Roma, undertaking activities to reduce dropout rates from school and to provide tutoring for university enrollment exams, as well as training for leaders where young Roma can develop leadership and conciliation skills. Similar projects have also been developed by other organizations. The government and the European Bank for Reconstruction and Development funded the construction of new apartments in Sofia for Roma families relocated from the Abyssinia Gypsy quarter.

More than 400 Romany nongovernmental organizations (NGOs) have been set up, as have more than 10 political parties in spite of a theoretical ban on ethnic parties. On 18 November 2002 in Sofia, the National Movement for Social Development–Roma was founded by 50 organizations under the leadership of MP Alexander Filipov. The goal of the umbrella group is to work for the improvement of the living standards of the Romany population. There are two Roma members of parliament in the 240-seat National Assembly elected in 2001: Alexander Filipov and Toma Tomov. In 2002 the EuroRoma party (a predominantly ethnic Roma political formation) was technically a member of the governing coalition, although it had no representatives in the Cabinet or the National Assembly.

Roma are gaining a higher profile in local politics; in the local elections held in October 2003, the number of Roma municipal councillors elected on the lists of Roma parties rose to 162, as compared with around 100 in the 1999 elections. Others were elected on the lists of other parties. However, the increased political participation of Roma in the election campaign has stirred up anti-Romany sentiment in some parts of the country.

In February 2003, more than 3000 Roma from the Stolipinovo neighborhood in Plovdiv took part in a demonstration. They were protesting against the local electricity company's decision to cut off power to the whole neighborhood after some people failed to pay their bills.

In December 1991, Circular 232 of the Council of Ministers permitted Romani to be taught in schools up to four hours a week on a voluntary basis, and an **alphabet** book was produced. From 1997, an experimental program of Romany culture has been available in some schools to all children. Figures collected in 2002 showed that less than 8 percent of Romany children had completed secondary education. Many Roma children starting school have problems from the outset, as a large number are not prepared for school and some are not proficient in Bulgarian. Romany and ethnic Bulgarian children usually attend separate schools, although integration programs, including busing, have been set up in several localities such as Vidin. The recognition that poverty has prevented many Romany children from accessing education has also led to the government and Romany NGOs providing free lunches and subsidizing textbook and tuition costs. In March 2002 a project in the Silistra region started providing weekend classes for Romany children under the age of 15 who did not attend school.

Desegregation of schools began in Vidin in 2000. The development of desegregated schooling with the support of the **Open Society Institute** is helping to raise educational standards among the Roma. In July 2002 the **Romani Baxt Foundation** started to implement the desegregation program for Roma schools in Sofia. In 2003, the University of Veliko Tarnovo opened a special department headed by **Hristo Kyuchukov** where teachers of Romani are being trained.

The Gypsy population of Bulgaria today is mixed Christian and Muslim. The recently settled nomads speak a variety of Romani dialects, both **Vlah** and non-Vlah, while the established sedentary communities speak mainly the **Erlia** dialect of Romani, Turkish, or **Romanian** as their first language. Thanks mainly to compulsory education in the Communist period, Gypsies are found at all levels of society, from surgeons to laborers, although unemployment is high (up to 80 percent of adult males in some districts). **Music** is a popular profession, and recent singers to attain general popularity include Azis and Sofi Marinova.

BUNYAN, JOHN (1628–1688). England. Baptist preacher and author. His major work was *Pilgrim's Progress* (1678). He said he came from a **tinker** family, but there is no evidence that he was an ethnic Romany. The surname, with the spelling Bonyan, however, was recorded as used by Gypsies in the 1590s in **England**.

BURGENLAND. Province in the east of **Austria**. Many Gypsies were settled there by Empress **Maria Theresa**. During the 1930s their economic position as casual farm workers was becoming difficult, and friction arose with local Austrians competing for work. They were among the first to be interned by the Nazis after **Germany** annexed Austria in 1938. Most perished in **Auschwitz**, Buchenwald, Chelmno, or Ravensbrück. There is a small surviving population, but few of the children speak Romani. A cultural center was set up in recent years. Attempts are being made with the help of the University of Graz to preserve the **dialect** (known as **Roman**) as a written language.

BURHAN, RAHIM (1949–). Macedonia. Theater director and actor. He founded the **Pralipe Theater** company in 1970. He was a joint winner of the 2002 **Hiroshima Foundation** Award.

BURTON, RICHARD (1821–1890). England. Writer, voyager, and linguist. One of his books was *The Jew, the Gypsy and El Islam* (1898). In spite of his probably being partly of Romany descent, he painted a bad picture of Gypsies in this work.

BUTTLER, LILJANA (1944–). Yugoslavia. Singer. Born in Belgrade, she later left **Yugoslavia** and stopped singing for several years. She has returned to the stage and has performed several times with the **Bosnian** band Mostar Sevdah Reunion.

BUZYLOV, LYONA. Russia. Contemporary singer. As a child she sang in the **film** *Gypsies Are Found near Heaven* (1976). Now she and her family form the Ensemble Buzylov.

BYZANTINE EMPIRE (BYZANTIUM). The name given to the Eastern Roman Empire, which covered modern **Greece** and what is now **Turkey**. The first Gypsies are recorded in Byzantium in 1054 at

Constantinople (present-day Istanbul). They were magicians, **fortune-tellers**, and veterinary surgeons. It is thought these Gypsies entered mainland Europe across the Bosphorus. Others crossed the Mediterranean to the Greek Islands and mainland.

– C –

CABRERA, MARIA (fl. c. 16th century). Spain. The first Romany woman in Europe to be publicly renowned for her beauty.

CAINE, MICHAEL (1933–). England. Actor. Born in Rotherhithe, he has a Romany heritage. His father, Maurice Joseph Micklewhite, was part Romany, and his parents and grandparents spent much time at the old horse repository at the Elephant and Castle in London.

CALCUTTA ASIATIC SOCIETY. United Kingdom. Est. 1784. Founder: Sir William Jones. It was established at a time when European interest in **Indian** languages was growing after scholars found a link between Latin and Sanskrit. This was to lead to the recognition of the **Indian origin** of the **Romani language** and the Gypsies.

CALDARAS, HANS (1948–). Sweden. Singer and composer. He has recorded mainly traditional **music** in **Swedish** and Romani. His autobiography *I betrakterens ögon* [In the Eye of the Beholder] was published in 2002. CD: *Romany Gipsy Songs* (with the Stefan Bucur Ensemble).

CALDARAS, MONICA (1943–). Sweden. Teacher, writer, and **musician**. A member of the music group **Gypsy Brothers**.

CALÓ. (1) A variety of Spanish with many Romani words. It replaced Romani as the language of Gypsies in **Spain**. **George Borrow**'s **Bible translation** is in Caló. (2) A term sometimes used instead of *Gitano* to describe a Spanish or **Portuguese** Gypsy. It is a Romani word meaning "black." *See also* KALO.

CAMARON DE LA ISLA. *See* CRUZ, JOSE MONJA.

CANADA. Vlah families have been moving to Canada since the 19th century, while recent years have seen several thousand asylum seekers from eastern Europe, many of whom have been given refugee status. The Romani Community and Advocacy Centre was set up in Toronto in 1998 and the magazine *Romano Lil* started publication that same year. In 2004 the Supreme Court began to deal with a case dating from 1997 where a group of skinheads in Ontario waved a placard saying "Honk if you hate Gypsies." The legal situation is that the term *Gypsies* does not necessarily refer to Roma.

CANNSTADT CONFERENCE. In 1871 during the Württemberg annual festival, the editor of a Stuttgart newspaper played a trick announcing that a Gypsy parliament would be held. Many curious people went to see this event. The trains coming to Cannstadt were apparently packed. In January 1872 the *Times* of London published a notice about the parliament, as did the *Evening Standard* a month later. From this joke, the conference has slipped into some books about Gypsies.

CANT. The term used for the language used by **Travelers** in **Ireland** and **Scotland**. These are two distinct varieties of English. The syntax and grammar are English, but the vocabulary comes from many sources, including the medieval vocabularies known as **Shelta** and **Gammon**. The vocabulary is taught from birth alongside the English equivalent, and as the children grow up, they learn which words are used by their community and which are the general English words. There is some overlap between **Scottish Travelers**' cant and that of **Irish Travelers**. Most Travelers know some 400 words. These words are used within the community to give a sense of identity and sometimes so that the Travelers can speak without being understood by outsiders. In the Scottish Highlands and Islands, a third variety of language is found—again a special vocabulary, but in this case with the syntax and grammar of Scottish Gaelic.

Examples of cant:

- Irish Travelers: *Bug muilsha gather skai* (Give me a drink of water)
- Lowland Scottish Travelers: I *slummed* the *pottach* in the *gowl* and then I *bing'*d *avree* (I hit the boy in the stomach and then I went out)

- Highland and Islands Scottish Travelers: *Dearc leagan cean a' ghlomhaich* (Look at the bad shoes of the man)

CANTEA, GEORGI. *See* KANTEA, GEORGI.

CARAVAN. The horse-drawn living caravan was not invented by the Gypsies, but was rapidly adopted by them in the 19th century. It first appeared in **France** and northern Europe about 1800. The earliest picture of a caravan in **England** dates from 1804. In 1817 Vincent Van Gogh painted Gypsy caravans in France. There are a number of different types, such as the Reading wagon. The horse-drawn caravan is called a *vardo* in the **Romani language**, a word earlier used for a more primitive type of cart. *Caravans* today are trailers or recreational vehicles.

CARAVAN SITES ACT OF 1960. United Kingdom. This Act introduced new planning controls on **caravan** sites in **England** and **Wales**. As a result, it became difficult to open new sites, and many existing sites were closed if they had not been operating long before 1960. The Act gave local authorities the power to build sites for Gypsies, but very few did so.

CARAVAN SITES ACT OF 1968. United Kingdom. This Act placed a duty on county councils in particular to build sites for Gypsies "residing in and resorting to their area." At the same time, new powers were introduced to make parking a **caravan** in an area illegal when the area was "designated" as having provided enough caravan pitches or when the government judged it was not "expedient" for the area to do so. Progress under the Act was slow, and by 1994 only some 30 percent of Gypsies were housed on official caravan sites. Others had obtained permission for private sites in accordance with a number of circulars that followed the passing of the **Caravan Sites Act of 1960**. The Act also gave some protection to tenants on Gypsy caravan sites. The section of the Act relating to Gypsies was repealed in 1994 by the **Criminal Justice and Public Order Act**.

CARI, OLIMPIO (1942–). Italy. Painter, **poet**, and songwriter. His first solo exhibition was in 1987, and he showed his **art** at the second **Mondiale of Gypsy Art** in Budapest in 1995.

CARINTHIA. Now a province of **Austria**; previously (1276–1918) part of the Austro-Hungarian Empire. Gypsies are mentioned in the area for the first time in 1692 at Villach. There was a small Gypsy population of Romanies and **Sinti** in the period up to World War II. Many of them were **transported** to Lackenbach internment camp, and others were put on a train heading in the direction of Tschenstochau. It is possible that they never reached Tschenstochau as the route passed near **Auschwitz**. Plans are under way to erect a memorial in Villach to the victims of the Nazi regime.

CARMEN. Carmen, the fictitious story of a **Spanish** Gypsy, was written by Prosper Mérimée in 1846 after he visited a Spanish cigarette factory, and it was turned into an opera by Georges Bizet in 1875. It is said that Mérimée wrote the story in just eight days. The story of a love triangle (or quadrilateral, if we count Carmen's husband) has been filmed by, among others, Jean-Luc Godard, Cecil B. De Mille, Francesco Rosi, and Carlos Saura. It has recently been turned into a **flamenco** opera by **Antonio Gades** and an ice-show—the latter with a sequence of **Irish** step-dancing on skates that has no parallel in the original story or opera. It was adapted as the musical *Carmen Jones*—with a black cast—in 1943 (and later filmed). James Robinson produced a play in 1997 at the Court Theater in Chicago based on the original novel with moderate success. In 2004 South African film director Mark Dornford-May set the story in a shantytown with the libretto delivered in the Xhosa language (*U-Carmen Ekhayelitsha*). The story carries the essentially misogynistic message that female sexual liberation is ultimately punishable by death, but this has not served to diminish its enduring appeal.

CARRASCO, MANUELA (1954–). Spain. **Dancer.** Since her first public performance at the age of 10, she has danced at many festivals in **Spain** and abroad.

CASH, JOHNNY (1932–2003). United States. Singer and **musician.** In his last biography, Cash said that he was part **Traveler.** There is a family of Traveler musicians in **Ireland** that performs as the Cashes.

CATALONIA. In 1447 the first Gypsies were recorded in Catalonia. In 1512 they were ordered to leave the region. Catalonia became administratively part of **Spain** later in the 16th century.

CATHOLIC CHURCH. *See* ASOCIACIÓN SECRETARIADO GENERAL GITANA; PONTIFICAL COUNCIL FOR THE PASTORAL CARE OF MIGRANTS AND ITINERANT PEOPLES; POPES.

CENTER FOR DOCUMENTATION AND INFORMATION ON MINORITIES IN EUROPE–SOUTHEAST (CEDIME-SE). Greece. The center works in cooperation with the Ethnocultural Diversity Resource Center in Cluj-Napoca, **Romania**. It has reported on the situation of Roma and other minorities in central and southeast Europe.

CENTRAL EUROPEAN UNIVERSITY. Budapest, Hungary. The university runs an academic **summer school** with a program on the Roma community.

CENTRE DE RECHERCHES TSIGANES. Paris, France. The center held a data base of organizations, books, and articles and until recently published the journal *Interface*. At its peak, three action research groups were managed by the center—on history, **education**, and language—leading to the **Interface** Collection. The director was the sociologist and writer Jean-Pierre Liégeois. The center ceased operation in 2003 when it lost its funding.

CENTRE MISSIONAIRE ÉVANGÉLIQUE ROM INTERNATIONAL (CMERI). France. Est. 1995. President: Loulou Demeter. A **Pentecostal** group, mainly **Kalderash**, that split from the original Vie et Lumière (Life and Light) group in 1995 and formed its own association. They have a central church in Bondy, **France**, and some 65 churches mainly in **Germany** and **Sweden**. They use the **Romani language** in services. The Roma congregation in London belongs to CMERI.

CENTRO STUDI ZINGARI. Italy. Est. 1966. Director: Mirella Karpati. An **Italian** cultural and **educational** organization. It published the journal *Lacio Drom* and organized several international meetings, including the **Ostia Conference**. The center ceased activity around 2000.

CERIFINO, JIMÉNEZ MALLA. *See* MALLA, JIMENEZ CERIFINO.

CHACHIPE. Spain. Contemporary **dancer**. He began his career performing for tourists. At the age of eight, he went to Paris, and by the time he was 15 he had danced in the major cities of **Spain** and throughout **South America**.

CHALGA. The name given in **Bulgaria** to Gypsy **music** backed by a **dance** beat and delivered with the hedonistic drive of American hip-hop. Exponents include Azis.

CHANDIGARH FESTIVALS. The **Indian** scholar **W. R. Rishi** organized two festivals so that European Romanies could come to their original homeland India and meet their long-lost cousins. Receiving the European delegates to the 1984 festival was one of the last public engagements of Indira Gandhi before her assassination.

CHAPLIN, CHARLES (1889–1977). England. **Film** star. His best films included *The Great Dictator* and *Limelight*. In his autobiography, he wrote that his mother was half-Gypsy and that his grandmother's maiden name was Smith. According to other sources, she was called Mary Ann Terry, and yet a further possibility is that his maternal grandfather Charles Frederick Hill, a shoemaker, was an **Irish Traveler**. Chaplin's biographer, Joyce Milton, felt that he was well aware of his heritage and that his tramp character recalled the image of the eternal Romany wanderer.

CHERENKOV, LEV (1936–). Union of Soviet Socialist Republics. Civil rights activist and writer. For many years after World War II, he corresponded with Western scholars and through them contributed to learned journals on the subject of Romani.

CHERGASHI (CHERHARI) (TENT DWELLER). The name given to a number of Gypsy **clans**, including (1) The Chergashi of **Bosnia**, many of whom emigrated to Western Europe after 1966. On their visits to London, flower-selling was a major source of income. (2) The Cherhari of eastern **Hungary**.

CHINCHIRI, HASAN (1932–1994). Bulgaria. Band leader, singer, and composer. He started performing after 1945 and made several recordings before the clampdown on Romany culture. He is included in the LP *Great Masters of Bulgarian Instrumental Folklore*.

CHOCOLATE, EL. *See* MONTOYA, ANTONIO NUÑEZ.

CHUHNI. Originally a pejorative term in **Russian** for **Finns**, it is now used by other Gypsies as a pejorative term for Russian Gypsies living in the Baltic states.

CHUNGA, LA. *See* AMAYA, MICAELA.

CHUNGUITA, LA. *See* AMAYA, LORENZA FLORES.

CHURARI. A Gypsy **clan** that evolved in **Romania**. Later, after the end of serfdom in the 19th century, many emigrated. The term is considered by some to be derived from the Romani word *churi* (knife). but this is disputed.

CIBULA, JAN (1932–). Slovakia. Political activist and medical doctor. He currently resides in **Switzerland**. He served as president of the **International Romani Union** from 1978 to 1981.

CICA, DZINTSARS (1993–). Latvia. Student and singer. He represented **Latvia** in the Junior Eurovision Song Contest held in Copenhagen in 2003 with his own composition "You Are Summer" and placed ninth. Cica sings in a children's choir in the town of Talsi and has performed with several Romany groups. CD: *Come and Sing*.

CIMBALOM. It is thought that the cimbalom was brought to Europe by the Gypsies. It is a stringed instrument played with sticks and is related to the Indian *santur*. In the 19th century it was enlarged and provided with legs, which is the way it is played in **Hungary** today, though elsewhere in the Balkans it is still hung from the neck.

CIOABA, FLORIN (1955–). Romania. Political activist. He was elected **king** of all the Gypsies in 1997 to succeed his father, **Ioan Cioaba**. The marriage of his 12-year-old daughter in 2003 aroused great public interest.

CIOABA, IOAN (1935–1997). Romania. Political activist. An elder of the **Kalderash clan**, he kept in contact with the **Comité International Tzigane** and agitated for Gypsy rights during the Communist period. In 1986 he was jailed on a trumped-up charge of cheating the government on a copper contract. After the fall of Nicolae Ceausescu, he was a member of the Provisional National Council. He and his son **Florin Cioaba** ran for the Senate in 1995 but were not elected. In September 1992 in **Romania** he was proclaimed **king** of all the Gypsies. His authority as king was limited to the Kalderash clan, but many other Romanian Gypsies also saw him as their spokesman. His daughter Lucia is married to the son of Emperor Iulian of All the Gypsies, who was crowned in Romania in August 1993, while a second daughter **Luminita Mihai Cioaba** is a well-known writer.

CIOABA, LUMINITA MIHAI (1957–). Romania. **Poet** and journalist. Daughter of **Ioan Cioaba**, she won first prize for poetry in the second Amico Rom contest. Her poetry includes the *Romeo and Juliet*–themed ballad "Mara thai Bakro" and the poetry collection *Die Wurzel der Erde* [The Roots of the Earth], published in Romani, Romanian, German, and English. She has also produced the **film** *Romane Iasfa* [Romany Tears]—a documentary on the deportation of the **Romanian** Roma during the **Holocaust**. Luminita Cioaba has set up a Social Cultural Foundation in memory of her father.

CIOCÂRLIA (FANFARE). Romania/Moldavia. Brass band headed by singer, clarinetist, and alto saxophonist Ioan Ivancea. An 11-strong cadre of horn and reed players, drummers, and singers, ranging in age from 22 to 68, their CDs include *Baro biao* [Big Wedding] and *Gigli garabdi* [Hidden Song].

CIULLI, ROBERTO. Milan, Italy. Contemporary **theater** director. Abandoned an academic career in 1960 to run a mobile theater. Currently director of the Theater an der Ruhr in Mühlheim, **Germany**, which was for several years used as a base by the **Pralipe** Company. His support for this company over many years earned him a share of the 2002 **Hiroshima Foundation** Award.

CIVIC UNION OF ROMA. Czech Republic. An umbrella organization of groups in Hodonin and other towns in the **Czech Republic.** Its activities include preschool **education** and a **music** festival.

CIVIL RIGHTS. *See* HUMAN RIGHTS.

CLAN. This term is used in this dictionary in preference to *tribe* as a collective noun for groupings of Gypsies sharing a common cultural and linguistic heritage. These include the **Sinti**, who do not use the word *Rom* as a self-ascription, as well as for those groups that in addition to the general word *Rom* call themselves by names related to their traditional trade, for example, **Kalderash** (Coppersmiths) or **Sepedji** (Basket Makers). Some clans have a geographic name (e.g., Istriani Sinti). In **Spanish**, the word *clan* is used—by the press in particular—to describe the extended families of Gypsies.

CLINTON, WILLIAM JEFFERSON (BILL) (1946–). United States. Politician; former president of the United States, 1993–2001. He is descended from **Scottish** Gypsies. Clinton was originally called William Jefferson Blyth. His great-great-great-great-uncle Charles Blyth, who held the title of Charles I of the Gypsies, was crowned at **Kirk Yetholm** in 1847. Charles's brother Andrew settled in the American South, and his son Andrew Jefferson Blyth was born in 1801 in South Carolina. He is the great-great-grandfather of Bill Clinton.

Bill Clinton's wife, Sen. Hillary Rodham Clinton, has taken a great interest in the living conditions of the Roma in Europe. She made the keynote address at a conference "The Plight of the Roma" at Columbia University in November 2004.

CODONA, CLIFFORD. England. Contemporary political activist. He is chair of the **National Travellers Action Group** and vice chair of the **Trans-European Roma Federation.**

COLOCCI, ADRIANO (1855–1941). Italy. Author. An **Italian Gypsy-lorist**. He met Gypsies during a visit to the Balkans and wrote a book about them, *Gli Zingari: Storia di un popolo errante* [Gypsies: History of a Wandering People; 1889]. He was later elected president of the **Gypsy Lore Society**. He was not just an amateur student of Gypsy lore, for he also took up the defense of the Gypsies in 1911 at the First Ethnographic Congress in Rome, where he denounced intolerance against Gypsies. He also opposed a proposal in the Italian Parliament to ban the immigration of Gypsies.

COLOGNE CONFERENCE (1989). Conference and arts festival in February 1989 attended by more than 450 persons, mainly Romanies, from towns in **Germany** and elsewhere. A manifesto was issued at the end of the conference—the "Cologne Appeal for the Implementation of **Human Rights** for **Sinti** and Roma."

COLUMBUS, CHRISTOPHER (1451–1506). Genoa, Italy. Explorer. On his third voyage to the Americas in 1498, supported by the Spanish king and queen, it is said that he was accompanied by four Gypsies.

COMBAYS. Trio from Zaragoza playing rumbas. They made one record in **Spain** and were the support for the **Gypsy Kings** at the Nimes Festival in 1989. The trio no longer plays together.

COMITÉ INTERNATIONAL ROM. *See* COMITÉ INTERNATIONAL TZIGANE.

COMITÉ INTERNATIONAL TZIGANE (CIT; INTERNATIONAL GYPSY COMMITTEE). France. Est. 1965. President: **Vanko Rouda**. This committee sought to overcome **religious** and **clan** differences within the Romany community to create a united body. Muslim, Catholic, Orthodox, and Protestant all worked together. The CIT formed several branches in other countries and adopted non-Gypsy strategies, such as demonstrations, to gain publicity for its aims. These aims included preserving Gypsy culture and language and promoting the right of Gypsies to nomadize. It launched the first **World Romany Congress**, held near London in

1971. The CIT later changed its name to Comité International Rom (CIR). The CIR's international role was gradually taken over by the **International Romani Union**. The CIR continues to operate on a small scale in Paris.

COMMITTEE FOR THE DEFENSE OF MINORITY RIGHTS. Bulgaria. The **Bulgarian** partner in a project under the auspices of the British **Minority Rights Group**. It later changed its name to Interethnic Initiative for **Human Rights**.

COMMONWEALTH OF INDEPENDENT STATES (CIS). A loose confederation of states formerly in the **Soviet Union**. *See also* BELARUS; ESTONIA; LATVIA; LITHUANIA; MOLDOVA; RUSSIA; UKRAINE.

COMMUNAUTÉ MONDIALE GITANE (CMG). France. Est. early 1960s. Founder: **Vaida Voevod III**. An international organization, it was banned by the French government in 1965, and most of its work was taken over by the **Comité International Tzigane**. The CMG nevertheless continued to operate unofficially, until 1984 at least, under the presidency of M. Stefanovic.

CONFERENCE ON SECURITY AND COOPERATION IN EUROPE (CSCE). Established in 1975 at a meeting of world leaders in Helsinki. One of its aims was to increase democracy in Europe, and a development of this has been the protection of minority rights. Both the participating states and the associated nongovernmental organizations have taken on board the Gypsy issue. At the CSCE follow-up meeting in Helsinki in 1992 and the CSCE Council meeting in Rome in 1993, it was proposed and confirmed that the **Office for Democratic Institutions and Human Rights**—an institution of the CSCE—would organize a number of specialized meetings. The seventh of these seminars dealt with Gypsies in the CSCE region and took place in Warsaw in September 1994. A consolidated summary of the discussions was published by the CSCE. In 1994 the CSCE became the **Organization for Security and Cooperation in Europe**.

CONGRESS. *See* CONGRESS OF LOCAL AND REGIONAL AU-
THORITIES OF EUROPE (CLRAE); EUROPEAN CONGRESS;
LODZ CONGRESS; ROMANI DEMOCRATIC CONGRESS; RO-
MANI NATIONAL CONGRESS; SOFIA CONGRESS; WORLD
ROMANY CONGRESS.

**CONGRESS OF LOCAL AND REGIONAL AUTHORITIES OF
EUROPE (CLRAE).** The CLRAE works as part of the **Council of
Europe**. It was among the first international bodies to concern itself
with Gypsies, though recently it has done little. In 1979 its Cultural
Committee organized a hearing on the subject of the problems of
populations of **nomadic** origin (Roma and Sami).

In 1981 a "Resolution on the Role and Responsibility of Local and
Regional Authorities in Regard to the Cultural and Social Problems
of Populations of Nomadic Origin" (Resolution 125) contained a
number of recommendations that were mainly directed at the Council of Europe and other bodies. They included the recognition by
countries of the Romanies and the Sami as ethnic minorities and the
provision of camping and housing facilities.

In July 1991 a second hearing was held in Strasbourg, **France**,
with representatives of Gypsy communities from 12 countries. One
of the results of this hearing was the setting up of the **Standing Conference for Cooperation and Coordination of Romani Associations in Europe**.

In 1993 the CLRAE passed a resolution specifically on the Gypsies. This was Resolution 249 on Gypsies in Europe, concerning the
role and responsibility of local and regional authorities. It called on
various authorities to integrate Gypsies into their local communities
by providing camping sites and housing and to consider the possibility of launching a European Gypsy Route as part of the European
Cultural Routes program.

In October 2003 the CLRAE discussed the Romanies at its meeting in Rome. An earlier proposal to establish a network of municipalities with Gypsy populations was relaunched.

CONNORS, JOHNNY (POPS). Ireland. Contemporary civil rights activist and songwriter. After moving to **England**, he was active in the
early days of the **Gypsy Council**. His songs and fragments of his au-

tobiography (*Seven Weeks of Childhood*) have been published in various ephemera.

CONSEIL DE COOPÉRATION CULTURELLE (CDCC). France. Est. 1983. The CDCC organized a series of training courses and seminars for teachers on schooling for Gypsy and **Traveler** children. It commissioned, from sociologist Jean-Pierre Liégeois, an expanded edition of a **Council of Europe** report on the Gypsies of Europe, which has now been published under the title *Roma, Gypsies and Travelers* (with a number of translations).

CONTACT POINT FOR ROMA AND SINTI ISSUES (CPRSI). Est. 1994 in Warsaw. The Contact Point was set up by the Budapest meeting of the **Organization for Security and Cooperation in Europe (OSCE)** in 1994. Its first coordinator was Jacek Paliszewski, followed by **Nicolae Gheorghe** in 1999. The CPRSI logs all reported instances of violence against Romanies and **Sinti** and informs the national authorities in the respective countries. In January 1996 the CPRSI organized a "Workshop on Violence against Roma" in Warsaw attended by representatives of 35 Romani and Sinti organizations and nongovernmental organizations. On 21 November 1996, alongside the **Council of Europe**, it held a meeting in Budapest with representatives of governments and Romani organizations to discuss minority rights and the legal situation of Romanies. This meeting took place at the same time as a gathering of the **Standing Conference for Cooperation and Coordination of Romani Associations in Europe** in Vienna. The CPRSI has also prepared a special report on violence against Gypsies for the OSCE Permanent Council and published a newsletter for OSCE's **Office for Democratic Institutions and Human Rights**.

COOK, ALBERT. *See* ESSEX, DAVID.

CORFU. In the 14th century, Gypsies were already living on the Ionian island of Corfu under the leadership of one of their own **clan**.

CORSICA. Gypsies were first recorded on the island of Corsica in the latter half of the 15th century.

CORTÉS, JOAQUÍN (1969–). Cordoba, Spain. **Dancer** and choreographer. His passion for dance was inspired by his uncle, Cristobel Reyes, who performed **flamenco** in local bars and persuaded his nephew to study ballet. His grandfather was the flamenco singer **Antonio Reyes**. Cortés joined the Spanish National Ballet at 15 and soon became the principal dancer but left five years later to pursue a solo career. In 1992 he established his own company—the Joaquin Cortés Flamenco Ballet—and began to develop his individual style. Combining ballet and flamenco, he caused an instant sensation in the Spanish national press but was also criticized for diluting Gypsy culture. He has appeared in two major **films**: *The Flower of My Secret* and *Flamenco*. His first show as producer and choreographer was *Cibayi*, followed by *Pasión Gitana*, which went on a world tour during 1995–1997. Cortés insists that his style is in fact a combination of "precision and passion, symbolizing the pride of a marginalized tribe, and that just as the younger generation of Gypsies is now adapting to white culture and wants to be absorbed, so Gypsy culture is adapting too." In 2005 he toured with his latest show *Mi soledad* [My Loneliness].

CORTÉS, LUIS. Spain. Contemporary sculptor. He is currently living and working in **Italy**.

CORTIADE (COURTHIADE), MARCEL (1948–). France. Linguist, lecturer, and translator. He has served as vice president of the **International Romani Union**. He has been active in promoting a standard **alphabet** and a common language for literary purposes and organizes annual language **summer schools**.

COUNCIL OF EUROPE. Based in Strasbourg, **France**, and including the majority of European countries, the Council first took an interest in Gypsies in 1969 when the Consultative Assembly adopted Recommendation 563 on the "Situation of Gypsies and other **Travelers** in Europe." It recommended to the Committee of Ministers (of the Council) that it urge member governments to stop discrimination, provide a sufficient number of equipped **caravan** sites and houses, set up special classes where necessary, support the creation of national bodies with Gypsy representation, and ensure that Gypsies and other Travelers have the same rights as the settled population.

Six years later, in 1975, the Committee of Ministers adopted Resolution 13 containing recommendations on the "Social Situation of Nomads in Europe." This again stressed the need to avoid discrimination; provide caravan sites, **education**, and training for adults; and ensure that nomads could benefit from welfare and health services.

In 1983 the Committee of Ministers adopted Recommendation R1 on "Stateless Nomads and Nomads of Undetermined Nationality," recommending the linking of such nomads with a particular state.

In 1993 the Parliamentary Assembly adopted Recommendation 1203 on "Gypsies in Europe." It again proceeded by making recommendations to the Committee of Ministers. Recognition was given to the existence of large settled Gypsy populations in many countries. These recommendations were far-reaching, covering the teaching of **music** and the **Romani language**, training of teachers, the participation of Gypsies in processes concerning them, the appointment of a mediator, and programs to improve the housing and educational position of Gypsies.

A first reply was given by the Committee of Ministers to the Assembly in January 1994. The Committee then instructed the European Committee on Migration to conduct an in-depth study of the situation of Gypsies in Europe. Further, in September 1995 the Committee of Ministers replied again. The report of the study was declassified and made available to the Assembly. The Committee of Ministers has transmitted the Committee on Migration's report to the European Commission against Racism and Intolerance and other bodies.

In 1996 the Council of Europe set up a **Specialist Group on Roma/Gypsies**, chosen from nominees by the different member states. Its first meeting was held in March in Strasbourg. The council appointed a coordinator of activities on Roma/Gypsies, John Murray, who was based in Strasbourg. He has been succeeded by Henry Scicluna. The new coordinator has visited Romany settlements in several countries, including **Albania**.

Regular meetings are organized by the council. In October 2002, for example, the seminar "Roma Political Participation: A Way Forward" was held. A newsletter (*Activities on Roma, Gypsies and Travelers*) is published regularly, giving an account of the council's work with respect to Gypsies. *See also* CONGRESS OF LOCAL AND REGIONAL AUTHORITIES OF EUROPE (CLRAE).

COUNCIL OF SLOVAK ROMA (RRS). Slovakia. Est. 2003. Chairperson: Frantisek Gulas. The council held its first conference in Košice in January 2003 and has more than 15,000 members. It aims, in cooperation with other Romany organizations, to work with the **Slovak** government to improve the situation for the country's Roma population.

COUNTESS MARITZA. Operetta by the **Hungarian** composer Emmerich Kalman (1882–1953). The heroine in the aria "Höre ich Zigeunergeigen" [When I Hear Gypsy Violins] praises the spirit of Gypsy **music**, where one can fulfill all one's romantic desires.

CRABB, JAMES **(1872–1940).** England. Cleric. He set up a number of **educational** projects for Gypsies, including a center for Gypsies in Southampton, and tried to promote Christianity among them.

CRETE. Gypsies were recorded on Crete in 1322, living in black tents. It is likely that they returned to the coast of present-day Lebanon. Others came later, and the presence of Gypsies, living in poverty, was noted again in 1528.

CRIMEA. *See* UKRAINE:

CRIMINAL JUSTICE AND PUBLIC ORDER ACT OF 1994. United Kingdom. This Act repealed the provisions relating to Gypsies in the **Caravan Sites Act of 1968** and introduced new penalties for camping on private land without the permission of the owner.

CRIPPS REPORT. The Labour Party government in the United Kingdom in 1977 commissioned John Cripps (later Sir John Cripps) to write a report on the working of the **Caravan Sites Act of 1968**. He wrote a detailed report with many recommendations. Some of these were incorporated in a new Caravan Sites Bill that, however, was never passed due to the fall of the Labour Party government in 1979.

CRIS. *See* KRIS.

CRISS. *See* RROMANI CRISS.

CROATIA. Estimated Gypsy population: 100,000. Official census figures were 313 Gypsies in 1961, rising to 1,257 in 1971, 3,858 in 1981, and 6,695 in 1991. The first written record of Gypsies on the territory of present-day Croatia dates from 1362 and refers to two Gypsies in Dubrovnik. Other early arrivals noted in the next century were a trumpeter and a lute player.

Until 1918 Croatia was included in the Austro-Hungarian Empire. It then became part of **Yugoslavia**. During World War II, after the **German** occupation of Yugoslavia, a puppet state was set up covering Croatia and **Bosnia-Herzegovina** under the control of the fascist Ustashe movement and Andre Paveli. The Ustashe considered all Gypsies, **Jews**, and Orthodox **Serbs** as enemies. Muslim Gypsies had a certain amount of protection from the Muslim authorities, though, because Germany wanted the friendship of Muslim leaders in the Middle East.

Under Decree No. 13–542 of the Ministry of the Interior, all Gypsies had to register with the police in July 1941. They were forbidden to use parks and cafés. By 1943 most of Croatia's Gypsies were put in the Ustashe-run concentration camps: **Jasenovac**, Stara Gradiska, Strug, and Tenje. At the time of the creation of the Independent State of Croatia, there had been over 30,000 Gypsies, either nominally Orthodox or Moslem. At least 26,000 perished between 1941 and 1945.

Croatia again became part of Yugoslavia from 1944 to 1991. At the end of the war, very few Gypsies had survived in Croatia itself, but there was a steady immigration from other parts of Yugoslavia.

Croatia became independent in 1991. During the 1991–1995 war in Yugoslavia, many Romanies who did not manage to escape from Baranja (in western Slavonia) were killed by the Serbian occupiers. On 31 November 1991, Serbian irregular units burned down the Gypsy quarter of the village of Torjanici and killed 11 inhabitants. Because the Gypsies were Catholics, they were accused of collaborating with the Croats. In 1993 Romanies were driven out of Dubac, a suburb of Zagreb, by Croats returning from fighting the Serbs and had to resettle elsewhere in Croatia. Several attacks have taken place in Zagreb. In February 2003, while searching for scrap metal, Safet Muratovic was attacked by 10 youths who set his van on fire with a Molotov cocktail.

Segregation in **education** is common. In September 2002 around 100 ethnic Croatian parents prevented Romany children from entering a school in the village of Drzimurec-Strelec in northwestern Croatia in protest over the formation of integrated classes. Meanwhile Romany parents in Čakovec filed a lawsuit against the Education Ministry alleging that their children are racially segregated.

The Cidinipe Romano (Romany Society) was founded in 1991 with its headquarters in Virovitica and Vid Bogdan as president. In 1994 the bulletin *Romano Akharipe/Glas Roma* [Romany Voice] was established, and this was followed by *Romengo Čačipe* in 1997, the organ of the first Romany political party Stranak Roma Hrvatske (Croatian Romany Party). In 1997 the party elected Cana Kasum as its president and he stood unsuccessfully for parliament.

In 1994, the first **summer school** was organized in Zagreb for Romany children, and a youth organization was established in 1998. There are other Romany associations in Rijeka, Zagreb (Zajednica Roma Grada Zagreba and Cidinipe Roma ani Zagreb), and other towns.

CRUZ, JOSE MONJE (CAMARON DE LA ISLA) (1950–1992). Spain. Singer. Cruz began to sing **flamenco music** at the age of eight and made his first album in 1969. In 1979 he began to expand his repertoire importing influences from rock, jazz, and oriental traditions. His first gold album (*Soy Gitano*) came out in 1989. *Alma y corazón flamencos* is a three-CD compilation of his music.

CSARDAS (CZARDAS). A popular couples' **dance** in **Hungary** and **Romania**. The Gypsy csardas differs by being traditionally danced with the man and woman not holding hands. The dance may go on for some time, with a new man or woman taking over the role of one of the partners.

CYPRUS. Estimated Gypsy population: 4,000 (in both parts of the island). The first recorded presence of Gypsies on the island is from 1468, but it is thought that they were there some years earlier. In 1549 a report described them earning their living from making and selling nails and belts. Now they trade in jewelry and meat skewers, tell **fortunes,** and sell donkeys. They also travel to different parts of the island to help with the harvest. Many villages and towns have allocated sites where the **nomadic** Gypsies can stop.

In 1974 Cyprus was divided into two parts, **Greek** and **Turkish**. In that year, Muslim Gypsies fled to the Turkish-held part of the island and Christian Gypsies to the Greek part, whereas previously both groups had circulated freely throughout Cyprus. Shortly after Turkish troops entered Cyprus, rumors circulated that the Turkish government was bringing in large numbers of Gypsies. This proved to be false—the new immigrants were Laz (a Turkic group). The traditional circuit for harvest work in the west of the island for carob and olives and then to the east for grapes has been stopped by the partition.

All reports suggest that the small Gypsy population in Greek Cyprus lives in comparative harmony with the Greek-speaking population, although there is little social mixing. In Greek they are known by two names: *Yieftos* (**Egyptians**) and *Tsignos* (from **atsingani**).

Asylum seekers in the United Kingdom from Turkish Cyprus have stated that the situation there of several thousand Gypsies, known as *Gurbet* or *Çingan*, is not as good as in the Greek part. There is a great deal of racism and discrimination in employment. Many tried to seek asylum in Britain to join relatives who came legally as citizens of Cyprus when it was a British colony. In 1994 more than 350 Gypsies sought asylum on one day and all were refused. In 1994, too, some Turkish airline companies refused to sell tickets to Romanies, saying they gave Turkey a bad name by seeking asylum in the West. A well-known personage in the community is painter Asik Mene. The majority of the Gypsies in Turkish Cyprus live in the town of Guzelyurt, in the center of the olive-growing area.

CZARDAS. *See* CSARDAS.

CZECH REPUBLIC (CZECHIA). Estimated Gypsy population: 200,000. The 1991 census (taken before **Czechoslovakia** was divided) recorded only 33,000 Romanies. The 2001 census recorded 72,000 with Romani as their mother tongue but only 11,000 declared themselves as belonging to the ethnic group (*narodnost*).

The Czech Republic was established in 1993 when Czechoslovakia became two separate states. Most of the families in the Czech part had come from **Slovakia** after 1945. Some of these had difficulties in obtaining citizenship in the new republic despite long residency in the Czech lands (Bohemia and Moravia) and were in danger of becoming stateless. The law stated that applicants for citizenship had to have had a clean criminal record for at least five years. This requirement was criticized because many Romanies had been punished for acts that would not have been considered crimes in a democratic state. Young unmarried **women**, for example, who stayed at home were sentenced as "work-shy" and others obtained a criminal record by committing the "crime" of moving from one town to another without permission. A new citizenship law passed in September 1999 remedied the situation for individuals (predominantly Roma) who lacked voting and other rights due to restrictions under the previous laws.

Prejudice against Gypsies persists and incidents of discrimination and harassment have been reported. In April 2003 the Czech weekly newspaper *Respekt* reported that according to a survey of the Prague-based Center for the Study of Public Opinion, 79 percent of respondents would not want Roma as neighbors.

Attacks on Gypsies by skinheads and right-wing elements that began before the breakup—as early as 1990—have increased and have led to many deaths. At least 12 Romanies are known to have died in racist violence since 1993 in the Czech Republic. In 1995 skinheads attacked Gypsies in Breclav and on a train from Chomutov to Klasterec. Tibor Berki was killed in May 1995 in Zdar nad Sazavou. In June 2001, three friends (two of them Roma) were stabbed by a group of skinheads who attacked them in a pedestrian subway in Ostrava.

An estimated 5,000 skinheads were active in the country in 2003, and many observers believe the figure is much higher. In June of that year, three drunken youths attacked a Romany couple in their home in the northern Moravian town of Jesenik. The youths slashed the husband in the face and chest with a knife and hit his wife in the eye with a cobblestone. A police spokesman stated that the attack appeared to be racially motivated.

There is also evidence of police harassment. In June 1994 Martin Cervenak died in police custody. In May 2003 five off-duty officers in the northeastern Bohemian town of Jicin forced their way into the home of the Danis family in the Popovice quarter and beat up three people, including a pregnant woman. The government's **human rights** commissioner criticized a June 2003 ruling by a Karlovy Vary court that the 2001 beating of Karel Billy by five police officers was not racially motivated. The Ministry of the Interior has since issued special instructions for police searching Romany dwellings.

The government is actively trying to recruit Roma to serve as police officers and improve police relations with the Roma community. Police trainees attend the National Police Academy's course in Romany language and culture.

There is discrimination in admission to restaurants, bars, and discotheques throughout the country. Signs are often posted to prevent Roma from entering public places. Segregation in hospitals and schools has also been reported. While overall unemployment was 10 percent in 2003, unemployment among the Romany population was estimated at over 70 percent. Although the law prohibits discrimination based on ethnicity, employers refuse to hire Romanies and ask local job centers not to send Romany applicants for advertised positions. In 2003, Marcela Zupkova, a Romany woman from Hradec Kralove in the northeast, was denied employment on the basis of her ethnicity. Individual Roma do not have the legal right to file discrimination complaints; such action must come from governmental authorities.

Roma continue to face discrimination in housing, leading to segregated neighborhoods. In 2002 the central government admitted that the housing law allowed municipalities to discriminate, and the situation has not changed. In 2003 it was reported that many municipalities, including the central Bohemian town of Slany and the northeastern Bohemian town of Jaromer, forced Romany families to leave their accommodations. Tactics employed included evicting Roma from municipally owned homes for alleged lapses in rent payments and coercing Roma to sign agreements they do not understand, which are then used to curtail their existing housing contracts. While the human rights commissioner criticized such practices publicly, the law allows municipalities substantial autonomy to take such actions. *Respekt* highlighted the case of Mrs. Ratzova from Slany. After four months looking for alternative accommodation without success and sleeping outdoors, she handed her children over to state care and went to live with her psychologically ill brother, who later killed her.

In the town of Bohumin, the local authorities expelled some 200 Roma from a building where they had been legal tenants. Four families, including the Scukovas, stayed on in spite of harassment from the council. On 4 October 2005 a number of prominent national personalities entered the building with some difficulty in an action called "Guests of Mrs. Scukova" to show solidarity with the beleaguered Roma.

Romany children continue to be sent to special schools for children with mental or social disorders at a disproportionate rate, thereby perpetuating their marginal position in society. According to unofficial government estimates, 60 percent or more of pupils placed in these special schools were Romany children, although less than 3 percent of the population are Roma. Not only are they receiving an inferior **education** but schooling is also provided only until age 14 in special schools, as opposed to age 15 in standard schools. Children from special schools can also start work at 14—one year earlier than normal. While the government reported that approximately 90 percent of children attended school in 2003, official estimates indicated that less than 20 percent of the Romany population was still at school at the age of 14, and less than 5 percent completed secondary school. Students leaving special schools are not barred from attending secondary schools, but the curriculum does not prepare students to pass the tests required to transfer to mainstream schools. Some Romany parents still choose not to send their children to school regularly due to fear of violence and the expense of books and supplies. The **European Court of Human Rights** agreed in May 2005 to take up the case of *D. H. and Others v. the Czech Republic*, involving 18 children who had been assigned to special schools.

The Ministry of Education independently started to implement some changes. It began to work on altering the psychological tests given to Czech children that many claim are psychologically biased against Roma children. Children are assigned to "special schools" based on poor results in these tests. In January 2002, the education minister announced a long-term plan to phase out the special schools and move pupils from them into regular classrooms.

Many districts with large Romany populations hold yearlong programs to prepare children for their first year in school; these programs are funded by the government and administered by local nongovernmental organizations (NGOs). More than a hundred of these schemes were operating throughout the country in 2003. Some districts tracking local Romany students reported that up to 70 percent of students who attended this preparation successfully entered and remained in mainstream schools. Other positive initiatives include the placing of Romani-speaking teaching assistants in primary and special schools and the use, by 2003, of bilingual Romani-Czech language textbooks in 60 elementary schools. The Ministry of Education has also commissioned a textbook for use in schools on the cultural and historical roots of the Romany minority, highlighting successful members of the Romany community. Local NGOs also have supported additional studies and private initiatives to prepare Romany children for mainstream schools.

The continued high numbers of Roma seeking asylum in the United Kingdom during 2002 led to the imposition of preinspection controls at Prague's international airport. Roma activists in Britain criticized the controls as "racist" because they appeared to target only Roma. In August 2002, the Czech prime minister issued an unprecedented call for Roma to remain in the country and work with the government and majority population to address their economic and social problems.

The new freedom to form organizations, travel, and publish after the fall of Communism in 1989 led to a flourishing of activities. The **Brno Museum** obtained its own building, and Romani was introduced as a degree subject in Prague University in 1991, taught by **Milena Hübschmannová**.

The state funds **radio** programs for Roma on public stations and also supports Roma publications. A new magazine entitled *Romano Vodi*, financially supported by the Czech Republic Ministry of Culture and based in Prague, first appeared in February 2003. There are many Romany and pro-Romany organizations operating, such as the **Foundation for the Renewal and Development of Traditional Romani Values** and the Rajko Djurić Foundation.

In 2003, in continuation of its Plan for Roma Integration, the government allocated tens of millions of crowns (several million dollars) at various times during the year for projects designed to promote the integration of the Roma. Allocations supported the construction of community centers and educational assistance.

The Inter-Ministerial Commission for Roma Community Affairs includes 12 government and 14 Romany representatives, as well as the commissioner for human rights and his deputy. There are, however, currently no Roma in the Parliament. David Dudas became one of the first Romany priests in history when he was selected to serve the Roma community living near the Holy Trinity Church in Rokycany in January 2003.

There is an increasing number of **musicians** who have a following also among non-Roma. These include **Ida Kelarova** and the Prague-based band Bengas.

CZECHOSLOVAKIA. In 1399 the first Gypsy on the territory of Bohemia is mentioned in a chronicle. There are further references, and then in 1541 Gypsies were accused of starting a fire in Prague.

In general, while the provinces were under the **Habsburg** and **Holy Roman** empires, Gypsies were seminomadic in the Czech lands—Bohemia and Moravia. They were largely protected over the centuries against central legislation by noblemen who found their services useful on their estates, even though Leopold I in the 17th century, for example, declared that all Gypsies were outlaws, ordering them to be flogged and then banished if found in the country. In **Slovakia** they were pressed to settle by both **Maria Theresa** and **Joseph II**.

The modern state of Czechoslovakia was formed in 1918. In 1921 Gypsies were recognized as a minority and allowed to organize some sports clubs. However, both the nomads and those living in settlements were viewed with mistrust by the majority population. Nineteen Gypsies were tried for cannibalism in Kosice in 1924 (and eventually found not guilty). In 1928 there was a pogrom against Gypsies in Pobedim after some crops had been pilfered. Slovak villagers killed four adults and two children and wounded 18 more.

Nomadism by **Vlah** Romanies was strongly discouraged. Law 117 of 19 July 1927 placed controls on a wide variety of nomadic tradesmen. All Romany nomads had to carry a special pass and be registered if they were over the age of 14. Over the next 13 years, the number of identity cards issued reached nearly 40,000. Local regulations prohibited Gypsies from entering certain areas.

Germany invaded Czechoslovakia in 1938. The country was divided, and the Czech lands (Bohemia and Moravia) became a German protectorate in 1939. The first anti-Gypsy decree during the Nazi occupation by the Protectorate Ministry of the Interior on 31 March 1939, prohibited nomadism in the border zones and in groups larger than an extended family. In May 1942 a further decree was passed (on the Fight to Prevent Criminality) by which Gypsies were not allowed to leave their residence without permission and all Gypsies could be taken into "protective custody." A count of Gypsies on 2 August 1942 registered 5,830 pure and "half-breed" Gypsies. Two existing work camps at **Lety** and Hodonín were turned into concentration camps for Gypsies. Gypsies were also sent to the main camp at **Auschwitz** in December 1942 and January 1943. The Lety camp received a total of more than 1,200 prisoners, and Hodonín a similar number. Conditions in these camps were poor. Food and medical attention were in short supply, and the Czech guards brutally beat the inmates. More than 500 prisoners died in the camps before they were closed in 1943. Then the majority of the surviving inmates were transferred to the Gypsy Family Camp in Auschwitz, together with more than 3,000 Czech Gypsies who had previously been left in supervised liberty. Only some 600 persons all told survived the Nazi occupation of the Czech lands.

In contrast to the multinational state that had existed before World War II, Czechoslovakia in 1945 was restored as a state for the Czechs and Slovaks, and there was no place in it for the Romanies as a nationality or even as an ethnic group. Little changed with the takeover in 1948 by the Communists, who decided on a policy of assimilating the Gypsies.

The first step was to end nomadism, and a law to this effect was passed in 1958. The penalty for disobedience was imprisonment. The 10,000 nomads saw their horses taken away and the wheels removed from their **caravans**. In 1958, too, the Communists issued a statement saying that Gypsies constituted a socioeconomic group (not an ethnic group), which had problems to be solved in a specific manner. In 1965 the government passed the Resettlement Law. It was decided that no town or village should contain more than 5 percent Gypsies. This meant that large numbers would have to be resettled from Slovakia to the Czech lands. Both the Gypsies and the potential host communities resisted this transfer, although some Romanies had already moved west in search of work in the postwar years.

The government did allow the setting up of the Svaz Cikán Rom (Union of the Romany Gypsies) in 1968, operating throughout Czechoslovakia. Some 20,000 members joined in the first two years.

The Union established a recommended orthography for the **Romani language**, and for a time a number of publications were produced. A Czechoslovak delegation attended the first **World Romany Congress**, but no one was allowed to travel to the second or third congresses. Lessons in Romani for teachers were organized from 1971 to 1974. The **Soviet** invasion of 1968 led, however, to a change in the liberal policy, under Gustav Husak's government. In 1973 Gypsy and other independent organizations were closed, the magazines ceased to appear, and from then until 1989 there were to be very few publications in Romani.

The next attempt to control the Gypsy population was a sterilization program linked to a decree of 1972. Hints were passed on by word-of-mouth to social workers and doctors that Gypsies and other mothers of large families should be encouraged to be sterilized. Special inducements were offered to Romany **women**—classed as "socially weak" under the decree. After bearing a fourth child, a Czechoslovak woman could be sterilized on payment of 2,000 crowns; Romany women, on the other hand, were offered 2,000 crowns to be sterilized after the second child. Some women were operated on without them being aware that the procedure was irreversible. The civil rights movement Charter 77 organized protests against this program. It is believed that 9,000 Romany women were sterilized during the program, including some who had had no children. In 2004 more than 50 persons came forward to ask for compensation for their sterilization under the Communist regime. In November 2005, in the first ruling of its kind, the District Court in Ostrava found that the rights of "Helene F." had been violated when she was sterilized in 2001 shortly after giving birth to her second child.

In the last years of the Czechoslovak Republic, a revival of organizations and publications took place. In the 1990 elections the **Romani Civic Initiative** gained two seats in the federal parliament. In the period 1990–1992, there were 11 Roma in the three parliaments—national and federal. In 1992–1993, Czechoslovakia broke up into the Czech Republic and **Slovakia**.

CZIFFRA, GYÖRGY (1921–1994). Born in Hungary but later lived in France. Classical pianist.

CZINKA, PANNA. *See* PANNA, CZINKA.

– D –

DANCE. In most countries, so-called Gypsy dancing is—like **music**— a less inhibited and less formalized variation on the national dances. One exception is **Hungary**, where the **csardas** has evolved to suit the Roma's views on relationships between the sexes. It is danced by a couple who do not touch hands, and each partner is replaced at intervals by one of the onlookers. In **Spain**, it is generally accepted that the Gypsies created **flamenco**, which has traces of the **Indian kathak** dancing style. *See also* CORTÉS, JOAQUÍN.

DANIEL, ANTONIN (1958–1996). Czechoslovakia. Teacher and author.

DANIEL, BARTOLOMEJ (1929–2003). Czechoslovakia. Historian. A scholar working at the **Brno Museum** in the **Czech Republic**.

DANIHEL, VINCENT (1946–). Czechoslovakia. Author and cultural worker.

DANISH TRAVELERS. These are descendants of the first immigrants who came into the country from the 16th century on. References to the **Tatere** (a pejorative term) are found in Danish literature, especially in the writings of Steen Steensen Blicher. After World War II, the government stopped the children of the **Travelers** from living in **caravans** and closed such sites as there were. Very few persons (probably less than 100) would identify themselves as Travelers in **Denmark** today, although some estimates place the number between 4,500 and 6,000.

DARÓCZI, AGNES. Hungary. Contemporary civil rights activist and broadcaster. She was active in the cultural association Amalipe and has been part of the teams preparing the regular **radio** and **television** broadcasts aimed at the Romany population.

DARÓCZI, JÓSZEF CHOLI (1939–). Hungary. **Poet**, translator, and civil rights activist. He translated the four gospels into Romani as well as **Federico Garcia Lorca**'s *Romancero gitano*, which appeared in a trilingual edition (Romani, Hungarian, Spanish) in Budapest. He was a praesidium member of the **International Romani Union**. In 1979 he became the head of a new political organization for the Romanies in **Hungary**—the Orzsagos Ciganytanacs (**National Gypsy Council**).

DAVID SOTO, JOSE. *See* MERCE, JOSE.

DAVIDOVÁ, EVA. Czechoslovakia. Contemporary sociologist. She helped to keep Romany culture alive during the years 1958–1989 and was one of the founders of the **Brno Museum**.

DEATH. Customs vary from **clan** to clan. In Great Britain, it is still common to burn the **caravan** belonging to a man who has died. The **Kalderash** hold a memorial ceremony—the *pomana*—at regular intervals following a death, a practice probably borrowed from their Balkan neighbors.

DEBARRE, ANGELO (1962–). France. Contemporary **musician**. He is a guitarist in the style of **Django Reinhardt**. The Angelo Debarre Quintet produced their first CD, *Impromptu*, in 2002.

DEBICKI, EDWARD (1931–). Poland. **Poet**. His brainchild is the Gypsy music festival in Gorzów Wielkopolski, which has run annually since 1989. In addition to music, it has featured **films**, exhibitions, book promotions, and more recently seminars related to Gypsy culture. He is also director of the Gypsy **music** group Terno and has written a novel *Tel Nango Boliben* [Under the Open Sky] published in 1993 (available in Polish and Romani).

DECADE OF ROMA INCLUSION (2005–2015). This was a proposal of the **World Bank**, the **Open Society Institute (OSI)**, and the **European Commission**. It was formally launched at a meeting of prime ministers from central and southeastern Europe in Sofia on 2 February 2005. In June that same year, **Romania** was chosen to hold the rotating presidency of the Decade at a meeting in Bucharest attended by **George Soros** of OSI. The aim is by 2015 to end discrimination and ensure Gypsies equal access to **education**, housing, employment, and health care.

DEMETER, GEJZA (1942–). Czechoslovakia. Writer. His work includes the novel *O mule maškar amende* [The Dead Among Us].

DEMETER, NADEZHDA (1953–). Russia. Ethnographer and writer. Researcher at the Russian Academy of Sciences.

DEMETER FAMILY. Russia. Members of the **Kalderash** Demeter extended family now play a leading role in the Romani cultural life of Moscow, including the **Teatr Romen.**

DEMETROVA, HELENA (1945–). Czechoslovakia. Author. She has written a book of short stories entitled *Rom ke Romeste drom arakhel* [A Rom Finds a Way to Another Rom].

DENMARK. Estimated Gypsy population: 1,750. The first recorded Gypsies in Denmark came from **Scotland** in 1505 and then moved on to **Sweden.** They had a letter of recommendation from King James IV of Scotland to King Hans of Denmark, his uncle. In 1505 other Gypsies came across the border from **Germany.** Junker Jørgen of **Egypt** came to Jutland and got a letter of safe conduct from Duke Frederik. In 1536, however, *tatere* (Gypsies) were ordered to leave Denmark in three months; this order was not obeyed. In 1554 King Christian III circulated a letter accusing many noblemen and others of supporting the Gypsies, although they were believed to be "wandering around and deceiving the people." Anyone who gave them refuge would be punished, anyone who killed a Gypsy could keep his property, and any local official who did not arrest the Gypsies in his area would have to pay for any damage they did. The main effect of this letter was that the Gypsies started traveling in smaller groups. A further letter was issued in 1561 by Frederick II, in a milder form than Christian's. A certain Peder Oxe was sent to arrest all Gypsies in Jutland and bring them to Copenhagen to work as smiths or in the galleys.

In 1578 the bishop of Fyn told his priests not to conduct marriage ceremonies for Gypsies and to have them buried outside the churchyard as if they were **Turks.** In 1589 the original edict, ordering Gypsies to leave the realm within three months, was reissued with the addition of capital punishment for those who remained. Immigration ended and with the strong laws, the Gypsies resident in Denmark merged with the indigenous **nomadic** population forming a group of **Travelers**, popularly still called *tatere*. There was a small immigration of **Sinti** and **Jenisch** families at the beginning of the 19th century. The laws against Gypsies were eased in 1849, but reimposed in 1875 with the threat of a large-scale immigration of **Vlah** Romanies. From 1911 this law was carried out more effectively with the creation of a national police force. A traveling **musical** group known as Marietta's Gang was probably the last to be expelled, in 1913, and by 1939 very few families of Gypsies, if any, lived in Denmark and the Travelers had all but disappeared.

After 1945, the government banned anyone who had not been born in a caravan from nomadizing. Around 1970 there was a camping site at Islands Brygge near Copenhagen that was used by Scandinavian Travelers and Gypsies, and from time to time by Dutch Travelers. After the repeal of anti-Gypsy legislation in 1953, small numbers emigrated from eastern and central Europe. They are settled in houses and flats in Copenhagen and Helsingør. The **European Roma Rights Center** has criticized the practice of racial segregation in schools in Helsingør County. Whereas other special classes are designed for children with special requirements, the classes for Roma children are focused on a special ethnic group. Helsingør municipality has stated that the classes are for "Roma pupils, who can not be contained in normal classes or special classes."

Stevica Nikolić was the representative in Denmark of the **Comité International Tzigane** until he moved to the **Netherlands**. The organization Romano led by Eric Thomsen is currently active. *See also* DANISH TRAVELERS.

***DEPP, JOHNNY* (1963–).** U.S. actor. He played the part of a Romany in the **film** *The Man Who Cried* and a **Traveler** in *Chocolat*. Depp has taken a special interest in promoting the **music** group **Taraf de Haidouks**.

DERBY. England. Horse race. It has for a long time been one of the important events in the Gypsy calendar. Gypsies have gathered there for many years from the Sunday before the race (known as Show Sunday). Apart from being a source of income for **fortune-**

tellers and racing tipsters, it is also a social gathering. Gypsies maintain that they were the first to race on the Epsom Downs, where the Derby takes place. Since 1937 several attempts have been made to stop Gypsies from attending. In that year, Gypsies camped instead on the land of a sympathizer, Lady Sybil Grant. Currently a fenced-in field has been allocated for Gypsy families and their **caravans**, while the fortune-tellers park separately. The moving of the Derby from Wednesday to Saturday (when it clashes with the **Appleby Fair**) has led to a reduction in the number of Gypsies attending.

DEVEL (DEL). The Romani word for "God." It is cognate with the Latin *Deus* and Greek *theos*. Early writers on Gypsies were confused by the similarity of *Devel* and "Devil" and thought the Gypsies worshipped the Devil. The Romani word for "Devil" is *Beng*.

DEVLIN, BERNADETTE. *See* McALISKEY, BERNADETTE.

DEWUS, REINARD. The Netherlands. Contemporary singer. Reinard Dewus is a **Sinto** whose songs have lyrics in the **Romani language** set to well-known Dutch melodies. The **film** *Soeni* [The Dream] by Carin Goeijers combines elements of **music** video with intimate glimpses of his family.

DIALECTS, ROMANI LANGUAGE. At the time of the Gypsies' arrival in Europe there were perhaps two main dialects of the **Romani language** (Romani and **Sinti**), but since then different **clans** have developed separate features that may have been present in the speech of some speakers of the two original dialects. Sedentary Gypsies have also been affected by the language of the majority population where they live. Now, there are many dialects, of which the main living ones can be grouped in the following five clusters:

1. **Vlah**
2. Balkan
3. Northern
4. Central
5. The Romani of Calabria and Abruzzo in **Italy**

With recent migration, speakers of the Balkan dialects can now be found in most countries of western Europe. *See also* BALT-SLAVIC ROMANI; ERLIA.

DIMIC, TRIFUN (1945–2002). Serbia. Writer. He translated the New Testament and the *Epic of Gilgamesh* into Romani. He also wrote and produced a first reader for Gypsy children.

DIMITRIEVITCH, VALYA. Russia. Contemporary singer. She is married to the **Brazilian** consul in **France**, where she lives.

DIMOV, ZORAN. Macedonia. Contemporary cultural worker. He is head of the BTR **television** station. In 2004 he was elected as general secretary of the **International Romani Union**.

DIVORCE. Divorce is still rare and in practice for most **clans** means the wife returning to her family while the children remain with the husband.

DJURIĆ, RAJKO (1947–). Serbia. Journalist and **poet**. He studied in the Faculty of Philosophy at Belgrade University from 1967 to 1972 and went on to obtain a doctorate of sociology in 1986. Until 1991, he was editor of the cultural section of the daily newspaper *Politika*. As an opponent of the government and the war in **Bosnia**, he had to flee in October 1991 to **Germany** but has now returned to Belgrade. He has written poetry and prose in both Romani and Serbo-Croat. At the third **World Romany Congress**, he was elected secretary, and he served as president between the fourth and fifth congresses. His **literary** works have been translated into more than five languages. They include a collection of lyrics—*Than telal o kham* [A Place Under the Sun]—and a survey of Roma writers.

DODDS, NORMAN (1903–1965). England. Politician. He was a Labour member of Parliament in the United Kingdom who fought for Gypsy rights. At one time he opened a **caravan** camp on his own land. He was to die before seeing the fruits of his efforts in the **Caravan Sites Act of 1968**.

DOHERTY, JOHN (1895–1980). Donegal, Ireland. He took up the fiddle in his teens and soon was in much demand to play at the local village entertainment venues known as "Ceilidh houses." The Doherty family would travel around the Bluestack Mountain region calling in at cottages in this sparsely populated area. In the 1960s, Doherty was "discovered" and made a recording for the British Broadcasting Corporation. He went on to make several other recordings, such as *The Peddlers Pack*, *Bundle and Go*, and *The Floating Bow*. He was also the subject of a documentary, *Fiddler on the Road*, made by an Ulster **television** producer.

DOHERTY, TOMMY (1937–2003). Ireland. Political activist. Brought up in **Northern Ireland**, he founded the Society of Travelling People in 1959 in Dublin. After moving to **England**, he joined the **Gypsy Council** in 1966 and was for many years its chairperson. He continued working locally in Leeds and Sheffield, where he advised on a study conducted at the university on the health of Gypsies and **Travelers**. His last public appearance was at the **Irish Travelers'** Heritage Day in London in February 2003.

DOM. (1) An earlier form of the words *Rom* and *Lom*. Originally in Sanskrit it meant "man" and was the self-ascription of many **clans**, some of whom emigrated west and helped to form the Romany people. However, in some parts of **India**, it now has a pejorative meaning referring to a lower-caste person. (2) The **Nawwar** clan of Gypsies living in the Middle East.

DOMARI (THE SOCIETY OF GYPSIES IN ISRAEL). Est. 1999. Spokesperson: Amoun Sleem. There is an estimated population of 1,200 **Nawwar** (Dom) in the Old City of Jerusalem in the neighborhood Migdal ha-Chasidah. They are recognized as a separate community but classed as Israeli Arabs. They are no longer **nomadic**.

DORAN, CHRIS. Contemporary popular singer. Traveler who represented **Ireland** in the European Song Contest in 2004.

DORAN, FELIX (1915–1972). Ireland. **Musician**. A **Traveler**, piper, and brother of **Johnny Doran**. He won the first prize for the pipes at

Fleadh Ceoil na h-Eireann, the national competition in **Ireland**. He moved to Manchester, where he became a haulage contractor but continued to play and record.

DORAN, JOHNNY (1907–1950). Ireland. **Musician.** A **Traveler**, piper, and brother of **Felix Doran**. Johnny and Felix Doran were descendants of John Cash, a famous piper in Wicklow in the 19th century. Johnny Doran traveled in a horse-drawn **caravan** throughout Ireland but principally in County Clare, before he died in an accident.

DORTIKA. A variety of Greek with Romani words.

DOUGHTY, LOUISE (1965–). England. Author, journalist, and broadcaster. She has written three novels. The most recent of her books, *Fires in the Dark*, is the first of a trilogy based on the history of the Romanies. The next volume in the series is set in Great Britain and deals with the lives of Romanies in the late 19th and early 20th centuries.

DOUGLAS, CHARLES. Scotland. Contemporary campaigner for civil rights. A **Scottish Traveler**, he was active in the 1970s and was involved in setting up the Scottish Gypsy Council, which worked in cooperation with the **Gypsy Council**. He has been one of the members of the **Advisory Committee on Travellers** in **Scotland** and was awarded a Member of the (Order of the) British Empire.

DRAKHIN (GRAPEVINE). A website in the **Romani language**.

DRAMA. The establishment of the **Teatr Romen** in Moscow led to the writing of plays in the **Soviet Union** celebrating the transmutation of **nomadic** Gypsies into collective farmers and factory workers. Since 1945, a few writers have created original plays in Romani. The works of **Mustafa Aliev** (Romanov Manush) in **Bulgaria** were apparently confiscated by the police some years after the Sofia Gypsy theater was closed. *See also* GINA, ANDREJ; KRASNICI, ALI; LACKOVÁ, ELENA.

DRINDARI. Quiltmakers' **clan** in Kotel, **Bulgaria**. Their name comes from the sound made by a mallet carding wool for quilts. They are also known as Musikantsi (**Musicians**) and Katkaji—as they use the word *katka* (here) in their **dialect** as opposed to the majority of Bulgarian Gypsies who say *kate*. Bernard Gilliatt-Smith described in the *Journal of the Gypsy Lore Society* their dialect, which resembles that of Sliven and others in eastern Bulgaria.

DUBLIN TRAVELLERS' EDUCATION AND DEVELOPMENT GROUP. Ireland. Est. 1983. Part of its program includes legal advice and training courses for young adults. It is now known as **Pavee Point**, after the name of its headquarters and to reflect its nationwide role.

DUDAROVA, NINA (1903–?). St. Petersburg, Russia. Teacher and **poet**. In the 1930s, she was employed to teach Romani to some actors at the **Teatr Romen** in Moscow.

DUENDE. A Spanish term describing a mysterious power said to be held by some **flamenco** singers and **dancers**.

DUKA, JETA (1948–). Albania. Civil rights activist and collector of folktales. During the transition period after the end of the Communist regime in **Albania**, she was employed as an adviser on **women**'s issues. She currently works as a university language assistant and is coauthor of a Romani–Albanian dictionary covering several **dialects**.

DUNN, SYLVIA. England. Contemporary civil rights activist. She is a leading figure in the **United Kingdom Association of Gypsy Women**.

DUO Z. The professional name used by singers **Rudko Kawzcynski** and Torando Rosenberg from 1979. The "Z" stood for the concentration camp designation of Gypsies, *Zigeuner*. Their aim was to sing for the non-Gypsies to confront them with the problems of their people. One of their successes was a reworking of the German folk song "Lustig ist das Zigeunerleben" [Gypsy Life Is Carefree] with words referring to the persecution during and after the **Holocaust**.

DURBAN CONFERENCE (2001). Several Romany organizations, including **Aven Amentza** from **Romania**, took part in **South Africa**

in the meeting of nongovernmental organizations that was held alongside the World Conference against Racism.

DZENO FOUNDATION. Czech Republic. The foundation aims at the renewal and development of traditional Romany values. Among its activities are the magazine *Amaro Glendalos* and the Internet **radio** ROTA.

– E –

EAST ANGLIAN GYPSY COUNCIL. United Kingdom. Est. 1976. Secretary: **Peter Mercer.** A regional body based in Peterborough, **England.** The former Liberal MP Clement Freud is a patron.

ECONOMIC AND SOCIAL COUNCIL OF THE UNITED NA-TIONS (ECOSOC). In 1979 the **[International] Romani Union** was recognized by the United Nations Economic and Social Council (ECOSOC) as a nongovernmental organization representing Gypsies and **Travelers.** In 1993 it was upgraded to category II status, which gave it the right to speak at meetings. **Études Tsiganes** is also recognized by ECOSOC. *See also* UNITED NATIONS (UN).

EDUCATION. Education, in the sense of bringing up children to be members of adult society, is traditionally carried out by fathers with their sons and mothers with their daughters. Even before puberty, boys will learn their father's trade in a practical way, while girls will have to cook and look after their younger siblings. Schools are viewed by many parents with suspicion as places where children will come into contact with non-Gypsies and the dangers of drugs, bad language, and sex. Girls in particular may be withdrawn from schooling at puberty. The segregation of Gypsy children into special schools in many countries also leads to a high drop-out figure at secondary level. Nevertheless, individual Romanies have progressed through the system to university level.

EGYPT. There are two **clans** of **Indian origin** in Egypt—the Ghagar and the **Nawwar** (Dom). The Helebi, numbering perhaps a million, are probably originally industrial **nomads** of Middle Eastern origin. **Tony Gatlif's film** *Latcho Drom* features some **musicians** from Egypt who may have been of Indian origin.

EGYPTIANS. The name first given to Gypsies when they reached western Europe, as it was thought they came from **Egypt.** A number of groups in the Balkans previously thought to be Romany Gypsies but who no longer spoke the **Romani language** began in the last few years to claim that they were not Gypsies at all, but descendants of Egyptian immigrants to Europe. They number several thousand and are found in **Albania, Kosovo,** and **Macedonia.** In Albania they are known as *Evgjit* or *Jevg*, where their non-Romany origin has been accepted for longer. They asked to be recognized as an ethnic group for the **Yugoslav, Serbian,** and Macedonian censuses of 1991 but no separate figures have been published listing them. The Serbian-led government in Belgrade was pleased to welcome the emergence of the Egyptians, as they helped to diminish the percentage of Albanians in Kosovo and ethnologist Hadzi Ristic stated that he had found traces of Egyptian presence in Macedonia. It seems likely that the Egyptians emerged from the population of Albanian-speaking Roma who found, after 1990, that there was no advantage in being Albanian in either Kosovo or Macedonia. However, they had little inclination to call themselves Roma, because of the low social status of this group.

EINSATZGRUPPEN. Nazi task forces that murdered some 20,000 Gypsies in the occupied regions of the **Soviet Union** between 1941 and 1943. Their primary targets were "**Jewish** Bolshevists." During a visit to Minsk in August 1941, Heinrich Himmler extended the original orders of the Einsatzgruppen to also kill all Gypsies—men, **women,** and children.

EL CHOCOLATE. *See* MONTOYA, ANTONIO NUÑEZ.

EL PELE. *See* MALLA, JIMENEZ CERIFINO; MAYA, MANUEL MORENO.

ENCYCLOPEDIA. The fourth **World Romany Congress** set up an Encyclopedia Commission with the remit of preparing an encyclopedia in

Romani. The work was taken over by a working party under the auspices of the now defunct **Centre de Recherches Tsiganes**. Some draft entries and a call for contributors were circulated with *Interface* early in 1997. The future of the project is in doubt.

ENGLAND. Estimated Gypsy population: 100,000, including **Irish Travelers**. Some 50,000 live in **caravans**. The census figures for January 2005 show about 6,500 caravans on official council sites, more than 5,000 on authorized private sites, and 3,500 on unauthorized encampments. The latter figure includes caravans on Gypsies' own land but without planning permission.

It is likely that the first Gypsies in England came from **France** at the turn of the 15th century. The first written record dates from 1514 and refers to a **fortune-teller** from Lambeth who had left England some time previously. Further references occur between 1513 and 1530. A distinctive costume was common knowledge in England early in the 16th century, as we have records of court ladies dressing up as Gypsies as early as 1517.

There was soon a large enough number of Gypsies to worry the authorities and the first anti-Gypsy law was passed in 1530 under Henry VIII. This banned **"Egyptians"** from entering the country and ordered those already there to leave within 16 days or forfeit their possessions. In 1540 a group of Gypsies was released from Marshalsea Prison and put on a ship bound for **Norway**. Others were expelled to Calais, still an English colony. In 1554 (under Queen Mary) the death penalty was introduced and eight years later Queen Elizabeth strengthened the law with the penalties extended to anyone consorting with the Gypsies. In 1577 in Aylesbury, six persons were hanged under this law, a further five in Durham in 1592, and nine in York in 1596. At least 13 more were executed under this law (in Bury St. Edmunds around 1650) before it and most legislation concerning Gypsies were repealed in 1783.

Under the 1598 Act for the Punishment of Rogues, Vagabonds, and Sturdy Beggars many Gypsies were deported to the colonies in America (1614–1776) and later **Australia** (1787–1868). This was remembered for a long time in the Romani name for a magistrate—*bitcherin' mush* (sending-away man). In some parts of the country, however, no action was taken against Gypsies, and they were also protected by landowners who found it useful to have Gypsies available for entertainment and casual work.

Fortune-telling was evidently an important **occupation**. In 1602 **William Shakespeare**'s Desdemona refers to a handkerchief that an Egyptian woman who could read minds had given to her mother. The wife of the diarist Samuel Pepys went to see Gypsies at Lambeth with a friend to have their fortunes told. However, a male was apparently burned at the stake in Warwickshire for telling fortunes, if the story is to be believed.

The policy of expulsion from the country failed, and in the 19th century, settlement and assimilation became the aim. Various Christian missions took an interest in the Gypsy **nomads**, and special schools were opened. In 1815 John Hoyland was commissioned by the Society of Friends to collect information about the Gypsies with a view to improving their condition. This was the first survey made and gave James Crabb, among others, the impulse to start his mission. Assimilation was the goal, but this was thwarted by police and local authorities who continued to move Gypsies on.

In 1822 and 1835 (the Highway Acts), penalties were introduced for Gypsies camping on the highway. Attempts by **George Smith** to control the nomadic Gypsies with the **Moveable Dwellings Bills** in Parliament failed, however, owing to the opposition of circus and fair owners. The Gypsy population around this time has been estimated at about 10,000.

Popular novels in England—as elsewhere—featured Gypsies who stole children or pronounced curses that could not be avoided. In the late 19th century **Gypsylorists** emerged.

A new immigration started in the second half of the 19th century and there are reports of "foreign Gypsies"—certainly belonging to **Vlah clans**. At the beginning of the 20th century, England was visited by bear trainers, "German Gypsies" (probably **Lovari**), and the first of the **Kalderash** families who were to become regular visitors. Legislation against "aliens," aimed at **Jewish** immigrants from eastern Europe, was used to prevent Romanies from landing and to expel them rapidly. Nevertheless, in the 1930s, the Kalderash Stirio and Yevanovic families established themselves in England, and their descendants form a compact Romani-speaking community today. Irish **Travelers** have been coming to England and the rest of Britain particularly since the middle of the 19th century. They number some 10,000 in England.

Between the two world wars (1918–1939) much legislation was enacted affecting the nomadic Gypsies. The 1936 Public Health Act defined tents, caravans, and sheds as statutory nuisances. In 1937 the first of many attempts to stop the Gypsies' annual gathering for the **Derby** horse race failed. During both wars, however, Romanies served in the armed forces, and many were awarded medals for valor.

In the highly industrialized England that arose after 1945, nomadic Gypsies found life much harder. Their traditional camping places were built on, and, with increased and faster traffic, stopping on the roadside became dangerous and—in many cases—banned. The 1947 and 1950 Town and Country Planning Acts restricted the use of land by caravans and then the **Caravan Sites Act of 1960** led to the closure of many private sites, forcing the Gypsies back on the road.

A civil rights movement began to emerge in the 1960s with the Society of Travelling People in Leeds (1965) and Tom Jonell in the south. In 1966 the **Gypsy Council** was founded at a meeting in Kent. Under its secretary, **Grattan Puxon**, it began a campaign of passive resistance to the forced moving-on of caravans from public land, which obtained considerable press and **television** publicity. It organized the first caravan school at Hornchurch aerodrome, with volunteer teachers including **Thomas Acton**. Others followed. Under pressure from **Norman Dodds**, a member of Parliament, the central government began to take an interest in Gypsies. The Ministry of Housing and Local Government produced a report, *Gypsies and Other Travellers* (1967), which was the first official study of Gypsies in England and **Wales**.

With this pressure from both inside and outside Parliament, the **Caravan Sites Act of 1968** was passed, applying to England and Wales. This act placed a duty on county councils in particular to provide caravan sites. However, areas of the country could then be "designated" as areas where Gypsies could not park their caravans unless they found a pitch on the official sites. The first of these designations were made in 1973.

In 1980 the Local Government Planning Land Act removed the word "Gypsy" from the 1835 Highway Act. This was no longer necessary because of the provisions of the 1968 Caravan Sites Act. Gypsies were no longer singled out for punishment for camping on the roadside, unless it was a designated area.

In 1994 the **Criminal Justice and Public Order Act** imposed stronger penalties for camping anywhere in England or Wales outside official sites. At the same time the duty on councils (laid down by the 1968 Caravan Sites Act) to provide such sites was removed, and Gypsies were told that they had to buy land, get planning permission, and make their own caravan sites. Gypsies began buying land as a winter base but local councils often refused planning permission. The penalties for living in a caravan on one's own land without planning permission are higher than for trespassing. The local authorities then take them to court in order to remove them. The evictions of the 1960s from public land have been replaced by evictions from the Gypsies' own land. During 2004 and 2005 bailiffs cleared by force several such encampments. A particularly violent eviction took place in Chelmsford in 2004 during which many caravans were destroyed.

In 2001 the government set aside money annually for the refurbishment of existing council-run caravan sites. Later this was extended to apply to new transit sites, although approval has been given for only two. In November 2004 a House of Commons select committee recommended reintroducing the duty on councils to provide sites. However, this was rejected by the minister, John Prescott, with overall responsibility for Gypsies. In December that year it was announced that local authorities could bid for money to build new caravan sites. A sum of £8 million was set aside for fiscal year 2005/2006 for new sites and the refurbishment of old sites. The approved projects, announced in July 2005, included £1.5 million for a site in Bristol.

In February 2006 the deputy prime minister's department issued a Circular (1/2006) which in due course will lead to local councils allocating areas where Gypsies can buy land with the likelihood that they will be given planning permission.

In 1996 it was estimated by the authorities that 50,000 nomadic children age 16 and under lived in England. This figure includes some **New Travelers.** The majority of primary-age children (age 5–11) attend school, but the situation is not so satisfactory for secondary-school children (age 11–16). The Department for Education and Science funds Traveller Education Support services as part of the Vulnerable Children's Grant. Continuing **education** after the age of 16 is not common, although many Gypsies and Travelers attending further and higher education colleges conceal their origins and no figures are available.

There have been some incidents of stone-throwing at caravans but most anti-Gypsy violence has been directed at asylum seekers. In May 2000 Roma experienced three separate physical attacks across the country in a week. A refugee in Salford had a brick thrown through his window while attempts were made to kick down his door. He was also subject to racist abuse screamed from the street. The City Housing Service refused to help or rehouse the man. The North West Refugee Consortium said it had yet to determine whether the attack was racially motivated—it could have been attempted burglary. A group of Roma living in Middlesborough were so shaken by the attacks they experienced that some of them decided to return to **Slovakia**, saying that if they were going to die, they would prefer it to be in their own country. Several thousand Roma from eastern Europe had come to Britain in the years after 1990 as asylum seekers but very few were accepted as refugees. With the accession of several countries to the **European Union** in May 2004, however, many now have the right to remain in the country as workers.

Gypsies in England today are mainly self-employed with such trades as tarmacking and block-paving, landscape gardening, and house repairs. As **musicians** they are known in folk club circles but not to the general public. *See also* MESSING; NORTHERN IRELAND; SCOTLAND.

EPSOM DOWNS. A gathering place for English Gypsies at the time of the **Derby** horse race. Howard Brenton wrote a play *Epsom Downs* that was first performed by the Joint Stock Company at the Roundhouse, London, in 1977 and featured the Gypsy presence. Sporadic attempts by the authorities to stop Gypsies bringing their **caravans** to the Downs have failed.

ERKÖSE BROTHERS (ERKÖSE ENSEMBLE). Turkey. The three brothers Ali (zither), Barbaros (clarinet), and Salahaddin (lute) are contemporary folk **musicians**, originally from Bursa. They have played concerts abroad and made recordings. CD: *Tzigane*.

ERLIA (ARLIA). A term used by Romanies in the Balkans to describe sedentary Gypsies and their **dialects**, as opposed to **nomads**. The derivation is from the **Turkish** word *yerli* (local).

ESMA. *See* REDJEPOVA (REDZEPOVA), ESMA.

ESSEX, DAVID (ALBERT DAVID COOK) (1947–). England. Singer and **film** actor. He played the roles of Jesus in *Godspell* (1971) and Che Guevara in *Evita* (1978) on stage. Essex assisted at the official opening of the office of the **Gypsy Council for Education, Culture, Welfare and Civil Rights** (of which he is patron) in 1995. He has recorded the poems of **Charlie Smith** and is the presenter on **Jeremy Sandford**'s video *Spirit of the Gypsies*. CD: *Forever*.

ESTONIA. Estimated Gypsy population: 1,000 (mainly immigrants after 1945). The first record of a Gypsy in the territory of present-day Estonia dates from 1533 when the presence of at least two Gypsies in Tallinn was noted. Estonia was under the rule of various countries until 1918, and their laws would have applied. Numbers have never been high, and during the Nazi period, the German occupiers murdered almost all the Gypsies in 1941–1943. The dead included all the Lajenge Roma, a distinct **clan** with their own **dialect** of Romani. The Estonian writer Tuglas Friedbert is of Romany origin.

ETAPE 29. France. An organization that campaigns for better camping facilities, schooling for children, and the abolishment of strict laws that make it illegal to camp on public land.

ÉTUDES TSIGANES. France. Est. 1949. President: Jacqueline Charlemagne. Organization with mainly non-Gypsy members, founded in Paris after World War II. Since 1955 it has published the journal of the same name (current editor: Alan Reyniers) and has held two scientific conferences, the first in Sèvres in 1986 and the second in the Centre Pompidou in Paris.

EUROPEAN COMMISSION. A body of the **European Union (EU)**. It initiated a newsletter with project partners in **Bulgaria, Poland,**

Slovakia, and the **Minority Rights Group** in London. The newsletter's purpose was to inform anyone involved in Romany rights and **education**.

EUROPEAN COMMISSION ON HUMAN RIGHTS. Established by the **Council of Europe** in 1950, it merged into the **European Court of Human Rights** in 1993.

EUROPEAN COMMITTEE ON MIGRATION (CDMG). On the instructions of the Committee of Ministers of the **Council of Europe**, the CDMG carried out an in-depth study in 1994 on the situation of Gypsies in Europe.

EUROPEAN COMMITTEE ON ROMANI EMANCIPATION (ECRE). United Kingdom. Spokesperson: Len Smith. ECRE was established to promote common rights of equity of treatment, protection, and improvement in the conditions of the Roma in Europe.

EUROPEAN COMMUNITY. See EUROPEAN UNION (EU).

EUROPEAN CONGRESS (1994). Seville, Spain. The Congress was organized originally with the primary purpose of looking at **education**, but its remit expanded and it took on the air of an international congress. The king and queen of **Spain** patronized the proceedings.

EUROPEAN COURT OF HUMAN RIGHTS. Est. 1950. A court set up in Strasbourg by the **Council of Europe** to deal specifically with individual cases involving **human rights**. A number of cases involving Gypsies have been taken to this court. Several concerned with police harassment in eastern Europe have been successful, but attempts by English Gypsies (such as Mrs. Chapman in *Chapman v. UK*) to overturn negative planning decisions for private **caravan** sites have so far met with failure.

In December 2005 in *Bekos and Koutropoulos v. Greece*, the court ruled that **Greece** had violated Article 3 of the European Convention on Human Rights (degrading treatment) when two Roma were beaten in a Mesolonghi police station in 1998. On the other hand, in February 2006 a panel of the court—to the dismay of their representatives—

found in a test case (*D. H. et al. v. Czech Republic*) that 18 Romany children had not been discriminated against by being placed in special schools because "the system of special schools had not been introduced solely to cater for Roma children."

EUROPEAN DIALOGUE. United Kingdom. Est. 1990. An independent membership organization launched as part of the pan-European civic network of the **Helsinki Citizens' Assembly**. It sponsors a number of initiatives in the Romany field.

EUROPEAN PARLIAMENT. *See EUROPEAN UNION (EU).*

EUROPEAN ROMA (AND TRAVELLERS) FORUM. A proposal of the Committee of Ministers of the **Council of Europe** put forward by **Finland**, originally in 2001. Anne-Marie Nyroos chaired a working party (GT-ROMS) on the project, which came into effect in 2004. The aim is to set up a body to represent all the Gypsy organizations. It will meet twice yearly and have an office in Strasbourg, **France**. A ceremony to mark the signing of the partnership agreement between the Council of Europe and the European Roma and Travellers Forum took place in Strasbourg on 16 December 2004. Seventy elected delegates from 33 countries came together in that same town in December 2005 for the forum's first full meeting.

EUROPEAN ROMA RIGHTS CENTER (ERRC). Hungary. Est. 1996. Director: **Dimitrina Petrova**. An autonomous nongovernmental **human rights** organization in Budapest, **Hungary**, governed by a nine-member board to monitor and defend the human rights of Romanies in Europe. Initial funding came from the **Open Society Institute**. The ERRC publishes the quarterly magazine *Roma Rights* and has produced several reports on conditions for the Roma in various countries. It has assisted Roma from many countries to bring their cases to national and international courts. For example, in February 2006 it lodged an allegation with the **European Court of Human Rights** that police in **Romania** had used excessive force when evicting four members of the Pandeles family from their fruit stall in the market in Targu Frumos. The police wore masks and carried Kalashnikov rifles. In May 2005 the regional Court of Appeal in

Romania had dismissed a complaint by the family, prompting this appeal to the European Court.

EUROPEAN UNION (EU). The EU, previously known as the European Community (EC) and based in Brussels, **Belgium**, has taken a number of initiatives in Gypsy matters. In May 1984, the European Parliament passed a resolution on the situation of Gypsies in the EC. It called on member states to eliminate existing discriminatory provisions that may exist in their legislation and to make it easier for **nomads** to attach themselves to a state in accordance with recommendation R(83)1 of the **Council of Europe**.

Five years later, in May 1989, the council passed the School Provision for Gypsy and Traveler Children resolution. The program of action to be taken included experiments with distance learning and training and employing Gypsies and Travelers as teachers wherever possible. The EU has financed a number of projects in the spirit of these recommendations. Governments were to let the Union know the results of their measures so that a combined report could be presented to the council by 31 December 1993. The report was eventually published in 1996. This showed, as might have been expected, that some states had done more than others in implementing the recommendations.

Recent action has been less directed at nomads in the west but rather with improving conditions for the Roma in the countries in central and eastern Europe that have joined or are joining the Union. The EU Commission has sponsored a number of initiatives, including Pakiv, a program to train local activists in eastern Europe.

In April 2005 the Parliament passed a resolution "on the Situation of the Roma in the European Union." It again calls on member states to tackle racism and exclusion. In December of the same year, the European Parliament hosted an international conference entitled "Roma Diplomacy: A Challenge for European Institutions." It was part of a project to equip young Roma **human rights** activists with the skills necessary to represent their communities.

EUROROMA. A civil rights program run by the **Autonomia Foundation** of **Hungary**. It covers **Bulgaria**, Hungary, **Romania**, and **Slovakia** and is financed by the **European Union**. Its aim is to foster self-help initiatives among the Romany communities in the partner countries. The first meeting of the partner organizations from the four countries took place in Budapest in January 1996.

EVANGELICAL CHURCH. *See* CENTRE MISSIONAIRE ÉVANGÉLIQUE ROM INTERNATIONAL (CMERI); PENTECOSTALISM.

EVENS, GEORGE BRAMWELL (1884–1943). England. **Religious** leader. Known as "Romany," he was the son of Tilly Smith—the sister of **Rodney Smith**—and Salvation Army lieutenant George Evens. Reverend Evens was a broadcaster of BBC Children's Hour programs in Manchester from 1933 until his unexpected death in 1943. His wife, Eunice Evens, published a biography of her husband entitled *Through the Years with Romany*.

EVGJIT. *See* EGYPTIANS.

EXPERT GROUP (OF THE COUNCIL OF EUROPE). *See* SPECIALIST GROUP ON ROMA/GYPSIES (MG-S-ROM).

EYNARD, GILES (1941–). France. Civil rights activist. He was a member of the Comité Rom de Provence and the **West European Gypsy Council**. He has also acted as treasurer of **Tchatchipen**.

– F –

FAA (FAW). The surname of several **Scottish Traveler** families. The name was also adopted by some Romanies who came to **Scotland**. The current heir to the Faa "throne" is an Edinburgh housewife who has shown no interest in claiming the title.

FAA, JOHN (fl. 16th century). Probably a Romany rather than a **Traveler**. He called himself the Duke of **Little Egypt** and was recognized by King James V as the leader of the Gypsies in **Scotland**.

FAA, JOHNNY (fl. 15th century). Scotland. **Scottish Traveler**. According to legend, in 1470 he rescued two sisters from the clutches of their uncle who had thrown them into a cellar to make off with their inheritance.

FABIANOVÁ, TERA (1930–). Czechoslovakia. Writer. She was one of the first **Czech** Gypsies to write in Romani. In 2003, she received the **Roma Literary Award** for Fiction.

FAMULSON, VICTOR. Finland. Contemporary political activist. A **Vlah** Romani living in **Finland**, he is a vice president of the **International Romani Union** (elected 1990 and 1994).

FARRUCO, EL, AND EL FARRUQUITO. See FLORES, ANTONIO.

FAYS, RAPHAEL (1959–). Italy. **Musician.** An Italian **Manouche** guitarist and the son of guitarist Louis Fays, he plays classical as well as jazz and Latin American music. He is currently playing in the **Django Reinhardt** style with a trio.

FEKETE VONAT (BLACK TRAIN). (1) A name given to the train carrying Gypsy workers to and from Budapest for a weekend break in their homes in eastern **Hungary**. (2) A rap group featured on the CD *Rough Guide to Hungarian Music*.

FELDITKA ROMA. A term used for the Lowland Gypsies in **Poland**.

FERKOVÁ, ILONA (1956–). Rokycany, Czechoslovakia. Writer. She began to write in Romani after getting acquainted with the works of **Tera Fabianová** and **Margita Reiznerová**. Her writings include a short story, "Mosarxa Peske o Dzivipen" [She Spoiled Her Life].

FERRÉ, BOULOU (1951–). France. Gypsy jazz guitarist and the son of **Matelo Ferré**, both he and one of his brothers, Elios, tour widely as a duo in the style of **Django Reinhardt**. They have made several recordings.

FERRÉ, MATELO (1918–1989). France. **Musician.** A jazz guitarist, he was the last survivor of the senior Ferré brothers. A **Gitano** living in Paris, he and his brothers composed many waltzes. His three sons—Elios, Michel, and **Boulou Ferré**—all follow in his footsteps as musicians.

FICOWSKI, JERZY (**1924– **). Poland. Contemporary historian. He is an authority on Romany history and culture, his first major publication being *Cyganie Polscy* [The Gypsies of **Poland**] in 1953. He has since published several works in Polish as well as one book in English on the Gypsies in Poland. Ficowski was instrumental in introducing the Romani poet **Bronislawa Wajs** (Papusza) to the Polish public.

FILM. Gypsies have been a popular subject for filmmakers. More than 2,500 films from 30 countries with Romanies as their theme are recorded in the database of the Hamburg Cinemathèque. The first film to feature Gypsies was probably *Campement des Bohèmes* (Georges Melies, 1896). Other important titles are as follows:

- *Gypsy Wildcat* (**United States**, 1944)
- *The Gypsy and the Gentleman* (Great Britain, 1957)
- *I Even Met Happy Gypsies* [*Skupljace perja*] (**Yugoslavia**, 1967)
- *Angelo, My Love* (United States, 1983)
- *The Time of the Gypsies* (Yugoslavia, 1988)—**Rajko Djurić** was the adviser for this film
- *Black Cat, White Cat* (Yugoslavia, 1998)

Some other films have been made by Gypsies or with their involvement at production level. **Bob Hoskins** directed and starred in the title role (an army deserter dressed as a Gypsy girl) in *The Raggedy Rawney* (Great Britain, 1988). Dufunya Vishnevskiy directed *Ya vinovat*—a crime drama—in **Russia** in 1993; a second film by the same director, *Greshnye apostoly lyubvi*, is a fictitious story set during the Nazi occupation. The **Italian** film *Take Me Away* [*Prendimi*] by director Turido Zangardi (2003) is another example.

A large number of documentaries have also been made, including the first two parts of a trilogy by **Tony Gatlif**—*Les princes* and *Latcho drom*, completed by the fictitious *Gadjo Dilo* (1997). *American Gypsy* (1999) by Jasmine Dellal features Jimmy Marks and his family, while *Opre Roma* (1999) covers the evolving **Canadian** Gypsy community. A **Spanish** film, *The Three Thousand* [aka *Seville*

Southside], made in 2003, deals with Romany families resettled in Seville. *Bjørn* (2004) is a documentary based on the life of a **Norwegian Traveler** child taken from his family soon after birth. *Pavee Lakin* (2005) depicts the life of an **Irish Traveler** family in Dublin. *Romany Tears* (directed by **Luminita Cioaba**) is the story of the deportation of **Romanian** Gypsies to **Transnistria** during World War II.

The Golden Wheel Roma Film Festival has been held in **Skopje** since 2002. It features productions with Roma stories.

FINKS, E. Latvia. A Rom who was a renowned **fortune-teller**. It is said he predicted in the 1930s that **Latvia** would prosper under a **woman**'s leadership and that the country would reemerge from **Soviet** occupation in 1991. He was sent to a Gulag prison camp.

FINLAND. Estimated Gypsy population: 8,000. From approximately 1200 to 1809, Finland was under **Swedish** control. Eight work horses were confiscated from Gypsies on the island of Åland in 1559—the year of their arrival, reputedly the first Gypsies in Finland. Many of this group were sent back to Sweden. The first record on the mainland dates from 1580. In the 1600s Finland's Romany population grew, with immigration occurring from the east as well as from Sweden. A Swedish law of 1637—which applied to Finland, too—stated that all Gypsies should be banished or hanged, but this was ineffective.

In 1660 the ruler Per Brahe settled 140 Gypsies on farms in the Kajaani Castle area that had been abandoned by Finnish peasants after the crops had failed. He wanted the Gypsies to serve as spies and guards on the eastern border. It seems then that they did not settle down, and in 1663 Per Brahe issued a warning that if they did not settle by the next year on the plot of land given to them, they would be banished from the whole of the Swedish empire.

The Gypsy population carried out traditional nomadic trades in Finland—horse selling, veterinary care, castration of pigs, ironwork, smithing, making and selling lace, **fortune-telling**, and seasonal agricultural work.

In 1809 **Russia** occupied Finland. In 1812 a decree was issued that all the disabled, wandering **Tartars**, Gypsies, and other vagabonds of poor reputation who were not capable of ordinary work were to be dispatched to workhouses. In 1863, any Gypsies in ordinary workhouses were removed and placed in special stricter workhouses in Hameenlinna. The year 1862 saw Gypsies arriving from abroad being refused entry even if holding genuine passports. A census in 1895 recorded 1,551 Gypsies, a figure seen as too low.

Finland became independent in 1917. In 1906 a Gypsy mission had been founded by Oskari Jalkio, whose aim was to remove Gypsy children from their families and give them a normal **education**. The first attempts to set up children's homes in the 1920s were not successful. By 1953 a new commission adopted a number of recommendations, including once again the use of children's homes and enforcing school attendance. By 1963 five homes were established, and 100–150 children lived in them.

After World War II, the industrialization of Finland decreased the demand for the Gypsies' trades, and seasonal work was no longer available. In addition, the Gypsy community of Karelia, taken over by the **Soviet Union**, decided to migrate from their former living areas into Finland proper. Gypsies had to move into towns, where they soon found themselves living on welfare benefits. In 1960 a report of the Helsinki City Special Committee published a survey of the situation.

In 1967 the Suomen Mustalaisyhdistys Ry (Finnish Gypsy Association) was formed, with the aim of bringing pressure on the government to improve the standard of living of the Gypsies and to stop discrimination in Finnish society. For several years, the magazine *Zirickli* (Bird), edited by Kari Huttunen, campaigned for Gypsy civil rights.

In 1968 the State Committee for Gypsy Affairs was reestablished. The committee included three members representing the association and two from the Lutheran Gypsy Mission. They set about making two studies, one on the social needs of Gypsies and the other on housing, and these were published by the committee. In 1970 an Act of Parliament prohibited racial discrimination. In 1971 the Social Welfare Act was reformed, and the government then refunded half of any welfare assistance that the local authorities gave to their Gypsy population. At this time, three-quarters of the Gypsies were receiving welfare payments and faced diminished health, family breakdown, and unemployment. The aim of the reform was to make it easier to obtain welfare payments and provide more systematic and better planned support to promote assimilation. The Ministry of Education encouraged adults to join classes in literacy and technical subjects, as well as studying Gypsy history. The National Board of Education then printed a history book for the Gypsies. In 1972 the Work Group for Vocational Training set up by the Ministry of Labor proposed linking vocational and basic education into one course.

Two thousand Finnish Gypsies immigrated to Sweden in the 1980s. Most left for better housing and employment conditions, and the Finnish Romany Association in Stockholm was created to assist the Gypsies there. Meanwhile, living conditions in Finland itself improved.

At the end of the 1960s Gypsy **music** was very popular in Finland, with **Hungarian** and Russian Gypsy music proving particularly popular with people of all classes. The Folklore Archive of the Finnish Literary Society started to collect Gypsy songs in 1968 and now has more than 1,000 titles. In 1972 the Folklore Archive and Love Records jointly produced an anthology called *Kaale dzambena* [Finnish Gypsies Sing]. Singers and musicians include **Olli Palm**, the band **Hortto Kaalo**, **Anneli Sari**, and classical violinist Basil Borteanou. In September 2005 a festival was organized in Porvoo where the performers included **Bratsch** from France.

The language of the Finnish Gypsies is a distinct Romani **dialect** that had been falling into disuse among the younger generation. However, there has recently been a revival of the **Romani language**, and textbooks have been prepared for children.

FIRLE BONFIRE. Sussex. In November 2003 the Firle Bonfire Society burned a **caravan** with effigies of Gypsies looking out of the window and anti-Gypsy graffiti painted on it. This was in line with an annual tradition of burning effigies of political figures on Guy Fawkes Day, 5 November, but this time the authorities felt the ceremony had gone too far and several members of the organizing committee were arrested and charged with incitement to racial hatred. Following this, there were a number of initiatives to move forward in a constructive way, and the local Lewes Council formed a working party to develop new strategies relating to caravan sites. In 2004, more than 100 Gypsies staged a bonfire of their own at nearby Southerham. They were joined by a number of Firle residents.

FIZIK, LADISLAV. Slovakia. Contemporary political activist. He is the chairperson of the national Roma Parliament.

FLAG. In the years after 1945, a Romany flag with green, red, and blue horizontal stripes appeared. By 1962 its use had spread widely. It was said that the green represented grass, red fire, and blue the sky. Because of the alleged Communist connection of the red stripe, some groups changed it to a fire-shaped emblem. The most commonly used flag nowadays is one with blue and green horizontal divisions and a superimposed wheel. This flag was decided on at the first **World Romany Congress**. According to the congress, the wheel is to be identical with the *ashoka* symbol on the **Indian** flag.

FLAMENCO. A form of song and **dance** that emerged in the south of Spain in the 19th century. It is considered to be the result of a combination of Gypsy, Moorish, and Andalusian dance and **music**. There may be some traces of the **Indian kathak** style of dance. Gypsies are the prime performers of flamenco, which has spread from Andalusia to the rest of Spain. The Spanish word *flamenco* means "Flemish"—that is, "exotic." The **Presencia Gitana** research team has listed 240 Gypsy singers in Spain from 1749 to the age of the flamenco, while Bernard Leblon in his book *Gypsies and Flamenco* gives details of 200 and lists 100 further names. This dictionary has entries for some 40 of the best known from the beginning of the 20th century on.

FLORES, ANTONIO MONTOYA (EL FARRUCO) (1936–1997). Spain. **Dancer.** He performed with Pilar Lopez and José Greco. His son El Farruquito died tragically, and his grandson El Mani now performs under the name El Farruquito.

FLORES, LOLA (LA FARAONA) (1923–1995). Spain. Singer. She was a **flamenco** artist who considered herself to be a Gypsy *adentro* (through and through).

FOLK LITERATURE. The Romanies' oral **literature** consisted of ballads, songs, and tales, as well as riddles and proverbs. These began to be collected and published in the 19th century by non-Gypsies. Since 1945 several Gypsies have begun to collect their oral literature in anthologies that are listed in the bibliography.

FONSECA, ISABEL. United States. Contemporary writer. Currently, Fonseca resides in **England** and is married to the writer Martin Amis. After several visits to meet Gypsies in eastern Europe, she wrote the controversial travel book *Bury Me Standing.*

FORTUNE-TELLING. Although comparatively few Gypsy **women** practice fortune-telling, it provides a useful first or second income for those families who pursue this profession. Many **Kalderash** families specialize in fortune-telling, with the daughters learning from their mothers, but **Sinti** also have traditionally told fortunes. In western Europe, fortune-telling is usually done by **palm-reading** while in eastern Europe, coffee beans are often thrown to form a pattern.

In **England** and **Wales**, fortune-telling was controlled until recently by the Vagrancy Act of 1824. Any person professing to tell fortunes could be arrested without a warrant. In fact, prosecutions normally take place under section 15 of the Theft Act, where, for example, a fortune-teller takes money away "to be blessed" and does not return it. The Fraudulent Mediums Act of 1951 is rarely used against Gypsy fortune-tellers. *See also* TAROT CARDS.

FOUNDATION FOR THE RENEWAL AND DEVELOPMENT OF TRADITIONAL ROMANY VALUES. Czech Republic. Director: Ivan Vesely. An organization in Prague that is the **Czech** partner of the **Minority Rights Group**.

FRAMEWORK CONVENTION FOR THE PROTECTION OF NATIONAL MINORITIES. Est. 1998. Countries signatory to the declaration have to report their progress in protecting national minorities each year.

FRANCE. Estimated Gypsy population: 310,000. The first Gypsies came to France, to the town of Colmar, in 1418. In 1419 more arrived in Provence and Savoy. Nine years later the first Gypsies were recorded in Paris. In 1504 Louis XII issued the first of many decrees ordering the expulsion of the Gypsies. Further decrees followed in 1539, 1561, and 1682. In the latter year, Louis XIV recognized that it had been impossible to expel the Gypsies because of the protection they had received from nobles and other landowners.

During the 18th century, there were reports of armed Gypsies resisting arrest and expulsion. Others served in the French Army as soldiers and **musicians**. Often this was the only alternative to imprisonment. Jean de la Fleur, born in Lorraine, served as a mercenary in several armies.

In 1802 there was a determined campaign to clear Gypsies from the French Basque provinces. More than 500 were captured and imprisoned pending their planned deportation to the French colony of Louisiana. The colony was, however, sold in 1803 to the **United States**. It was 1806 before the last of the captives were released, after four years during which many had died from disease and malnutrition.

Gypsies, such as **Liance**, were well known in France as **dancers** and are mentioned several times by the playwright Molière. In 1607 they danced before King Henri IV at Fontainebleau Castle, although legally they had no right to be in France at all. It was not until the 20th century that **Django Reinhardt** and other instrumentalists again attained the fame of the Gypsy dancers.

The very first Romanies to come to France appear to have merged over the years with indigenous **nomads** to form the community known today as *Voyageurs* (**Travelers**). They no longer speak Romani but a variety of French with Romani words. In the south of France, many families speak **Caló**. There have been two migrations from **Germany** of families of the **Sinti** and **Manouche** clans. **Vlah** Gypsies arrived from the end of the 19th century on, both from **Romania** directly and via **Russia**.

It was probably the Vlah newcomers that led the French government to introduce new measures to control the nomadic population.

In 1898 a report gave the exaggerated figure of 25,000 persons traveling in bands with **caravans**. As a result, in 1912 the authorities introduced a special identity card—the *carnet anthropométrique*—for nomads. This carried the photograph and fingerprints of the owner and other details such as the length of the right ear. It was not abolished until after 1945.

In 1915 during World War I, the government arrested all the Gypsies in the disputed territory of Alsace-Lorraine—159 men, **women**, and children. They were interned in Crest, in the Department of the Drome.

At the beginning of World War II, Gypsies were again interned—this time from the whole of France. They were held in some 27 camps run by the French police even after the German occupation of the country. The camps at Jargeau, Les Alliers, Montreuil-Bellay, Rennes, and St. Maurice held internees for most of the war. Conditions in the camps were poor, and many prisoners died from disease and malnutrition. Some camps were closed as the conditions in them worsened, and the prisoners were transferred from camp to camp. In some places, Gypsies were allowed out to work under supervision. Small numbers were deported to concentration camps in **Poland**. Others who had Belgian nationality were released, only to be rearrested by the Germans in **Belgium** and northern France and sent to **Auschwitz**. House-dwelling Romanies were not affected by any special regulations.

The years following 1945 witnessed the arrival of large numbers of Gypsies from eastern Europe, in particular from **Yugoslavia**. They came as factory workers and settled in houses and flats in Paris and elsewhere. Meanwhile, nomadic Gypsies found that there were few official campsites, and many districts prohibited the stationing of caravans. It was on French territory that **Vaida Voevod III** and **Vanko Rouda** founded the first international Gypsy organization, while the **Études Tsiganes** association pioneered serious research into Romany history and culture. There are writers who have written in French, such as **Matéo Maximoff** and Sandra Jayat. In France, too, **Pentecostalism** first took hold among the Gypsies.

The 1999 **Loi Besson** encouraged the provision of council-run campsites, and in 2003 a new internal security act set fines of 3,750 euros for **Travelers** who occupy land belonging to someone else. In practice few sites have been built and in October 2002 a delegation representing a dozen Gypsy organizations met Minister of Home Affairs Nicola Sarkozy to press for more sites and better conditions on those that have been built. *See also* ETAPE 29.

FRANKHAM, ELI (1928–2002). England. **Poet** and political activist. He was the founder of the **National Romani Rights Association**.

FRANZ, PHILOMENA (1922–). Germany. Author. Now living near Cologne, she survived internment in **Auschwitz**, Ravensbrück, and Oranienburg concentration camps. Franz has written her autobiography and tales in the folk idiom.

FREDRIKSSON, MALIK FALTIN (1977–). Sweden. Entertainer. A **Traveler**, he is a break **dancer** and rap singer who performs under the name Tattarprinsen ("Gypsy Prince").

FRIENDS, FAMILIES AND TRAVELLERS' ADVICE AND INFORMATION UNIT. United Kingdom. Est. 1993. Founder: Steve Staines. Originally based in Glastonbury and working mainly with **New Travelers**, it now has its headquarters in Brighton and serves all Gypsies and **Travelers**.

FUHLER, LEE (1963–). Australia. Poet and political activist. President of the **Romani Association of Australia**. A collection of his poems was published under the title *Dog Days*.

FUREY, FINBAR (1946–). Ireland, Dublin. Piper and singer of **Irish Traveler** origin. In 1966 he moved to **Scotland** with his elder brother Eddie as a laborer but the two then developed a successful **musical** career. They have played at the Edinburgh Festival and toured widely in Great Britain and the **United States**.

In 1969 their brothers Paul and George joined them to form the Fureys. Apart from their recordings, the group appeared on both Scottish and English **television**. Their CDs include *Steal Away* (1992). Finbar left the group in 1993 to launch a solo career, with

CDs include *Chasing Moonlight*. His son Martin currently resides in **England** and plays in the folk-rock group Bohinta.

– G –

GADES, ANTONIO (1936–2004). Spain. **Flamenco dancer** and choreographer. He produced a stage version of *Carmen* as well a **film** version in conjunction with Carlos Saura.

GAJO. The Romani word for a non-Gypsy. The etymology is disputed but it probably comes from a Greek word for "farmer." Another suggestion derives it from the Sanskrit word *gramaja* ("villager"), which survives in some modern **Indian** languages as *gajja*. In Romani the feminine is *Gaji* and the plural *Gaje*. It is also spelled *Gadjo* and, traditionally in English, *Gorgio*.

GAMMON. (1) An alternative name for **Irish Travelers'** cant. (2) One of the suggested sources of vocabulary for this cant. It is a secret vocabulary from the Middle Ages formed by reversing or changing the order of the letters in a word. An example is the word *gred* ("money") from the Irish *airgead*. The name *Gammon* itself is probably formed from the word *Ogam*, an ancient alphabet used in Britain and **Ireland**.

GANDHI SCHOOL. Pecs, Hungary. Est. 1994. The school was set up to teach mainly children of the **Bayash clan**. There is a strong Romany cultural element in the curriculum. Its first graduating class had 18 pupils, 16 of them seeking higher **education**. Classes in at least two Gypsy **dialects** are compulsory at the school. It is hoped that the experience gathered by the school will prove invaluable for similar institutions elsewhere. The principal, Erika Csovcsics, received the U.S. **Human Rights** Prize.

GARCIA LORCA, FEDERICO **(1898–1936).** Spain. **Poet** and playwright. In 1922, he organized a festival in Granada that paid tribute to Gypsy traditions. His *Romancero gitano* [Gypsy Ballad Book] was published in 1928 and demonstrates his empathy with the Romany community. He had already shown this sentiment two years earlier by opposing the brutal expulsion of Gypsies from Alpujarra. Speaking of this book, he said, "I gave it the name *Gypsy Ballads* because the Gypsies are the highest, the deepest, and the most aristocratic people of my land." The **Pralipe** Theater performed Garcia Lorca's play *Blood Wedding* in their repertoire, and the **Hungarian** Romany poet **Jószef Choli Daróczi** has independently translated it into Romani.

GATLIF, MICHEL DAHAMANI (TONY) (1948–). Algeria. **Film** producer. He has been resident since 1962 in France where he has made several documentary films about Gypsies: *Corre gitano*, *Les princes*, and *Latcho drom* (1993). In addition, his productions include three fictional films: *Canto gitano* [Gypsy Song; 1981], *Gadjo Dilo* [Foolish Non-Gypsy; 1997], and the later film *Swing* (2002), featuring a boy in the world of Gypsy jazz. *Mondo* (1996) and *Vengo* (2000) also feature Gypsy culture.

GAZA AND THE WEST BANK. A number of Dom (**Nawwar**) families live in this territory.

"GELEM, GELEM." The Romany **national anthem**, chosen at the first **World Romany Congress**. The first lines are as follows:

> *Gelem, gelem lungone dromensa,*
> *Maladilem bahtale Romensa.*
> [We went, we went down long roads,
> We met happy Gypsies.]

The tune is traditional and was featured in the **film** *Happy Gypsies*. The new lyrics were composed by **Žarko Jovanović** during the Congress.

GENOCIDE. *See* HOLOCAUST.

GEORGIA (ASIA). The official figure for Gypsies is 1,744 (1989 census) but in fact there are several thousand living in the Republic. Their economic and social situation is not good. Few are **educated**, and they were taught **Russian** rather than Georgian, which puts them at a disadvantage in the job market. Many have **Moldovan** rather than Georgian citizenship, which debars them from welfare payments. Police harassment of market traders is common. In August 2003, a market incident in Tbilisi escalated into a pogrom: after a non-Roma woman was beaten up by a merchant, the local people then came together and began beating and menacing the Roma community, destroying their places of trade by burning them to the ground. It has been alleged that market officials provoked the incident in order to gain control of Romany trading stalls. A Roma Rights Defense Center has been established.

GEORGIEV, MIHAIL. Bulgaria. Contemporary political activist and **poet**. Executive director of the **Romani Baxt** Foundation in Sofia.

GEORGIEVDEN. *See* ST. GEORGE'S DAY.

GERMAN, ALEKSANDR (1893–1955). Russia. Writer and translator. A cultural worker and active in the All-Russian Union of Gypsies in the 1920s. He translated **Russian** literature into Romani as well as writing original works.

GERMANY. Estimated Gypsy population: 100,000. Records state that in September 1407 wine was given to Gypsies ("**Tartars**") while their papers were being checked at the town hall in Hildesheim. Another early description is of a group of acrobats in Magdeburg who danced on each others' shoulders and did "wonderful tricks." They were rewarded with food and drink. In 1416 we find the first anti-Gypsy action in Germany when the Margrave of Meissen ordered the expulsion of Gypsies from the territory under his authority. In September 1498 the Parliament of the **Holy Roman Empire**, as the German Empire was then called, meeting in Freiburg under Maximilian I, ordered them to leave the country by the following Easter. Any who did not leave would be regarded as outlaws, and it would then not be a crime to beat, rob, or even kill them. In 1658 Gypsies were outlawed in Bavaria. Adults found there were killed and their children taken into care.

By the 18th century, the laws were becoming more severe. Saxony ordered Gypsies to be executed if they reappeared in the state after once being expelled. In 1714 Mainz decreed the execution of any Gypsy men captured, while their wives and children would be flogged and branded. In Frankfurt-am-Main in 1722 it was stated that children would be taken away from their parents and placed in institutions, while their parents would be branded and expelled from the district.

The harsh laws led to some emigration when some of the **Sinti** and all of the **Manouche clans** left for **France**, and other Sinti went east to **Poland** and **Russia** or south into northern **Italy**. The existing laws gradually fell into disuse, and in the 19th century, assimilation programs began replacing expulsion. Schools for Gypsies were set up in a few places. However, when **Otto von Bismarck** became chancellor of Germany in 1886, he recommended the expulsion of all foreign Gypsies. Anti-Gypsy actions by the authorities then increased.

In March 1899 an Information Service on Gypsies was set up at the Imperial Police Headquarters in Munich. There, the registration and surveillance of the entire Gypsy population group was organized. This included the **Vlah** Romanies who were emigrating from the east. Alfred Dillmann, an officer of the Munich police, in 1905 published his *Zigeunerbuch* [Gypsy Book], giving details of more than 3,500 Gypsies and persons traveling as Gypsies. By 1925 the Information Service already had 14,000 individual and family files for Gypsies from all over Germany.

Two years after the Nazi Party came to power, the **Nuremberg Laws** made Gypsies, alongside **Jews**, second-class citizens. The first internment camps for **nomadic** Gypsies were established in the towns of Cologne and Gelsenkirchen in 1935. More camps followed, and settled Gypsies were removed from their houses and also interned. In 1936 the Race Hygiene and Population Biology Research Center was established under the direction of **Robert Ritter**. Its role was to search out, register, and classify Gypsies as pure or mixed race. The first mass arrests came in the week of 13–18 June 1938 when many Gypsies were deported to concentration camps. In October of the same year, the National Center for the Fight against the Gypsy Plague was set up. In 1940 a policy of making Germany Gypsy-free began when 2,800 Gypsies were deported to German-occupied Poland. Then, starting in March 1943, the mass deportation of some 10,000 Gypsies—both Romanies and Sinti—to the concentration camp of **Auschwitz** was organized. It is estimated that three-quarters of the Gypsy population of Germany (some 15,000 persons) died there and in other camps.

After the end of World War II, those who had survived found it difficult to get **reparations** as compensation for their suffering. In 1956 Oskar Rose founded the Union and Society for Racially Persecuted German Citizens of Non-Jewish Belief, the first organization for Sinti and Romanies. In 1979 the **Verband der Deutschen Sinti und Roma** was recognized throughout the republic as the representative body for Sinti. It also has some non-Sinti members. In 1997 a Documentation and Cultural Center was established in Heidelberg.

Many Romanies have come to Germany since 1945 as guest workers, particularly from **Yugoslavia**. Others arrived from Poland and, more recently, **Romania** as asylum seekers. This explains the high estimated Gypsy population. Many asylum seekers have, however, been sent back to Romania and **Macedonia**. **Rudko Kawzcynski** in Hamburg set up the **Romani National Congress**, which represents the interests of these recent arrivals.

The **Romani language** has been recognized as an official minority language in the state of Hesse. In general, the press and the public have little sympathy for the Gypsies. Some towns, however, have set aside stopping places for the few remaining nomadic families. *See also GESELLSCHAFT FÜR BEDROHTE VÖLKER.*

GESELLSCHAFT FÜR BEDROHTE VÖLKER (SOCIETY FOR ENDANGERED PEOPLES). Göttingen, Germany. An organization led by Tilman Zülch that helped the German **Sinti** develop their own representative bodies. It supported the third **World Romany Congress**, and its journal *Pogrom* often has articles on Gypsies in different countries.

GHEORGHE, NICOLAE (1940–). Romania. Sociologist and civil rights worker. He is active on the international scene and has represented Romany interests at many international conferences. Gheorghe organized the rebuilding of Romani communities that had suffered from pogroms in **Romania**. He has traveled extensively in Europe investigating the situation of the Romanies and has made reports to major international organizations.

GIESSEN. A town in **Germany** where a project to encourage the culture and **educational** prospects of Romanies and **Sinti** has been running. The program includes a publication called *Giessener Zigeunerhefte*.

GILDEROY, JACK SCAMP (1812–1857). England. Bare-knuckle boxer. **"King"** of the Kentish Gypsies. His several brothers worked in the scissors-grinding trade. His striking appearance in a top hat, given to him by Baron Rothschild in return for his vote in the Hythe Parliamentary elections, was well known to contemporaries. Gilderoy also took part in pony-trap races.

GILLIAT-SMITH, BERNARD (1883–1973). England. Diplomat and amateur scholar of the **Romani language**. He was a regular contributor to the *Journal of the Gypsy Lore Society* and also translated St. Luke's Gospel into Romani.

GINA, ANDREJ (1951–). Czechoslovakia. Writer. He has written a novel in Romani entitled *Biav* [Wedding]. He received the 2003 **Roma Literary Award** for fiction.

GINA, ONDREJ (1936–). Czechoslovakia. Contemporary **musician** and political activist. He is a leading member of the Romany community in **Rokycany**. He was a member of Parliament in the first post-Communist parliament in **Czechoslovakia**.

GIRCA ASSOCIATION. Switzerland. Est. 2000. The association, under the direction of **May Bittel**, organizes actions aimed at obtaining recognition for Gypsy communities' rights and more specifically to get indemnification for the death of many thousands of Gypsies in the Nazi period.

GITAN; GITANO. The French (alongside *Tsigane*) and Spanish names for Romanies, deriving from the words *Egyptien* and *Egitano* ("**Egyptian**"). The terms are particularly used of Romanies in **Spain** and the South of **France**.

GJUNLER, ABDULA (1965–). Macedonia. **Poet**. Gjunler currently resides in the **Netherlands**. A book of his poems in Dutch and Romani was published in 1995 under the title *Bizoagor/Eindeloos* [Without End].

GOLEMANOV, DIMITER (1938–1994). Bulgaria. **Poet** and teacher. His father was active in trade union politics as early as the 1930s and was honored as a fighter against fascism. Golemanov became known to the world of Gypsy studies through a version of the Balkan tale, "Song of the Bridge," that **Lev Cherenkov** had published in the *Journal of the Gypsy Lore Society*. Golemanov had a great love of the **Russian** language, which he had studied at Sofia University, and he wrote poetry and songs in Russian as well as **Bulgarian** and Romani. He attended the second **World Romany Congress** in Geneva. He died of a heart attack shortly after the political changes in Bulgaria.

GOMEZ, HELIOS (1905–1956). Spain. Political activist. Born in Seville, he was one of the founders of the Anarchist Trade Union, but then joined the Communist Party. Gomez was detained by the police 72 times, faced 42 criminal charges, and was expelled from **Spain**, **France**, **Belgium**, and **Germany**. He then worked in the Kuznetsoy factory in Siberia. He returned to Spain in 1936 after the election victory of the left-wing government. He was in Barcelona when the civil war broke out and fought there and later in Aragon. He was the political commissar of the Balearic command. During the war, many Gypsies were members of the Catalan Nationalist Party and fought for the government. After the defeat of the government, he sought refuge in the **Soviet Union** again.

GORGIO. *See* GAJO.

GRANICA. Town in **Kosovo, Yugoslavia**. Since 1945 it has become a place of Gypsy pilgrimage on the Orthodox Feast of the Assumption (August 27–28).

GRASS, GÜNTHER **(1927–).** Germany. Author. He told a conference against racism that Gypsy representation in international bodies was the only way to overcome the discrimination they encountered in many European states. "It should be possible to make room and give a voice to the Roma nation, Europe's largest minority, in the European Parliament," he said. He was awarded the Spanish **Premio Hidalgo**.

GREAT BRITAIN. *See* ENGLAND; NORTHERN IRELAND; SCOTLAND; WALES.

GREECE. Estimated Gypsy population: 350,000. At an early date, Gypsies were recorded on the islands of the eastern Mediterranean. By 1384 Gypsy shoemakers were established on the mainland of Greece in **Modon** (then a part of the Venetian empire), and by the end of the 14th century a large number of Gypsies were also living on the Peloponnese Peninsula. As the **Turks** advanced into Europe, many Romanies fled to **Italy** and other countries of western Europe. Under the **Ottoman Empire** those Gypsies who remained were given comparative freedom provided they paid their taxes to the Turkish rulers. In 1829 Greece gained its independence. There have been a number of population exchanges between Greece and Turkey, and some Muslim Gypsies have taken the opportunity to migrate eastward to Turkey.

Toward the end of World War II, the **Germans** began to arrest Gypsies to use them as hostages, but the majority survived unscathed.

In Greece today, many Gypsies are settled in housing and their existence as an ethnic minority ignored, except by some **educational** authorities. Perhaps half are living in barely tolerated tent and shantytowns. In 1997 some 3,500 Gypsies living in tents were ordered to leave the land in Evosmos (Salonica) where they had been living for 30 years. It was intended to rehouse them in a converted army barracks. A number of other Gypsy settlements have been destroyed, some in preparation for the 2004 Olympic Games, and the promised compensation has not been paid. As the Olympics began, a score of Roma families were evicted from their settlement in Patras. Evictions from this area continued until June 2005. In the same year, 70 families were evicted from Votanikos (Athens).

As many of the adults in shantytowns are not registered as citizens, their children are refused entry by schools. Elsewhere segregated classes are common. Children in Aspropyrgos on the outskirts of Athens were at first refused enrollment and then placed in special classes. The international **Helsinki Foundation for Human Rights** protested about this situation in an open letter to the minister of education in February 2006.

A positive note is the establishment of a **museum** of basket making in Thrace. Also, in 2004 a government circular banned the use of derogatory references to Roma by the police.

Gypsy **musicians** are popular. They include the singers Vasilis Paiteris, Kostas Pavlides, and Eleni Vitali, together with the clarinetist Vasilis Saleas. An extremely popular **television** soap opera entitled *Whispers of the Heart* transformed public attitudes toward the Roma for a short time in 1998. Chronicling the love story of an upper-class Greek architect and a young Romany woman, it was one of the most successful shows ever on Greek television. *See also* BYZANTINE EMPIRE.

GRELLMANN, HEINRICH (1753–1804). Germany. Author. He wrote a treatise in 1783 entitled *Die Zigeuner: Ein historischer Versuch*, which was translated into English as *A Dissertation on the History of the Gypsies* in 1787. The English edition was influential in affecting thinking on the treatment of Gypsies and inspiring the evangelical movement of persons such as John Hoyland and Samuel Roberts to start missions to the Gypsies in Britain in the 19th century. Some Dutch academics see Grellmann as the founder of a Gypsy identity that did not exist before his book.

GROOME, FRANCIS HINDES (1851–1902). England. Writer and scholar. Possibly related to **George Borrow**. He left university without taking a degree and lived with Gypsies in **England** and Europe, including an English Romany named Esmeralda Locke whom he later wed, although the marriage was not to last. He was joint editor of the first series of the *Journal of the Gypsy Lore Society*. Groome also wrote a novel *Kriegspiel* with a Romany theme and edited a collection of Gypsy folktales.

GROTA BRIDGE. A bridge in Warsaw, **Poland**. In 1994 hundreds of Romany refugees from pogroms in **Romania** found shelter under this bridge. In 1995 the settlement was broken up by police.

GURBET. (1) A **clan** in **Yugoslavia**. Archaic features in their **dialect** suggest that they were among the first Roma to reach Europe. (2) A name given to the Muslim Gypsies of **Cyprus**.

GYPSIES FOR CHRIST. A **Pentecostal** movement in **England** and **Wales**. It is now independent of any international organization.

GYPSY. In this dictionary, *Gypsy* is used as a synonym for *Romany* except in articles on the Middle East and Asia. There the term applies to industrial nomads (**peripatetics**), mainly of **Indian origin**. The word is derived from "**Egyptian**" because, when the Romanies first came to western Europe, it was wrongly thought they had come from **Egypt**. Alternatively, some authors suggest that the name may come from a place called Gyppe in **Greece**. Early **English** laws and authors such as **William Shakespeare** used *Egyptian* (e.g., in the play *Othello*). The **Spanish** word *gitano* and the French *gitan* are of the same derivation.

Gypsy is not a Gypsy word, and there is no single word for Gypsy in all Romani **dialects**. *Rom* (plural *Rom* or *Roma*) is a noun meaning "a man belonging to our ethnic group" but not all Gypsies call themselves Roma. The **Sinti**, the **Manouche**, and the **Kaale** of **Finland** use the word *Rom* only in the meaning of "husband." There is, on the other hand, a universal word for non-Gypsy, *Gajo*.

In the western European image of a Gypsy, the idea of **nomadism** and self-employment is predominant. So we find, for example, a site on the World Wide Web proclaiming: "We are Cyber Gypsies—we roam the Net." A leading tennis player or international footballer is described in the media as leading a "Gypsy way of life." In eastern Europe, on the other hand, nomadism is not seen as a fundamental meaning of the equivalent of the word *Gypsy* (usually *Tsigan*) in eastern European languages. We find other paradoxes in their **stereotype**, with the Gypsies considered lazy but also as taking on the dirtiest work, foolish and at the same time cunning.

In British planning law (cf. Office of the Deputy Prime Minister's Department Circular 1/2006), the term *Gypsy* does not apply to an ethnic group but rather to anyone traveling or who has traveled in a **caravan** for an economic purpose. With regard to race relations legislation, however, *Gypsy* is considered to be a synonym for the ethnic term *Romany*.

GYPSY AND TRAVELLER LAW REFORM COALITION. United Kingdom. Est. 2002 (as Traveller Law Reform Coalition). Coordinator until March 2006: Andrew Ryder. A pressure group comprising Gypsies, **Irish Travelers**, **New Travelers**, and non-Gypsies. It has been campaigning for Parliament to pass the proposals in the **Traveller Law Reform Bill**. A further aim was to get the government to address the Gypsies' accommodation needs, principally by placing on local authorities a duty to provide or facilitate site provision. The deputy prime minister to some extent has done this with his Circular 1/2006 but Gypsies in the coalition have expressed their dissatisfaction with its lack of progress.

GYPSY BROTHERS. Malmö, Sweden. Group playing traditional **music**, comprising keyboard player Ivan Nikolizsson, **Monica Caldaras**, and their three sons. CD: *Gypsy Brothers*.

GYPSY COUNCIL. United Kingdom. Est. 1966. The first secretary was **Grattan Puxon**. It carried out a campaign of passive resistance to the moving on of **caravans** by the police and local authorities. The campaign was a major factor in persuading the government to take some action over the problem of sites for Gypsies, culminating in the **Caravan Sites Act of 1968**. In 1973 the **Romany Guild** joined with the Gypsy Council to form the **National Gypsy Council**. The Guild was later reestablished as an independent body, but the National Gypsy Council continued under that name. The National Gypsy Council has recently readopted the name Gypsy Council and uses this on its stationery. *See also* GYPSY COUNCIL FOR EDUCATION, CULTURE, WELFARE AND CIVIL RIGHTS.

GYPSY COUNCIL FOR EDUCATION, CULTURE, WELFARE AND CIVIL RIGHTS. United Kingdom. Chair: Vacant following the death of **Charles Smith**. Vice chair: Daniel Baker. This was for several years the new name of the **National Gypsy Education Council**. It took over the former's constitution but has had a wider area of responsibility than **education** alone (as the name indicates).

Recently it has been using the abbreviated title Gypsy Council. *See also* GYPSY COUNCIL.

GYPSY CZARDAS. (1) A poem written by the 19th-century **Russian** poet Appolon Grigoriev after his beloved Leonida married another man. Ivan Vasiliev, conductor of a Gypsy choir, composed the **music**, and it became popular with Gypsies in both St. Petersburg and Moscow. The tune is often sung with different words, but in recent years the original lyrics have returned to popularity. (2) A variety of the Hungarian **csardas danced** by Gypsies without hand contact.

GYPSY EVANGELICAL MOVEMENT. *See* PENTECOSTALISM.

GYPSY GROOVZ. Gypsy brass band from Vranjska Banja in **Serbia**. The leader is trumpeter Ekrem Sajdic. Its album *Rivers of Happiness* relates to the struggle of the villagers to get their water supply restored.

GYPSY KINGS. A band playing folk rock. It was first formed under the name Los Reyes in 1972 by younger members of the Reyes and Baliardo families in the south of **France** and in 1982 adopted the name Gypsy Kings. Their first record appeared in 1987, and they have toured widely since. An early hit was the song "Bamboleo," which reached the Top 10 in the United Kingdom. Another well-known song is "Djobi, Djoba." The group sings in a number of languages, including **Caló**. *See also* BALIARDO, RICARDO.

GYPSY LORE SOCIETY. United States. Est. 1888. Founder: David McRitchie. It ceased activities in 1892 and was revived in 1907. Current secretary: **Thomas Acton**. The oldest society for the study of Gypsies. In the early years, few meetings were held, but it published the *Journal of the Gypsy Lore Society (JGLS)*. Members of the newly created U.S. chapter of the society took over its running in the 1980s, and it has since had a substantial number of American members on its Management Committee. In addition to the journal (now called *Romani Studies*, edited by **Yaron Matras**), there is a newsletter. Annual conferences are usually held in the **United States**, but six have taken place in Europe—at Budapest, Florence, Leicester, Leiden, Newcastle, and most recently Granada (2005).

GYPSY RONDO. The final movement of a piano trio by Franz Josef Haydn.

GYPSY SCALE. Also known as the "Hungarian scale." This is a **musical** scale with the notes C–D–E-flat–F-sharp–G–A-flat–B–C, popular in **Hungary** in the 19th century.

GYPSY SITES MANAGEMENT AND WELFARE COMMITTEES. United Kingdom. These are two committees set up in 1977 by the **Association of Gypsy Organisations (AGO)** that still operate a small number of projects originally established by AGO.

GYPSY STUDIES. Gypsy studies were largely amateur until the 1950s. Since then, departments for or courses in Gypsy Studies have been set up at a number of academic institutions in Europe—for example, St. Charles University in Prague (**Romani language**), Greenwich University in **England**, and the pedagogical college in **Košice** in **Slovakia**—at the University of Texas in the **United States**, and elsewhere.

GYPSY WELFARE COMMITTEE. *See* GYPSY SITES MANAGEMENT AND WELFARE COMMITTEES.

GYPSYLORISTS. A term used for non-Gypsy amateur scholars in the 19th and early 20th centuries who saw the Gypsy life as romantic, at least for short periods in the summer. They used to travel in horse-drawn wagons and make campfires around which they sang their own translations into Romani of popular songs. So, the student song *Gaudeamus igitur* was translated as *Kesa paias kana 'men tarniben atchela* (Let us make merry while we still have youth). They have been criticized for ignoring the harassment suffered by the Romanies they studied.

– H –

HABSBURG EMPIRE. The Habsburg family ruled much of central Europe from 1438 to 1745. **Maria Theresa** and her son **Joseph II** inherited part of the Habsburg Empire.

HADLOW. On 20 October 1853, 30 Gypsy hop-pickers were drowned when the flooding river swept away their wagons as they were crossing Hartlake Bridge near Hadlow. The people of Hadlow decided to erect a memorial to the dead Gypsies in the form of a pyramid-shaped tablet in the corner of the graveyard beneath a yew tree. The names of those who perished are now displayed inside the church doorway. The event was also commemorated in a song.

HAGA, ANTONIA (1960–). Hungary. Teacher, political activist, and politician. She has been a member of the Hungarian Parliament and is currently president of the Ariadne Foundation, a cultural organization.

HALADITKA (XALADYTKO). The name given to a large **clan** of Gypsies living in **Russia** and adjoining countries. Their **dialect** is called *Haladitko*. Many members of the clan consider the term (which means "soldier") pejorative and prefer being called Russian Gypsies.

HALITI, BAJRAM (1955–). Kosovo. **Poet** and journalist. From the town of Gniljane, Haliti was the editor of the journal *Ahimsa*. He set up a Memorial Center for Holocaust Studies, holding some 4,000 books and other items, all of which were lost when his house was burned down. He was seen as pro-Serb during the hostilities of 1999–2001 and was barred from entering the **European Union** countries for a time. Later, he was to flee to Zemun in **Serbia** after being denounced as a collaborator and war criminal by **Albanians**.

HALL, GEORGE **(fl. 19th century).** England. Cleric. He was a supporter of the Romany way of life in the Midlands.

HANCOCK, IAN (1942–). England. Lecturer, writer, and political activist. He has been teaching in Texas since 1984. He was at one time vice president of the **International Romani Union** and on the board of the U.S. **Holocaust** Museum.

HAVEL, VACLAV **(1936–).** Czechoslovakia. Political leader. The last president of **Czechoslovakia** and the first of the **Czech Republic**. Addressing the international Romani festival, Romfest, in Brno in July 1990, he stressed the right of Romanies to their own ethnic consciousness and said that they should enjoy the same rights and duties as all citizens of the nation.

HAYWORTH, RITA (1918–1987). United States. **Film** actress. Born in Brooklyn, New York, she was the daughter of an American mother and a Spanish Gypsy father. Starting her career as a dancer at age 12, she became the star in many popular Hollywood films.

HEARN, PATRICIO LAFCADIO (1850–1904). Greece. Author. Son of a Cypriot Romany mother and a British Romany father, he was one of the first writers to create modern-day journalistic style. He studied in the United States, where he met his wife, who was African American, and spent the end of his life living in Japan.

HEDERLEZI (HIDRELLEZ). Turkish feast celebrated by Gypsies, coinciding with **St. George's Day** (6 May in the old calendar).

HEDMAN, HENRIK (1954–). Finland. Pastor. He is leader of the Lutheran Mission to Gypsies in **Finland** and a translator of the New Testament.

HEINSCHINK, MOZES (1939–). Austria. Civil rights activist and scholar. Without having pursued an academic career, he received an honorary title of professor from the University of Vienna for his studies of Romani speech and music. His involvement with the **Romano Centro** in Vienna takes up much of his free time. His documentation of widespread and rarer Romani **dialects** is legendary. His collection of more than 700 hours of speech and music is housed in the Phonogram archives in Vienna.

HELSINKI CITIZENS' ASSEMBLY (hCa). Est. 1990. The Helsinki Citizens' Assembly is an international coalition of civic initiatives, east and west, working for the democratic integration of Europe. At its Ankara assembly, several workshops were devoted to the problems of the Romanies, and an hCa Roma Committee with Romany and non-Romany members was established in March 1994. It has its headquarters in Brno, **Czech Republic**, where **Karel Holomek** is the contact.

HELSINKI FOUNDATION FOR HUMAN RIGHTS. Warsaw, Poland. The foundation's aims include producing a handbook to enable activists and nongovernmental organizations to gain access to information about Romanies' rights and **educational** possibilities.

HEREDIA, JOSE. Spain. Contemporary scholar. He is professor of modern Spanish literature at Granada University.

HEREDIA, JUAN DE DIOS. *See* RAMÍREZ HEREDIA, JUAN DE DIOS.

HIGGINS, LIZZIE (1929–1993). Singer. A **Scottish Traveler**, she was **Jeannie Robertson**'s daughter and related to the **Stewart family** of **musicians** and singers. Albums include *What a Voice* (1985).

HIROSHIMA FOUNDATION. The foundation works to support peace activities in the cultural field. It was founded after her death in memory of Swedish-born author Edith Morris, whose best-known novel is *Flowers of Hiroshima*. In 2002, the foundation elected to bestow its awards on individuals who have played key roles in preserving and promoting Romany culture—including **Valdemar Kalinin**, **Rahim Burhan**, and **Roberto Ciulli**.

HOLLAND. *See* NETHERLANDS.

HOLOCAUST. The Nazi genocide of **Jews**, Gypsies, and others, particularly in the period following 1941.

When the National Socialist Party came to power in **Germany** in 1933, it inherited laws against **nomadism** already in operation. From the beginning, the Nazis considered the Romanies and **Sinti**—whether nomads or sedentary—as non-Aryans. Together with the Jews, they were classed as alien and considered a danger to the German race. Already by 1935 they had been deprived of citizenship and given the second-class status of "nationals." In the same year, the Law for the Protection of German Blood made marriages between Gypsies and other Germans illegal. There was no place in the image of Germany under the New Order for a group of people who traveled around the country freely, worked as craftsmen, and sold their wares from door to door.

A quasi-scientific research program was set up in Berlin under the leadership of **Robert Ritter**. Later this program was carried out at the Race Hygiene and Population Biology Research Center. The researchers had to accept the historical and linguistic fact that the Romany and Sinti peoples were of **Indian origin** and therefore should count as Aryan, but they claimed that on the route to Europe they had intermarried with other races and as a "mixed race" had no place in Nazi Germany. Allegations were made against the whole race in pamphlets and articles.

Internment camps were set up on the outskirts of towns in Germany, and both **caravan**- and house-dwelling Gypsies were sent there. Discipline was strict and the internees were allowed out only to work. In 1938 several hundred Gypsy men were deported to Buchenwald and Sachsenhausen concentration camps as "people who have shown that they do not wish to fit into society" under the Decree against Crime of the previous year.

Heinrich Himmler, who became police chief in 1936, was particularly interested in the Gypsies and led the campaign against them. In 1938 he signed the Decree for Fighting the Gypsy Menace under which Ritter's Research Center was linked with an established Gypsy Police Office and the new combined institution was put under the direct control of police headquarters in Berlin. The first task of this institution was to classify all nomads by their ethnic origin. To be classed as a "Gypsy of mixed race," it was sufficient to have two great-grandparents who were considered to have been Gypsies, which meant that part-Gypsies were considered to be a greater danger than part-Jews: In general, a person with one Jewish grandparent was not affected in the Nazi anti-Jewish legislation whereas one-eighth "Gypsy blood" was considered strong enough to outweigh seven-eighths of German blood.

Alongside the program of registration and classification, new laws were imposed on the Romanies and Sinti. Any children who were of foreign nationality were excluded from school; the German Gypsies could also be excluded if they represented a "moral danger" to their classmates. The race scientists discussed what should happen next. Eva Justin proposed sterilization except for those "with pure Gypsy blood," while Ritter himself wanted to put an end to the whole race by sterilization of those with at least one-eighth Gypsy blood. In fact, a law of 1933 had already been used to carry out this operation on individual Sinti and Romanies.

In the end, the Nazi leaders decided in 1940 that deportation was the means to clear Germany of Gypsies. Adolf Eichmann was responsible for the transporting of Gypsies alongside the Jews. In a first operation 2,800 were sent to Poland and housed in Jewish ghettoes or hutted camps.

In 1941, however, the Nazi leaders had carried out an experiment with Zyklon B gas at **Auschwitz** where they had murdered 250 sick prisoners and 600 **Russian** prisoners-of-war in underground cells. The discovery of this cheap and rapid method of mass murder led to a change in the treatment of the Jews. Deportation was replaced by death, and in 1942 Himmler decided that the same "final solution" should be applied to the Gypsies.

On 16 December 1942 he signed an order condemning all the German and **Austrian** Gypsies to imprisonment in Auschwitz, and in February 1943 the police began rounding up the Romanies and Sinti. Within the first few months, 10,000 persons had been transported to the camp. Children were taken out of orphanages and Germans were asked to inform the police of any Gypsies living in houses that might have been missed. We are not yet in a position to say how many German Gypsies remained outside the camps. They can be numbered in the hundreds and lived under strict police control.

When Austria was annexed to Germany in 1938, it was announced that the Gypsies there would be treated like those in Germany. Two years later a camp was opened in Lackenbach just for the Austrian Romanies and Sinti. The western part of **Czechoslovakia** was also annexed, but many Romanies succeeded in escaping across the border to the puppet state of **Slovakia**. Two internment camps were opened in 1942 in the German-controlled provinces of Bohemia and Moravia. The majority of the nomads were immediately locked up in the new camps, and later several hundred of them were sent to Auschwitz from the camps when they were closed—together with the sedentary Gypsies. Only a handful of the Czech Gypsies survived the occupation.

The Romany population in eastern Europe was mainly sedentary and integrated into the life of town and village. Many had been to school and had regular work. They had cultural and sports clubs and had begun to develop Romani as a **literary** language. Nevertheless, the German troops carried out the same policies of murder against these populations as against the nomads.

The Romanies who lived in **Poland** were crammed into the Jewish quarters of towns and villages. The Germans forced the Jews to give up their houses and move in with other families, and then the Romanies were allocated the empty houses. In addition, a transport of 5,000 Sinti and Romanies were brought from Germany and Austria and housed in the Jewish **Lodz Ghetto.** An epidemic of typhus broke out, but no medical help was provided. In the first two months, 600 died. When spring arrived, the survivors were taken to Chelmno and gassed.

The task of murdering the Romanies in the occupied areas of the **Soviet Union** was allocated to **Einsatzgruppen**, which were given their orders soon after the invasion. Their instructions were to eliminate "racially undesirable elements," and most of their reports mention the killing of Gypsies. In all, they murdered more than 20,000 Romanies.

After the rapid capture of **Yugoslavia** in 1941, **Serbia** came under German military rule and the Romanies were compelled to wear a yellow armband with the word "Gypsy" on it. Trams and buses bore the notice "No Jews or Gypsies." A new tactic was used to kill the Romanies. They were shot as hostages for German soldiers who had been killed by the partisans. In Kragujevac, soldiers with machine guns executed 200 Romanies, alongside many Serbians, in revenge for the death of 10 German soldiers. These executions were carried out by regular soldiers of the German Army. After so many of the men had been shot, the occupying forces were faced with the problem of a large number of **women** and children with no breadwinners. A solution was easily found. Mobile gas vans were brought from Germany, and women and children were loaded into these vans, taken to the forests, gassed, and buried. Their possessions were sent to Germany to be distributed by charitable organizations to the civilian population.

In most of the countries that came under German rule, the alternative was often between death on the spot and a journey without food or water to a concentration camp. Nearly all the larger camps had their section for Romanies: Bergen-Belsen, Buchenwald, Mauthausen,

Natzweiler, Neuengamme, Ravensbrück, Sachsenhausen, and others. From 1943 on, the camps were merely waiting rooms for the journey to death by gas or shooting. Chelmno, Sobibor, and Treblinka were names that meant immediate death on arrival. From all the camps where Romanies and Sinti were held, the best records available are for Auschwitz, where Jewish prisoners kept secret notes.

It is also known that Romanies and Sinti were used in the camps for experiments with typhus, salt water, and smallpox, but perhaps the most horrifying were the attempts to find new quick methods of sterilization. These were to be used on all the races considered inferior so that they could be used as a workforce while preventing the birth of a new generation.

As Soviet and Allied troops advanced in 1944, the last tragic phase began in the life of the concentration camps. The remaining prisoners were evacuated on foot in the direction of Austria and Germany. Anyone who could not keep up during these marches was shot.

During the Hitler period, the Romanies and Sinti of Europe suffered a terrible blow from which they have not yet fully recovered. Some estimates of deaths are as high as 500,000. It should not be forgotten that this figure does not give the whole extent of the persecution of the many thousands more who suffered internment or other repressive measures. *See also* REPARATIONS.

HOLOMEK, KAREL (1937–). Czechoslovakia. Son of **Thomas Holomek**. Political activist. He is currently the Roman contact, based in Brno, for the **Helsinki Citizens' Assembly**. He was a member of the national Parliament before the breakup of **Czechoslovakia**. He also edited the journal *Romano Hangos*.

HOLOMEK, MIROSLAV (1925–1989). Czechoslovakia. Political activist and sociologist. He was active in the Romany civil rights and cultural movement in the Republic in the 1970s.

HOLOMEK, THOMAS (1911–1988). Czechoslovakia. Lawyer and writer. He was one of the founders of the Romany civil rights and cultural movement in the Republic in the 1970s. He is the father of **Karel Holomek**.

HOLY ROMAN EMPIRE (962–1806). This term was applied to the German Empire, and from 1438 it can be considered for practical purposes the same as the **Habsburg Empire**. Its boundaries varied. For the policy of the empire toward Gypsies, *see* GERMANY; JOSEPH II; MARIA THERESA.

HORSMONDEN. The Horse Fair at Horsmonden in Kent in October, together with the Barnet Fair, was one of the last events in the **English** Gypsies' calendar before the winter sets in. Unlike some of the other fairs, Horsmonden has been an all-Gypsy event. It is not governed by an ancient charter and is popularly believed to have grown out of a 19th-century Hop-Pickers' Sunday holiday. Attempts have been made over the years to stop the fair or move it to another location. In 2001, the local authorities made their most determined effort yet to halt the fair and the home secretary declared the village an "exclusion zone." Gypsy activists have maintained a token presence each year since then in the hope of keeping the tradition alive and eventually seeing it restored.

HORTTO KAALO. Finnish Gypsy music group, playing traditional **music**, founded in 1970 by the two brothers Feija Akerlund and Taisto Lundberg. together with Marko Putkonen. Their first record was a protest song against discrimination, "Miksi ovet ei aukene meille?" [Why Are the Doors Not Open for Us?], which reached the Top 10 in Finland. Their repertoire is varied: Russian-style Gypsy songs, folk songs from various countries, and their own compositions. They have toured in Scandinavia and appeared regularly on **television**.

HORVATH, ALADAR (1964–). Hungary. Civil rights activist. Once a teacher, now a politician, Horvath was president of the Roma Parliament in **Hungary**. Standing for the Free Democrat Party, he was one of the first two Romani MPs in the Hungarian Parliament (1990–1994). Since 1995 he has run the Foundation for Romany Civil Rights in Budapest and set up the Roma Press Center.

HOSKINS, BOB (1942–). British. **Film** actor and producer. His films include *The Raggedy Rawnie* in which a deserter disguises himself as a Gypsy girl.

*HOST (HNUTI OBĆANSKE SOLIDARITY A TOLERANCE; CITI-
ZENS' SOLIDARITY AND TOLERANCE MOVEMENT).* Czech
Republic. Est. 1993. The movement was founded in Prague late in
1993 after four people, including two Romanies, were killed in violent attacks in one month. Its aims include monitoring ethnic violence and opposing discrimination. Gypsies are only part of HOST's
work.

HÜBSCHMANNOVÁ, MILENA (1933–2006). Czechoslovakia.
Scholar and civil rights activist. She helped to keep Romany culture
alive during the period 1973–1989 when it was discouraged by the
government in **Czechoslovakia**. She was instrumental in small-scale
publishing during this period, including *Romane Gil'a*, a book of
songs in Romani, as well as teaching the language. Hübschmannová
wrote many articles and books in and on the language. She was the
editor of the learned journal *Romano Džaniben* (Romani Knowledge)
and taught Romani at Prague University.

HUMAN RIGHTS. Human rights are enshrined in the Charter of the
United Nations and its Universal Declaration of Human Rights
(1948). Europe also has its own Convention of Human Rights, which
has been ratified by most European countries. The Convention includes the following rights, which Roma are being denied in many
European countries:

- *Article 2: Right to Life.* Police and private security guards in
  eastern Europe are shooting and killing without justification
  young Roma (even children) who commit minor crimes, for example, theft of wood from a forest.
- *Article 3: Prohibition of Degrading Treatment.* Also in many
  eastern European countries, police are subjecting Roma to degrading treatment. In **Romania**, for example, they have been
  arrested, made to clean the police station, and then sent away
  without being charged with any crime.
- *Article 8: Right to Respect for Private and Family Life.* There is
  discrimination in housing, including attempts to set up "ghettoes," for example, in **Slovakia** and **Spain**. Shanty towns have
  been destroyed without any alternative accommodation being

offered in **Greece, Italy**, and **Serbia**. Roma living in **caravans** are being forced to give up **nomadizing** in **France**, Great Britain, and **Ireland** where central government policies to help the nomadic Roma with a supply of caravan sites are being thwarted by local authorities.

• *Protocol 1, Article 2: Right to Education.* Roma children are put into "special schools" for mentally and physically handicapped pupils even though they are normal. **Hungary** and Slovakia are guilty in this respect. The children cannot then take the normal school-leaving examinations and go on to further study or technical courses.

See also EUROPEAN COURT OF HUMAN RIGHTS; HUMAN RIGHTS PROJECT.

HUMAN RIGHTS PROJECT. Bulgaria. Est. 1992. Director: Dimiter Georgiev. The organization documents human rights abuses against Romanies and others, as well as providing free legal services to combat discrimination. It publishes a newsletter, *Focus*, as well as a number of reports and arranges training meetings for activists. It is based in Sofia, with branches in Montana, Pleven, Shumen, and Stara Zagora. In 1999 the project initiated work on the Framework Plan for integrating the Romanies into **Bulgarian** society.

HUNGARIAN GYPSY MUSIC. Apart from the groups playing what is popularly regarded as Gypsy **music** in **Hungary**, such as waltzes and polkas by Strauss, there is also a strong singing tradition among the **Vlah clans** in the country. This includes slow songs for listening and fast songs for **dancing**. The slow song (*loki gili*) is often sung in harmony when others join in with the soloist, often improvising the words. The **dance** song (*khelimaski gili*) is used for the Gypsy **csardas**, and much of the text consists of nonsense syllables (mouth music). They are accompanied by other singers imitating various instruments such as the double bass and percussion (snapping fingers, spoons, etc.). Finally there are the "stick songs," which usually have short verses and accompany stick and other solo dances (*csapás*). Groups such as **Kalyi Jag**, playing a type of folk rock, have become popular among both Gypsies and Hungarians.

HUNGARY. Estimated Gypsy population: 750,000. Gypsies may have reached Hungary by 1316, but the first certain reference to Gypsies refers to **musicians** who played on the island of Czepel for Queen Beatrice in 1489. However, others certainly passed through the country earlier in the 15th century. Sigismund, the king of Hungary and of the **Holy Roman Empire**, attended the empire's Great Council in 1417 at Constance. While he was spending some free days in the neighboring town of Lindau, some Gypsies arrived from Hungary and asked him for a letter of safe conduct. In 1423 Sigismund gave a safe conduct letter to another Gypsy leader, Ladislaus and his company, in **Slovakia** (then part of the Hungarian Empire). These Gypsies then traveled to **Germany**, where they used Sigismund's letters to get food and lodging from the authorities. Later, in 1476 Gypsies were sent to work by King Matthias Corvinus as smiths in Sibiu in Transylvania (part of Hungary at that time). In these early years, Gypsies in Hungary were under the jurisdiction of their own leaders.

Things were to change with the rule of **Maria Theresa**. From 1758 legislation demanded the assimilation of the Gypsies, or "New Hungarians" (*Ujmagyar*) as they were thenceforth to be called. They were to settle and farm the land. Her son **Joseph II** continued his mother's policies. The 1893 census recorded 275,000 Gypsies, of whom more than 80,000 spoke Romani. The vast majority were sedentary, as a result of Maria Theresa's intervention.

Apart from the musicians, Gypsies have been viewed with mistrust. From the mid-1930s, calls were made in the Hungarian Parliament for the internment of Gypsies in labor camps. However, although Hungary was allied to **Germany** in World War II, it was not until German troops occupied Hungary in March 1944 that mass deportations of Romanies to concentration camps began. The accession to power of the fascist Arrow Cross Party in October 1944 gave a new impetus to the persecution. With the **Soviet** army approaching Budapest, killing increased. More than 100 were shot in the woods near the town of Varpalota in February 1945. One postwar report suggests that 50,000 died in the camps, but this figure may be too high.

After the liberation of Hungary in 1945, the official policy was that the Romanies had the same rights and responsibilities as other Hungarians. This policy was meaningless, however, because it did nothing to remedy the neglect of years and the general prejudice against the Roma. They continued to live in isolated settlements, and many children were not accepted into schools.

On coming to power the following year, the Hungarian Workers Party adopted a policy of assimilation. Prime Minister Matyas Rákosi referred to them as New Hungarian Citizens, echoing Maria Theresa. **Nomadism** was prohibited. The regime of János Kadar (after the 1956 counterrevolution) took more interest in the Romany population, and in 1958 the Politburo of the Hungarian Socialist Workers Party adopted a policy of active support for minority culture and **education**. Part of this policy included the creation of the Cigányszövetség (Gypsy Union), the first Romany organization officially operating in Hungary (1958–1961). A report revealed that two-thirds of the Gypsies then lived in substandard housing, mainly in rural Gypsy settlements or separate quarters in towns. A rehousing program began in 1964 with low-interest, long-term loans.

A debate in 1961 concerning whether the Romanies were an ethnic minority resulted in the conclusion that they were not and that Romani should not be taught in schools. The Gypsy Union was closed in the same year. *Rom Som* (I am a Romany), a bilingual journal, published its first issue in January 1975. It was produced with stencils by the Romany cultural club in District 15 of Budapest but circulated outside the capital. By 1982 it had disappeared, although the title has now been revived in a printed format.

In 1976 the government ordered measures to ensure full employment for men and preschool nursery education for children in an attempt to integrate the Gypsy population. By 1986, the need to support a political organization for the Romanies was acknowledged, and the Orzsagos Cigánytanacs (National Gypsy Council) came into being. The head of the new body was **Jószef Choli Daróczi**. The establishment of the national body was soon followed by the creation of councils in each county to deal with individual cases of discrimination. A further body, the Ungro-themeske Romane Kulturake Ekipe (Hungarian Romany Cultural Association), was created in 1986 to encourage and sponsor Gypsy **artists** and support Romany culture. It received a large grant to assist more than 200 cultural groups and 40 **dance** troupes. The president was **Menyhért Lakatos**. In 1979 the Gypsies in Hungary were finally recognized as an ethnic group.

In 1989 multiparty democracy came to Hungary, and Dr. Gyula Naday formed the Magyar Cigányok Demokrata Szövetség (Democratic Union of Hungarian Gypsies), while Pal Farkas became chairman of the Social Democratic Party of Gypsies of Hungary. The Hungarian Roma Parliament was set up in the same year, as was the organization **Phralipe** under **Bela Osztojkan**. The Minorities Law, passed in July 1993, defined the rights of minorities in Hungary and led to the creation of the short-lived Minorities Round Table, a body that negotiated with the government Office of National and Ethnic Minorities. In 1994 the Romanies were able for the first time to elect local Romany councils, and in April 1995 a Hungarian National Council of Romany Representatives was formed, with Florian Farkas as its president.

Independent Romany political parties have been able to put up candidates at the recent general elections: the Magyarorszagi Cigányok Bekepartja (Hungarian Gypsies' Peace Party), led by Albert Horvath; Magyar Cigányok Antifasiszta Orszagos Szervezet (National Organization of Gypsy Antifascists); and Roma Parliament Választási Szövetség (Romanies' Parliamentary Electoral Alliance). The Magyar Cigányok Szolidaritás Partja (Hungarian Gypsies Solidarity Party) presented three candidates, including Bela Osztojkan.

Ethnicity is not registered officially in Hungary, so voting on the recently established local minority self-governments is not limited to the minorities themselves. The Democratic Romany Coalition, under the chairmanship of **Aladar Horvath**, swept to victory in the National Gypsy Minority Self-Government elections, defeating Lungo Drom.

In 2003, there were four Romany MPs, Romany mayors headed four municipal governments, and 544 Roma sat on local and county government assemblies. A Rom, Laszlo Teleki, was appointed as first secretary for Roma affairs in June 2002. The government is appointing special commissioners for Gypsy affairs at six ministries.

Democracy has also meant freedom for right-wing nationalists and skinheads to organize, and racist attacks against Romanies have occurred in Eger and other towns. Three Romanies were killed in 1992, but the government denied any racist motivation. In September 1992 there was an arson attack on Romany homes in Ketegyhaza. Heavy-handed police raids have taken place in Arantyosapoti, Orkeny, and elsewhere. In 1999 Laszlo Vidak from the town of Bag filed a complaint alleging that he had been beaten by police officers during interrogation in October of that year, and three police officers were later given suspended sentences. Following on from this, it has been suggested that a February 2001 incident where police raided a Romany settlement in Bag may have been intended to intimidate Vidak. More recently, in November 2003, a Romany man burned to death in a "rubber cell" at a prison in Zalaegerszeg, Zala County. It took nine years for the **European Court of Human Rights** to rule in 2004 that Sandor Balogh had been mistreated by the police in Oroshaza.

Physical attacks by right-wingers are at a lower level than in other eastern European countries. Nevertheless, prejudice remains. A petition signed by 827 residents in Szentetornya in 1994 called for the expulsion of all Gypsies in the area. A poll taken earlier by Helsinki Watch found that one-third of the Hungarian population supported the idea of compulsory repatriation of the Romanies to **India**. In another poll by the Median agency, three-quarters of those asked expressed anti-Gypsy sentiments. Roma continue to be widely discriminated against, even by the judiciary. In one recent case, two Roma men who had served 15-month prison sentences were released from custody in November 2003, having been found innocent. They decided to sue for compensation but, despite the existence of an anti-discrimination law, were not awarded the requested amount, as the court stated that the individuals were more "primitive" than average and did not merit the greater compensation. An appeals court went on to uphold the judgment; however, the prime minister was later to reprimand the presiding judge.

In January 2003 a police investigation into the minority affairs ombudsman's allegation of housing discrimination against Roma removed to villages surrounding the town of Paks in September 2002, concluded that there was no violation of the law, and the case was closed. However, in 2005, after proceedings stretching over three years, a court awarded damages of 2,400 euros to two Romany men who had been refused entry to the Zold Pardon discotheque in Budapest.

The unemployment rate for Roma is estimated at 70 percent, more than 10 times the national average. That the government reduced the limit on unemployment benefits from one year to nine months in 2000 has only served to exacerbate the poverty of the Roma. The central government has, however, recently committed two billion forints ($24 million) toward improving the plight of the Gypsy minority. Some Gypsy leaders have called for a larger 20-year program.

Romany children are often segregated by being placed in special schools, designed for children with mental disabilities or poor academic performance. The government states that these schools are intended to provide intensive help for disadvantaged children. The opening of a selective English-style private school in the 30-percent-Romany town of Jaszladany caused great resentment for the town's Romany population, who feel discriminated against and socially excluded because the high tuition fees at the school mean that their children are essentially barred from attending.

There are, however, signs that the government is committed to increased efforts at various levels of Gypsy **education**. Pecs University launched the country's first postgraduate program in Gypsy studies, with a department of Romology. The teachers' training colleges in Pecs and Zsambek also have departments of Romany studies and the Romaversitas program supports Roma students completing higher education degrees. A high school with special responsibility for Gypsy education has been opened at Szabolcs, a deprived region of eastern Hungary. A kindergarten catering almost exclusively to Gypsy pupils has also been opened in Csepel, a poor Budapest suburb. The cities of Ozd and Szolnok have just signed an agreement with the Ministry of Education for the creation of student hostels providing 400 spaces to Gypsy pupils engaged in further education. Additionally, there are scholarships available to Roma at all levels of education through the public Foundation for the Hungarian Roma. Nevertheless, it took three years up to 2004 for a complaint against the primary school in Tiszatarjan to be upheld and for the school to have to pay damages to nine families whose children had been taught in a segregated class.

More than 50 percent of Romany households in Hungary do not have access to hot running water, and 35 percent do not have access even to cold running water. More than half of the houses do not have indoor toilets, and one in 10 has one or more members of the family sleeping on earthen floors. Discriminatory rules preventing Gypsies from obtaining social housing have been reported from Budapest, Debrecen, and Miskolc.

Music has always been a popular profession for the Gypsies of Hungary. In 1683 it was said that every nobleman in Transylvania had his own Gypsy—either violinist or locksmith. In 1839 the first Hungarian Gypsy orchestra visited western Europe, and in 1847 **Barba Lautari** met composer **Franz Liszt**. In 1938 the Federation of Hungarian Gypsy Musicians arranged a Gypsy music festival to commemorate the 500th anniversary of the Gypsies' first appearance in Hungarian territory. Apart from the polkas and waltzes that they play in restaurants, there is **Hungarian Gypsy music**. The **Vlah** Romanies have a lively culture of their own, with ballads and songs to accompany **dancing**.

Three main groups of Gypsies live in Hungary: the Hungarian Romanies, who form some 70 percent of the population, very few of whom speak (the Carpathian **dialect** of) Romani; the Vlah, some 20 percent; and the **Bayash**, who speak a dialect of **Romanian**.

Weekly **radio** and **television** programs are aimed at Gypsies but also have a Hungarian audience. **Agnes Daróczi** was originally on the teams that produce these programs. In 2001 Budapest's Roma gained their own radio station with the launch of Radio C, a station run by and for Gypsies. The current director is David Daróczi. The station is noted for its breadth of musical coverage, including Romany rap, such as the band **Fekete Vonat**. *See also* MINORITY SELF-GOVERNMENT (HUNGARY).

– I –

ICELAND. Apart from short visits early in the last century by horse dealers from Scandinavia (and one woman and her child on their way to the **United States** in 1933), there has been no migration of Gypsies to Iceland.

ILIEV, JONY. Bulgaria. Contemporary **musician**. In his own country, he plays turbo-folk but his CD *Ma maren ma* [Don't Beat Me] is more traditional.

INDIA. It would take a volume on its own to look at tribes and castes in India and **Pakistan** who might be related to the Romanies of Europe and the Doma (**Nawwar**) of the Middle East. We would need to consider all the groups of industrial nomads who speak a North Indian language. However, there are three names that spring to mind because of links that have already been made. The first is the **Banjara**, who took an active part in the second **World Romany Congress** in Geneva. Dr. Shyamala Devi, who later was to be one of the first of the **clan** to go through university, has visited Europe many times and written about the Banjara–Romany connection. Roma writers from Europe were invited to participate in the second Writers Festival in 2006 and a special session was arranged for them.

The Sapera (snake charmers), also known as **Kalbelia**, live mainly in Rajasthan. Sapera dancers have visited Europe several times and are featured in **Tony Gatlif's film** *Latcho drom*. **English** Gypsies were invited by the Indian High Commission to a showing of a documentary on this tribe in 1984. The Romany viewers immediately claimed to recognize the whistles used to call dogs—which had survived in their folk memory for nearly a millennium since the departure from northern India. The Kalbelia themselves are not as politically organized as are the Banjara.

It has been suggested that—at the same time the ancestors of the European Gypsies moved west—a small group of **nomads**, the **Vaghri** or Nari-kuravar, migrated south. They speak a North Indian language and their main **occupation** today is catching birds—*nari-kuravar* in Tamil. The Vaghri—like the Kalbelia—have not reached the political maturity of the Banjara and links between them and European Romanies have been solely through the missionaries of the **Pentecostalism** movement. *See also* INDIAN ORIGIN.

INDIAN INSTITUTE OF ROMANI STUDIES. Chandigarh, India. Founder: **W. R. Rishi**. The institute is now under the directorship of his son, **Veerendra Rishi**.

INDIAN ORIGIN. Some references to Indian origin are made in the early accounts of Gypsies in Europe. This was then forgotten both by Gypsies and non-Gypsies and replaced by the theory that they came from **Egypt**. However, investigations into the **Romani language origins** showed that it came from northern **India** and had been brought to Europe by the Gypsies. A small number of writers have recently denied the Indian origin and claim that the Gypsies are Europeans who acquired the language through contact with Indian merchants. Many Gypsies are actively aware of the Indian connection. They like to watch Indian **films** and play the **music** of these films, while some even have statuettes of Indian gods in their houses. The **Teatr Romen** in Moscow includes translations of Indian plays in its repertoire. Some contemporary writers—in particular, **poets**—have introduced Hindi words into their works. In India itself, the connection has been recognized by Prime Minister Indira Gandhi, the two **Chandigarh Festivals**, and the activities of the **Indian Institute of Romani Studies**.

INDORAMA. Bulgaria. Est. 1991. President: Vasil Danev. The association's vice president was the businessman and sometime poet Georgi Parushev.

INFORMAL CONTACT GROUP ON ROMA OF THE INTER-GOVERNMENTAL ORGANIZATIONS. The group is composed of representatives from the **Organization for Security and Cooperation in Europe**, the **Council of Europe**, the **European Commission**, and the **European Union**.

INFOROMA. Bratislava, Slovakia. The organization collects documentation and runs training courses. It is supported partly by the **Open Society Institute**.

INSTITUTO ROMANÓ. (1) A cultural and welfare organization in Barcelona, **Spain**, affiliated to the **Union Romani**. The secretary is Juan Reyes Reyes. (2) The Romani title used by the **Romany Institute** of Great Britain.

INTERFACE. (1) The Interface Collection, a publication program of **educational** books by the **Centre de Recherches Tsiganes**. (2) The newsletter of the Centre de Recherches Tsiganes. It was published in several western European languages.

INTERNATIONAL CONFERENCE ON ROMANI LINGUISTICS. The first conference was held in Hamburg in 1993, evolving from a workshop entitled "Romani in Contact with Other Languages." Further conferences have been held in Amsterdam, Graz, and Manchester.

INTERNATIONAL COVENANT ON ECONOMIC, SOCIAL, AND CULTURAL RIGHTS (ICESCR). The Covenant was set up by and is monitored by the **United Nations (UN).** The **European Roma Rights Center** and other bodies have regularly submitted evidence to the UN showing that many countries, most recently **Russia** and **Slovakia**, are not following the Covenant.

INTERNATIONAL MEETINGS. The first meeting mentioned in some books is the **Cannstadt Conference** of 1871, but recent research has discovered that this was a story made up by a newspaper. Some books also mention an international **Sofia Congress** in 1905. However, it seems that this gathering was just for Gypsies living in **Bulgaria**. In 1934 the Romanian Gypsy Union organized what can be considered the first international meeting, the **Bucharest Conference**, although few—if any—foreigners participated. After World War II, six international congresses have been held, as well as a European Congress in Seville, **Spain**. Both Catholic and Protestant organizations arrange international conferences and meetings. *See also* LODZ CONGRESS; PARIS CONFERENCE; WORLD ROMANY CONGRESS.

INTERNATIONAL ROMA WOMEN'S NETWORK (IRWN). Sweden. President: Soraya Post. The IRWN was launched on 8 March 2003 (International Women's Day) by Roma **women** from 18 European countries to lobby governments for better living conditions and to fight for Roma women's rights. Activists are drawn from Roma, **Sinti**, and **Traveler** communities and cover western, central, and eastern Europe.

INTERNATIONAL ROMANI UNION (IRU). Est. 1978. President: **Stanislaw Stankiewicz.** Since the second **World Romany Congress** in 1978, the union has operated between congresses as the official body representing Roma, taking over the role of the **Comité International Tzigane**. It is recognized as a representative body by the major international organizations and was awarded roster status by theUnited Nations **Economic and Social Council** as long ago as 1979 and later by the United Nations Children's Fund. It has been the prime mover in setting up the European Roma Information Office in Brussels.

The names of the other current officers of the IRU will be found under the entry for World Romany Congress.

INTERNATIONAL ROMANI WRITERS ASSOCIATION. Finland. President: **Veijo Baltzar**. Arising initially from a meeting in Cologne in November 2001, the association was formed in July 2002 when some 30 Roma writers from nine countries came together in Karis, **Finland**. The main aim of the organization is to promote multilingual Romani **literature** and to strengthen the language and culture of the Romany people.

INTERNATIONAL UNION OF THE ROMA OF THE BALTIC STATES AND THE COMMONWEALTH OF INDEPENDENT STATES. The union was established at a conference in Smolensk, **Russia**, in early 2003. It links 32 Romany organizations throughout the region. Oleg Kozlovski was elected as chairperson but his appointment has not been recognized in all the states.

IRAN. The Roma passed through Iran on their journey from **India** to Europe, enriching their language with loans from Farsi. Some remained in the country. Their descendants include the **Koli**.

IRAQ. The 1976 census recorded 5,519 "Gypsies" (presumably **Nawwar**) and 2,569 Karach (indigenous commercial **nomads**) but the real figure is perhaps 10 times this. In 1979 the government granted citizenship to all the Gypsies provided they knew Arabic and had a trade. Saddam Hussein settled several hundred in Abu Ghraib and Qamaliya near Baghdad, where they came into conflict with the locals for selling alcohol. After the overthrow of Saddam Hussein in 2003, the local population forced most of the Gypsies to leave their homes in the capital.

IRELAND (IRISH REPUBLIC). Estimated population of **Irish Travelers**: 45,000 in **caravans** and houses. They form a separate social group and are distinguished by mainstream Irish society even when they are settled in houses. About 1,500 families live in camps run by local councils or all-**Traveler** housing schemes; 2,000 are in standard municipal housing, while some 1,000 **nomadize** or settle on unofficial sites. No figures are collected for those who have made their own provision in housing or private camp sites. Their main **occupation** is recycling waste material. There is considerable discrimination, for example, in entry to hotels and bars. A farmer who recently battered and then shot a Traveler he found on his property in Cross was cleared of murder.

In 1960 the Irish government established a Commission on Itinerancy, whose report was published three years later. This report was the basis for a later assimilation program. Around this time, a civil rights movement emerged among the Travelers.

In 1963 a school for Travelers, St. Christopher's School, was built by Johnny MacDonald and others on an unofficial site at the Ring Road, Ballyfermot, Dublin. On 6 January 1964 it was burned down by Dublin Corporation employees, together with several huts used as accommodations. The school was later rebuilt on Cherry Orchard.

At the end of 1963, the Itinerant Action Group was set up to fight for better living conditions and access to **education**. The first demand was for a water supply at the Ring Road site. In 1981 Travelers took a test case to the International Court of Human Rights in Strasbourg. They claimed that their constitutional right to educate their children was denied by their being moved constantly without caravan sites being available. Families sought the ruling that they could not be evicted unless an alternative site was provided. The court ruled favorably. So, in that same year, a new report was requested, and the Travelling People Review Body was set up by the minister of health. It consisted of 24 members, including representatives of the National Council for Travelling People (a network of settlement committees) and three Travelers. Its remit was to review current policies and services for the "travelling people" to improve the existing situation. The thrust of the council's 1983 report, like that of 1963, was the need to provide official stopping places for the Travelers' caravans and to help with education and employment.

The Task Force on the Travelling People was set up in 1993 and published yet another report two years later. In March 1996 a National

Strategy for Traveller Accommodation was announced to provide 3,100 units of accommodation. This would consist of 1,200 permanent caravan pitches, 1,000 transit pitches, and 900 houses. A Traveller Accommodation Unit was established at the Department of the Environment to oversee the strategy. It was intended to initiate legislation that would require local authorities to draw up five-year plans for Traveler accommodation. This emerged in the Housing (Traveller Accommodation) Act of 1998.

Provision of caravan sites has been slow, and only some 850 units of accommodation have been provided. Nevertheless, in 2002 the government introduced the Housing (Miscellaneous Provisions) Act, which made trespass a criminal act. The **Irish Travellers Movement** picketed the Dáil (Parliament) on 2 July to protest against the law. Many Travelers have been evicted from unauthorized camps, and in some cases their caravans were confiscated, forcing them to sleep in their cars.

The real effect of this Housing Act has not been to start an exodus to mainland Britain, as some predicted, but to create intolerable conditions on already existing local-authority accommodation. Over the first three years after the passing of the Act, the number of Traveler families living on unauthorized sites—that is, the roadside—has fallen from about 1,000 to 630, while at the same time the numbers of families living on temporary official sites or sharing bays/pitches with other family members on official sites has increased by some 400. This would indicate that families in fear of the trespass legislation have opted to move on to already overcrowded or poorly serviced legal sites.

From 1999 to 2002 the government funded the Citizen Traveller Campaign to improve the negative attitude of the public toward Travelers. The main self-help organizations are the Irish Travellers Movement and **Pavee Point** (previously known as the Dublin Traveller Education and Development Group). There is also a national coordinator employed by the Department of Education. *See also* NORTHERN IRELAND.

IRISH TRAVELERS. Estimated population: 45,000 in the Irish Republic, 22,000 in the United Kingdom and Northern Ireland, 10,000 in the United States. The origins of the **Travelers** are unknown. Some writers would trace the Irish Travelers back in history to as early as 2000 B.C. when newly arrived metalworkers traveled around **Ireland** with their families. These families would then have been joined by itinerant **musicians** and later by some Druid priests as Christianity gained in popularity, forming the core of the Traveler population. Others may have joined them when tenants were much later dispossessed of their lands. By 1834 the traveling community was clearly distinguished from other poor who wandered the land in the report of the Royal Commission on the Poor Laws in that year.

Migration of Irish Travelers to **England** probably started soon after invaders from Britain landed in the country in 1172. It may be more than a coincidence that the first appearance of **"tinker"** as a trade or surname in Britain was nine years later. In 1214 a law was passed for the expulsion of Irish "beggars" from England, and in 1413 all Irish (with a very few exceptions) were to be expelled.

Several hundred Irish Travelers immigrated to mainland Britain from 1880 onward. There are now well over 1,000 Irish Traveler families living in **caravans** in Great Britain, including children who were born in that country. In spite of some intermarriage with the English Romanies, they form a separate ethnic group, partly because of their strong Catholicism. It is estimated that there are also 10,000 people of Irish Traveler descent in the **United States**, whose ancestors left Ireland even before the 19th-century famine.

The Travelers used to speak Irish with two special vocabularies called **Cant** and **Gammon** by their speakers and **Shelta** by scholars. By the 20th century the vast majority spoke English, still with a special vocabulary.

Irish Travelers were recognized as an ethnic group in England and **Wales** in 2000 as a result of a court case concerned with discrimination (*CRE v. Allied Domecq*). They had already been acknowledged in **Northern Ireland** in 1997 in the Race Relations (Northern Ireland) Order. The Irish Republic protects Travelers against discrimination in section 2 of the Equal Status Act of 2000, though without accepting them as an ethnic group.

A strong musical tradition thrives among the Travelers. There are many of their musicians listed in this work, while Michael Collins has achieved fame as an actor. *See also* IRISH TRAVELLERS MOVEMENT; IRISH TRAVELLERS MOVEMENT (ITM) BRITAIN.

IRISH TRAVELLERS MOVEMENT (ITM). Ireland. Est. 1990. Chairperson: Catherine Joyce. A national association in the Irish Republic, linking a number of local groups from all parts of **Ireland** in its membership. The ITM is a partnership between **Irish Travelers** and settled people committed to seeking full equality for **Travelers** in Irish society. This partnership is reflected in all of the structures of ITM. *See also* IRISH TRAVELLERS MOVEMENT (ITM) BRITAIN.

IRISH TRAVELLERS MOVEMENT (ITM) BRITAIN. United Kingdom. Est. 1999. Chairperson: Joe Browne. The aim of ITM Britain is to establish and facilitate a national network of groups, organizations, and individuals working with and within the **Traveler** community to promote the interests and welfare of the **Irish Traveler** community in Britain. The ITM was formed due to a recognized need that arose from conferences organized by Brent Irish Advisory Service in consultation with local Traveler projects throughout the country. These three conferences highlighted a lack of representation at a local and national level for Irish Travelers. The main activities of the organization are to promote the recognition of Irish Travelers as a **nomadic** ethnic group, to bring together in partnership Travelers and those settled people who are committed to achieving full equality for Travelers, and to challenge the racism and discrimination—individual, cultural, and institutional—that Irish Travelers experience. *See also* IRISH TRAVELLERS MOVEMENT (ITM).

ISLE OF MAN. Gypsies are rare on the island. Around 1950 a Gypsy **caravan** stopped on Douglas Head, then disappeared because of the banning of camping on the island. In 1975 a **fortune-teller** operated in Douglas. There were also at that time a few families—some dealing with scrap metal—living in houses, also in Douglas.

ISRAEL. A small community of **Nawwar** (Dom) live in Jerusalem and are well organized politically. *See also* DOMARI.

ISTANBUL ORIENTAL ENSEMBLE. The ensemble that plays alongside **Burhan Ocal** brings together some of the best Roma musicians of **Turkey** playing Turkish and Thracian Gypsy music of the 18th and 19th centuries.

ITALY. Estimated Gypsy population: 100,000. In 1422 the first company of Gypsies came from the north into Italy, to the town of Bologna, in the shape of Duke Andrew of **Little Egypt** with a party some 100 strong. They had a letter of safe conduct from King Sigismund of **Hungary** and said they were on their way to Rome to see the **pope**. The local priests in Bologna threatened to excommunicate anyone who had their **fortune** told by the Gypsies. There is no record of them being received by the pope at that time.

We later find a series of edicts from different parts of Italy that, on the one hand, enable us to follow the travels of the Gypsies but, on the other, reveal the antipathy toward these **nomadic** groups. The first edict was in 1493 in Milan, where the duke ordered all the Gypsies in the area to leave under the threat of execution. Similar decrees followed in Modena (1524), the Papal States (1535), Venice (1540), Tuscany (1547), and Naples (1555). These decrees did not succeed in banishing the Gypsies from Italy, however. We find them depicted by Leonardo da Vinci and Caravaggio, among others. In Lombardy and Piedmont, Gypsies nomadized with their crafts without attracting the same attention of lawmakers as had the companies led by the dukes.

Following a different route, across the sea from the Balkans, Gypsies came to central and southern Italy—Abruzzi and Calabria—in the period 1448–1532, along with **Greeks** and **Albanian** immigrants, fleeing from the advancing **Turks**. They settled here and traveled only in limited areas, up to and including Rome. Later, **Sinti** Gypsies came from **Germany** into northern Italy, and toward the end of the 19th century, **Vlah** Gypsies arrived from **Romania**. Some **Yugoslav** Gypsies nomadized in Italy between the two world wars (1918–1939).

Under the fascist regime of Benito Mussolini, Gypsies were harassed and imprisoned. Even before World War II, many were arrested and expelled from the mainland to Sicily and smaller islands. Then from September 1940, internment camps were set up and the first official instructions for the incarceration of Italian Gypsies were issued. From 1942 Agnone in the south was a camp solely for Gypsies. When Italy signed an armistice with Great Britain and the Allies in September 1943, the Germans took over the north of the country and began to send Gypsies to the concentration camps in **Poland**.

The years after 1945 witnessed a great influx of Romanies from Yugoslavia. Most of these live in shantytowns on the outskirts of the cities. There have been a number of anti-Gypsy actions by right-wingers. In March 1995 a bomb was thrown at two children who were begging by the roadside near Pisa. Local authorities have evicted nomadic families from sites in Florence, Milan, Turin, and Verona. The right-wing National Alliance has organized demonstrations against Gypsy camps in Rome and elsewhere. The Northern League in Verona has distributed a pamphlet alleging that "Gypsies are parasites." In Genoa in June 1996 two demonstrations against Romany immigrants were held. Heavy-handed police action against new immigrants has been alleged, and at least one death in police custody has occurred, that of Zoran Ahmetovic in 1996.

On the other hand, the voluntary **Opera Nomadi** organization has worked to get **education** to the children of nomadic families and those in the shantytowns, while the **Centro Studi Zingari** published for many years the informative journal *Lacio Drom*. Vittorio Pasquale Mayer and Zlato Levak are among the Romanies who contributed to the journal. One of the foremost cultural activists is **Santino Spinelli**.

ITINERANTS. A pejorative term sometimes used in **Ireland** for **Travelers**.

– J –

JAKOWICZ, WLADYSLAW (1915–?). Poland. Writer and **dancer**. Born in Krakow, from 1939 to 1945 he lived in **Russia**. On his return to **Poland**, he earned his living as a dancer and then immigrated to **Sweden**, where he worked as a teacher. Jakowicz wrote the poem "O Tari thaj e Zerfi" [A Ballad of Two Lovers] in the **Romani language** in 1981.

JAROKA, LIVIA. Hungary. Contemporary politician. She is a former **radio** announcer and graduate in English who — in 2004 — became only the second Gypsy member of the Parliament of the **European Union** in Brussels. *See also* RAMÍREZ HEREDIA, JUAN DE DIOS.

JASAROVA (REDJEPOVA), USNIJA (1946–). Skopje, Macedonia. Singer. She also appeared in the **film** *Dervis i smrt* [Dervish and Death; 1974]. CD: *The Best of Usnija Redjepova.*

JASENOVAC. Concentration camp set up by the puppet **Croatian** government in 1941. Some 28,000 Gypsies were killed there, alongside **Jews, Serbs,** and left-wingers, by the fascist Ustashe guards. The majority were killed on arrival. Men and **women** were separated and then taken across the Sava River to extermination units at Gradina and Ustice. A small number of men were sent to forced labor in a brick factory where they soon perished due to the poor conditions. A few Gypsy survivors escaped while being led to execution.

JAYAT, SANDRA. Italy. Contemporary **poet** and artist. A self-taught **Manouche** Gypsy, she describes herself as "a daughter of the wind." Jayat is related to the renowned guitarist **Django Reinhardt.** She left Italy, where her parents lived, as a teenager and worked as a commercial artist in Paris. Small exhibitions culminated in having her work shown in the Grand Palais Salon. In 1985 she organized an international exhibition of Gypsy **art** in Paris and in 1992 exhibited at the Musée Bourdelle. The French government then commissioned her to create a postage stamp depicting "traveling people" in the same year.

Among her collections of poems are *Herbes Manouches* (1961), illustrated by Jean Cocteau, and the 1963 publication *Lunes nomades.* She has also written a novel, *El Romanes.* Her many honors include the 1972 Children's Literature Prize (Paris), the Poetry Book Prize (Stockholm) in 1978, and an international prize for painting also in 1978. The book *Nomad Moons* (1995) contains translations into English by Ruth Partington from four of the poet's volumes, mainly, but not exclusively, from *Lunes nomades.*

JENISCH (YÉNICHE). A **clan** of **Travelers** originally established in Germany, some of whom later migrated to **Austria, Belgium, France,** and **Switzerland.** They may well number 10,000. They speak a variety of German, with loan words from Romani as well as Yiddish. Traditionally they were basket makers and peddlers. Some scholars say they originated with a group of basket and broom makers in the Eifel region of Germany, from where they spread out.

During the Nazi period in Germany, many of the Jenisch were sent to concentration camps as "antisocial" and perished. In occupied France, they were kept alongside Romanies in internment camps for **nomads** during the period of World War II. For many years, a Swiss mission took Jenisch children away from their parents and sent them to be brought up in children's homes. In both France and Germany, small numbers continue to survive as seminomads. The Jenisch in Austria have formed their own cultural organization.

JENTINA. *See* ROSE, JENTINA.

JETHRO. It has been said, with little justification, that Jethro (Moses' father-in-law) was a Romany.

JEVREMOVIĆ, DRAGAN. Yugoslavia. Activist at the **Romano Centro** of Vienna, where he now lives. He is also chairman of the **Parliament** of the **International Romani Union**.

JEWS. The destinies of the Gypsies and the Jews have been intertwined ever since the former arrived in Europe centuries after the latter. For example, in **Spain** the deportation of the Moors and the Jews and the attempted deportation of the Gypsies happened at about the same time. In the **Russian** Empire, some Gypsies were converted to Judaism. They survived the Nazi occupation because they were thought not to be ethnically Jewish or Gypsy.

Many Jews have written about the genocide of the Roma and Sinti during the **Holocaust** (e.g., Ben Sijes in the **Netherlands** and **Miriam Novitch**) while **Dora Yates** served many years as the voluntary secretary of the **Gypsy Lore Society**.

JOHN, AUGUSTUS **(1878–1961).** England. **Artist**. He painted Romanies and Gypsy themes. John learned many Romani words, which he used in correspondence with his closest friends.

JONES, JOHN WOOD (1800–?). Wales. Harpist. Jones was also a teacher of the harp to blind and lame children in a school at Carmarthen. In 1843, a year before his death, he accompanied Thomas

Gruffydd to Buckingham Palace to perform on the harp before the Prince of Wales, Prince Albert, and Queen Victoria, to their apparent satisfaction.

JONES, NELLA (née SAUNDERS) (1932–). England. Psychic and healer. A Romany Gypsy who was brought up at Belvedere Marshes in Kent. She reputedly assisted in solving many cases for police headquarters at Scotland Yard. They included the famous Yorkshire Ripper case—that of Peter Sutcliffe who was sentenced at the Old Bailey in 1981 for the murder of 13 women. She also helped to locate Stephanie Slater, a kidnap victim.

JORDACHE, TONI. Romania. Contemporary **musician**. He played the **cimbalom** in the years after World War II.

JOSEPH II (1741–1790). Austria. Emperor of Austria-Hungary (part of the **Habsburg** and **Holy Roman** empires) from 1765. He was the son of **Maria Theresa** and continued her assimilationist policies toward the Gypsies. The **Romani language** and dress were banned, and **music** was allowed only on feast days. Schooling and church attendance were made compulsory. Resistance by the Gypsies led to Joseph modifying some of his decrees.

JOSEPH, CHARLES LOUIS (1833–1896). Austria. Writer and politician. The Archduke of **Austria**, he published a number of works at the end of the 19th century on the **Romani language** in **Hungary**.

JOVANOVIĆ, ŽARKO (?–1997). Serbia. Balalaika player and singer. During World War II, he escaped from the concentration camp of Zemun and joined the Partisans. Jovanović made many recordings in the years after 1945. He wrote the lyrics of the Romani **national anthem**, "**Gelem, Gelem.**"

JOYCE, NAN. Ireland. Contemporary civil rights activist. An **Irish Traveler** herself, she stood unsuccessfully in Dublin in 1982 for election to the Irish Dáil (Parliament) to draw attention to the **Travelers'** needs.

JUSTIN, EVA. Germany. 20th-century scientist. She worked with **Robert Ritter** in the Race Hygiene Research Center in Nazi **Germany.** She saw sterilization as the way to solve the "Gypsy problem." *See also* HOLOCAUST.

JUSUF, SHAIP (ŠAIP) (1932–). Skopje, Macedonia. Teacher and writer. He helped in the establishment of the **International Romani Union** and was a scholar of Romani grammar. Jusuf visited the first **Chandigarh Festival** and used many loans from **Indian** languages in his writing. He published a biography of Tito in Romani in 1978 and a Romani grammar in 1980.

– K –

KAALE. The term used for self-ascription by **Finnish** Gypsies. It is from the Romani word *kalo*, meaning "black."

KAL. Serbia. Band playing traditional **music.**

KALBELIA. Nomads in Rajasthan, also known as Sapera, one of whose **occupations** is snake charming. They are considered by many scholars to be close cousins of the European Romanies. Kalbelia **dancers** have appeared several times in western Europe with folk dance groups from **India.** Gulab and Mera, who danced with the Surnai Company in Rajasthan, came to London and performed at the Albert Hall in March 1986. They also appear in the first part of the documentary **film** *Latcho drom* [Good Road].

KALDA, JOZEF. Czechoslovakia. Contemporary **poet.** A Moravian poet who had success with a series of poems supposedly written by a farmer's son who falls in love and runs off with a Gypsy. The poems inspired the composer Leos Janaćek to write the song cycle *The Diary of One Who Disappeared.*

KALDERASH. (1) Name of a **clan** derived from the **Romanian** word *calderar* (coppersmith). Many emigrated from Romania after the end of slavery in the 19th century. They are probably the largest Romany clan, numbering nearly one million, spread throughout the world. Many men still work in the traditional trade of repairing copper utensils, while their **women** practice **palm-reading**. (2) A **dialect** of the **Romani language**.

KALI. An incarnation of God in the Hindu **religion**. When the Gypsies came to Europe, they transferred their adoration of Kali to the many black statues of the Virgin Mary in **Poland** and elsewhere, as well as of St. Sarah at **Saintes Maries de la Mer**. There is a report from 1471 of Duke Paul of **Egypt** making a pilgrimage to Santiago de Compostela in **Spain** to see the Black Virgin of Guadalupe.

KALININ, NIKOLAI (1977–). Belarus. Lawyer. The son of **Valdemar Kalinin**, he is a counselor for Roma at the **Belarus** branch of the International Society for Human Rights.

KALININ, VALDEMAR (1946–). Belarus. Teacher, **poet**, and translator. He currently resides in London. Kalinin translated the New Testament into Romani and is currently preparing the Old Testament for publication. In 2002 he was a joint recipient of the **Hiroshima Foundation** Award, and he won the **Roma Literary Award** for Translation in 2003.

KALO. The Romani word for "black." The north **Welsh** and **Finnish** Gypsies use *Kalo* or *Kaale* as a self-ascription rather than *Rom*. It is likely that many of the Finnish Gypsies moved there from **Spain** via Great Britain, and there are some similarities in the **dialects**. The connection with the **Koli** clan in **Iran** is unclear.

KALYI JAG ("BLACK FIRE"). Hungary. The first group to play **Vlah music** in a popular style for a wider audience. Their music has developed from traditional **dance** tunes with the accompaniment of mouth music and improvised percussion instruments. CDs include *Gypsy Love*.

KALYI JAG ROMA SCHOOL. Hungary. Vocational comprehensive school in Budapest.

KANNAUJ. A city in **India** on the Ganges captured by the Muslims in 1018. All of its inhabitants were apparently taken as captives to Khorasan. Linguist **Marcel Cortiade** has put forward the hypothesis that these captives were the ancestors of the Romanies.

KANTEA, GEORGI. Moldova. Contemporary **poet**. A member of the **Ursari clan** who has collected and published folklore from **Moldova**.

KARDERASH. A **Vlah clan** in **Bulgaria**.

KARRNER. A **clan** of **Travelers** in **Austria**.

KARWAY, RUDOLF. Poland. Contemporary civil rights leader. A **Lovari** who immigrated to **Germany**, Karway was president of the Zigeunermission, a civil rights movement based in Hamburg that was active in the 1960s. In 1968, the mission organized a delegation to the **European Commission on Human Rights** in Strasbourg protesting against discrimination.

KATHAK. *Kathak* is the major classical **dance** form of northern **India**, derived from the dance dramas of ancient India. Under the influence of the royal court, there was a change in the overall emphasis, which shifted from the telling of **religious** stories to one of entertainment. It is often said that **flamenco** retains elements of the Kathak dance style.

KATITZI. Largely autobiographical character in a series of 13 books for children written by **Katarina Taikon** in 1975–1976. In 1979 the books came out in cartoon form, and there was also a **film**. **Hans Caldaras** recorded the song "Katitzi" in Taikon's honor. In 2003 the books were turned into a play. The books are still popular and have been translated into several languages.

KAWZCYNSKI, RUDKO. Poland. Contemporary civil rights activist. He came to **Germany** as a refugee in the 1970s. He was a singer in the **Duo Z**. Later, he entered the Gypsy civil rights movement and set up the **Romani National Congress** in Hamburg. He was also active in establishing Eurom. Kawzcynski has organized many demonstrations, such as the Bettlermarsch, a march across Germany to the Swiss frontier, and the occupation of the Neuengamme concentration camp site. He recently arranged the international **Lodz Congress** and takes part in conferences sponsored by intergovernmental organizations.

KAYAH (1960–). Poland. Singer of popular **music**. She made the largely folk music CD *Kayah and Bregović* (1999). There is no connection with the **Finnish** pop group of the same name.

KEENAN, PADDY (1950–). Ireland. **Musician. Irish Traveler** piper in the style of **Johnny Doran**. He was a member of the **Pavees** group and a founder member of the Bothy Band and also has recorded as a soloist. CDs include *Na Keen Affair*.

KELAROVA, IDA (1956–). Czech Republic. Singer. She has performed in the **Czech Republic** and abroad. CDs include *Gypsy Blood* (2001).

KENITES. A tribe of **nomadic** smiths in biblical times living in Judah who appear on a map in at least one book in circulation. They are, however, unrelated to the Romany Gypsies.

KERIM, USIN (1929–1983). Bulgaria. **Poet.** He wrote in Bulgarian and later, Romani. His first book of poems was *Songs from the Tent* (1955).

KETAMA. Contemporary folk rock group in **Spain** founded by Ray Heredia, Jose Soto, and Juan Carmona. Later they were joined by Antonio Carmona. Their first recording was issued in 1985. Heredia left the group to be a solo act. Josemi Carmona—a cousin of Jose and Juan—then joined the group. Their third recording, *Songhai 1*, incorporated a fusion of **flamenco** and Mali music. In 1992 the sixth recording, *Pa gente con Alma*, was again fusion, in collaboration with the Dominican jazz pianist Michel Camilo. Soto has now left the group, and Ketama consists of the three Carmonas. In their first disc as a family trio, *El arte de lo invisible*, salsa predominated over flamenco. Ketama has also played in **films** such as Carlos Saura's *Flamenco*. CDs include *La pipa de Kif* and *Aki a Ketama*—a mixture of flamenco, jazz, and funk.

KHAMORO ("LITTLE SUN"). Cultural festival first held in Prague in 2000.

KIEFFER, JANE. France. Contemporary **poet**. The collection *Cette sauvage lumière* [This Savage Light] appeared in 1961, followed by the volume *Pour ceux de la nuit* [For Those of the Night] in 1964.

KINGS. When the Romanies first came to Europe, their leaders adopted European titles; we find in the records references to dukes in particular. The use of the titles *king* and *queen* started perhaps in the 19th century. In some cases, the person designated king is not the real leader—a device to deceive the authorities. Most modern "kings" and "queens" have authority only over their own extended family. *See also* SHERO ROM.

KIRK YETHOLM. Village near Kelso, Scotland. In 1695 a Gypsy named Young saved the life of Capt. David Bennet at the Siege of Namur. In a gesture of generosity, the grateful officer gave some cottages to the Gypsies in Yetholm. The twin villages of Yetholm and Kirk Yetholm then became home to as many as 250 Gypsies for more than two centuries. They wintered in the villages and took to the roads in the spring to sell their wares and their horses. Smuggling tea, salt, and alcohol from across the border in **England** is said to have provided a valuable additional source of income. The romantic but harsh lifestyle changed radically in 1839, when the Rev. **John Baird** became minister at Yetholm. He persuaded the elders of the tribe to board out their children with local families so that they could attend school.

A so-called Gypsy Palace—in reality a modest-sized cottage—still stands, but otherwise there are no tangible signs that generations of Romanies settled there. Descendants of the original Yetholm gypsies continue to live in the area. The Romanies are now to be honored with a memorial in the village, which claims to be **Scotland**'s Gypsy capital.

KISFALU CONFERENCE (1879). A meeting of Gypsies held in **Hungary** in 1879. The participants were from Hungary only.

KLIMT, ERNST (?–1992). Germany. Political activist. A post-1945 political leader of the **Sinti** in Hildesheim and Lower Saxony. Klimt's family lived in the Sudetenland, where his father was a miner. The family was arrested and taken to **Auschwitz**, where Klimt arrived still wearing his Hitler Youth uniform. He was transferred, as being fit for work, to Buchenwald, where he took part in the internal camp resistance movement and helped to free the camp just as the U.S. Army arrived. In 1965, he gave up his business activities and devoted himself to civil rights. His life story was turned into a musical play at the Fahrenheit Theater in **Germany**.

KOCHANI (KOĆANI). A brass band from **Macedonia**. They have toured widely abroad. CD: *Gypsy Follies*.

KOCHANOWSKI, VANYA DE GILA (1920–2007). Poland. Linguist. Born in **Poland** but brought up in **Latvia**, he later lived in **France**. Kochanowski wrote *Gypsy Studies* (1963), for which he earned a doctorate, the novel *Romano atmo* [L'ame tsigane], and *Parlons Tsigane*.

KOCI, FERDINANT (FERDINAND). Albania. Contemporary **artist**. Now living in **England**, he has illustrated several publications, including *Bibaxtale berša*, a Romani edition of Donald Kenrick and Grattan Puxon's *Destiny of Europe's Gypsies*.

KOGALNICEANU, MIHAEL (1817–1891). Romania. Civil rights activist. A **Romanian** politician who strove for the emancipation of the Gypsy slaves in the 19th century.

KOIVISTO, VILJO. Finland. Contemporary writer and translator. He attended the first **World Romany Congress**. He writes for the **religious** bilingual periodical *Romano Boodos* (Romani Information) and has translated parts of the New Testament as well as producing a language primer.

KOLI. A **clan** of **Indian origin** in **Iran**. In recent years some members have visited **Italy**, mainly trading in gold.

KOPTOVÁ, ANNA. Slovakia. Contemporary writer. Founder of the **Romathan** theater in **Košice.**

KOŠICE. A town in **Slovakia** that is home to the **Romathan** theater and a college that has a faculty for training Romany teachers. *See also* LUNIK IX.

KOSOVO. Kosovo is a province in the Balkans, currently still a de jure part of **Serbia**, following a 12-week war in 1999 waged by the North Atlantic Treaty Organization (NATO) against the rump **Yugoslavia** to prevent the ethnic cleansing of the indigenous **Albanian** inhabitants. De facto, however, it is now controlled by Kosovar Albanians and the successors to their guerrilla force, the Kosovo Liberation Army (KLA). Estimated Gypsy population today: 40,000. The 1971 census showed 14,493 Roma in Kosovo, while in 1991 a more realistic figure of 45,745 was recorded. The estimated Romany population before the recent conflict was, however, at least 100,000. During the weeks preceding the 1971 and 1981 censuses both ethnic Albanians and **Turks** tried to persuade Roma to declare themselves as Albanians or Turks, respectively, while the Serbs encouraged them to register as Roma, in order to reduce the recorded numbers of Albanians in the country.

During World War II, Kosovo was garrisoned by Albanian fascists. Gypsies were made to wear distinctive armbands and recruited for forced labor. Many Romanies joined the Partisans. **Ljatif Sucuri** is regarded as having personally saved the Gypsies of Kosovo from massacre.

Kosovo was a strong center for Romany culture from 1945 until the recent hostilities. In 1983, **radio** broadcasts in Romani began in Priština, among the earliest in Europe, and these continued for many years, while weekly **television** broadcasts started in the same town three years later. There was a locally produced magazine called *Amaro Lav* (Our Word) and two other magazines—*Rota* and *Ahimsa*—being published in Priština. A group of young **poets** received acclaim well beyond the province largely because of the efforts of **Marcel Cortiade** in getting their work published. Formal education was rather less successful since, although some schools introduced Romani in 1985, this was without a curriculum or any textbooks. In this region, **Erlia** and **Gurbet** are the main **dialects** spoken. However, many parents bring up their children speaking Albanian because of the discrimination against Roma.

In spite of pressure both from Serbs and ethnic Albanians on the Roma to align themselves with one of the larger groups, the Association of Roma People of Priština had a membership of more than 10,000. Its president, Baskim Redjepi, was a deputy in the Priština city council, while poet **Bajram Haliti** worked in the Center for Minority Languages and Culture in Priština. In 1990, following the example of some Romanies in **Macedonia**, an **Egyptians** Association was set up in Kosovo. It claimed that several thousand "descendants of the Pharaohs" live in the province.

From 1981 the desire of many Kosovar Albanians for a fully independent Kosovo strengthened. Sometimes this turned to violence against Serbs but also against the Roma, whose leaders supported the Serbs. Such attacks only served to reinforce the alignment of the Roma with the dominant Serbs. When Yugoslav government tanks arrived in Priština prior to the autonomous status of Kosovo being revoked in 1990, the Romany population unwisely turned out to welcome them.

As economic and social segregation intensified, Albanians voluntarily or unwillingly had left their jobs under the Serbian-led administration and many Roma took over the vacant posts, a move that was not to endear them to the Albanians. In social life Serbs replaced Albanian **musicians** by Roma, while the Albanians themselves employed Albanian musicians in preference to Roma.

Albanian resistance against the Serbs continued and in 1998 the central government of Yugoslavia launched an offensive against the KLA, leading some 2,000 Roma to leave Kosovo for **Voivodina** in northern Serbia to flee the hostilities. After Serbian troops recaptured Orahovac from the KLA and massacred some 200 civilians, Roma were used to load corpses onto trucks. The use of Roma as gravediggers, reminiscent of how they were used by the Nazis in **Yugoslavia** to bury **Jews**, was to escalate during the period of the NATO raids the following year.

A decade later, in a rapidly deteriorating situation, the Yugoslav delegation to the Paris peace talks on Kosovo in 1999 included Albanians, Turks, Kosovar Roma, and the newly emerging minority of Egyptians, alongside a Serbian majority. Amid this claim of multiculturalism, the delegation refused for several days to have direct talks with the KLA, whom they persisted in calling "terrorists." For the Romani and Egyptian delegates, Ljuan Koka and Cherim Abazi, their participation in the talks was to lead to their enforced flight to Serbia to escape Albanian hostility.

Then came the period in 1999 during which NATO carried out intensive bombing raids. During this dramatic period when they were the victims of both warring groups, Roma were swiftly enrolled by the Serbs to help them terrorize the ethnic Albanians. Men of military age were forcibly recruited into the army and others were posted at the doors of food shops to keep the Albanians out. In self-defense, interpreted as complicity by the Albanians, the Roma in several villages marked an "R" on their doors to distinguish them from the Albanian houses when the Serbian auxiliaries arrived to burn and kill. Some Roma had worked as gravediggers before the bombing started. Now their services were called upon by the Serbs to bury their Albanian victims. But the number of victims was such that extra hands were needed and ordinary Roma were recruited for the task.

Other Roma fled the country, either to escape the NATO bombing raids or because—as Muslims—they, too, were being targeted by the Serbian auxiliaries. Some 2,000 fled to **Macedonia**, where they were helped by Romany organizations and individual families in the face of discrimination by Macedonian agencies. More than 20,000 took refuge in Serbia, over 800 in Albania, 8,000 in **Montenegro**, and a smaller number in **Bosnia-Herzegovina**.

In June 1990, after Serbian leader Slobodan Milosević agreed to peace terms with the NATO forces, the latter took over the province as peacekeepers in the Kosovo Force (KFOR). As the Serbian troops withdrew from Kosovo, they looted the houses of Albanians who had fled during the period of the air strikes. The Serbs forced the Roma to load the most valuable items onto their trucks and then told the Roma to take what was left. Undoubtedly, some did so.

The departure of the Serbian Army and police was soon followed by a series of retaliatory attacks by Albanians from Kosovo and from

Albania proper on both civilian Serbs and Roma. By 12 August 1999 the **United Nations** estimated that 170,000 Serbs had already fled in the days KFOR arrived, leaving only 30,000. The Roma were to follow.

Many of the Albanians who returned from refugee camps in Macedonia and Albania were to take revenge on the Romany community as a whole because of those members who had actively helped the Serbs. It is not yet clear how much of the ethnic cleansing of Roma that was to follow can be attributed to Kosovo Albanians and how much to intruders from Albania proper. Whoever the perpetrators were, the Roma were now to suffer what the Albanians had suffered from the Serbs.

Pogroms since the end of the conflict include the following. In June 1999 the Romani quarter in Mitrovica was burned down and the inhabitants fled to Priština. Roma in Kosovo Polje (near Priština) also came under threat, and 3,500 took refuge in a school. Roma and Egyptians in Djakovica and elsewhere were told they would be killed if they stayed. On 29 June, 12 houses were torched in Sitinica, a mixed village inhabited by Roma and ethnic Albanians. The Romany quarter of Dusanova in Prizren has also been burned down, as have many houses in Obilic and the quarter of Brekoc in Djakovica.

German KFOR troops discovered 15 injured Roma in a police office that had been taken over and used by the KLA as a prison in Prizren. A 16th man had been beaten to death. It was alleged the victims had taken part in looting. Romany victims of Albanian violence, however, have included many who could have taken no part in helping the Serbs. For example, a nine-year-old girl, "J. Q.," was beaten in the Fabricka Street quarter in Mitrovica, and in the same quarter, three elderly Roma died in their houses when these were set on fire by Albanians.

In addition to an improvised refuge in Kosovo Polje, KFOR built a camp housing 5,000 "internally displaced" Roma at Obilic (near Priština) in a pine forest and surrounded it with barbed wire covered with plastic sheeting. Albanians removed the protective sheeting so they could hurl insults and missiles against the Roma in the camp. In December 1999 the residents were moved to an army barracks in Plemetina. Roma elsewhere have complained that KFOR does nothing. There are countless reports of Roma seeing their homes looted and burned while British and other KFOR troops stood by unable or unwilling to help.

Although ethnic Serbian refugees from Kosovo were reluctantly accepted into Serbia proper, many Roma were stopped on the border and told to go back to their homes by the police. Meanwhile, thousands of Roma from Kosovo have taken refuge in other countries. As attacks increased, more than 2,000 Roma fled to **Italy** in June and July 1999, but in August the Italian authorities said they would no longer accept refugees from Kosovo because the fighting was over. Nevertheless, Roma still attempt the sea crossing, sometimes with tragic results.

A report by the **Organization for Security and Cooperation in Europe** in January 2000 suggested there were some 25,000 Roma of various **clans** still in the province, living in a precarious state, and the new millennium has seen further attacks. One report stated that seven Roma were murdered between February and May, an 11-year-old boy was beaten and thrown into the river at Klina in March, while 16 Roma families were forced out of Ogoste by ethnic Albanians displaced from an Albanian settlement on the other side of the Kosovan border in southern Serbia.

Most of the Roma intelligentsia have fled and, at the present time, it seems that the conflicts in this region have extinguished what had once been an inspirational example to Roma elsewhere. International agencies still say that life in the province is dangerous for Roma and, at the time of writing, Roma from Kosovo are generally not being returned to the area from the mainly western European countries to which many fled.

As early as 2000, investigations began into the alleged danger to human life being caused by the placement and retention of approximately 550 Roma people in three camps contaminated by lead poisoning in northern Mitrovica. At least one death—that of Dzenita Mehmeti, a two-year-old child—can be directly attributed to the lead contamination. In spite of expressions of goodwill by officers of the United Nations Mission to Kosovo, the Roma have not been moved to safer places.

KOSTURI, DEMIR (1928–1998). Albania. Internal judge for the Romany community in Korca and neighboring districts, he was the first

Albanian Rom to lead a delegation abroad when he attended the fourth **World Romany Congress** in 1990. He also organized **musical** and **theatrical** events in Albania.

KOUDELKA, JOSEPH **(1938–).** Czechoslovakia. Photographer. In 1961, he started to photograph the Gypsies of **Slovakia**. His pictures were exhibited in Prague in 1967. In 1968 he also worked with Gypsies in **Romania** and took photographs of the **Soviet** invasion of **Czechoslovakia** that were published anonymously abroad. In 1970, he was granted asylum in Great Britain and later became a French national. *Gypsies* (1978) contains his photographs from Slovakia. He had his first retrospective solo show in Perpignan, **France**, in 2003.

KOVALEVSKY, SONYA (1850–1891). Moscow, Russia. Academic. In 1884, Kovalevsky, whose mother was a Gypsy, became the first **woman** professor in **Sweden** when she taught mathematics at Stockholm University.

KRASNICI, ALI (1952–). Yugoslavia. Writer. As well as short stories, he has written two plays in Romani: *Čergarendje jaga* [Nomad Fires] and *Iripen an-o živdipen* [Return to Life].

KRIS. The legal system of some Romany **clans**. Some writers think this practice goes back to the village courts of **India**. The Kris is an assembly of adult members of a group of extended families or, in the case of a serious problem, the whole clan.

KUPATE. Bulgaria. Zlatko Mladenov is the main figure in this organization, which has a central office in Sofia and works with several local councils. A cultural center is planned for the capital.

KWIEK DYNASTY. Several families named Kwiek emigrated to **Poland** from **Romania**, via **Hungary**, at the beginning of the 20th century. They established a royal dynasty, which continued until shortly after World War II. These **kings** were not recognized by the long-settled Polish Romanies, who had their own chief with the title *Shero Rom*. In the period between the two world wars, there was sometimes more than one claimant for the title of king.

King Michal II (elected in 1930) was invited to the **Bucharest Conference** in 1934 and addressed a meeting in London's Hyde Park later that year, putting forward the case for a Gypsy state in Africa. Janusz Kwiek was crowned king in 1937 by the archbishop of Warsaw. He, too, was influenced by Zionism and asked Benito Mussolini to grant the Gypsies an area of land in recently conquered Abyssinia (present-day Ethiopia). He disappeared during the Nazi occupation of Poland. In 1946 Rudolf Kwiek was declared king but, living in a Communist state, he changed the title to that of president of the Gypsies. He died in 1964.

KYUCHUKOV, HRISTO (1962–). Bulgaria. **Educationalist.** He compiled the first Romani **alphabet** primer for children in **Bulgaria** and has produced teaching material on Romani culture for schools. He is currently training Roma teachers in Veliko Tarnovo.

– L –

LA CHUNGA AND LA CHUNGUITA. *See* AMAYA, LORENZA FLORES.

LABOUR CAMPAIGN FOR TRAVELLERS' RIGHTS. United Kingdom. Est. 1986. Secretary: Andrew Ryder. This is a recognized Labour Party group set up in 1986 and open to members of the British Labour Party. Its aims include sensitizing members of the party to the needs of Gypsies and **New Travelers.** Current activists are **Thomas Acton,** Mr. and Mrs. Codonas, and Ryder.

LACIO DROM ("GOOD ROAD"). (1) An academic journal founded in **Italy** in 1964 and, after 1966, published by the **Centro Studi Zingari.** It has ceased publication. The editor was Mirella Karpati. (2) The Lacio Drom schools, established to further the **education** of Gypsy children in Italy. (3) As *Latcho drom*, a **film** by **Tony Gatlif.**

LACKOVÁ, ELENA (1921–2003). Slovakia. Writer. Born in the Romani settlement of Velky Saris to a Polish mother and a Romany father, Lacková was one of nine children and the only girl in her community of 600 to complete primary school. In 1944 the settlement where she lived with her husband was set on fire by fascists. As a result, she was forced to flee into the forest, where one of her twin daughters died of hunger in her arms. Her first **literary** work, a play in the Slovak language, drew on her wartime experiences and was entitled *Horiaci cigansky tabor* [The Gypsy Camp is Burning; 1947]. Later on, she wrote in Romani. She set up and later became president of the Cultural Association of Romani Citizens and founded a Romani periodical, *Romano Lil* (Gypsy News). She continued to write, including her autobiography, published in English as *A False Dawn*.

LAFERTIN, FAPY (1950–). Belgium. **Musician.** A **Manouche** jazz guitarist and violinist, he is renowned for his performances in the Belgian-based Gypsy group Waso and for his forays into British jazz venues. Lafertin has been fascinated from childhood with the 12-string Portuguese guitar and mastered the *fado*, a Portuguese style of singing. He plays regularly with the British band Le Jazz and his own group, the Hot Club Quintet. In 2002, the Quintet toured the United Kingdom, including appearances at the Edinburgh Jazz Festival and London's Ronnie Scott's Club.

LAGRENE, BIRELI (1966–). France. **Musician. Sinto** Gypsy jazz guitarist béorn in Alsace. Taught by his father, Fiso, from the age of four, he began touring at an early age. He started recording at the age of 11, with *Routes de Django* (1981) and later *Acoustic Moments* and *Bireli Swing*. Switching to the electric guitar, he developed a style of fiery speed and versatility, moving away from mere imitation of **Django Reinhardt**.

LAGRÉNE, JEAN (fl. 19th century). France. Artist's model in Paris. Manet painted him in the picture *The Old Musician* (1862), now on display in Washington.

LAGUILLER, ARLETTE (1940–). France. Politician. A **New Traveler** who was an unsuccessful candidate for the European Parliament in southern **France** in 1995.

LAKATOS, ANKA. Hungary. Contemporary **poet**. The daughter of **Menyhért Lakatos**, she writes in Hungarian.

LAKATOS, MENYHÉRT (1926–). Hungary. Writer. A contemporary novelist who writes in Hungarian, his first novel *Füstös képek* [Bitter Smoke] has been translated into German as *Bitterer Rauch*.

LAKATOS, ROBY (1965–). Hungary. Violinist. He is descended from **János Bihari**. Drawing upon Gypsy folk **music**, classical, and jazz, his music's improvisatory spirit is what makes his style so distinctive. After graduating from Bela Bartok Musical Conservatory in Budapest in 1984 as top graduate of the year, he moved to Brussels, **Belgium**, where he began a residency at Les Ateliers de la Grande Île with an ensemble comprised of his oldest friends. Since 1996, numerous concert engagements throughout Europe have left Lakatos little time to play in his old club in Brussels. He has performed twice at the prestigious Promenade Concerts in London's Albert Hall. CD: *Lakatos*.

LALORE SINTI. Literally "dumb Gypsies." The name given by the **Sinti** Gypsies of **Germany** to all those in the country who did not speak their **dialect**. During the Nazi period, the Lalore Sinti were classed as German Gypsies because it was said they had lived among Germans in Bohemia and Moravia. However, this did not save them from the concentration camps.

LAMBRINO, ZIZI **(1898–1953).** Romania. The first wife of King Carol II of **Romania** (married in 1918), she was **Jewish** rather than—as some books suggest—a Romany.

LAS TRES MIL. A neighborhood in Seville, **Spain**, called Las Tres Mil Viviendas ("The 3,000 Apartments") built around 1970. Many Gypsies were moved there from the shantytown Triana. It is featured in Dominique Abel's documentary **film** *Seville Southside*.

LATVIA. Estimated Gypsy population: 14,000. The official population according to the 1989 census was 7,044, with 84 percent speaking Romani as their mother tongue. Latvia was an independent country in the period 1919–1940 and again from 1991. By the 20th century, the majority of Romanies living in the country had been sedentarized during the years of **Russian** rule. Soon after the **German** occupation in 1941, the **Einsatzgruppen** began killing Gypsies. At Ludza, Gypsies were locked up in a synagogue, then taken to the nearby forest and shot. Only in Talsen and Daugawpils were local Latvian officials able to protect the Gypsies. It is thought that about 2,000 were killed in all, a third of the population.

After 1944 when Soviet troops reoccupied the country, there was immigration by Gypsies from elsewhere in the **Soviet Union**. Some anti-Gypsy activity persists today. Joachim Siegerist, leader of the People's Movement for Latvia, was convicted in Germany for incitement to racial hatred as a result of distributing more than 17,000 circulars in which he said "Gypsies produce children like rabbits" and are "a seedy criminal pack who should be driven out of the country." His party gained 15 percent of the vote in the Latvian general election of October 1995.

In 1933 **Janis Leimanis** translated St. John's Gospel into Romani. Janis Neilands is the leader of a small **educational** movement that has opened two Romani schools and produced a language primer in the local **dialect**. **Karlis Rudjevics** is a contemporary artist.

LAU MAZIREL ASSOCIATION. Netherlands. Est. 1981. Founder: Jan Rogier. An organization in the **Netherlands** that has been working since 1981 for the interests of the Romanies. It published the journal *Drom* and also gives help to individual Gypsies and organizations in the Netherlands. The association is named after Lau Mazirel (d. 1974), a **Jewish** lawyer who supported the rights of minorities.

LAUTARI, BARBA (fl. 19th century). Moldavia. Violinist. He was an acquaintance of composer **Franz Liszt**.

LAWSON, HENRY (1876–?). Australia. Writer. Son of a Kentish Gypsy and a Norwegian sailor.

LAZURICA, LAZARESCU. Romania. 20th-century civil rights activist. At first he worked with **Popp Serboianu**, but then in 1933 he set up his own organization, Uniunea Generala a Romilor din Romania (General Union of the Gypsies of **Romania**). A year later he handed over the presidency to **Gheorghe Niculescu**.

LE COSSEC, CLEMENT (1921–2001). France. Missionary. A lay pastor in Brittany in the years after World War II, he was the initiator of **Pentecostalism** among the Gypsies in 1952. Le Cossec was preaching in Lisieux when a **Manouche** couple, Mandz Duvil and his wife, came to his prayer meetings and were converted. They spread the message among their relatives and friends. The number of converts grew, and in 1958 Le Cossec decided to devote himself to work among the Gypsies.

LEE, TOM (1923–2002). England. Political and civil rights activist. He was born in a horse-drawn wagon and fought in World War II. A seasoned campaigner, he made headlines in 1970 when he parked his **caravan** close to the prime minister's residence in Downing Street to persuade the government to pressure local authorities to provide fit sites for Gypsies to rent. Later, he began to regard officially provided sites as unsuitable and argued that individuals should be allowed to buy their own sites and plots for other Gypsy caravans. He set up a private caravan site in Stratford, East London, and, following the trend for urban farms, encouraged schools to visit the horses, chickens, and doves he kept on it. After falling out with members of the **Gypsy Council**, he founded the **Romany Guild** in 1972, although the two organizations later reunited for a short time as the **National Gypsy Council**.

LEIMANIS, JANIS (1886–1954). Latvia. Translator, writer, and civil rights activist. Leimanis devoted his life to organizing and providing aid to the Roma. From 1915, he worked alongside Romany refugees helping with welfare and taking care of their cultural needs. Involved in collecting the **literary** heritage of Gypsies in **Latvia**, in 1931 he established the society Ciganu Draugs (Friends of the Gypsies), an Orthodox Christian organization. In 1933 he translated the Gospel of John, the Lord's Prayer, and the 10 Commandments, and in 1939 he published the book *Cigani Latvjas mezzos un lakos* [Gypsies of the Forests and Lakes of Latvia]. During World War II, he served the Romany people on behalf of the Orthodox Church. He worked as a leader and tried to help the Roma to escape the concentration camps. After the war, until his death, he continued to take part in the ministry among the Roma.

LEKSA MANUŠ. *See* BELUGINS, ALEKSANDR ALEDZUNZ.

LESHAKI. A subdialect of **Polish** Romani.

LETY. Two work camps were established by the **Czech** government, at Lety and Hodonin, in 1939. Later they became camps for Romanies. The site of Lety is now occupied by a pig farm, and this has angered the survivors, but the Czech government has blamed the cost of removing the pig farm for its inaction.

LIANCE (fl. 17th century). France. Dancer. She was feted by poets and nobles and had her portrait painted by Beaubrun. Her husband was arrested for highway robbery and executed. After this incident, Liance wore mourning clothes for the rest of her life and never **danced** again.

LIFE AND LIGHT (VIE ET LUMIÈRE). A **Pentecostal** evangelical group founded 50 years ago that estimates it has 100,000 followers in **France** and 500,000 members in all of Europe. Its annual conventions in France attract several thousands. The French interior ministry has ordered that this large gathering be held at a different location each year in a bid to appease local officials.

LIMBERGER, TCHA. Belgium. Contemporary singer and violinist in the **Django Reinhardt** tradition.

LIOZNA. A collective farm in the **Soviet Union**, near Vitebsk, in the years between the world wars. Originally a **Jewish** collective farm, the authorities moved the Jewish farmers out and replaced them with Romanies. Later, the Gypsies in their turn were displaced, as Josef Stalin decided that Gypsy nationalism was dangerous.

LISZT, FRANZ (1811–1886). Hungary. **Musician.** Liszt was already fond of Gypsy music as a child, and between 1840 and 1847 he published 20 pieces based on **Hungarian Gypsy music**. These became the basis for his *Hungarian Rhapsodies* (1851–1853).

LITERATURE, GYPSIES IN. Many famous authors have put Gypsy characters into their novels and plays or written poems on Gypsy themes. Among them are Guillaume Apollinaire, Louis Aragon, Matthew Arnold, Charles Baudelaire, Vicente Blasco Ibáñez, Charlotte Brontë, Robert Browning, Miguel de Cervantes, Arthur Conan Doyle, the Greek writer Drossinis, George Eliot, Ralph Waldo Emerson, Henry Fielding, Johann Wolfgang von Goethe, Oliver Goldsmith, Ernest Hemingway, Ben Jonson, John Keats, Jack Kerouac, Blaže Koneski, D. H. Lawrence, **Federico Garcia Lorca**, Antonio Machado, Osip Mandelstam, Boris Pasternak, Ezra Pound, **Aleksandr Pushkin**, Walter Scott, Jules Verne, Tennessee Williams, and Virginia Woolf.

LITERATURE, GYPSY. Until the 20th century, Romany literature was almost entirely oral—songs and folktales. The temporary encouragement of the **Romani language** in the newly founded **Soviet Union** led to a flourishing of literature in the period between the world wars. Since 1945 much **poetry**, many short stories, and numerous **dramas** have been written. Many Gypsy writers, such as **Matéo Maximoff** and **Veijo Baltzar**, have written novels in the majority languages of the country where they live. *See also* FOLK LITERATURE.

LITHUANIA. Estimated Gypsy population: 5,500. The official population, according to the last **Soviet** census (in 1989), was recorded as 2,700, with 81 percent speaking Romani as their mother tongue. The earliest reference to Gypsies on the territory of present-day Lithuania dates from 1501, but it is likely that they had been there for some years before. In that year, Earl Alexander granted the right to Vasil to govern the Gypsy **clans** in Lithuania, **Poland**, and **Belarus**, the Gypsies being permitted to **nomadize** under the authority of their own leader.

In 1564, however, Gypsies were told to settle or leave the country. In 1569 Poland and Lithuania became one country, and a new decree was issued, confirming the existing policy of expelling nomads, in 1586. Some Gypsies left, some settled down, and a third group continued to nomadize in spite of the prohibition. In 1795 the **Russian** tsar became ruler of the country. From 1919 to 1940 Lithuania was independent, then it was taken over by the USSR for one year until Nazi **Germany** invaded.

During the German occupation (1941–1944) about half of the Gypsies were killed, with the collaboration of Lithuanian nationalists. One transport of 20 persons was sent to **Auschwitz**; the others were killed in Lithuania itself.

In 1944 the Soviet Union once more occupied Lithuania. The country finally became independent again in 1991. Nationalist feelings against the Russians spread to incorporate the Gypsy minority. In 1992 there was a pogrom in Kaunas. Some Gypsies were killed, cars were set on fire, and homes were ransacked.

The majority of the present population are Catholics, the rest Orthodox. A Gypsy organization has been set up, and a project to develop Romani as a written language is under way.

LITTLE EGYPT. When the Gypsies moved farther west in the 15th century, many came in large groups, sometimes over a 100 persons, led by a Duke of Little **Egypt**. It is thought that "Little Egypt" referred to a part of **Greece**.

LIULI. Previously **nomadic** Gypsies in the Asian republics that were part of the **Soviet Union**. Many of them have come into **Russia** in search of better conditions.

LODZ CONGRESS. This May 2002 congress was called by the organizers the "Second World Congress"—the coronation of the **Polish** Romani **king** in 1935 being counted as the first and ignoring the congresses organized by the **International Romani Union (IRU)**. The event was initiated by the **Romani National Congress** with the strong support of the **European Union**. It was preceded by a period of discussion via the Internet, and the congress was partially on line with the opportunity to vote via the Internet. There were some 50 participants, including Roma from 30 organizations.

The first day of the congress was taken up with keynote speakers, including **Nicolae Gheorghe**. On the second day, a ceremony was held at the site of the **Lodz Ghetto**, set up by the Nazis during World War II. That afternoon and on the following day, three working groups met. The three groups debated Romany representation at the international level, compensation for the **Holocaust**, and the question of refugees and other migrants.

The congress appointed an Executive Committee to serve for one year. Six members were elected, including **Agnes Daróczi**, **Ondrej Gina**, and **Rudko Kawzcynski**. The seventh place was to be left open for a representative of the IRU. The committee was given the task of setting up a body to be called the Romany Council of Europe. The congress supported the idea of a **European Roma Forum** with membership open to all Roma organizations and leaders.

The organization Drom from Kumanovo, **Macedonia**, had featured the peace song "Is Love Enough?" for its celebrations of 8 April—**Roma Nation Day**—and the song was adopted as the song of the congress.

LODZ GHETTO. In October 1941 the **Germans** ordered the **Jews** already imprisoned in the ghetto at Lodz, **Poland**, to evacuate several streets, which were then wired off and used to house 5,000 Gypsies, mainly from **Austria**. An epidemic of typhus broke out, and several Jewish doctors volunteered to treat the sick. Apart from those who died of typhus, many Gypsies were beaten to death in the first weeks. The fate of 120 adults who were apparently sent to work in a factory in Germany is not known. Early in 1942 the remaining Gypsy prisoners were taken to the Chelmno extermination camp and gassed.

LOI BESSON. France. The adoption by the French Parliament in 1999 of Article 28 of the Loi Besson was intended to lead to the establishment of **caravan** sites for **nomads**. It requires every town with a population greater than 5,000 to provide camping facilities for the "*Gens du Voyage*" (traveling people). It was hoped to attain a figure of

30,000 plots. By 2000, only a third of these had been provided, and further progress has been slow.

***LOLI PHABAI* ("RED APPLE").** The first international journal entirely in Romani was published in Greece in the 1970s under the editorship of **Grattan Puxon**. Three issues appeared. The contents included articles by **Shaip Jusuf** and others, as well as folktales and reprints from **Soviet** literature of the interwar period.

LOM. A **clan** of Gypsies calling themselves Lom who are believed to have originated in northwest **India** together with the Roma and who are now resident in **Armenia**, other parts of the former **Soviet Union** (e.g., **Georgia**, Nagorno-Karabakh), and **Turkey**. In Armenia they live in the capital, Yerevan, and in a number of villages. The Lom of Armenia migrated there from the Erzerum region of so-called western Armenia (eastern Turkey) following the Russo-Turkish war at the beginning of the 19th century. The name *Lom* is considered to be derived from *Dom*.

The Lom make their living from trade: selling handmade sieves, candles, straw baskets, and boxes; they also deal in honey. The **women**, unusual for Gypsy clans, do not tell **fortunes**. They are practicing Christians and attend the Armenian Orthodox Church, although they often marry cousins, which is not permitted under Armenian Christian tradition. They no longer speak Romani but a variety of Armenian with words of **Indian origin**, known as Lomin or Lomavren.

LONGTHORNE, JOE (1955–). England. **Musician**. A contemporary singer who performs in concerts and on **television** in the country-western idiom.

LORCA, FEDERICO GARCIA. *See GARCIA LORCA, FEDERICO.*

LOVARI. A **clan** living mainly in **Hungary** (numbering many thousands) and in **Poland**. In the past, many were horse-dealers and some still carry on this trade. From 1870 on, small groups **nomadized** in western Europe, though they were never as numerous as the **Kalderash**. The Romani spoken by the Lovari belongs to the **Vlah**

dialect cluster. The Lovari rarely play **music** for the public, though they have a strong tradition of singing and **dancing** within their own community.

LOVERIDGE, SAMUEL. The alleged author of *Being the Autobiography of a Gipsy*, published in 1890. Although supposedly written by Loveridge and edited by a "Francis Carew," it was the work of Arthur Way.

LOYKO. A partly Gypsy trio of **musicians** from **Russia**, including Sergei Edenko and Oleg Ponomarev, now resident in **Ireland**. Vladim Koulitskii replaced the original guitarist, Igor Staroseltsev. They have toured widely in Europe and made several recordings. The name comes from a legendary Russian Gypsy musician. CD: *The Fortune Teller* (1995).

***LUBBOCK, ERIC* (1928–2000).** England. Political activist. A Liberal member of the British Parliament, he added a section on Gypsy sites to a bill he was introducing in Parliament to champion the rights of non-Gypsies living in mobile homes. This became the **Caravan Sites Act of 1968**. As a result, he became to some extent the guardian of Gypsy rights, a role that he continued as Lord Avebury in the House of Lords.

LUGHA. A secret vocabulary of the Middle East probably developed by Arabic-speaking Dervishes. Many of the words are found in languages spoken by Middle Eastern Gypsies. *Lugha* is the Arabic word for "language."

LULUDJI ENSEMBLE. A song-and-dance group from Moscow. Leading members are the singer and guitarist Slava Vasiiev and Vladimir Kutenkov who teaches the children's ensemble Gilori.

***LUNDGREN, GUNILLA* (1942–).** Sweden. Author who writes mainly children's books, especially biographies in collaboration with Romany children.

LUNIK IX. A housing project on the edge of the town of **Košice** in **Slovakia**. The population of Lunik IX is already 70 percent Romany, and the city council of Košice has proposed moving the remaining Gypsy population of the city there.

LURE. Every summer, Gypsies from across **France** and elsewhere in Europe travel to Lure, in eastern France, for an annual **religious** meeting.

LURI. Iran. (1) The name by which the writer Firdausi called a group of **musicians** who came from **India** in the 10th century. (2) A **clan** of singers and musicians living in **Iran** at the time of Hafiz and other poets. (3) A Gypsy clan in today's Iran, possibly of **Indian origin**. They are craft workers and blacksmiths who move around, offering their services to the seminomadic tribes. They also prepare food for weddings and ceremoniously wash the groom. Their language is a variety of Beluchi with a jargon vocabulary. They are not to be confused with the indigenous Luri of Iran.

LUTE. It is thought that some of the Gypsies of Europe are descended from lute players brought from **India** to **Iran** by the Shah Bahram Gur. There are early records of a Gypsy lutanist in Dubrovnik. With the dying out of the lute as a popular instrument, lute players adopted the violin and other stringed instruments.

LUXEMBOURG. Estimated Gypsy population: 150. The first Gypsies appeared during the 16th century. They struggled against newcomers from **Germany** and **France** to preserve their trading area. In 1603 a mercenary, Jean de la Fleur, was put on trial for entering the country contrary to a decree forbidding Gypsies to enter the Grand Duchy. During World War II, the Germans deported a handful of Gypsies from the country to camps in **Poland**. Since 1945, immigration control has remained strict using a law against vagrancy.

LYULI. A **clan** of Gypsies living mainly in Uzbekistan and Tajikistan, though some families have moved to **Russia**. The Lyuli probably left **India** later than the Roma, because they have not integrated with the local population as have other Gypsy groups in what was **Soviet Asia**.

– M –

MacCOLL, EWAN. *See* MILLER, JIMMIE.

MACE, JEM (1831–1910). England. Boxer. A bare-knuckle fighter known as the "Father of Modern Boxing." At one time he also ran a fairground known as Strawberry Gardens in Liverpool. A memorial was recently erected by his grave at Anfield Cemetery in Liverpool. Nicknamed "the Gypsy," Mace was the bare-knuckle English boxing champion in 1861.

MACEDONIA, REPUBLIC OF. (This entry deals with Macedonia from 1941 onward. Previously it was part of the **Ottoman Empire** and then the kingdom of **Yugoslavia**. There is also a province of **Greece** called Macedonia.) The estimated Romany population is at least 200,000, although the 1994 census listed only 42,707, a decrease from the 55,575 recorded in 1991 in spite of the availability of census forms in the **Romani language**.

During World War II, Macedonia was handed over by the **Germans** to the **Bulgarians** and **Italians**. Most of the Romanies managed to persuade the occupiers that they were **Turks** or Muslim **Albanians**. Those who were identified as Romanies had to wear yellow armbands. Some were taken as forced laborers to Bulgaria and a small number to camps in **Poland**. Many joined the Partisans, and it was said that Tito promised them their own state after the war. This promise—if it had been made—was not carried out, as the Yugoslav government would have seen a smaller Macedonia as a prey for Greek and Bulgarian expansionist ambitions.

The largest Gypsy community in Europe developed in **Shuto Orizari** on the outskirts of **Skopje** in the aftermath of the earthquake of 1963. About 90 percent of the inhabitants are Gypsies.

In May 1980 Naša Kniga, a publishing house in Skopje, produced the first Romani grammar written in the Romani language. The author was **Shaip Jusuf**. The **Pralipe** Theater operated until 1990 when the Communist Party forced the company to vacate its premises and the actors immigrated to **Germany**.

In 1990, too, the Egyptian Association of Citizens was founded in Ohrid by Nazim Arifi, consisting of some 4,000 residents of Ohrid and neighboring Struga, who—although many scholars consider them to be of Romany origin—claim to be descendants of **Egyptians** brought to the Balkans during the rule of the Ottoman Empire. The association claimed 20,000–30,000 adherents, and "Egyptian" was included as a separate identity in the 1994 census in Macedonia.

On 1 September 1990, the leaders of the Macedonian Romany community called on all Romanies to stop identifying themselves as Albanians simply on the basis of a common **religion**, Islam, and declared 11 October 1990—already a public holiday—to be a day of celebration of the cultural achievements of Romanies in Macedonia. Nevertheless, in the census of 1994, many declared themselves to be Macedonians or—if they were Muslims—Albanians or Turks.

In 1991 Macedonia became de facto independent. President Kiro Gligorov publicly acknowledged the Romanies as "full and equal citizens of the Republic of Macedonia." They were recognized as a nationality in the new constitution. Romani-language **radio** and **television** programs from Skopje joined those already being broadcast from Tetovo. A few bilingual (Macedonian and Romani) magazines are published.

A Romani **educational** program in schools began in principle in September 1993, consisting of language classes for grades 1–8. A 40,000-word Macedonian–Romani dictionary and other teaching material are still being prepared. The main **dialects** are **Erlia** (Arlia), the most widely spoken and the mother tongue of an estimated 80 percent of Macedonia's Romanies, Burgudji, Djambazi, and **Gurbet**. It has been agreed to use Erlia as the basis for a standard language using the Latin **alphabet** for educational purposes. In addition to the planned introduction of the Romani language in primary education classes from the 1993/1994 academic year, there are proposals for Skopje University to inaugurate a Department of Romani Studies for the study of, and research into, the language, history, and culture. Some 100 potential teachers of Romani attended a seminar convened by the Ministry of Education at Skopje University in October 1993. The full implementation of the Romani language program has been slowed down by the lack of materials and qualified teachers. There are more than 50 Romany students attending various full-time courses at the university.

The main political party for the Gypsies in Macedonia is the Party for the Complete Emancipation of Romanies in Macedonia (PSERM), claiming a membership of 36,000. Its president, **Faik Abdi**, has also been a member of the Macedonian parliament, representing Shuto Orizari. The PSERM has been the prime mover in securing Romany rights.

Many Romanies from all over the country took part in the festivities on 8 April 1993, marking the de jure creation of the new state and coincidentally **Roma Nation Day**. In general, Macedonia can be considered a country where the Roma enjoy equal recognition at all levels. However, some interethnic conflict, mainly between Albanians and Romanies, has been reported as well as occasional instances of police brutality, for example, in Kumanovo and Prilep. The Romany ethnicity of alleged perpetrators of crimes is increasingly emphasized by the Macedonian media, creating a link between Roma and crime. For example, on 22 February 2003 the Skopje dailies *Dnevnik* and *Vesti*, reporting a violent fight between two group of teenagers in which a young non-Romany man was killed, stressed that two of the perpetrators were Roma.

MACEDONIAN ROMA UNION. An organization in northern **Greece** whose president is Savas Georgiadis.

MacFIE, ROBERT ANDREW SCOTT (1868–1935). England. Businessman and amateur scholar. Contributor to the *Journal of the Gypsy Lore Society*, he sometimes wrote under the Romani pseudonym Andreas Mui Shuko ("Dry Face"). His collection of books was donated to the Liverpool University Library.

MACHVAYA. A Gypsy **clan** originating in the Balkans.

MacPHEE, WILLIE (1910–2002). Scotland. **Scottish Traveler, musician**, tinsmith, basket maker, piper, and singer. He was a regular performer at folk clubs and festivals.

MAGERIPEN. A **Sinti** term for the hygienic rules of the Romany community. Romani names in other **dialects** for the same concept are the adjectives *mockerdi* (in England) and *mahrime* (**Kalderash**). There is a broad set of concepts of cleanliness and a system of taboos maintaining the opposition of the socially or spiritually clean to persons or objects seen as unclean or dirty. Traditionally Gypsies have placed much emphasis on the uncleanness of **women** at the time of their menses and after childbirth. Dogs are considered as having the potential to make things dirty and are excluded from the **caravan** or home. To preserve cleanliness, a strict separation is observed when washing clothes, food, and the human body. Many of these rules are observed by the majority populations in the Balkans. Some western European Gypsies consider all non-Gypsies to be dirty by definition and reserve special cups and even chairs for visitors.

MAGNETEN. A company of Gypsy **dancers, musicians,** and singers from many countries, formed by Andre Heller, that toured **Germany** and elsewhere with great success in 1993. The ensemble included **Kalyi Jag, Kálmán Balogh, Loyko,** and **Esma Redjepova.**

MAGYARI, IMRE. Hungary. 20th-century musician. He was a well-known violinist in **Hungary** in the 1930s.

MAHRIME. *See* MAGERIPEN.

MAJARI CALI (BLACK VIRGIN). Statue in Valencia showing a black Virgin Mary, sculpted by José Luis Vicent in 1978.

MALIKOV, JASHAR (1922–1994). Bulgaria. Composer. A composer of songs and collector of folk **music** and tales in **Bulgaria**. While still at school, he played the trumpet and accordion in a band at weddings. He learned to write music and took up playing light music, including the so-called town songs. In 1949, he was in charge of music at the **Roma Theater** in Sofia. He was one of the first Gypsy musicians to be recorded by the company Balkanton. He was also the author of the first Romani–Bulgarian dictionary.

MALLA, JIMENEZ CERIFINO (EL PELE) (1861–1936). Spain. Originally a cattle dealer, in 1926 he became a brother in the Third Order of the Holy Friars. At the outbreak of the civil war, he defended an imprisoned priest and was himself thrown into prison. He refused the offer of freedom and was shot in August with other brothers of the Order. His beatification took place in 1997.

MALTA. There are no Gypsies currently living on the island and no historical record of their presence in the past.

MANISCH. *See* JENISCH.

MANITAS DE PLATA. *See* BALIARDO, RICARDO.

MANOLESCU, STELLA. Romania. Contemporary **artist**. She paints with oil and acrylic. The daughter of **Ioan Cioaba**, she lives in Austin, Texas.

MANOUCHE. A **clan** of Gypsies living mainly in **France** and **Belgium** but whose ancestors spent many years in **Germany**. The word *manouche* means "man" in Romani. Their **dialect** has many German loan words and is close to that of the **Sinti**.

MANUŠ, LEKSA. *See* BELUGINS, ALEKSANDR ALEDZUNZ.

MARCINKIEWICZ, JAN (fl. 18th century). Russia. Bear trainer. In 1778, he set up a school for bear trainers in **Russia** and held the title of "Gypsy **king**." After the failure of the so-called Katyushka Revolt against the tsar, he fled to **Turkey**.

MARIA THERESA **(1717–1780).** Hungary. Empress of Austria-Hungary (1740–1780). From 1758, she announced a series of decrees with the intention of turning the Gypsies into *Ujmagyar,* "New **Hungarians**." Government-built huts replaced tents, while travel and horse-dealing were forbidden. Gypsy children were taken away, often by force, to be fostered by Hungarians. Her son **Joseph II** continued her policies.

MARKOVIĆ, BOBAN. Serbia. Contemporary trumpet player and leader of **Serbia**'s biggest brass band, the Boban Marković Orkestar. CDs include *Srce Cigansko* [Heart of a Gypsy] and *The Promise*.

MARSHALL, BILLY (1672–1792). Scotland. **Scottish Traveler** and early civil rights activist. In 1724, he led an alliance of extreme Protestants and peasants against land enclosures and the imposition of the Presbyterian Church. After initial success, they were defeated.

MATRAS, YARON **(1963–).** Chicago, Illinois. Linguist and writer. He teaches at Manchester University (United Kingdom) and has been active in organizing international **linguistic conferences** on the **Romani language**.

MAXIMOFF, MATÉO (1917–1999). Barcelona, Spain. Writer, translator, and preacher. He moved to **France** with his family as a child. As a young man he was involved in an interfamily dispute concerning an abducted girl and was sent to prison, where he met lawyer Jacques Isorni. Isomi suggested that he write about his life and thus he began his writing career.

Maximoff has written many novels, including *The Ursitory* (1946), one of the few books that gives an account of Gypsy life from a Gypsy perspective. He then wrote several more novels, including *Le Prix de la Liberté* [The Price of Liberty; 1955], about the revolt of Romani slaves in Romania. He has published ghost stories told to him by his mother, and he translated the Bible into Romani after becoming a convert to **Pentecostalism**. He worked on his Old Testament translation for more than nine years, finishing in 1981. So far, only two parts have been published. His New Testament was finally published in 1995.

MAYA, MANUEL MORENO (EL PELE) (1954–). Cordoba, Spain. **Flamenco** singer. The first member of his family to become a professional singer, he has won many awards. CD: *La fuente de la jondo* (with Vicente Amigo).

MAYA, PEPE HEREDIA (JOSE HEREDIA) (1947–). Spain. **Flamenco** teacher and dancer, He founded a company whose first production was the history of the Gypsies in **Spain** portrayed through a flamenco presentation, *Camelamos naquerar* (1976). This was made into the **film** *Let Us Be Heard* (1983).

McALISKEY, BERNADETTE (née DEVLIN) (1947–). Ireland. Political activist. She is from an **Irish Traveler** family and is a nationalist politician in **Northern Ireland**. McAliskey was for a time a member of the British Parliament.

McPHEE, ROSEANNA, AND SHAMUS McPHEE. Scotland. Contemporary **Scottish Travelers**. Roseanna is a **poet**, and her husband Shamus a painter.

MEDZITLIJA. Town on the Greek-Macedonian border. In June 2003 some 700 Roma from **Kosovo** whose refugee camp in **Macedonia** had been closed tried unsuccessfully to cross the border into **Greece**. They remained in poor conditions on the border for several weeks while negotiations took place as to their fate. Finally, with a partly kept promise of satisfactory accommodation, they returned to **Skopje** in Macedonia.

MERCE, JOSE (JOSE SOTO) (1955–). Spain. Singer. His professional career as a **flamenco** singer began at the age of 15. He has worked with **Antonio Gades**'s company and took part in the **film** *Bodas de sangre* [Blood Wedding]. Merce took part in the 2004 Flamenco Festival at London's Sadler's Wells Theatre with his own company.

MERCER, PETER. England. Contemporary community worker and civil rights activist. He was active in the original **Gypsy Council** and the **National Gypsy Education Council** as well as setting up the East Anglia Gypsy Council. Mercer is the British representative on the Praesidium of the **International Romani Union** and has been awarded a Member of the (Order of the) British Empire.

MEREJAN, MEHMED. Bulgaria. Contemporary **poet**. He received the 2003 **Roma Literary Award** for poetry.

MÉRIMÉE, PROSPER (1803–1870). France. Writer. He worked in the civil service and, under Napoleon III, was employed on unofficial missions. After a visit to a tobacco factory in **Spain** in 1846, he wrote the novel *Carmen*, which was the basis for Georges Bizet's opera of the same name.

MESHARE (MESHARYAVA). An internal legal system, similar to the **Kris**, operated by the elders of the Bulgarian **Karderash**.

MESSING. Essex, UK. The village of Messing in Essex became infamous for evicting its Gypsy families in 2003. After rumors that U.S. president George Bush might want to visit his ancestral home there whenever he came to **England**, it was thought he might be offended by the sight of Gypsies. This visit never actually occurred, but some Romany families still had to look for a new place to stop.

MÉSZÁROS, GYÖRGY (?–1987). Hungary. An expert on Gypsies, he lived in Eger, where at one time he worked at the local museum. He wrote numerous articles and a dictionary. The eyewitness accounts Mészáros collected from victims of the Nazi period are an invaluable record.

METECH, JULIETTE. France. Contemporary painter. She grew up as an **artist** in her father's circus until the age of 19, when her father died. She then went into business selling carpets door-to-door, and it was not until the age of 52 that Metech began to paint seriously. Many of her pieces can be seen in French galleries.

MICHALCZUK, KAZIMIERZ (?–1996). Poland. Political activist. The vice president of the Roma Organization of **Poland**, he was killed by an unknown assassin on 1 September 1996.

MIHAILOVA, DANIELA. Bulgaria. Contemporary political activist. She is legal director of the **Romani Baxt** Foundation in Sofia, **Bulgaria**.

MILLER, JIMMY (EWAN MacCOLL) (1915–1989). Scotland. Singer. He recorded the Gypsies' own stories of their life and composed the **music** for a popular documentary—a "**radio** ballad," as it was called by the BBC—*The Travelling People*. Many of the songs he wrote have become part of the repertoire of Gypsy singers, such as "The Moving On Song" and "A Freeborn Man."

MINA, LA. High-rise suburb of Barcelona, **Spain**, where many Gypsies were resettled during the rule of Francisco Franco. It was the scene for the documentary **film** *La Mina* by British photographer Hannah Collins and local leader Manuel Fernandez Cortés. The film is made to be shown on five TV screens simultaneously and was first shown at the Toulouse image festival in 2003.

MINORITY RIGHTS GROUP (SLOVAKIA). Partners in a project with the **Minority Rights Group (UK)**. The group is concerned with offering training to young Romanies in central and eastern **Slovakia**.

MINORITY RIGHTS GROUP (UNITED KINGDOM). Among its many activities, the group runs projects for Romany rights and **education** with partners in **Bulgaria**, **Poland**, and **Slovakia**. These are the **Committee for the Defense of Minority Rights** (Bulgaria), the **Helsinki Foundation for Human Rights** (Poland), and the **Minority Rights Group (Slovakia)**. It has also published three reports on Romanies.

MINORITY SELF-GOVERNMENT (HUNGARY). The law in **Hungary** provides for the establishment of local minority self-governments as a necessary precondition for the enforcement of the rights of ethnic minorities. With some funding from the central budget, these local self-governments seek to influence matters affecting minorities, particularly in the fields of **education** and culture. Local minority self-government elections, in conjunction with local government elections, have been held since 1994. Any of the 13 designated minorities can set up a minority self-government.

Since ethnicity is not registered officially, voting on minority self-governments is not limited to the minorities themselves. All voters receive a minority ballot in addition to the local government ballot. Minority self-government has been criticized mainly on two grounds. First, several minority representatives have objected to the fact that members of the majority can vote for minority candidates and thus influence minority politics. Second, critics have called for an increase in the power of the minority self-governments and considerably more financial resources for them.

There were cases of candidates who did not belong to the ethnic minority being elected to minority self-governments in the 1992 elections. In Jaszladany, the votes of members of the Hungarian majority in the Roma minority self-government elections resulted in four non-Roma being elected to the five-member body. Roma rights observers viewed this move as a deliberate attempt to undermine the local Roma community. The Ministry of Justice and the state secretary for Roma affairs criticized the election outcome, but there were no legal grounds to overturn it.

In October 2002 there were 1,004 Roma minority self-governments elected in the local minority elections, an increase over the 770 elected self-governments in the minority elections held in 1998. Of those elected in 1998, a number of self-governments had ceased functioning due to a lack of resources, knowledge, and leadership. In contrast to other minorities, for whom the preservation of their identity and culture is the basic goal, the elected Roma representatives also have to face the task of improving the lives of their constituents with no additional financial resources.

MINORITY STUDIES SOCIETY. Bulgaria. Est. 1992. Cochairs: Elena Marushiakova and Veselin Popov. The society was founded in 1992 as a center for studying the minorities in **Bulgaria**. As the situation of the Gypsies is the most complicated, this topic has been the main focus of the group's work. Its aims include popularizing Gypsy culture, stopping discrimination, and researching the history and culture of the Gypsies of Bulgaria. The society publishes the journal *Studii Romani*. Members have taken part in a number of international projects, such as the History Group once based at the **Centre de Recherches Tsiganes** in Paris.

MINUNE, IONICA. Romania. Contemporary **musician**. One of the leading accordion players in the world, his repertoire ranges from folk music to jazz played in the style of **Django Reinhardt**.

MIRANDO, TATA, JR., AND TATA MIRANDO SR. The stage names of the brothers Kokalo and Meisel Weiss, who are the leaders of two contemporary bands playing Balkan-style music in the **Netherlands**.

MISS ROMA INTERNATIONAL BEAUTY CONTEST. An annual contest since 1991, organized by TV BTR Nacional, a Roma **television** station in **Skopje, Macedonia**. The contest has attracted criticism from some traditionalists.

MITTEILUNGEN ZUR ZIGEUNERKUNDE (BULLETINS ON GYPSY CULTURE). At least two publications have had this title. (1) *Organ der Gesellschaft für Zigeunerforschung*, vol. 1 (January 1891), is identical with volume 7 of the journal *Ethnologische Mitteilungen aus Ungarn* and contains a **German** translation of **Charles-Louis Joseph**'s Romani grammar. (2) Several issues of a journal with this title were published in Mainz, Germany, in the 1970s.

MLADENOV, TOMA NIKOLAEV. Bulgaria. Contemporary political activist. He set up the organization Spasenie (Rescue) in **Bulgaria**. During a stay in **England**, Mladenov served as vice chair of the **Trans-European Roma Federation**.

MLADENOV, ZLATO. Bulgaria. Contemporary civil rights activist. He is the president of the organization Kupate (Together) and was elected treasurer of the **International Romani Union** in Prague in 2000.

MLAWA. Town in **Poland** that was the scene of an anti-Gypsy pogrom toward the end of the Communist period in 1991, during which many houses were burned down. Many of the town's Romanies fled to **Sweden** but were refused residence and returned to Poland.

MOCKERDI. Adjective used by **English** Gypsies for "ritually unclean." *See also* MAGERIPEN.

MODON. Greece. Town with a Gypsy settlement of 300 huts in 1483–1486. This number dropped to 100 in 1497, and by the time the

Turks took Modon in 1500, most of the inhabitants had fled to escape their advance; in 1519, only 30 occupied huts remained. The Gypsies living there were shoemakers. Their fate is unknown. There is no trace of the arrival of any Gypsy shoemakers in the West, and the trade is generally considered unclean by today's Gypsies as it involves working with the skins of dead animals.

MOLDAVIA. Province of **Romania**.

MOLDAVIAN SOVIET SOCIALIST REPUBLIC (1945–1991). *See* MOLDOVA; SOVIET UNION.

MOLDOVA. Estimated Gypsy population: 22,500. The official Gypsy population (based on the **Soviet** 1989 census) was 11,517, of whom 85 percent had Romani as their mother tongue. It occupies part of the territory known as **Bessarabia** and belonged to Russia from 1812 to 1917 and to **Romania** from 1917 to 1940. From 1945 to 1991, the greater part of the territory was the Moldavian Soviet Socialist Republic, and it is now an independent state. A collection of oral **literature** from the region made by **Georgi Kantea** was one of the few publications in Romani to emerge in the Soviet Union after 1945.

MONDIALE OF GYPSY ART. The first Mondiale was held in Paris in 1985 and the second in Budapest from 31 August to 31 October 1995. Alongside the exhibition of paintings, the second Mondiale had a program of **music** and **dance**.

MONTENEGRO. Estimated Gypsy population: 2,000. The 1971 census recorded 396 Romanies. Montenegro was independent or semi-independent from 1389 until 1918, when it became part of **Yugoslavia**. Until 1940 the Gypsies in Montenegro were almost entirely **nomadic**, unlike elsewhere in the Balkans. During the 1930s, police prevented them from entering the then capital Cetinje. Montenegro was occupied by the **Italians** during World War II. Some Gypsies organized an independent Partisan unit in the mountains but eventually succumbed to the Italian Army. Many Romanies from Montenegro immigrated as workers to Western Europe in the 1970s.

Roma in Montenegro have not escaped prejudice—a pogrom in Danoilovgrad when the Gypsy quarter was burned down being the most visible manifestation of this feeling. The small Romany population has been expanded by refugees from **Kosovo**, who may stay and bring their cultural heritage to build a larger and more vibrant community.

MONTOYA, ANTONIO NUÑEZ (EL CHOCOLATE) (1931–2005). Spain. Singer. Montoya made his debut at the age of nine in Seville. He took part in the 2004 **Flamenco** Festival at London's Sadler's Wells Theatre with **dancer** Manuela Carrasco.

MORELLI, BRUNO (1957–2000). Italy. Artist. A self-educated painter, he specializes in graphics and realistic portraiture and has had many exhibitions since his first in Avezzano in 1981. He exhibited at both the first and second **Mondiale of Gypsy Art**.

MOTHER TERESA. *See* BOJAXHIU, AGNES.

MOVEABLE DWELLINGS BILLS. These bills were proposed as legislation in the British Parliament between 1885 to 1908, under the instigation of **George Smith**. In 1891, for the first time, Gypsies from **England** went on delegations to Parliament. There were two delegations—one led by the similarly named George Smith and the other led by a Gypsy, George Lazzy Smith—to oppose the bill. The bills were never passed because the opposition of the owners of circuses and fairs persuaded members of Parliament to vote against them.

MRÓZ, LECH. Poland. A contemporary **Polish** ethnologist and writer, teaching at the University of Warsaw.

MUNTEANU, BORIS (1949–2000). Union of Soviet Socialist Republics. Medical doctor and civil rights activist. He is now living in **England** and involved in national Gypsy politics.

MUSEUMS. Museums devoted to Gypsy culture operate in **Brno, Czech Republic**; Pecs, **Hungary**; and **Saintes Maries de la Mer,**

France, and there is the private **Boswell Museum** run by Gordon Boswell in Spalding, Lincolnshire, **England**. Sections are devoted to Gypsy history and culture in the district museum in **Tarnów, Poland**; the Sami provincial museum in Rovaniemi, **Finland**; and Paultons Leisure Park in Hampshire, England. The Museum für Völkerkunde in Hamburg, **Germany**, owns the Max Haferkorn Gypsy collection, but this is not on permanent display. Gypsy handicrafts and wagons are exhibited in a number of museums, including a small display as far afield as the National Museum of Ethnology in Osaka, Japan.

A museum illustrating Romany basket making was opened in 1995 in Komotini in Thrace, **Greece**. An application by the **Romany Guild** for planning permission for a museum in Essex, England, was refused by the Planning Inspectorate, as was a later application for a museum in Bedfordshire.

MUSIC. There is probably no such thing as Gypsy music—that is to say, relics of the music brought from **India**—except, some would claim, in **Albania**. But there is a Gypsy style of playing that is often improvised and always dramatic. A small selection of the many professional Gypsy musicians and ensembles have individual entries in the dictionary, including **Ferus Mustafov** and **Django Reinhardt**. *See also* CIMBALOM; DANCE; FLAMENCO; HUNGARIAN GYPSY MUSIC.

MUSTAFOV, FERUS. Macedonia. Contemporary **musician**. He plays the clarinet, saxophone, and most other instruments and currently leads a band in **Skopje**. He has toured widely and has recorded various albums.

– N –

NA CHMELNICI. A **theater** in Prague that has a Romany company attached to it.

NAFTANAILA, LAZAR. Romania. 20th-century civil rights activist. He was a farmer from Calbor in Transylvania who was the first to fight for Gypsy civil rights in **Romania**. In the 1920s, he set up the society Infratirea Neorustica (Brotherhood of New Farmers), which organized lectures and **theater** events to raise the cultural level of the Romanies. In 1933, he founded the journal *Neamul Tiganesc*.

NAGY, GUSZTAV. Hungary. Contemporary translator. Winner of a 2003 **Roma Literary Award** for Translation.

NARI-KURAVAR. *See* VAGHRI.

NATIONAL ANTHEM. The internationally recognized anthem for the Gypsies is "**Gelem, Gelem**." In **Hungary**, a second song is popular, sung to words by **Károly Bari**.

NATIONAL ASSOCIATION OF GYPSY WOMEN. *See* UNITED KINGDOM ASSOCIATION OF GYPSY WOMEN.

NATIONAL DAY. *See* ROMA NATION DAY.

NATIONAL EMBLEM. *See* FLAG.

NATIONAL GYPSY COUNCIL. United Kingdom. Est. 1979. President: Hughie Smith. The de facto successor to the **Gypsy Council**. It was formed in 1973 after a merger of the Gypsy Council and the **Romany Guild**. The Romany Guild later withdrew and again became an independent body. The council also uses the abbreviated name Gypsy Council on its stationery.

NATIONAL GYPSY EDUCATION COUNCIL. United Kingdom. Est. 1970. Founded with a committee of Gypsy activists and non-Gypsy **educationalists**. Lady Plowden, author of the **Plowden Report**, was invited to be the patron of this body, and it was able to obtain substantial grants from charitable funds and the government. A program of education by volunteers was set up that continued for several years until local authorities gradually took over the work of teaching Gypsy children, whether they were living on official sites or still traveling. In 1988 the council split, with some members forming the **Advisory Committee (later Council) for the Education of Romanies and Other Travellers**. The National Gypsy Education Council later changed its name to the **Gypsy Council for Education, Culture, Welfare and Civil Rights** and finally the **Gypsy Council.**

NATIONAL ROMANI RIGHTS ASSOCIATION. United Kingdom. Civil rights organization founded by **Eli Frankham**. It was active in the 1990s.

NATIONAL ROMANI TRAVELLER ALLIANCE. United Kingdom. 2004. Chairman: Barrie Taylor. This alliance was set up at a meeting in Peterborough hosted by **Peter Mercer**. It is supported by the **National Travellers Action Group** and the **United Kingdom Association of Gypsy Women**. It crosses the boundaries between the **International Romani Union** and the **Romani National Congress**, as Mercer is the British representative on the Union praesidium and Taylor of **Unified Nomadic and Independent Transnational Education** is linked with the congress. One reason for setting up the alliance was the feeling among its members that the **Gypsy and Traveller Law Reform Coalition** was dominated by its non-Gypsy members and was lobbying for a new Act of Parliament without sufficient consultation with grassroots Gypsy opinion.

NATIONAL TRAVELLERS ACTION GROUP. United Kingdom. Est. 2003. The leading members are Clifford Codona and his wife Janie.

NAUMCHEV, ILIA. Prilep, Macedonia. In 1867 in the newspaper *Macedonia*—published in Istanbul—a letter to the editor was printed that was signed "an **Egyptian**." In it, Naumchev defended the right of each nation to have **religious**, civic, and national equality and pleaded for right of the Gypsies as a people with an ancient history to develop their own **education** and religious institutions. This is among the first documented evidence of the struggle of the Gypsies for civic emancipation. Naumchev initiated the establishment in Prilep of separate Gypsy guilds (smiths, violinists, porters) with their own patron saints. He ended his life as a priest in his hometown.

NAWKIN. A name the **Scottish Travelers** use for themselves. Also spelled "noggin." The word is possibly from the Gaelic *an fheadhainn*—pronounced "an nyogin" and meaning "the people."

NAWWAR (NURI). A **clan** of Gypsies living in Lebanon, Syria, and elsewhere in the Middle East. They call themselves **Dom** and speak a language of **Indian origin**, related to Romani. The name may have originally meant "blacksmith"—from the Arabic word *nar* (fire). In 1912 two Nuri **women** from Jaffa traveled through **Germany** with a circus troupe. Since about 1970 a number of individuals and families have come to western Europe, including Great Britain.

NEILANDS, JANIS (FRIC) (1919–2000). Latvia. Writer and cultural worker. He founded the first Romany school in his country in the post-1945 period and was coauthor of a Romani–**Latvian** dictionary in 1997.

NETHERLANDS. Estimated Gypsy population: 37,500 (including the *Woonwagenbewoners*, Dutch **Travelers**). In 1420 the first Gypsies appeared in Deventer, in the shape of Andrew, Duke of **Little Egypt**, with a company of 100 persons and 40 horses. In 1429 a similar group appeared in Nijmegen. In 1526 Gypsies were forbidden to travel through the country by **Holy Roman Emperor** Charles V, who had authority at that time over much of the Netherlands. The punishment would be a whipping, and their noses would be slit. In the 16th century, placards begin to appear throughout the country warning the Gypsies of punishments if they remained in the district.

In 1609 the Netherlands became independent. With the emergence of a central government, it became more difficult for Gypsies to escape persecution in one province by fleeing to another. "Gypsy hunts" (*Heidenjachten*) at the start of the 18th century were to be the means by which the Gypsies were finally driven out of the country. Soldiers and police combined to scour the woods for Gypsies. An edict of 1714 forbade citizens to harbor them. Ten Gypsies were executed at Zattbommel in 1725. It is likely that all Gypsies left the country by 1728, the year that saw the last of the hunts, and that there were none in the country for over a century until the 1830s when new **Sinti** Gypsy immigrants arrived from **Germany**.

After 1868 there are reports of the arrival of three groups of Gypsies: **Hungarian** coppersmiths (**Kalderash**), **Bosnian** bear leaders, and Sinti with circuses from Piedmont. These immigrants had money and valid travel documents but were nevertheless put under strong control, which made it difficult for them to earn a living. At the beginning of the 20th century, **Lovari** horse dealers arrived from Germany. In 1918 the **Caravan** and Houseboat Law was instituted to control the indigenous Travelers and the newly arriving Gypsies. A few caravan sites were set up.

During World War II, the German-controlled government made all caravan dwellers live on fixed sites. Fearful of what might happen to them next, many of the Travelers and Gypsies abandoned their caravans to live in houses. The Germans deported all the Romanies they could lay their hands on to **Auschwitz**—245 prisoners in all, of whom only 30 survived.

After the end of the war, the Dutch government decided to tackle the problem of caravans. In 1957 local authorities were allowed to link up and build sites. The government gave a grant per caravan and 50 percent of the running costs. Then in 1968 it was made compulsory for all local authorities to take part in the program. The aim was 50 large regional sites, on the scale of a village with a school, shop, and church. Soon 7,000 Travelers were on the large sites, and a similar number on smaller sites. Recent policy has been to close the larger sites and move the Travelers to smaller ones so that there is less competition for work in a particular area.

After 1945 there was a steady immigration of Romanies from **Yugoslavia** in particular. Incoming nomads were made unwelcome by the authorities, and their caravans were moved on by the police. Some were pushed over the border into neighboring countries. In 1978 the Dutch government decided to legalize those Gypsies who had come into the country from eastern Europe after 1945. This followed adverse publicity in the media on the situation of these largely stateless aliens and lobbying by the Rom Society. In 1977 Minister of Justice Zeevalking legalized some 500 of these Gypsies. A separate civil servant with responsibility for Gypsies was appointed to the Department of Caravan Affairs, which had until then mainly been concerned with the indigenous Dutch caravan dwellers. In fact, the majority of the immigrants have been settled in houses. The late **Koka**

Petalo was recognized as a leader by many of the **Vlah** Romany families.

The Sinti in the Netherlands first organized themselves into an association, the Zigeunerorganisatie Sinti, in 1989. In 1991 the Stichting Sinti-werk was set up and currently the Landelijke Sinti Organisatie represents the Dutch Sinti.

A feature of the Romani and Sinti community is the large number of **musicians** among them, such as the Gipsy Swing Quintet, Hotclub de Gipsys, Het Koniklijk Zigeunerorkest **Tata Mirando Jr.**, Zigeunerorkest Tata Mirando Sr., the Rosenberg Trio, and many others.

NETOTSI. The name given to a group of Romanies in the 19th century who, according to one account, escaped from slavery in **Romania** and lived in the forests, resisting all attempts to recapture them. An alternative explanation of their origin is that they fled much earlier — from **Maria Theresa**'s efforts to sedentarize them.

NETWORK OF CITIES. The Network of Cities Interested in Roma/Gypsy Issues was set up by the Standing Conference of Local and Regional Authorities of Europe following its Resolution 249 of 1993. It has held a series of hearings on **human rights** and legal issues. The second hearing took place in **Košice, Slovakia**, and the third in 1996 in Ploesti, **Romania**. *See also* CONGRESS OF LOCAL AND REGIONAL AUTHORITIES OF EUROPE (CLRAE).

NEVIPENS ROMANI. A periodical in Barcelona, **Spain**, published in Spanish by the **Instituto Romanó**. About once a year, there is a special issue in **Romanó-kaló**, which the institute supports.

NEW TRAVELERS. United Kingdom. From around 1960, a number of non-Gypsy house dwellers started living in **caravans** and buses. Some did this for economic reasons, others because of frustration at town life. By 1986 the numbers had grown to several hundred, and they are mentioned in a report on Gypsies prepared in that year for the secretary of state for the environment by Prof. Gerald Wibberley of London University. The government brought in the concept of trespassing on private property as being a crime, to deal with what it saw as a new problem. This was introduced into the Criminal Justice Act of 1986 and strengthened in the 1994 Criminal Justice Act. New Travelers are generally classed as Gypsies in English law if they travel for an economic purpose. The term "New Age Travellers" is sometimes loosely applied to people who do not travel at all but live in tents and grow food on organic principles.

NICULESCU, GHEORGHE. Romania. 20th-century civil rights activist. A flower dealer from Bucharest, in 1934 he took over the presidency of the Uniunea Generala a Romilor din **Romania** (General Union of the Gypsies of Romania) from **Lazarescu Lazurica**. This organization continued its activities until 1940.

NIKOLAEV, TOMA. See MLADENOV, TOMA NIKOLAEV.

NOMADISM. The Romanies were never cattle-raising nomads who moved from place to place with their flocks. Many of them were, however, industrial nomads (sometimes termed "**peripatetics**") who traveled from place to place practicing their crafts, whether they were smiths, acrobats, or **fortune-tellers**. The word *Gypsy* has become a synonym for *nomad* in western Europe. However, it is not certain that all Gypsies were nomadic by choice in the past. The Gypsies of **Modon**, for example, lived in a settlement and worked as shoemakers for several generations until the **Turkish** occupation of the town. Often Gypsies moved because they were forced to do so. Nomadism was almost impossible during World War II, and afterward many countries in Eastern Europe banned nomadism. In western Europe it became more difficult to travel as land became scarce. At present, it is doubtful that more than 10 percent of European Romanies are nomads.

NORDISKA ZIGENARRÅDET (NORDIC GYPSY COUNCIL). It was founded in 1973 to link Gypsy organizations in the Scandinavian countries.

NORTHERN GYPSY COUNCIL. United Kingdom. Est. 1992. Chairperson: William Nicholson. A regional association in the north of **England**.

NORTHERN IRELAND. Traveler population: 1,100. Northern Ireland is from time to time ruled directly from London, depending on the political situation there. The first legislation concerning **caravan** sites was contained in the Local Government (Miscellaneous Provisions) Order of 1985. This gave 100 percent grants for site provision and gave councils the power (but not the duty) of providing sites. In 1986 an Advisory Committee on Travellers was set up to advise the Department of the Environment for Northern Ireland. It has some Traveler members.

The Travelers in Northern Ireland have the same lifestyle as those in the Irish Republic. About 7 families out of every 10 live on authorized sites, including those run by local authorities. Four districts have been designated under the 1985 order as areas where Travelers cannot stop except on official sites. In 1997 the Race Relations (Northern Ireland) Order was passed. The outlawing of discrimination on racial grounds in this order also applies to discrimination against **Irish Travelers**. As a result, it was proposed to repeal the designation paragraphs of the 1985 order. The Traveller Support Movement is a network of local groups that works for the civil rights of Travelers, along with the Belfast Travellers Education Development Group. *See also* IRELAND.

NORWAY. Estimated **nomadic** or seminomadic population: 400 Romanies and some 5,000 **Travelers**. Norway had become part of **Denmark** in 1380, and Danish laws applied. So, when the Danish king Christian III expelled Gypsies from his kingdom in 1536, this action applied to Norway as well. It is thought that, because he and his people became Protestant in that year, his tolerance waned for immigrants claiming to be pilgrims. There may well have been no Romanies in Norway at the time. One group was deported from **England** to Norway in 1544, and others entered from **Germany**. In 1554 the king again ordered their banishment from his territories. If they then returned, the magistrates were to set them in irons to work for up to a year, following which they were to be expelled again. A further order from King Frederick II in 1589 became valid for Norway on 1 August, when Gypsies were to be imprisoned, their possessions confiscated, and the leaders executed without mercy. The followers would be killed as well if they did not leave. Mayors of towns would forfeit their property if they did not denounce Gypsies, and anyone protecting or sheltering them for the night would be punished, as would the ferrymen and captains of ships that brought Gypsies into the country.

Some Romanies then left—for **Finland**, probably—and others went underground in the country, mixing and intermarrying with Norwegian nomads to form the group known as Reisende or **Norwegian Travelers**.

In 1814 Norway set up its own Parliament. The immigration of Romanies from **Romania** and **Hungary** was helped by the relaxation of the Passport Law in 1860, and in 1884 the first Romany birth in the country for many years was recorded. In 1888 a new law stating that citizenship depended on descent, not birth, was introduced. That meant that Romanies born in Norway did not get Norwegian citizenship until 1914, when the law was changed and between 30 and 40 Romanies acquired Norwegian citizenship. However, between 1918 and 1939 the Norwegian government tried hard to keep Romanies out, specifically invoking the Foreigners Law of 1901, which meant they could not get permission to enter the country to work as nomadic craftspeople; only a few who had relatives already in the country were allowed to come. In 1924 the Justice Department accused the Catholic Church of issuing false baptism certificates to Romanies. The following year, the department said that all Norwegian passports held by Romanies were false and should be withdrawn. In 1927 all the Romanies left the country, precipitated by the Aliens Law, which said that "Gypsies or other Travelers who cannot prove they have Norwegian citizenship shall be forbidden access to Norway."

An international incident occurred in 1933 when a group of Romanies, some with Norwegian passports, wanting to go to Norway were stopped on the frontier between Germany and Denmark. The Danish government would not allow them transit until the Norwegian government agreed to take them, which it refused to do. These Gypsies were held in an internment camp in Germany for some months and then pushed over unmanned border crossings into **Belgium**. During the Nazi occupation of Belgium, some of these Gypsies with Norwegian nationality were arrested and sent to **Auschwitz**.

Between 1927 and 1954 there were no Romanies in Norway. After 1954 a number of Gypsy families came into the country from **France**, but there has never been a large population. Some families were able to regain Norwegian citizenship. In 1955 Oslo social workers ordered a Romany family to move from their two tents to the workhouse at Svanvike. The parents refused because they had heard about the place from Travelers. Their six children were then taken away by force. The press took up the story, and the authorities then agreed to return the children to the parents. In 1956 a new Law on Foreigners left out an earlier provision about Gypsies (*Sigøiner*) that was seen as racist and replaced it with a section on nomads: "Foreigners shall be refused admittance at the border if it is thought that they will try and support themselves as nomads."

In 1956 some Romany families regained their Norwegian citizenship and permission to live in the country. Temporary camps were set up around Oslo. In 1961 the authorities in Oslo discussed the problem of Romany children not going to school. The Mission for the Homeless, set up for the Norwegian Travelers, was still involved and suggested sending families to work in a kind of labor camp. A Gypsy committee was set up by the Social Services Department in 1962 for a Romany population of about 40 people. A new Gypsy committee was set up in 1969, excluding the Mission for the Homeless, although in fact there were no Romanies in Norway at this time. In 1970 and again in 1973 the government published reports and proposals for the Romanies. By this time some families had returned, and in 1973 Parliament passed a decree on support for Gypsies. In 1975 all immigration was stopped, affecting newcomers but not the existing population of about 100.

Several initiatives of 1978 were aimed at Romanies in Oslo: the opening of the first nursery school, an agreement that all Romany children were to have mother tongue tuition, and the appointment of a special employment adviser. The Romanies in the country were not, however, classed as immigrants but had a special status. In 1979 a language primer in Romani was printed, *Me ginavav Romanes* [I Read Romani], and two years later a reader for primary-age children appeared. In the last few years, there has been renewed immigration from eastern Europe.

An annual international **music** festival called Iagori ("Little Flame") has been held since 1999, organized by **Raya Bielenberg**. The king of Norway attended the 2004 event.

NORWEGIAN TRAVELERS. The some 5,000 indigenous **Travelers in Norway** have many names but they prefer to be known by the less pejorative name of Reisende (Travelers). They are traditionally divided into two groups by both themselves and outside experts—the *storvandringer* and *småvandringer* (long- and short-distance Travelers). The long-distance Travelers are generally considered to be the descendants of Romanies who went underground to avoid deportation in the 15th and 16th centuries and intermarried with local **nomads**. On the other hand, the short-distance Travelers are thought to be of Norwegian origin, with some intermarriage with **German Jenisch**, who came to Norway to trade.

By the 19th century, the existence of the Travelers was worrying the government, and in 1841 a Commission of Enquiry was set up. Three years later the discussion of "the problem of the *Fanter*" (another name for the Travelers) in the Norwegian Parliament resulted in a new Poor Law. Aimed specifically at the Travelers, it imposed a punishment of two years' imprisonment for any of them who nomadized in bands. The government voted in 1855 an annual sum of money to **educate** Travelers. This budget was later used for placing them in workhouses, where they were forced to labor. The policy failed due to a lack of suitable institutions. In 1893 the Church Department, which had responsibility for Travelers, estimated that there were some 4,000 of them. In 1896 a law was passed permitting the state to remove children from parents to state institutions. In some cases, the child could be detained until the age of 21. This law was also invoked against some Romany families into the 20th century.

In 1897 Pastor Jacob Walnum followed **Eilert Sundt** as the official expert on Travelers. He became general secretary of the Association for the Fight against Nomadism, which, under the new name of Norwegian Mission for the Homeless, operated until 1986. In 1934 about 1,800 Travelers were said to still be living as nomads. Articles written by J. Scharffenberg appeared in the press recommending their sterilization, and many Traveler **women** were operated on from 1935 until 1950 or even later.

During World War II and the German occupation, moves were made to intern the Travelers in work camps. A story is told that some Traveler families painted swastikas on their caravans to convince the

Germans that they, too, were of Aryan origin, but this has not been substantiated. The proposal of the puppet Norwegian government was to submit the Travelers to tests to see to what extent they were of Romany origin and sterilize those who were. Government minister Jonas Lie compared the Traveler question with the **Jewish** question, while the Norwegian Mission for the Homeless offered its card index of Travelers to the police and recommended more stringent laws. Fortunately, the German occupation of Norway ended before these plans could be put into effect.

Two varieties of Norwegian are spoken by the Travelers, known as *romani* and *rodi* (or *rotipa*). The grammar of both is Norwegian, but there are many loans of vocabulary from Romani as well as from Jenisch. Many Travelers played the violin and contributed to Norwegian folk **music**, including in the 19th century Karl Frederiksen and his pupil Fredrik Fredriksen. Another Traveler musician was Nils Gulbrand Frederiksen. The songs and melodies of the Travelers have been collected and form part of the repertoire of contemporary folk singers. Gjertruds Sigøynerorkester produced the album *Jeg er på Vandring*. A cultural center for the Travelers is being established.

NORWOOD, VERA. England. Contemporary political activist. For many years, she was a member of the Stow Parish Council (now called Town Council) and later the mayor of Stow. She was a long-time active member of the Conservative Party but like all other Stow Councillors, Norwood stood as an independent. Disillusioned by the Conservative stance on Romanies and some other issues, she stood in 2001 for the District Council against the official candidate and won. This is possibly the first time when someone who was refused an official candidacy for being too pro-Gypsy has gone on to win an election. She also joined the **Gypsy Council** and has campaigned for the retention of the **Stow-on-the-Wold Fair**.

NOVITCH, MIRIAM (?–1990). Poland. Political activist and historian. She escaped death during World War II because she was arrested as a resistance worker—not as a **Jew**—and was therefore sent to a prison rather than a concentration camp. She was among the first to become interested in the fate of the Gypsies during the **Holocaust**. In 1961, she wrote her first article on the subject—"Le second génocide" [The Second Genocide]—and followed this up in 1965 with a 31-page report on the killing of the Gypsies and a pamphlet supporting a campaign to get a monument erected for the Gypsies killed in **Auschwitz**. She addressed the second **World Romany Congress**. After immigrating to **Israel**, Novitch established an exhibit on Gypsies in the Museum of Kibbutz Lohamei ha-Ghettaoth.

NUREMBERG LAWS. From 1933 to 1938 the **German** Nazi Party held rallies in the town of Nuremberg. During the 1935 rally, three decrees were announced, including two on nationality and marriage. They made non-Aryans second-class citizens and forbade marriage between the Aryan Germans and persons of "foreign blood"— defined as **Jews**, Gypsies, and blacks.

NUREMBERG TRIBUNAL. After the end of World War II, a series of trials of war criminals was held at Nuremberg from 1945. Former SS general Otto Ohlendorf told the court that in the campaigns of killing in the East "there was no difference between Gypsies and **Jews**." The accused at the first trial (1945–1946) included Ernst Kaltenbrunner, who had been involved in the murder of Jews and Gypsies. He was sentenced to death and hanged.

NUSSBAUMER-MOSER, JEANETTE (1947–). Switzerland. Author. A **Jenisch nomad**. She has published an autobiography, *Die Kellerkinder von Nivagl*, describing the life of her family, with a winter base in a small village and traveling in the summer with her grandfather.

– O –

OCAL, BURHAN (1953–1950). Turkey. **Musician**. Born in Kirklareli, a town in Thrace near Istanbul, he is a virtuoso on a variety of **Turkish** percussion instruments, including the bendir, darbouka, kos, and kudum. He is also a skilled player of Turkish string instruments and a vocalist. Ocal plays with the **Istanbul Oriental Ensemble** and has made numerous recordings, winning many awards.

OCCUPATIONS. Certain occupations are associated with Gypsies such as **fortune-telling**, **music**, metalwork, and horse trading, but Gypsies are to be found in many other fields as well. There are surgeons, lawyers, and other professionals especially in eastern Europe, where most Gypsies are sedentary and **educational** opportunities better. It is not always easy to identify professionals who are Gypsies (Romanies), as they may hide their origin because of real or imagined prejudice.

OFFICE FOR DEMOCRATIC INSTITUTIONS AND HUMAN RIGHTS (ODIHR). Est. 1992. An institution of the **Organization for Security and Cooperation in Europe (OSCE)**. Founded in 1992, its aim is to promote **human rights** by assisting participating states to build democratic societies. Its field of work includes the Romanies, and it organized the first Human Dimension Seminar on Roma in the OSCE Region in Warsaw as early as 1994. It also published for some time a newsletter for the **Contact Point for Roma and Sinti Issues**, which works within ODIHR. In October 2003 ODIHR brought together 200 participants in Vienna for a supplementary meeting during its eighth Human Dimension Implementation Seminar in order to boost the OSCE's Action Plan for Roma and **Sinti**.

OLAH, DEZIDER. Slovakia. Contemporary political activist. President of the Demokraticky zvaz Romov na Slovensku (Democratic Union of Romanies in **Slovakia**) and the Strana Socialnej Demokracie Romov (Romany Social Democratic Party).

OLAH, VLADO (1947–). Slovakia. Teacher and writer. Now living in the **Czech Republic**. A collection of his **poetry** was published in 1996 under the title *Khamori Lulud'i* [Sunflower]. He is a founder of Matice Romska, a Christian-oriented **educational** organization, and coauthor of a children's Bible in Romani. Olah is now translating the New Testament.

OPEN MEDIA RESEARCH INSTITUTE (OMRI). Prague. **Soros Foundation**–supported organization whose field of interest includes Gypsies.

OPEN SOCIETY INSTITUTE (OSI). Budapest, Hungary. Est. 1993. The institute was created by **Jewish** investor and philanthropist **George Soros** to support his foundations in central and eastern Europe and the former **Soviet Union**. Those foundations had been established from 1984, to help former Communist countries in their transition to democracy. The OSI is a privately operated grant-making foundation that implements a range of initiatives to promote an open society by shaping government policy and supporting **education**, media, public health, **human rights**, and **women**'s rights, as well as social, legal, and economic reform. To foster an open society on a global level, the OSI aims to bring together a larger Open Society Network of other nongovernmental organizations, international institutions, and government agencies. The OSI has expanded the activities of the **Soros Foundation**'s network to other areas of the world where the transition to democracy is of particular concern. The network encompasses more than 50 countries, but Roma remain an important priority for funding.

OPERA NOMADI. Italy. Est. 1963. Organization concerned with promoting the **education** of Gypsy children. It was founded at Bolzano by Bruno Nicolini.

OPRE ("UPWARDS"). Zurich, Switzerland. **Music** producers whose aim is to preserve the authenticity of Romany music and further its development. They have issued several CDs to date.

ORGANIZATION FOR SECURITY AND COOPERATION IN EUROPE (OSCE). The OSCE was set up at a meeting of the Great Powers in 1975 as the Conference on Security and Cooperation in Europe. Its present name and structure date from 1994. It has included Gypsy affairs in its meetings and other activities. In September 1995 it organized a hearing of 23 Gypsy **women** from all over Europe. During the meeting of the OSCE in Warsaw in October 1995, a workshop on networking was run for Romany associations.

In November 2003 its Permanent Council published a detailed Action Plan on improving the situation of Roma and **Sinti** within the OSCE area. In December the OSCE Ministerial Council adopted the plan. It covers the police, mass media, housing, health, **education**, and other issues. A working group to develop the plan is chaired by Liviu Bota of **Romania**. *See also* CONTACT POINT FOR ROMA AND SINTI ISSUES (CPRSI); OFFICE FOR DEMOCRATIC IN- STITUTIONS AND HUMAN RIGHTS (ODIHR).

ORIGINS. The Romanies have their origins in North **India**, though they emerged as a distinct people only after their emigration west- ward. *See also* INDIAN ORIGIN; ROMANI LANGUAGE ORIGINS.

OSTIA CONFERENCE (1991). Under the title "East and West," the **Centro Studi Zingari** organized a conference for Gypsies and non- Gypsy experts at New Ostia near Rome in 1991. The arrangement of workshops by topics gave an opportunity for the members of the working parties elected at the fourth **World Romany Congress** to meet. The results of the conference were published in the journal *La- cio Drom*.

OSWIECIM (AUSCHWITZ). Town in **Poland** that was the site of the largest Nazi concentration camp, **Auschwitz**. In the town of Os- wiecim itself, there was a small Gypsy population after 1945, but in 1981 local Poles organized a pogrom against them and most then left the town.

OSZTOJKAN, BELA (1948–). Hungary. Poet. He is the chief editor of *Phralipe*, a monthly Romani literary magazine and the president of Phralipe, the Free Organization of Gypsies, a **Hungarian** Roma Rights group. His publications include a book of **poems**, a collection of short stories titled *Nincs itton az isten* [God Isn't Home], and the novel *Atyin Joskanak nincs, aki megfizesse* [Nobody Will Pay for Atyin Joska].

OTTOMAN EMPIRE. The Ottoman **Turks** conquered Constantinople (present-day Istanbul) in 1453. They were to expand and rule parts of eastern Europe for hundreds of years, beginning in the 16th century. The Gypsies were generally treated like other minority ethnic groups, with their own leaders often being responsible for tax collection. Gypsies of all faiths paid higher taxes than the Turkish Muslims but were exempt from most obligations to the state. Under Ottoman rule, many Gypsies in the Balkans became converts to Islam, while others who were already Muslims came into Europe with the Turkish conquerors as soldiers, **musicians**, and courtiers of various kinds. From time to time the Ottomans banned **nomadism**, probably because of the difficulty of collecting taxes from nomads rather than any special ill will toward nomadism as such.

– P –

PAINTING. *See* ART.

PAKISTAN. Although today there are no direct commercial or family links between European Gypsies and **nomadic** artisan clans in Pakistan, it is possible that some of these groups share a common ancestry with European Romanies. This entry is confined to the *Paryātan* communities—nomadic artisans and entertainers—as it is these that would most likely have links to Europe's Romanies.

There are perhaps eight separate communities of Paryātan living in Pakistan, each with distinct **occupations**. First there are the Jogi. These communities, which are also found across western and northern India, live mainly in tents and are renowned as snake charmers. Many of them are also peddlers and make potions for a living. Next are the Kanjar, who live in grass tents. The Kanjar are most famous for the terra-cotta toys they produce and are often greeted warmly by the children in local villages, who know they have toys for sale! The Kanjar are also nomadic entertainers and, along with families who provide carnival rides, many of them are particularly renowned for their **dancing** and singing.

The Mirasi are another **peripatetic** group known for their singers and dancers. Living in tents, Mirasi people travel from village to village entertaining the locals with their singing, dancing, and impersonations. Many families are also trained to be genealogists for the majority population. A fourth group of peripatetic entertainers are the Qalandar. Like the Mirasi and Jogi, they live in tents similar to the bender tent of Romanies in Great Britain—a tarpaulin thrown over a framework of poles. The Qalandar make a living by performing circus acts. As well as being jugglers, acrobats, and magicians, they are famous as animal trainers.

The remaining four Paryãtan communities are known for their specialist skills as artisans. The Chungãr are basket and broom makers and live in grass tents, like the Kanjar. The Chriga are peddlers of bangles and jewelry and live in bender tents. The Kowli are groups of peddlers and **tinkers** who also live in bender tents. Lastly there are the Lohãrs, whose main occupation is smithing.

Many of these communities speak their own languages and can also be found in areas of northwest **India**. As with peripatetic groups in India, Paryãtan populations in Pakistan tend to be excluded from the usual social rules governing caste and class interaction, which has enabled them to be flexible in their economic activities and to supply specialized services not offered by sedentary clans.

PALESTINE. *See* GAZA AND THE WEST BANK.

PALM, KAI, AND PERTTI PALM. Finland. Contemporary **musicians**. They are two brothers who play rock music. They have lately begun to introduce songs in the **Romani language** into their repertoire.

PALM, OLLI. Finland. Contemporary singer. He combines the tradition of the **Finnish** tango with the American folk-rock style. Among his repertoire are jailhouse blues.

PALM-READING. **Fortune-telling** was one of the **occupations** mentioned in the early reports of Gypsies—for example, in 1422 in **Belgium** and in the same year in **Italy**. The first record of palmistry in **England** is in 1530. The art probably originated in **India**. Many **clans** have continued the tradition, though the increasingly popular **Pentecostal** Church disapproves of any form of fortune-telling. It is predominantly **women** who read palms.

PALMROTH, ARVO VALTE (1916–). Finland. Singer and songwriter. He began his **music** career in 1962 after his wife's death. He had been involved in music on a casual level for many years, but was then inspired to record a disc in 1973 that included Gypsy songs, romances, and airs and some original compositions. Some of his family accompanied him. This recording launched Palmroth on his singing career.

PANKOK, OTTO (1893–1966). Germany. **Artist**. Pankok drew many Gypsy subjects. His "Passion" was based on visits to a Gypsy camp in Heinefeld near Düsseldorf in 1933–1934. In July 1937 came the opening of the National Socialist propaganda exhibition attacking "degenerate art" (*Entartete Kunst*). Among the works on display was Pankok's lithography "Hoto II," the portrait of a **Sinto**. A prize named in his honor has been awarded since 1999 for Romany cultural achievements.

PANKOV, NIKOLAI (1895–1959). Russia. Journalist and writer. With only a primary **education**, he translated **Prosper Mérimée's** *Carmen* and works by **Aleksandr Pushkin** into Romani. He worked as a journalist, first on a **Russian** newspaper and then on the Romani magazine *Romani Zorya*. He strove from 1924 on to persuade the Romanies to settle down and have an education. His writings include *Buti i džinaiben* [Work and Knowledge; 1929] and *Džidi buti* [Living Work; 1930]. Pankov taught in the Gypsy technical school in Moscow from 1933 to 1938. In 1942, he suffered from an illness brought on from working as a night watchman, after which he wrote little. He was elected a member of the Union of **Soviet** Writers in 1944.

PANNA, CZINKA (1711–1772). Slovakia. **Musician** and composer. Coming from a musical family, she was encouraged to study music and later played the violin in her own band with her husband and brothers-in-law. Her repertoire included folk songs and her own compositions. Panna was honored both during her life and after her death as a great musician. Since 1970, musical festivals in her honor have been organized in the Gemer, the county of her birth. She has also appeared on an official postage stamp.

PAPASOV, IVO (1952–). Kardzhali, Bulgaria. Clarinet player who first made his name with the Ensemble Trakiya. He is an exponent of so-called wedding **music**, a combination of folk music in Gypsy style and jazz. CDs include *Fairground* and *Balkanology*.

PAPP, KATALIN. Slovakia. Contemporary artist. Papp is a **Hungarian** Rom from **Slovakia** presently residing in the **United States**. Her work has been exhibited in several locations, including New York City.

PAPUSZA. *See* WAJS, BRONISLAWA.

PARA-ROMANI. Name given by some linguists to varieties of non-Romani languages that have been influenced by the **Romani language**. *See also* CANT.

PARIS CONFERENCE (1986). A conference—which some books wrongly call the fourth **World Romany Congress**—that took place in Paris on 22–23 February 1986. It has been called variously an open meeting of the Presidium of the **International Romani Union (IRU)** or a meeting of the **Comité International Tzigane**. The main purpose of the conference was to consider the campaign to get **reparations** from the **German** government for victims of the Nazi period. This meeting saw one of the last public appearances of **Vaida Voevod III**, the founder of the modern Gypsy civil rights movement. Some delegates regarded it as a prelude to holding a fourth congress of the IRU in Paris, but efforts to obtain financial backing failed, and that congress was eventually held in **Poland**.

PARLIAMENT, ROMANY (HUNGARY). *See* ROMA PARLIAMENT.

PARLIAMENT OF THE INTERNATIONAL ROMANI UNION. The Chairman of the **International Romani Union** Parliament is **Dragan Jevremović**. The Parliament was set up at the fifth meeting of the **World Romany Congress**.

PASHOV, SHAKIR (fl. 20th century). Bulgaria. Editor, politician, and political activist. In 1933, he was editor of *Terbie* (Education) but a year later the right-wing government banned all the minority and opposition magazines and organizations. Following the establishment of a Communist government in 1945, he became head of the new Gypsy organization Ekhipen (Unity) and editor of a new magazine for Gypsies. He became a member of Parliament but was interned at Belen prison camp during the later Communist clampdown on Romany nationalism.

PATRIN. An international periodical in Romani and English. Two issues appeared with Galjus Orhan as editor.

PAVEE. A word used by **Irish Travelers** for self-ascription.

PAVEE POINT. The name given to the headquarters of what was the Dublin Travellers' Education and Development Group and the new name of the group itself. Its membership consists of settled people (non-Travelers) and **Irish Travelers** who are committed to the right of **Travelers** to equality in Irish society. It runs training courses, has publications, and tries to influence local and national policy in **Ireland**.

PAVEES, THE. An Irish folk band from the 1980s that had mixed membership, including non-**Travelers**. .

PELE, EL. (1) Cleric. *See* CERIFINO, JIMENEZ MALLA. (2) **Flamenco** singer. *See* MAYA, MANUEL MORENO.

PEN. *See* ROMANI PEN.

PENTECOSTALISM. The start of a Pentecostal revival among Gypsies came in 1952 when a French **Manouche**, Mandz Duvil, asked the Breton pastor **Clement Le Cossec** to baptize him and his partner. Duvil spread the news of his new faith among his family and friends. Two years later, the hundred or so converted Gypsies chose four of their number to be elders. Also in 1954, the first large convention was held in Brest. From 1960 the movement spread outside **France** to **Germany**, **Spain**, and most countries in Europe, as well as the **United States**. Along with the Manouche, who were the original converts, members of other Gypsy groups (**Kalderash** and **Gitanos**) also became converted. By 1982 it was estimated that 70,000 Gypsies had already been converted and rebaptized.

The first contact with **England** came when an English Gypsy visited a convention of the Pentecostals in Montpellier, France, in 1954.

The first convention in England was held in 1983 at Fox Hall Farm, Nottinghamshire, and the second—also in the Midlands—in 1984. *Vie et Lumière* is the organ of the movement. In 1995 the Romani-speakers (Kalderash and others) decided to form their own organization known as **Centre Missionaire Évangélique Rom International**. *See also* LIFE AND LIGHT.

PERIPATETICS. Term used by some authors to describe industrial or commercial nomads, as opposed to traditional **nomads** who move around with cattle or other livestock.

PERUMOS. A popular **music** group from the **Czech Republic**.

PETALO, KOKA (?–1996). The Netherlands. Civil rights activist. He was a spokesman for Gypsies in the **Netherlands** in the first years after World War II.

PETROV, MIHAIL (1968–). Bulgaria. **Poet**. A collection of his poems, *Mo vogi* [My Soul], was published in 1996.

PETROVA, DIMITRINA. Bulgaria. Contemporary political activist. Previously director of the **Human Rights Project** in **Bulgaria**, she is now director of the **European Roma Rights Center** in Budapest.

PETROVIC, ALEXANDER (1890–1942). Russia. Medical practitioner. Petrovic aided victims of the dysentery epidemic in Smolensk, **Russia**. He was a military doctor in **Corfu** during World War I and later in **Yugoslavia**. Between 1920 and 1931, he was a medical assistant at the University of Odessa, after which he returned to Yugoslavia to the Central Institute of Hygiene. He was murdered by unknown assailants in September 1942.

PETULENGRO. The Romani word for a blacksmith, used by several authors named Smith as a penname. One of these, Xavier Petulengro, wrote *A Romani Life* (1935). **George Borrow** used the name in his books to disguise the actual identity of Ambrose Smith.

PHRALIPE (BROTHERHOOD). (1) The name given to a number of Gypsy organizations, particularly in **Yugoslavia** after 1945. One of the most significant was a national organization founded in **Hungary** in 1988. (2) A Hungarian bilingual monthly literary magazine. *See also* PRALIPE.

PIKER; PIKEY. Originally a derogatory term for a Gypsy. It is probably derived from the word *turnpike*—a toll gate on a road. It is also used in contemporary English slang for someone who is always looking for bargains and ways of saving small sums of money.

PISTA, DANKO (1858–1903). Hungary. Composer. He specialized in so-called urban folk songs. These can perhaps be compared with the Victorian music hall repertoire in England.

PITO, JOZKO (1800–1896). Slovakia. **Musician.** Born in southwest **Slovakia**, he was a popular violinist in the town of Liptovsky Mikulás. Pito collected and played folk songs. His sons and grandsons have followed in his musical footsteps.

PLOWDEN REPORT. United Kingdom. Following an inquiry chaired by Lady Plowden, a report was published entitled *Children and Their Primary Schools* (1967). It found that Gypsies were "probably the most severely deprived children in the country." Lady Plowden was later to become president of the **National Gypsy Education Council**, set up to help Gypsy children obtain schooling.

PLYUNI (PLYUNIAKI). A subgroup of the **Polish** Roma.

POETRY. Romani poetry has developed from song. Some verse was written during the early years of the **Soviet Union** before the use of the **Romani language** was discouraged. **Aleksandr German** and O. Pankova were the outstanding names in a repertoire that followed the state policy in seeing **nomadism** as romantic but outdated. Poetry has become a common literary form only since 1945. Well-known poets include **Rajko Djurić**, **Aleksandr Belugins** (Leksa Manuš), and **Bronislawa Wajs**. A number of anthologies are listed in the bibliography.

Increased settlement and **educational** opportunities have also produced poets who use the majority language of the country where they
live. They include **Dezider Banga (Slovakia), Károly Bari** and
Jószef Kovacs **(Hungary), Slobodan Berberski (Serbia), Luminita
Mihai Cioaba (Romania),** and **Sandra Jayat (France),** together
with many in the Commonwealth of Independent States (CIS). Their
themes often mirror those of non-Gypsy poets.

In the former **Yugoslavia,** where **radio** and periodicals have fostered the language, a circle of poets in **Skopje** and its satellite town of
Shuto Orizari developed alongside a flourishing **theater** in Romani.
The lyric writers of **Kosovo** are better known. Characteristic of this
school is the creation of neologisms from Romani roots rather than using loan words from Serbo-Croat or **Albanian.** From the score of
writers in the province, mention can be made of three: Dzevad Gasi,
Iliaz Šaban, and Ismet Jasarević. The latter, in his rhymed autobiographical poem "Te džanel thaarako ternipe" [That Tomorrow's Youth
Might Know], tells of his hard struggle against poverty and illness.

On a lesser scale than in the 1920s and 1930s, the CIS has seen a
small revival with Nikolai Satkievitch and Djura Makhotin. Gypsy poets in Hungary have seen their work appear in a number of anthologies
and in magazines, one of the earliest being *Rom Som* (I Am a Rom).
Jószef Choli Daróczi takes his inspiration from Berthold Brecht and
the Hungarian poet Jószef Attila. Ervin Karsai, on the other hand, is
best known for his children's poems. Characteristic of **Czech** and Slovak writers was that they had often been manual workers with little
formal schooling. Worthy of mention are **Bartolomej Daniel, Tera
Fabianová,** Frantisek Demeter, **Elena Lacková,** Vojtech Fabian, and
Ondrej Pesta.

Vittorio Pasquale writes in the less used **Sinti dialect** and, together
with Rasim Sejdić, has been published in **Italy.** There are other occasional poets such as **Matéo Maximoff** (better known for his novels), **Dimiter Golemanov** (primarily a composer of songs), and **Rosa
Taikon** (an **artist** in metal).

An outstanding achievement of post-1945 Romani poetry is the
full-length verse ballad *Tari thaj Zerfi* [Tari and Zerfi] by the **Lovari** dialect writer **Wladyslaw Jakowicz,** recounting the story of
two lovers. It has been published in **Sweden** with a glossary in
Kalderash, thus making it accessible to a broader circle of read-

ers. The poets writing in Romani are part of the wider European tradition and important figures in Gypsy cultural life. *See also* LITERATURE, GYPSY.

POGADI CHIB (JIB) ("BROKEN LANGUAGE"). The name given in some books to the variety of English spoken by Gypsies in **England** and southern **Wales**. Scholarly articles use the term *Anglo-Romani*. It has a large vocabulary borrowed from Romani but with the grammar and syntax largely based on English. This form of speech spread during the 19th century, replacing the **Romani language** proper. There are conflicting theories about its origin. An example of a sentence in Pogadi Chib is as follows: *The rakli jelled to lel some pani* (The girl went to fetch some water). Similar varieties of the majority language have been developed in **Ireland** (**Cant**), **Norway, Scotland, Spain** (**Caló**), and **Sweden**.

POLAND. Estimated Gypsy population: 35,000; according to the last national census (2003), there are 12,900 Roma in Poland. Romanies first arrived on the territory of present-day Poland during the 15th century. By the end of that century, several places were named after the Gypsies (such as Cyhanowa Luka), where they had presumably settled. Following harassment in **Germany** and other countries, more Gypsies followed. In 1501 a Gypsy named Vasil was appointed by Earl Alexander of **Lithuania** to govern the Romani clans in Poland, as well as in Lithuania and **Belarus**. However, in 1557 the Polish Parliament ordered the expulsion of Gypsies from the country. This was not carried out, as is shown by the passing of similar laws five times between 1565 and 1618. From around 1650, Polish kings began to appoint Gypsies as heads of their own **clans**. Even when this role was given to non-Gypsies, the Romanies continued to have their own recognized leaders. The Polish Lowland Gypsies still acknowledge the **Shero Rom** (Gypsy chief) as their leader.

In the 18th century, Gypsy families emigrated from **Slovakia** and settled in the Carpathians. These Gypsies settled in permanent communities and formed the group now known as **Bergitka Roma** (Mountain Gypsies) as opposed to the longer established Lowland or Polish Romanies. In 1791 the Settlement Law was passed, abolishing the previous decrees on expulsion but—again unsuccessfully—banning

nomadism. By 1793 Poland ceased to exist as a separate nation, being partitioned between **Russia** and Prussia (Germany).

The first writings on the Gypsies in Polish were by Tadeusz Czacki at the end of the 18th century and in 1824 by Ignacy Danilowicz. In the 19th century, **Kalderash** and **Lovari** Gypsies from **Romania** arrived on Polish territory. Poland regained its independence in 1918 after the end of World War I. The Kalderash then elected their own **kings**, forming the **Kwiek dynasty**. These kings were recognized by the Polish government.

In 1939 Germany occupied part of Poland and as early as 1940 began to deport Gypsies and **Jews** there from Germany. These Gypsies were put in ghettoes and work camps. In 1941 Germany occupied the rest of Poland, and the following year massacres began. At Karczew, 200 Gypsies were killed, 115 in Lohaczy, 104 at Zahroczyma, and smaller numbers throughout the country. Hundreds were deported to the extermination camps at Belzec, Chelmno, Sobibor, and Treblinka. These camps, as well as **Auschwitz (Oswiecim)**, also witnessed the death of Romanies brought from outside Poland. Probably some 13,000 Polish Romanies were killed during the Nazi occupation.

In the first years after 1945, the Polish authorities did not regard the Romanies as a problem, in contrast to the attitude of other countries of eastern Europe. Romanies made up only 1 percent of the population, and many had been sedentary for generations. There was also little fear that the Polish Catholics would be outstripped in births by the Romanies, and any racist feelings were directed toward the **Jews**. After the election of a Communist government in 1947, Romanies were required to take up employment in factories and farms alongside the rest of the population, and private trading was restricted. Many Lovari and Kalderash were allowed to leave for **Sweden** or West Germany and were provided with exit visas.

A government resolution of 1952, the "Resolution on Assistance to the Gypsy Population in Moving toward a Settled Style of Life," aimed at integrating the Gypsy population, but this had little effect at the local level. Then in 1964 nomadism was completely stopped by strict interpretation of the laws on schooling, camping, and so on. Many young Gypsies subsequently moved into towns to work in factories. Until 1989 national minorities were supervised by the Ministry of Internal Affairs, and Romanies were de facto classed as an ethnic minority.

In 1963 the first Romany cultural organization in Poland was founded in Andrychów. However, all cultural associations were in those years controlled by the government. The only publishing in Romani in that period were the poems of **Bronislawa Wajs** (Papusza). There was also a small number of books in Polish about the Romanies, by **Jerzy Ficowski**, **Lech Mróz**, and others. Some **musical** ensembles were formed, including the Roma Ensemble in Kraków, founded in 1948, which toured in Poland and abroad. A cultural club was established and a Gypsy exhibition put on permanent display in **Tarnów**.

In the late Communist period, there were pogroms in Konin and **Oswiecim** in 1981. Houses were broken into, plundered, and set on fire. As Poland moved toward democratic government, an annual Gypsy music festival was started in Gorzow Wielkopolski, and the bilingual newspaper *Rrom p-o Drom* (Romanies on the Road) began to appear in 1990 under the editorship of **Stanislaw Stankiewicz**. Since 1998 the Roma have been considered a national minority.

After the end of the Communist regime, surplus unskilled laborers —mainly Gypsies—were sacked from their jobs. On the other hand, many Gypsies have established small businesses and attracted the envy of their poorer Polish neighbors. Since the breakup of the Communist state, there has been one big pogrom, in **Mlawa** in 1991 where the houses of Gypsies were set on fire, following an incident in which a car driven by a Gypsy hit three pedestrians. Also in 1991, three Gypsies were killed in a second incident elsewhere. In 1992 there was an attack on the house belonging to one of the only seven remaining Gypsies in Oswiecim, the majority having left after the 1981 pogrom. Windows were smashed, and anti-Gypsy slogans were painted on nearby walls. The political party Narodowy Front Polski (Polish National Front) circulated leaflets during 1993 complaining about an exaggerated figure of 90,000 Gypsies and campaigning for them all to be expelled from the country. In March 1995 a Romany couple was killed in Pabianice, and in October of the same year a mob attacked a house in the Warsaw suburb of Marki. In July 1997, the police opened an inquiry into an incident in which a grenade was left by the door of a Romany family's flat.

The locally-based **Helsinki Foundation for Human Rights** report in September 1997 said that after 1989 the treatment of Roma by the authorities in Poland changed markedly and that the situation was better than in other countries in central and eastern Europe. The problem of harassment is, however, widespread. Incidents of skinheads clashing with Roma and racially motivated violence directed at Roma continue to be reported. In April 1998 there were five separate attacks in Zabrze, including the beating of a five-year-old boy. In November 1999 a group of Poles from Pilsudski Street, Limanowa, demanded that councillors evict their Romany neighbors. They also insisted that no flats be allocated to Roma in the future and that they be accommodated in separate, walled-off quarters. In the event of local authorities refusing to meet their demands, protesting residents threatened to take matters into their own hands.

In September 1998 a skinhead attacked a Romany home in Bytom, throwing a gasoline bomb into a room in which two girls were sleeping. The swift action of the girls' parents prevented lives being lost, but as a result of the attack, 12-year-old Pamela received second- and third-degree burns to 20 percent of her body and was in a critical condition. In June 1999 the skinhead responsible for the attack was sentenced to five years' imprisonment. During the trial, the girl's family was repeatedly threatened by the defendant's associates, who stoned their home and, shortly before the sentence was passed, attacked the girl's 14-year-old brother.

At the end of September 1999, British prime minister Tony Blair sent the Polish prime minister a letter demanding better treatment of Roma in Poland, threatening to introduce entry visas for Polish citizens if this was not done. The request was a response to some 400 Polish Roma seeking political asylum in England, citing the racist persecution they continually suffered in Poland.

In April 2000 anti-Semitic and anti-Roma graffiti were painted on the wall of the Jewish cemetery at Oswiecim. In August 2000, a Romany woman was attacked in her home with an axe by two men wearing masks whom she believed to be skinheads. She suffered serious injuries and had to be admitted to a hospital. Police detained two suspects but were reportedly unable to proceed with the case for lack of evidence.

Violent attacks against Roma have also been perpetrated by the police, including an incident in July 1998 in which three Roma were beaten up in a spa park following a festival of Romany culture and song.

The law provides for the **educational** rights of ethnic minorities, including the right to be taught in their own language, but there is currently a shortage of qualified teachers with a knowledge of Romani **dialects**. Most Roma children do not complete primary schooling; education for these children ends at age 12, and many are illiterate. In the majority of cases, Roma are integrated into mainstream classes, and some schools, recognizing economic disadvantage, language barriers, and parental illiteracy, have introduced special preparatory classes for Romany children. In July 2001 the ombudsman called for the implementation of institutional and long-term solutions in Roma education that took account of the history, specific culture, and traditions of the community. He expressed the opinion that the low level of education among Roma was not only the result of attitudes and lifestyle but also caused by a lack of initiative in this area on the part of the Polish authorities.

The central government made several moves to improve the situation of the Roma prior to entry into the **European Union**. The school enrollment rate among Roma children increased from 30 percent to 80 percent, and a number of new homes are being built specifically for Roma.

In 2000 the Interdepartmental Group for National Minorities discussed the issues of Bergitka Roma, who have been recognized as the poorest Roma group in Poland. As a result, the Pilot Government Program for the Roma Community in the Malopolska Province for the years 2001–2003 was prepared and launched in March 2001. The aim was to end the disparities between the Malopolska Roma and the rest of society. The program covers education, employment, health, and accommodation conditions. In addition, two plenipotentiaries for Roma issues were appointed in 2000 in two Malopolska counties in which there are significant Roma populations.

Several hundred Romanian Gypsies have immigrated to Poland. At the same time, large numbers of Polish Romanies have sought to settle in western Europe—some as asylum seekers on the grounds of racial persecution.

The Gypsy population consists of a number of different groups speaking different dialects. Apart from those already mentioned (Lowland Gypsies, Bergitka, Kalderash, and Lovari), there are also Russian Gypsies who have immigrated since (and even in some cases before) 1945 and **Sinti** Gypsies. Organizations currently operating include the Central Council of Polish Roma (chairman: Stanislaw Stankiewicz), which has representatives of the five largest associations: the Fundacia Mniejszosci Roma w Polsce (Association of the Roma Minority in Poland), the Romanies Social and Cultural Association in Tarnów, the Friends of Romany Culture in Gorzow Wielkopolski, the Kraków/Nowa Huta Romany Association, and the Solidarity Association for the Romany Minority in Kielce. There is also the independent Romany Association in Poland (chairman: Andrzej Mirga), with headquarters in Oswiecim; it has published a number of books under the title of the Polish Library of Gypsy Studies (Biblioteczka Cyganologii Polskiej). In addition, there is a monthly **television** program aimed at the Romany population. Fr. Edward Wesolek, a Jesuit, has been appointed the national Catholic minister to the Romany community.

PONOMAREVA, VALENTINA. Union of Soviet Socialist Republics. Contemporary singer and **musician**. She blends her vocals with electronic orchestral accompaniment. She toured internationally in the late 1990s with the Volgograd (Stalingrad) band Orkestrion, which incorporates made-up instruments recycled from rubbish dumps, giving a unique performance of **poetry** and music.

PONTIFICAL COUNCIL FOR THE PASTORAL CARE OF MIGRANTS AND ITINERANT PEOPLES. Cardinal Hamao, president of the council, on 28 February 2006 issued a new document entitled *Guidelines for the Pastoral Care of Gypsies*. This recognizes their separate culture and the need to welcome them into the Catholic Church.

POPES. Over the years, a number of popes have interacted with the Gypsies — in a positive or negative way. In 1423, Pope Martin possibly gave a safe conduct letter to Duke Andrew of **Little Egypt**. A copy of the presumed document has survived, and there is a record of

Andrew and his followers setting off for Rome, but no record of a meeting. Between 1550 and 1557, several edicts were passed in the Papal States declaring that Gypsies had to leave the territory or the men would be sent to the galleys and the **women** whipped.

In his Christmas message of 1942, Pius XII spoke of the "hundreds of thousands of people who, solely because of their nation or their race, have been condemned to death or progressive extinction." He has been criticized for not opposing the Nazi regime more actively.

In September 1965, Paul VI addressed 2,000 Gypsies at Pomezia. He talked of his "dearest **nomads**—perpetual pilgrims who have found a home in the heart of the Catholic church" and named Mary as "queen of the Gypsies." This was followed by a Mass and a concert in St. Peter's Square, Rome. The Holy See then set up the International Secretariat for Apostolate of Nomads, which later became the **Pontifical Council for the Pastoral Care of Migrants and Itinerant Peoples**.

John Paul II attended the **Ostia Conference** organized by the **Centro Studi Zingari** in 1991 and addressed its delegates. He stressed the Gypsies' love of the family and the fact that they were not using weapons in their fight for their rights. Later, in 1993, he wrote a letter of solidarity to the Gypsy memorial gathering at **Auschwitz**. John Paul included Romani as one of the languages of his regular greetings. *See also* PONTIFICAL COUNCIL FOR THE PASTORAL CARE OF MIGRANTS AND ITINERANT PEOPLES.

PORRAIMOS ("TEARING APART"). A Romani term used to describe the genocide of the Gypsies under the Nazis, corresponding to the Hebrew term *Shoah*. *See also* HOLOCAUST.

PORTUGAL. Estimated Gypsy population: 60,000. Although there are no reports of the first Gypsies to arrive in Portugal, references to them appear in literature in 1516 and 1521. The number in the country must have been significant, since in 1525 a law on Gypsies was passed, followed by 26 subsequent edicts. A law of 1573 ordered that Gypsies be arrested and used as galley slaves. In 1579 the wearing of Gypsy dress was banned. Deportation to the colonies in Africa and South America was a common way of dealing with Gypsies in Portugal from the 16th century.

In 1920 a law defining the role of the National Guard contained special provisions concerning Gypsies. The members of this police force were told to "exercise strict vigilance over the Gypsy population to suppress their habitual stealing" and "to detain immediately any Gypsy accused of any crime." In 1980 after the political changes in the country, the provisions of the law of 1920 were declared unconstitutional because they conflicted with paragraph 13 (against racial discrimination) of the new Portuguese constitution.

The majority of Portugal's Gypsies live in the poorer areas of towns or on the outskirts. There was some migration to **Spain** during the 20th century. There is no active national Gypsy organization in Portugal, although the Catholic Church has a body working with Gypsies. Marcellino Cabeca is a leader within the community, and his son Inocencio has attended international meetings.

POSHA. *See* LOM.

POVERTY 3. The third European antipoverty program from 1990 to 1994. This was a European Community program to support experimental projects to eradicate local poverty. A number of Gypsy projects received funding through Poverty 3, as either Model Actions or Innovatory Measures.

PRALIPE. Macedonia/Germany. Est. 1970. Director: **Rahim Burhan**. A **theater** company originally from **Skopje** performing in Romani. It moved to Mühlheim in **Germany** after the **Yugoslav** Communist Party evicted it from its theater building and its grants were stopped. It toured widely, using the buildings of the Theater a.d. Ruhr in Mühlheim as a base but moved to Cologne. Pralipe's repertoire included **William Shakespeare**'s *Othello* and *Romeo and Juliet* and **Federico Garcia Lorca**'s *Blood Wedding*. The name of the group came from the Romani word for "brotherhood," generally spelled *phralipe*. The company has now closed down.

PREMIO HIDALGO. Spain. Est. 1979. A prize awarded by **Presencia Gitana** in Madrid. It is awarded each year to two personalities, one Spanish and one international, who have contributed to the development of Gypsy culture or rights. Laureates include **Günther Grass**.

PRESENCIA GITANA. Spain, Madrid. An organization with Gypsy and non-Gypsy members. It promotes **education** through projects and publications and awards an annual prize, the **Premio Hidalgo**.

PRESLEY, ELVIS (1935–1977). United States. Singer. The legendary singer reportedly comes from a Romany background, with his mother Gladys Love Smith being an English Romany. His surname, common as Priestley among **Scottish Travelers**, may indicate that he also has **Traveler** blood from his father's side.

PRESS. Before 1939 a small number of short-lived journals for the Gypsy community were published, including the following:

- *Glasul Romilor* (Voice of the Romanies)—**Romania** (bilingual)
- *Neamul Tiganesc* (Gypsy News)—Romania, 1933–? (bilingual)
- *Nevo Drom* (New Way)—**Soviet Union**, 1928–? (Romani)
- *Romani Zorya* (Romani Dawn)—Soviet Union, 1927–? (Romani)
- *Romano Lil* (Romani Paper)—**Yugoslavia**, 1935–? (bilingual)
- *Terbie* (Education)—**Bulgaria**, 1933–1934
- *Timpul* (Time)—Romania, 1933–? (bilingual)

The rise of fascism put a stop to these periodicals, and it was not until around 1970 that new magazines began to appear. Since 1989 there has been a spate of publications, particularly in eastern Europe, some short-lived and some that have lasted longer. Others have closed and then revived as money again became available.

PRO JUVENTUTE. Switzerland. Est. 1920s. A Swiss charitable organization that in the period 1926–1973 took many Gypsy and **Jenisch** children away from their parents and sent them for adoption.

PROJECT ON ETHNIC RELATIONS (PER). United States. Est. 1991. A nongovernmental organization founded to encourage the peaceful resolution of ethnic conflicts in the new democracies of central and eastern Europe and the former **Soviet Union**. It has organized a number of conferences in Europe on the position of Romanies. There is a council composed of Gypsies who advise PER, known as PERRAC (PER Romani Advisory Council).

PUSHKIN, ALEKSANDR (1799–1837). Russia. Writer. His lyric poem *The Gypsies* took three years to write and was completed in 1827, depicting the Romanies of **Bessarabia** as ideal representatives of a natural state of human society. While celebrating the freedom of the Gypsy way of life, the poem also describes a fateful union between a Gypsy and a non-Gypsy. This inspired Mikhail Lermontov's 1829 poem *The Gypsies* and was later turned into a play—with moderate success—by the Moscow **Teatr Romen**.

PUXON, GRATTAN (1939–). England. Journalist and political activist. Puxon went to **Ireland** and there became involved with the campaign of the **Travelers** to get **caravan** sites. After returning to **England** in 1966, he helped set up the **Gypsy Council**, of which he was the first secretary. In 1971, he organized the first **World Romany Congress** and became secretary of the **International Romani Union**. He served as its secretary until the third World Romany Congress. He is currently the organizer of **Ustiben**.

– Q –

QUENITES. *See* KENITES.

QUINQUILLEROS (QUINQUIS). Estimated number: 150,000. The Quinquilleros (Spanish for "tinkers") were semi**nomadic** in **Spain** until the 20th century, trading from village to village. Some think they are of **German** origin, as many are blond and blue-eyed. Another theory traces their origin to landless Castilian peasants. Until the 1950s they were completely nomadic, but punitive laws barring nomadism—with the penalty of from six months to five years in prison or forced settlement—have caused them to settle. Some 85 percent now live in urban slums. They prefer to be called *Merceros* (Haberdashers).

QUITO CONFERENCE (2001). Alongside the Forum of the Americas for Diversity and Plurality, the Roma organized their own meeting in March 2001. Representatives attended from several Romany organizations, including those of Argentina, Chile, Colombia, and Ecuador, as well as Sa Roma from the **United States**, the American Romani Union, Romano Lil from **Canada**, and the Western Canadian Romani Alliance. They issued a declaration on behalf of four million Roma in the Americas asking for recognition as a people with full rights rather than as an ethnic minority.

– R –

RACZ, ALADAR (ALADAR JASZBARENY) (1886–1958). Hungary. **Cimbalom** player of international standing. Racz was well known for his interpretations of Bach, Beethoven, and other classical composers by playing the technical equivalent on a reconstructed sounding board. He played in Budapest in a Gypsy band for 16 years. His recitals in Europe included a 1910 performance in Paris, a 1926 recital at the Concert Hall in Lausanne, **Switzerland**, and a 1938 concert in Rome, after which he was invited to join the Academy of Music in Budapest.

RADIO. No broadcasts for Gypsies were aired until after 1945. Now a number of stations regularly broadcast programs in Romani or aimed at Gypsy audiences. The earliest was perhaps in 1973 when a radio program started at Tetovo, **Macedonia**. There are stations currently broadcasting such programs for Romany listeners in Belgrade, Budapest, Paris, Prague, and **Skopje**. In addition, there are some **religious** radio programs broadcast from stations such as Trans World Radio. The proposed broadcasts from Peterborough, **England** (which are mentioned in some books and articles), were never started though BBC Three Counties local radio has begun a weekly program aimed at Gypsies and **Travelers**. *See also* TELEVISION.

RADUCANU, GHEORGHE (1960–). Romania. Civil rights activist, politician, and academic. He is a professor of economics at the Academy of Science. As a member of the political party Partida Romilor

(Romanies' Party), he was the first Romany to be elected to the **Romanian** Parliament, in 1990.

RADULESCU, IULIAN (1937–). Romania. Contemporary political activist. A **Kalderash** head of family. He was crowned "Emperor of All the Gypsies" in August 1993 in **Romania**. His son is married to Lucia, the daughter of his one-time rival, the late **Ioan Cioaba**.

RAFTO FOUNDATION. Norway. Est. 1997. The foundation in **Norway** awarded the Thorolf Rafto Memorial Prize to the Romany People in 1997. The prize was accepted by Prof. **Ian Hancock** on their behalf.

RAJKO DJURIĆ FOUNDATION. Prague. Named after the writer **Rajko Djurić**, the foundation carries out a number of charitable and civil rights activities. It organizes a national festival, Romfest, each year in Moravia and has produced a number of programs for Czech **television**.

RAJKO SCHOOL. A school for gifted Romany children in **Hungary** where they specialize in **music**.

RAMÍREZ HEREDIA, JUAN DE DIOS. Spain. Contemporary political activist. A former teacher and community worker in Barcelona, he is now a politician. He was elected to the Spanish Parliament and was for a time a member of the Parliament of the **European Union** in Brussels. He is active in the **Union Romani**, based in Barcelona, and writes for the journal *Nevipens romani* (Romani News). He helped to organize the **European Congress** in Seville.

RANJIČIĆ, GINA (1831–1890). Serbia. Singer. Her songs were recorded by Heinrich von Wlislocki and published in the book *Vom Wandernden Zigeunervolke* [About the Wandering Gypsy People] in 1890.

RAOUL WALLENBERG FOUNDATION. Budapest. Est. 1997. President: Baruj Tenembaum. Civil rights organization in Budapest named after the famous World War II figure. It has investigated cases of discrimination or harassment against Gypsies in **Hungary**.

RASUMNY, MIKHAIL "KING" (1890–1956). Actor. He played the Gypsy grandfather, Nino Koshetz, opposite Jane Russell and Cornel Wilde in the film *Hot Blood* (1955).

RAYA. *See* BIELENBERG, RAYA.

RAZVAN, STEFAN (?–1595). Romania. Politician. The son of a slave and a free woman in **Romania**, he became ruler of **Moldavia** in April 1595. He was deposed four months later and murdered in December of the same year.

REDJEPOVA (REDŽEPOVA), ESMA (1943–). Skopje, Macedonia. Singer. She has her own ensemble, originally set up with her late husband. They have made many recordings and have toured widely in Europe and North America. She sang the Romanies' **national anthem**, **"Gelem Gelem,"** to open the fourth **World Romany Congress** and performed at the grand concert for **television** during that conference.

REDJEPOVA (REDŽEPOVA), USNIJA. *See* JASAROVA (REDJE-POVA), USNIJA.

REINHARDT, BABIK (1944–2001). France. **Musician.** Guitarist son of **Django Reinhardt**. He initiated the annual Django Festival in Samois-sur-Seine, **France**.

REINHARDT, DJANGO (JEAN-BAPTISTE) (1910–1953). Born in **Belgium**, though he spent most of his life in **France**. **Musician.** Reinhardt was in fact his mother's surname, while his father was called Weiss. As a young Gypsy musician, Reinhardt began his career busking in Paris. In 1920, a French accordionist heard him playing his guitar and offered him a professional engagement in a dance hall, from where he earned his first real money. Jack Hylton, the famous British bandleader, traveled to Paris twice to find him to offer him a contract. The night of their meeting, tragedy struck when a candle set fire to Reinhardt's **caravan** and his left hand was burned. It was a year before he could play in public again. Yet, because of this disability, he spent hours working out how to play with the three fingers usable on his left hand, and his technique was said to reinvent guitar playing. At this stage, he discovered jazz and formed a quartet with his brother Joseph and two non-Gypsies, Louis Vola and Stefan Grappelli. A fifth player was added, and they formed the quintet, which gained fame as the Hot Club de France.

In September 1939 the quintet was playing in London on the eve of World War II, which prompted the guitarist to return to France. When that country was conquered by the **Germans**, jazz was condemned as "Negro music." Concerts were no longer advertised as jazz. While playing later in occupied Belgium, at the Club Rythmique de Belgique, Reinhardt was asked to tour **Germany**. He knew Gypsies were being arrested there and sent to the death camps, so he avoided this danger by requesting 120,000 francs per concert, knowing the Germans would not pay such an amount. Toward the end of the war, he sensed danger again and moved from Paris to near Thonon-les-Bains at the Swiss border, where he once dared to play "La Marseillaise" in front of German officers. From there he tried to slip across the border, but was arrested and found to have a membership card of the British Society of Composers. The German officer who interrogated him was a jazz fan and let the musician go free.

His being cut off from the international world of jazz in occupied France led to a lukewarm reception in New York when later he did play there in 1946. Café society there no longer felt jazz was an art with mass appeal, and the Reinhardt name was not enough to make up for his lack of professionalism. On his return to France, he began to learn the electric guitar but died in Samois after refusing to call a doctor when suffering from a brain hemorrhage.

Contemporary performers of Gypsy jazz include Lollo Meier, Andreas Oberg, Ritary Gaguenetti, and Matcho Winterstein, as well as others who are listed individually in this dictionary.

REISENDE. *See* NORWEGIAN TRAVELERS.

REIZNEROVÁ, MARGITA (1948–). Slovakia. Writer and political activist. President of the Organization of Romany Authors, she translated Anton Chekhov into Romani. Her work includes **poetry**, and her most recent publication is *Kali*, a collection of stories about the **Indian** goddess **Kali**, in Romani with an introduction in Czech.

RELIGION. Gypsies have tended to adopt the religion of the country where they live or travel, so we find Protestant, Catholic, and Orthodox Christians, as well as Muslims. It is said that some customs, such as burning the possessions of the deceased, are relics of Hinduism. Recently many Romanies have adopted **Pentecostalism**.

REPARATIONS. After the end of World War II, the Bonn Convention said that persons who were persecuted because of their race should be compensated. However, in 1950 the Interior Ministry in the **German** state of Württemberg told judges to remember that Gypsies were persecuted not because of their race but because they were antisocial. In 1953 a law on reparations (Bundesergänzungserlass zur Entschädigung für Opfer des NS) made reparations available but only to Gypsies who were of German nationality, stateless, or refugees. A later arrangement (from 1959) was that West Germany would pay global reparations to Western European countries, which they would then use to pay their nationals who had suffered. In the case of Eastern European countries, a number of Gypsies who had been used for medical experiments have received reparations, but otherwise very few others have been compensated for their suffering in this period.

In 1956 there was an important decision of the Higher Court (Bundesgerichthof) that a Gypsy woman should not be compensated for the 1940 deportations to **Poland** as these, the court said, were not for racial reasons but because of the fear of espionage. In 1962, however, the Higher Court accepted that persecution had started as early as 1939 (the Blum case). In 1965 a new law (Bundesentschädigungsschlussgesetz) confirmed that Gypsies did not have to prove that persecution from 1938 was racial — this was assumed. Finally, a new law provided for reparations to be paid for those victims who had not yet been compensated.

Requests have been made for block reparations to be paid to international Gypsy organizations, in particular for families where all the members perished and no one survived to claim compensation. Following the third **World Romany Congress**, the **International Romani Union** has been pursuing such a claim against first the West German and then the Federal German government. The **Indian** government informally offered to be the trustee for such payments. The German government has given money to German

Sinti organizations for cultural and **educational** purposes but these payments have not been seen by the government as being a form of global reparations. Since that Congress, no progress has been made on this question, although two international funds have now been set up to provide pensions for survivors. *See also* HOLOCAUST.

REPUBLIKA SRPSKA. When **Bosnia** was partitioned, the political entity known as Republika Srpska was set up which is de facto under **Serb** rule. The current total Romany population figure is unknown but there are around 200 living in the area of Banja Luka and a similar number in Bijeljina. The Romany population is small because during the three years of fighting those Roma who were Muslims—the majority—were expelled from this area. Roma expelled from Bratunac, for example, now live in Virovitica in **Croatia**. Almost the entire prewar populations of Banja Luka and Bijeljina, both numbered in thousands, have left. The Roma in Bijeljina were told to "leave or be killed," and the majority fled. The Romany settlements of Jasenje and Staro Selo have been destroyed. In 1994 the 200 Roma in the village of Klasnice in northern Bosnia, in Republika Srpska, asked the **United Nations** High Commissioner for Refugees to arrange their evacuation. Reports say that Roma continue to be harassed and persuaded to leave the country. Several thousand Roma who formerly lived in the area now under Serb control are living as refugees in western Europe, in particular **Germany**, **Italy**, and the United Kingdom, and they, too, like those from Bosnia proper, are unlikely to be accepted as citizens if they return.

RESANDE. *See* SWEDISH TRAVELERS.

REYES, ANTONIO (EL MONO) (1946–). Spain. Contemporary singer. He is the grandfather of **Joaquín Cortés** and sings in the **flamenco** style.

REYES, JOSE (1930–). Spain. Singer. Metalworker, carpet seller, and amateur **flamenco** singer. A cousin of **Ricardo Baliardo**, Reyes sings largely for his own pleasure.

REYES, JOSE ANTONIO (1983–). Spain. International soccer star. Seville's top-scoring player in 2002–2003, he signed with **English** team Arsenal in January 2004. He wears a No. 9 shirt and plays forward. He signed his first semiprofessional contract with Seville at 15 years of age and made his debut for the **Spanish** national squad at 19. He has been described as a "play station footballer" who will take the ball as close to goal as he can at the fastest pace.

REYES, LOS. *See* GYPSY KINGS.

RIEFENSTAHL, LENI **(1902–2003).** Germany. **Film** director. She made propaganda films for Adolf Hitler during the Nazi regime. For the film *Tiefland* (1942), she used Gypsies from two internment camps as extras, 68 from Marzahn near Berlin and 50 from Salzburg.

RIGHTING THE ROMA FOUNDATION. Canada. Est. 2005. President: Monica Odenwald. A charity dedicated to relieving suffering in eastern European Roma settlements.

RIPPLE (ROMA INFLUENCE ON POLICY AND PRACTICE IN LOCALITIES IN EASTERN AND CENTRAL EUROPE). Est. 2000 by **Minority Rights Group** International. A two-year project intended to progressively develop the knowledge and skills of national- and regional-themed networks of young Roma in seven countries in eastern and central Europe to enable them to influence public opinion, policy, and practice.

RISHI, VEERENDRA. India. Son of **W. R. Rishi.** He has continued his father's interest in the Romany world.

RISHI, W. R. **(1917–2002).** India. Interpreter in the diplomatic service. He spent some time during his service in Europe studying the Romanies. He attended several congresses and conferences and was a strong link between the Romanies in Europe and their motherland **India.** After retiring and returning to the Punjab, he set up the **Indian Institute of Romani Studies** and edited the journal *Roma,* as well as organizing the two **Chandigarh Festivals.** In the 1990s, he founded a Gypsy **museum** in Chandigarh, the Nehru Romano Kher (Gypsy

House). His publications include two Romani dictionaries, a Romani–Punjabi phrase book, and *Roma: The Punjabi Emigrants and India*. He was elected honorary president of the **International Romani Union** in 1978.

RISTIĆ, DUSAN. Serbia. Contemporary **artist** and **musician**. He has played in the band **Kal**, as well as organizing cultural events. From 2004, he has been working with **Voice of Roma** in the **United States**.

RITTER, ROBERT (?–1950). Germany. Psychologist and doctor. A race scientist during the Nazi regime who in 1936 founded an institute that later became the Race Hygiene and Population Biology Research Center of the Ministry of Health in Berlin. He took over existing records on Gypsies. His aim was to track down every Gypsy in the country and classify them as pure- or part-Gypsy. By 1942, he claimed to have files on 30,000 persons living in **Germany** and **Austria**. The policy he proposed was to intern part-Gypsies in work camps and sterilize them. Pure Gypsies should be allowed to travel but kept apart from mixing with Germans.

ROBERTSON, JEANNIE (1908–1975). Scotland. Singer. A **Scottish Traveler** and performer of folk songs, Robertson's parents traveled principally in the northeast of **Scotland**. She first came to prominence in folk-song circles in 1953, when she was recorded by Peter Kennedy. Acknowledging her mother as the main source of her **musical** knowledge, she gained a reputation as one of the finest ballad singers in western Europe. She made several records and videos and was honored by Queen Elizabeth II with the Member of the (Order of the) British Empire. Her daughter **Lizzie Higgins** and nephew **Stanley Robertson** were also singers.

ROBERTSON, STANLEY (1940–). Scotland. **Musician** and singer. A **Scottish Traveler** and the nephew of **Jeannie Robertson**, he is a piper and singer in the folk tradition as well as a storyteller. He joined the Mormon Church and with its encouragement became a professional entertainer. Robertson has toured in the **United States** and Europe.

ROKYCANY. Town in Bohemia (**Czech Republic**) with a large Romany population that emigrated soon after 1945 from **Slovakia**. The community has a strong **musical** tradition, and performers include the Gina family, which formed a folk band first called Ginovci and later, playing more modern music, Rytmus 84.

ROM. The name used to describe themselves by the majority of ethnic Gypsies in their own language. The etymology is unclear but the term may come from an old **Indian** word *dom*, the original meaning of which was "man." Derivation from the god Rama is unlikely. The plural is *Rom* or *Roma* according to the **dialect**. Other Gypsy groups—for example, the **Sinti** and **Manouche**—have the word in their dialect but only in the sense of "husband." The term is commonly employed when western European media are writing about Romanies from eastern Europe, and we have adopted this usage in this dictionary alongside *Romany*.

The primary unifying concepts of the Romany people are their awareness of a common history and destiny and of a language (even if no longer spoken). Gypsy culture preserves a spirit of **nomadism**, whether exercised or not, a preference for self-employment, and—for most groups—laws of hygiene (**Mageripen**). *See also* ROMANI; ROMANY.

ROMA. Plural form of *Rom*.

ROMA CULTURAL SOCIETY. Poland. Est. 1966. It is still active.

ROMA DAY. *See* ROMA NATION DAY.

ROMA ENSEMBLE. Poland. Est. 1946. Founding director: Michael Madziarowicz; he was followed by Wladyslaw Iszkiewicz in 1967. This Romany song-and-**dance** ensemble was originally formed in Kraków in 1946 by some ex-members of Moscow's **Teatr Romen**. It toured abroad frequently and in 1970 came under the management of the state-owned Estrada Agency in Poznan. It made two recordings in **Poland** before some of the ensemble left for **Sweden** to form the group **Svarta Pärlor**.

ROMA INFORMATION CENTER (RIC). Serbia. Est. 1999. Director: Rozaliza Ilić. Its mission is to improve the Roma's life and to preserve their culture and traditions. The center is dedicated to the emancipation of Roma through **education**, and it runs several workshops for adults and children offering psychological support, numeracy and literacy projects, and creative activities such as **art** and **drama**. It also runs cross-cultural projects and houses a library within its offices containing some 1,200 titles. RIC works alongside other Roma support groups and is supported by the **Open Society Institute**.

ROMA LITERARY AWARDS. Established in 2002 by the **Open Society Institute** in Budapest to honor Roma artistic achievement in **literature** and first awarded in 2003. An international jury of Roma select finalists from four categories: Fiction, Nonfiction, **Poetry**, and Translation.

ROMA NATION DAY (ROMANO DIVES). The first **World Romany Congress** chose 8 April—the day it opened in 1971—to be celebrated by all Gypsy communities as a national day. It was at first sporadically commemorated. For example, in 1993 the Cidinipe Roma (Gypsy Association) of Zagreb held a formal meeting in the Hotel Intercontinental. In recent years, there has been a growth in celebrations, including adopting the **Indian** custom of throwing flowers into a river, first used in 2002 in London when the booking of a hall had to be canceled as earmarked funds were diverted to helping victims of floods in India.

ROMA OPRE ("ARISE ROMA") (BELGIUM). Est. 1998. Chairperson: Wolf Bruggen. An organization that offers a range of activities and services. It promotes Romany culture, tradition, and history and defends the interests of all groups within the larger Romany community in **Belgium** and Europe. Liberation and development, emancipation, and equal participation are the key principles of the organization.

ROMA OPRE ("ARISE ROMA") (UNITED KINGDOM). Est. 2002. President: **Toma Nikolaev Mladenov.** The organization of **Bulgarian** Roma refugees and asylum seekers in Great Britain.

Roma Opre is a constituent body of the **Trans-European Roma Federation.**

ROMA PARLIAMENT. (1) The Roma Parliament set up at the fifth **World Romany Congress.** It has met several times, putting forward proposals for the democratization of the **International Romani Union**'s statutes and for reconciliation with its main rival, the **Romani National Congress.** (2) A **Hungarian** institution that has been very dynamic in Romany politics since 1989, perhaps as it was built up by local organizations. It protects and promotes the interests of Roma through negotiations with the government during the development of new legislation for minorities.

ROMA PRESS AGENCY (RPA). Slovakia. Est. 1999. Director: Ivan Hriczko. This organization began with the aim of improving the presentation of Roma in the **Slovak** media. The agency was set up on a voluntary basis, but since 2002, at the request of the **Open Society Institute** and with the support of the U.S. Peace Corps, it is now more formally constituted. The agency also provides training of young Roma for the profession of journalism.

ROMA RIGHTS AND ACCESS TO JUSTICE IN EUROPE (RRaJE). United Kingdom. Est. 2001. President: **Peter Mercer.** Originally a three-year program supported by the British Department for International Development, it aims to tackle the social exclusion of the Romanies in central and western Europe. In 2003 it produced a background report for the British **All-Party Parliamentary Group on Roma Affairs.**

ROMA SUPPORT GROUP. United Kingdom. Est. 1998. Previously known as the Romany Support Group, it is a community organization working to improve the quality of life of immigrants from eastern European countries, especially **Poland.** The group runs an advice/advocacy service as well as a football (soccer) club, indoor sports activities, a summer program, visual **art** workshops, and a **music** and **dance** project (**Romani Rad**) in East and West London.

ROMA WOMEN'S ASSOCIATION IN ROMANIA (RWAR).
Bucharest, Romania. Est. 1996. Coordinator: Violeta Dumitru.
RWAR's mission is to defend the rights of Roma **women** and support
the development and expression of the ethnic, cultural, linguistic, and
religious identity of its members.

ROMADEX (ROMA DEVELOPMENT EQUITY EXCHANGE).
Europe. Est. 2003. Technical director: Hector McNeil. Extensive
fieldwork by the **European Committee on Romani Emancipation**
and the Agricultural Development Foundation led to the development
of RomaDEX in 2003. RomaDEX wants to address the specific problems facing rural Roma. It will provide market identification, the selection of appropriate technology, and training and business development and thereby help jump-start, in the short to medium term, a
substantial rise in the real incomes of those involved.

ROMAN. The name given by its speakers to the Romani **dialect** of
Burgenland, spoken by some 2,000 persons.

ROMANE DYVESA (ROMANY DAYS). An annual international
meeting of Gypsy **music** groups held in Gorzow, **Poland**, and organized by a local committee. The first gathering was in 1989.

ROMANES. An adverb in the **Romani language** meaning "in the Romany manner." For example, we find the usage "to speak *Romanes*."

ROMANESTAN (LAND OF THE ROMANIES). The name given to a
planned Gypsy homeland in the 1930s on the lines of the Zionist movement's vision at that time of creating a **Jewish** state. The idea was first
proposed by the **kings** of the **Kwiek dynasty** in **Poland**. World War II
put an end to these dreams. The idea of a Gypsy state was revived after
1945 by **Vaida Voevod III**, but nowadays most Gypsies would perhaps
follow the thoughts of the **Canadian** Gypsy writer Ronald Lee, who has
said, "Romanestan is where my two feet stand."

ROMANEZ, ESMERALDA. Contemporary writer. Her mother was a
Romany from Andalusia and her father a French **Manouche**. She has
published numerous books.

ROMANI. (1) Originally a feminine adjective formed from *Rom*, the term most Gypsies use for themselves. It is replacing the old English spelling *Romany*. (Check also for entries listed under ROMANY, as both spellings are still widely used.) (2) The **Romani language**. It is in this sense that the word is used in this dictionary.

ROMANI ASSOCIATION OF AUSTRALIA (RAA). Est. 1990. First president: Jimmy Storey. The RAA is affiliated to the **International Romani Union**.

ROMANI BAXT ("GOOD FORTUNE") FOUNDATION. Sofia, Bulgaria. Est. 1996. Chairperson: Michali Georgiev. The organization focuses on legal and social programs designed to promote the Roma people's inclusion in society and to promote **human rights** and equal treatment. Within this framework, the team monitors and reports on the situation in **Bulgaria** and provides **educational** as well as legal and social services. It offers free legal advice to Roma as well as working alongside the Sofia municipality to develop a strategy for improving education. In 2002, the foundation was selected from 50 nominees to win a **Body Shop Human Rights Award**. It also receives the support of the **Open Society Institute**.

ROMANI CHEL. *See* ROMANY CHAL.

ROMANI CIVIC INITIATIVE (ROI). Czechoslovakia. Est. 1981. Chairperson: **Emil Ščuka**. A political party that fields candidates in local and national elections in the **Czech Republic**. A similar organization operates in **Slovakia**.

ROMANI DEMOCRATIC CONGRESS. Czech Republic. Est. 1992. A nationwide forum in the **Czech Republic** to which many leading Romany figures contribute. It has no activities as such.

ROMANI LANGUAGE. The Romani language belongs to the North **Indian** group and is close to Punjabi and Hindi. It was brought to Europe by the Gypsies and has retained more of its earlier structure than the modern Indian languages. The sound system includes up to four aspirated consonants. There are five or six cases, and verbs have a number of tenses. Words are inflected to show changes of tense, person, gender, and case. There are masculine and feminine genders.

Romani is taught at INALCO (Paris University V), Charles University in Prague, Bucharest University, Manchester University, United Kingdom, and some other colleges and schools. It remained largely a spoken language until the 19th century, when it began to be written. In accordance with the European Charter for Regional or Minority Languages, **Finland**, **Germany**, **Netherlands**, **Slovenia**, and **Sweden** officially recognize Romani as a minority language. *See also* DIALECTS, ROMANI LANGUAGE; LITERATURE, GYPSY; ROMANI LANGUAGE ORIGINS.

ROMANI LANGUAGE ORIGINS. During the 1700s, a Hungarian pastor named Istvan Vályi, when at the University of Leiden in the **Netherlands**, met some fellow students from west **India**'s Malabar coast. They made a list of more than a thousand Sanskrit words for him, which the pastor took back to **Hungary**. Comparing them with words Romanies used in his region, he found some similarities. An article about this study was published in Vienna in 1776 and was noticed by the **German** linguists **Heinrich Grellmann** and Jakob Rüdiger, who each compiled a table of **Romani language** words and compared these with a number of languages. The latter saw the similarities between Romani and Hindustani (Urdu) and in 1781 first recorded his discovery. A further publication by Rüdiger a year later, demonstrating a scientific comparison between the two languages, aroused more attention. Another student of languages, Christian Büttner, then found similarities between Romani and the Pashto language. Grellmann saw the young man's work and went on to publish in 1783 a book that included a section on the **Indian origin** of Romani.

Meanwhile in **England**, independently of all this, Jacob Bryant, an amateur coin collector and historian, compared Romani words with a printed vocabulary of Hindustani around 1780. He revealed the similarities between words such as the Romani *rup* (silver) and the Hindustani *rupee*, but he also identified **Greek** words that Gypsies had borrowed on their journey across Europe to England. However, some of his links were unlikely, and more important discoveries were made by William Marsden, who was famous for his work on the Malay language. He made the Romani–Hindustani link in 1783, compiling a paper that was presented to the London Society of Antiquaries on 3 February 1785. The society then published his findings.

The news of the relationship between the two languages (Romani and Hindustani) spread across Europe and with it the forgotten truth as to the North Indian origin of Europe's Gypsies. The **Russian** academician Petr Pallas mentioned this in his collection of comparative dictionaries published in St. Petersburg as early as 1787. *See also* INTERNATIONAL CONFERENCE ON ROMANI LINGUISTICS.

ROMANI NATIONAL CONGRESS. Germany. An organization based in Hamburg and largely supported by Romanies from eastern Europe. It has links with individuals and groups in other countries and publishes the bulletin *Romnews*. It organized the **Lodz Congress**. The leading figure is **Rudko Kawzcynski**.

ROMANI PEN. President: **Rajko Djurić**. Secretary: Johano Strasses. The center is a member of international writers organization PEN. Membership is open to authors using Romani and to those writing about Romanies. The newsletter *Stimme des Romani PEN* first appeared in 1996. After the death of its editor Reimar Gilsenbach, Djurić took over the running of the organization. In 2003 it held an international competition for literary work on the **Holocaust**. *See also* INTERNATIONAL ROMANI WRITERS ASSOCIATION.

ROMANI RAD. London, England. Band and **dance** ensemble run by and for **Polish** Roma in London. They have performed with Terry Hall and Mushtaq. CD: *Journey*.

ROMANI RESOURCE CENTRE. London, England. Est. 2004. Under the leadership of **Florina Zoltan**, the center aids refugees and asylum seekers from **Romania** and elsewhere.

ROMANI UNION. *See* INTERNATIONAL ROMANI UNION.

ROMANI WRITERS ASSOCIATION. *See* INTERNATIONAL ROMANI WRITERS ASSOCIATION.

ROMANIA. Estimated Gypsy population: 1,000,000. According to the 2002 census, the Roma population numbered some 500,000. The majority belong to **Vlah clans**, but there are also **Ursari** and Muslims. Gypsies may have arrived with the invading **Tartars** in the 13th century. By the end of the next century, they were already treated as slaves. They had even fewer rights than the native serfs, as families could be split up and the members sold or given away as gifts. The first recorded transfer of Romany slaves took place in 1385. The Gypsies may have been brought to Romania as slaves by the Tartars and remained in the country with this status when the Tartars were driven out. Alternatively they may have been forced to sell themselves into slavery through debt. Like the slaves in the **United States**, they had no rights and could be beaten by their masters. The slaves included both farm workers and craftspeople.

A ruler of the **Wallachia** region of Romania, Vlad IV (Dracula), is said to have brought back 11,000–12,000 Gypsies to his capital to be tortured or executed for his entertainment.

The Gypsy slaves have a place in Romanian **literature**. Bogdan Hasdeu wrote the play *Razvan si Vidra* [Razvan and Vidra], in which he tells the true story of a slave (**Stefan Razvan**) who was liberated in the 16th century and became a local leader in **Moldavia**. *Istoria unui galban* [The Story of a Gold Coin] was written by Vasile Alecsandri in the 19th century. Its heroine is Zamfria, who is bought by a cruel owner. A Gypsy kills him and saves her, but he is executed while Zamfria is gripped by insanity. In 1878 Barbu Constantinescu made the first countrywide collection of Romani folklore.

In Transylvania, slavery was not widespread. However, in Moldavia it was not abolished until 1855 and in Wallachia (Muntenia) one year later. Even then, liberty did not mean equality. A trickle of emigration then became a flood, and hundreds, if not thousands, of liberated slaves left Romania for other countries. Many Gypsies of the Vlah clans went as far as **Australia** and the Americas.

A census in 1930, which counted only sedentary Gypsies, recorded 262,000, but this figure was recognized as too low. In the period between the world wars, Gypsies began to organize themselves and demand social equality. In 1933 the journal *Glasul Romilor* (Voice of the Romanies) appeared, continuing until 1939. It was followed by other newspapers, such as *Neamul Tiganesc* (Gypsy Nation), and associations were set up in different parts of the country. In 1926 the first local Gypsy organization was founded in Calbor, and in 1933 the Asociatia Generala a Tiganilor din Romania (General Association of Gypsies in Romania) was formed. **Gheorghe Niculescu** and **Popp Serboianu** were among the leaders at this time. In 1934 the General Association arranged an international meeting, the **Bucharest Conference**, although there were few, if any, foreign participants. A number of resolutions were passed on **education**, employment, and civil rights, but little was done to put these into practice.

At the same time, as fascist ideas spread through the country, racist commentators such as Ioan Facaoru put forward a policy of preventing contact between the Gypsy and Romanian peoples to avoid contaminating Romanian blood. This meant in theory that the **nomadic** clans that did not intermarry with Romanians should be allowed to continue their traditional life.

Romania allied itself with **Germany** during World War II. It began a policy of deporting Gypsies to land in the east captured from the **Soviet Union**. During 1942, the government removed 25,000 Romanies to this land, known as **Transnistria**, where some 19,000 died.

When the Communists came to power after the war, the lot of the Gypsies changed again. The nomads were forced to settle down and abandon the nomadic life. The sedentary Gypsies found themselves placed in high-rise flats in the minitowns created later by Communist leader Nicolae Ceausescu's policy of destroying villages and resettling the population. At an official level, the Romanies did not even exist during this period. There were no books about them and, in contrast to, say, **Bulgaria**, Romany **musicians** were not advertised as such even for the tourist trade. Only one scholar, Olga Nagy, was able to publish work on Romany culture. For an idea of the treasures that were being lost through neglect, consider the fact that she alone produced eight volumes of folktales, all gleaned from Romanies.

During the Communist period, Gypsies were given jobs on state farms and in state factories. Prejudice against Gypsies continued, however. It was alleged that often police would raid their houses and steal their gold jewelry, claiming that it was the result of black market dealings. Visits from Romany leaders from the West were not made easy by the law that imposed a heavy fine on anyone allowing a nonmember of the household to stay in their accommodation after darkness. Leaving Romania was also difficult and costly. Only two Romanian Gypsies were able to attend the third **World Romany Congress**. **Pentecostal** missionaries worked underground, and in 1979 St. John's Gospel was translated into Romani and printed in the **Netherlands** by Open Doors for smuggling into Romania. During this period, **Ioan Cioaba** was an intermediary between his people and the government.

The census of 1979 counted 225,000 Gypsies (less than had been recorded in 1930) because many registered themselves as Romanian or **Hungarian**.

The fall of Communism in 1989 brought both good and bad results for the Gypsies. In the first place, they were free again to form associations and publish magazines. On the other hand, the new governments and many Romanians often blamed the Gypsies for the economic difficulties that the change to a free market brought. There were many pogroms in the following years. One of the worst attacks was in Bucharest in 1990 when Prime Minister Petre Roman brought in miners to help him to retain power. After beating up opposition students and others in the center of Bucharest, the miners, together with secret police, then attacked the Gypsy quarter, causing much damage and many injuries.

In March 1993 a report in a Bucharest newspaper concerned the Ion Antonescu Command, a vigilante organization with a national network and considerable financial capital whose proclaimed aim was to "kill Gypsies who commit crimes against society." A representative of the group stated that its members were not concerned about European public opinion and that the Gypsies were not a minority but a "curse on the Romanian nation." Romanies formed paramilitary self-defense groups in response to the authorities' failure to protect them.

Since 1990, some 50 villages in Romania have experienced ethnic conflict wherein Romanians and/or Hungarians have come together to burn Gypsies out of their homes. More than 300 houses belonging to Romanies have been burned down and 10 persons killed by mobs since, and no one has yet been convicted of arson or murder. In January 1995, houses were set on fire in Bacu and Botosani. In the same year, there were heavy-handed police raids in Akos Bontida, Sectorul Agricol Ilfov, and Tandarei. In the town of Curtea de Arges, 21 houses were burned down in June 1996. The majority of those who lost their homes have been unable to return to them. Many now live in very poor circumstances as "illegal residents" in other towns.

There are many examples of Roma being forced to leave their places of residence: In May 2002, city hall representatives pulled down the tents of 20 families who had been living in the Vacaresti Lake area of Bucharest, after the families failed to obey a notice to leave. In July of the same year, Roma were forcibly removed from public land in Sector 6 of the city of Bucharest and made to return to their counties of origin. In 2003, the same thing happened to Roma living on the outskirts of Bucharest's Militari district.

In 1997 four persons were finally arrested for trial in connection with events in 1993 in Hadareni where three Romany men had been killed. These were the first arrests of anyone for this series of attacks. The four who were convicted were released in 2000, after serving short sentences. In 2005 the Romanian government reached a settlement with the 18 surviving victims of the pogrom. The attacks in Hadareni had led to a second exodus, and Romanian Gypsies can now be found in **Poland** as well as many western European countries, where they have been usually tolerated for a short time and then sent back to their birthplace.

An action initiated on 5 December 2002 by 52 policemen from the county of Bacau and Neamt in the Orbic region on the outskirts of Buhusi, intended to locate several wanted criminals, ended in bloodshed. One of those wanted by the police for theft and his father were shot dead by the police forces. Many Roma were beaten, including a 72-year-old woman. The police concerned in Buhusi were later rewarded for their courage in entering the Romany community.

Instances of police brutality toward Roma continue in the 21st century with numerous reports of police torture and mistreatment that fail to result in due punishment of the officers concerned. In June 2002, 18-year-old Nelu Balasoiu died in detention in Jilava Prison near Bucharest. Witnesses claimed he was beaten every day by the police during his three months in prison. In June 2003, Mihai Dumitru was also the victim of a police officer in civilian clothes who was involved in a raid in Tulcea. Dumitru suffered a severe beating and was subsequently hospitalized. Although the Ministry of Administration and Interior acknowledged the officer's guilt, his punishment had not been determined by the year's end and although the case had been referred to court for criminal prosecution, it has still not been decided.

Roma children have been subjected to police brutality: In February 2002, 14-year-old Calin Sterica was beaten in a Galati schoolyard by local police using fists and clubs. They were there to investigate a disturbance in which she was not involved. Calin's mother, who arrived to see what was happening, was fined four million lei ($120) for "disturbance of the public order." The Roma County Bureau subsequently discouraged the mother from filing a complaint.

It is clear from the above that the police in many towns in all parts of Romania have until recently been themselves persecuting the Roma, not defending them. There are not any reports of police brutality against Roma since those listed above. There have, however, been cases where civil security guards have used excessive violence against Roma.

The *Country Report 2004* for Romania from the **European Commission** states: "A particular concern is the occasional excessive use of violence by law enforcement officers, including the unlawful use of firearms. Reports of [such] violence have been most common in the case of disadvantaged categories such as Roma."

On a more positive note, an emergency ordinance passed in January 2002 prohibited discrimination based on a number of factors, including ethnicity, and established the ability to sue on the grounds of discrimination. The National Council for Combating Discrimination, the agency enforcing the ordinance, fined two private companies for denying access to Roma. In January 2006 the National Council for Combating Discrimination ruled that a speech by Vadim Tudor, leader of the extreme right-wing Greater Romania Party, labeling Gypsies as "rapists and thieves" was in breach of the national law against discrimination.

At the end of November 2003, the ruling Social Democratic Party signed an agreement of cooperation with the Roma Party. It called for the continued monitoring of the Roma situation, the hiring of Roma to work in state institutions, and programs to educate the public about racism and discrimination. A partnership protocol that sets out cooperative measures to ensure that Roma have access to health care continued during the year.

In June 2003, the Department for Interethnic Relations and the National Office for Roma were placed under the General Secretariat of the government. The government reported that 60 percent of the goals of the 2001 National Strategy for the Improvement of the Situation of Roma had been achieved. Under this strategy, some 400 Roma experts and counselors were appointed in ministries, prefect's offices, and some mayoral offices. Ministerial Committees for Roma were subordinated to a joint committee to monitor the implementation of the strategy, and joint working groups at the local level have been set up. Roma nongovernmental organizations have asserted that, with the exception of the establishment of bodies to implement the strategy, there were few practical achievements. In April 2004 the government stated that it would desegregate education and ensure equality of access to Roma children.

The situation today is that, while in some parts of Romania Gypsies live in fear of attack by their neighbors and the police, elsewhere the community has been able to develop associations and magazines. The Bible is being translated and published legally, and the **Romani language** is taught in several schools and colleges. There was a move to replace the pejorative term *Tigan* by the word *Rom*, but in 1995 the government changed it back officially to *Tigan* on the grounds that there was confusion with the word *Roman* (a Romanian). Some schools continue to segregate children, but the situation is being addressed. In 2005 the government agreed to a detailed **European Union**–inspired education project that includes integrating Roma children into the main school system.

Romany organizations currently operating include the Ethnic Federation of Roma, the Young Generation of Roma, the United Association of Roma, the **Aven Amentza Foundation**, and **Rromani CRISS**. The last is a national body linking Gypsy associations. One Gypsy is in the upper house of Parliament. In 2003 there were two Romany members of the lower house (Chamber of Deputies). The former Romany minority representative joined the PSD party and sat in the Chamber, while the constitution and electoral legislation then allowed an extra seat for the Roma.

After being discouraged under Ceausescu, Romany musicians are now active. Aside from the band **Taraf de Haidouks**, Taraf din Baiai and Mahala Rai Banda are other popular groups. There are also many solo artists, such as the fiddlers Romica Puceanu, Faramita Lambru, and Alexandru Titrus, the last of whom performed at the third **World Romany Congress.**

ROMANO. Denmark. The country's oldest Gypsy organization, founded by Johannes and Fanny Folkessen. The current spokesperson is Erik Stöttrup Thomsen, elected in 2000.

ROMANO CENTRO. Vienna, Austria. Est. 1991. President: Dragan Jevremović. A cultural and welfare center that publishes a regular magazine. *See also* RROMANO CENTAR.

ROMANO CHAVO ("ROMANY YOUNG PERSON"). A term used by some groups in eastern Europe as a self-denomination.

ROMANO DIVES. *See* ROMA NATION DAY; RROMANO DIVES.

ROMANO DROM ("ROMANY WAY"). Hungary. **Music** group, some of whose members were previously in the band **Ando Drom.** They play **Vlah** music in a popular style. Antal Kovacs (?–2005) was their leader, succeeded by his son Antal. CDs: *Ando foro* [In the Town] and *Ande lindri* [In a Dream].

ROMANO DROM SCHOOLS. United Kingdom. The Romano Drom (Romany Way) schools were established in **England** and **Wales** by the **Gypsy Council** around 1970 to provide **education** in **caravans** for **nomadic** Gypsies. They were absorbed into official Traveller Education Services.

ROMANO ROM. Hungary. A **clan** of **Vlah** Gypsies.

ROMANO THEM. *See* SLOVENIA; THEM ROMANO.

ROMANO VODI. Czech Republic. This magazine, financially supported by the **Czech** Ministry of Culture and based in Prague, was first published in February 2003.

ROMANÓ-KALÓ. A development of **Caló** in **Spain**. Its aim is to reintroduce the lost grammar of the **Romani language** with the preserved vocabulary of Caló. The magazine *Nevipens Romani* (Romani News) sometimes publishes in this form of speech. **Juan de Dios Heredia Ramírez** is one of the leading proponents of this program.

ROMANOV, MANUSH. *See* ALIEV, MUSTAFA.

ROMANY. An older spelling of *Romani.* This dictionary uses *Romany* for all purposes except for the **Romani language**.

ROMANY AND TRAVELLER FAMILY HISTORY SOCIETY. United Kingdom. Coordinator: Janet Keet-Black. A nonprofit self-help group for those interested in research on Gypsy and **Traveler** family history, particularly in the United Kingdom. The society has published a number of booklets.

ROMANY CHAL (CHEL). The name of a **clan**, sometimes used as self-ascription by Gypsies in **England** and Scandinavia. In **France**— in the form *romanichel*—it has become a pejorative term. *Chal* is possibly a loan from Hungarian *csalad* (family).

ROMANY GUILD. United Kingdom. Est. 1972. Founded in 1972 by Gypsies, this group was led by the late **Tom Lee**, who felt that the non-Gypsy members of the **Gypsy Council** were too influential. Later it reunited for a short time with the Gypsy Council under the name **National Gypsy Council**. After the death of Lee, its activities waned but members of the Lee family are trying to reestablish it as a cultural nonpolitical organization.

ROMANY GYPSY COUNCIL. United Kingdom. Chair: Mrs. Bendell-Smith. Local organization in southwest **England** that supports and advises Gypsies and **Travelers** in the fields of accommodation and welfare.

ROMANY INSTITUTE. United Kingdom. Est. 1968. Set up in Great Britain after the first **World Romany Congress** with the support of

Slobodan Berberski. It carried on the work of the Cultural Commission of the Congress until the third **World Romany Congress.**

ROMANY STUDIES. *See* GYPSY STUDIES.

ROMANY THEATRE COMPANY. Ipswich, England. Est. 2002. Artistic director: Daniel Allum. The **theater** company aims at helping young Romanies have an opportunity to act. In its choice of plays, it hopes to build a bridge between the Gypsy and non-Gypsy.

ROMANY TOWER. United Kingdom. Est. 2003. An organization in London, running English-language, **drama**, and **dance** classes, mainly for **Polish** Romanies.

ROMATHAN. Slovakia. Est. 1992. A **theater** in **Košice** using the **Romani language.**

ROMEN THEATER (MOSCOW). *See* TEATR ROMEN.

ROMERIA. The name given to Gypsy festivals in **Spain.**

ROMEROS, THE. Contemporary **music** group from the French Camargue region, influenced by **flamenco** and rumba. CD: *Torero.*

ROMI. Spain. Est. 1990. Association of **women**. Its aims include raising the status of women within the Gypsy community and increasing their participation in **education** and public life.

ROMINTERPRESS. Yugoslavia. Est. 1995. Initiator: **Dragoljub Acković**. RomInterpress is a cultural organization set up with the main aim of publishing **films**, books, and periodicals. It intends to coordinate the activities of the Gypsy elite in **Yugoslavia**, to establish a Gypsy news agency, and to arrange cultural events, including film shows, of Romany interest.

ROM-LEBEDEV, IVAN (1903–1989). Russia. Author and songwriter. He was active in the 1930s. Some of his songs have been recorded by artists of the **Teatr Romen.**

ROMNEWS. A fax and e-mail news service from the **Romani National Congress** in Hamburg.

ROSE, JENTINA. England. Contemporary singer. She was brought up in Woking, Surrey, in a large traditional Romany family alongside seven brothers and six sisters. She is much appreciated by the "chavs"—teenagers who follow the latest clothes fashions. Her debut single, "Bad Ass Stripper," reached number 20 in the **music** charts in 2004. In the same year, she released another single, "French Kisses."

ROSE, ROMANI. Germany. Contemporary civil rights activist. A **Sinto**, he is secretary of the **Verband der Deutschen Sinti und Roma**. He has written extensively on Gypsy rights, in particular those of the Sinti as a long-standing minority living in **Germany**.

ROSTÁS-FARKAS, GYÖRGY. Hungary. Contemporary writer and political activist. He is president of the cultural association Cigány Tudományos és Müvészeti Társaság (Gypsy Scientific and Art Society) and organizer of several international Gypsy conferences held in Budapest since 1993.

ROTARU, IONEL. *See* VAIDA VOEVOD III.

ROTWELSCH. A variety of German and the speech of the **Jenisch**, non-Romany nomads in **Germany**. It was used before the arrival of the Gypsies, but has since borrowed words from Romani.

ROUDA, VANKO. Algeria. Contemporary civil rights activist. He worked for Romany rights in postwar Europe together with his brother Leulea. In the early 1950s, while living in North Africa, he read a newspaper report of a speech by **Vaida Voevod III**. He then came to Paris and worked with the latter in the **Communauté Mondiale Gitane**. Later, Rouda was to set up the **Comité International Tzigane**.

RROM. In the standard **alphabet** adopted by the fourth **World Romany Congress**, *Rom* is spelled *Rrom*. There are two *r* sounds in most Romani **dialects**. The one that is retroflex or guttural (depending on the dialect) is written *rr* in the standard alphabet, and the trilled *r* is written with a single *r*. (For names beginning with Rromani or Rromano, try also looking under entries for Romani/Romany and Romano.)

RROMANI BAXT ("ROMANY GOOD FORTUNE"). Poland. Est. 1991. Chairperson: **Marcel Cortiade.** An international organization developing **educational** and cultural projects in **Albania** and elsewhere.

RROMANI CEXRAIN ("ROMANI STAR"). Spain. A contemporary cultural and social action organization.

RROMANI CRISS. Romania. Est. 1993. Director: **Nicolae Gheorghe.** The Center for Social Intervention and Studies (CRISS)is based in Bucharest. The center is currently engaged in **human rights** activities, including local social action mainly in **Romania**, the documentation of violence, and training for mediators.

RROMANO CENTAR. Austria. Contemporary band, led by fiddler Pera Petrovic, whose members are originally from **Voivodina** but now live in Vienna. CD: *Pilem, pilem* [I Drank].

RROMANO DIVES ("GYPSY DAY"). Albania. Band, founded in 1991, which has toured to other countries. The lead female singer is Astrit Qerimi (Titi). CD: *Chaj Zibede*.

RUDJEVICS, KARLIS (KARLO RUDEVITCH). Lithuania. Contemporary writer.

RUMANIA. *See* ROMANIA.

RUSSIA. The 2002 Census for the Russian Republic recorded 183,000 Gypsies, which may be closer to the real figure than earlier estimates of 400,000. There are two main **dialects** of Romani spoken in Russia: **Haladitko**, the dialect that was used in the **education** program of the 1930s in the **Soviet Union**, and Servi in southern Russia. A contemporary **poet** writing under the pen name

Sandor uses the latter dialect. Toward the end of the 19th century, there was an influx of **Vlah** Romanies. The overwhelming majority of Roma in Russia are Orthodox; a small group of Crimean Roma are Muslims.

The first record of Gypsies in territory that would later become part of Russia dates from around 1500. They entered from **Wallachia** but are distinct from the later arrivals of Vlah Gypsies. On the whole, there was less persecution under the tsars than in western Europe. In 1759 a law promulgated by Empress Elizabeth prohibited **nomadic** Gypsies from entering St. Petersburg. Passports were imposed in an attempt to control nomadism in 1775. In 1783 Gypsies were given equal rights as citizens, and in 1856 a decree confirmed that they were liable to military service.

Many **musicians** were adopted by nobles and made a good living, as Gypsy music and songs were much appreciated. Count Orlov set up one of many Gypsy choirs formed from families living and working on the large estates at the beginning of the 19th century, and the Tolstoy family, among others, patronized these choirs. Leo Tolstoy's brother and son (Sergei) both married Gypsies. Aleksei N. Apukhtin wrote *The Old Gypsies* in 1870 to commemorate the growing love between Sergei Tolstoy and Maria Shishkin. In 1919, when the tsarist government collapsed, some Gypsy singers accompanied their patrons to the west. One of these was V. Dimitrova. A record of hers was pessimistically, though not realistically, entitled *La dernière des voix tsiganes* [The Last of the Gypsy Voices].

After the Bolshevik Revolution of 1917 and the subsequent civil war, Russia became part of the Union of Soviet Socialist Republics until 1991. Information on this period will be found under the SOVIET UNION entry.

Following the political changes in 1991 and the breakup of the USSR, the social situation slowly became worse for Gypsies in Russia as the curbs on open expression of racial hatred disappeared. Under Mikhail Gorbachev, right-wing and nationalist groups were still kept under control, but after the succession of Boris Yeltsin, the hatred toward minorities came into the open. Anti-Gypsy pogroms have been reported from Nyevil, Ostrov, Safornovo, and Yeroslavni, in the Urals, and near Moscow. Among many reported incidents, in

September 2003 a group of skinhead teenagers attacked a family of Gypsies from the **Lyuli** clan in St. Petersburg with knives and chains, killing a six-year-old girl. The attackers were given light prison sentences while the police detained all the residents of the Gypsy camp and expelled them from the town. In June 2004 Roma had to leave Pskov after threats from skinhead gangs. The remaining Roma left the town of Iskitim (Novosibirsk region) after a series of attacks culminating in November 2005 when a child died as a result of an arson attack on two houses.

However, the overall political situation has gradually improved, and in 1999 the Russian government granted the Romany Association (Romano Kher) full cultural autonomy. The president of the association is Prof. George Demeter. There are currently some 16 branches of the association in different regions and cities of Russia, organized by Alexander Bariyev. There is also an influential Romany council of elders headed by Gen. Yan Rechetnikov. It deals with disputes between Roma and the authorities and operates throughout the Commonwealth of Independent States (CIS) and the Baltic States. Moscow holds an annual international festival of Romany **music** and **dance**, run by Y. Mauer and Georgi Tsvetkov, and there are numerous local competitions, concerts, festivals, and fairs. Roma from Russia helped to establish the **International Union of the Roma of the Baltic States and the Commonwealth of Independent States**.

Some cultural activity has taken place in Russia since the political changes. For example, a dictionary of the **Kalderash dialect** has been published.

– S –

SAARTO, TUULA. Finland. Contemporary writer. She has written a biography of her father-in-law, Kalle Hagert, a well-known figure in Gypsy circles, as well as a book for young people entitled *Suljetut ovet* [Closed Doors], which aims at dispelling the prejudice against Gypsies.

ST. GEORGE'S DAY. This day is celebrated by both Christian and Muslim Gypsies on 5/6 May according to the Orthodox calendar.

Scholars have seen relics of the **Indian** Baisakhi (New Year's Day) rituals in the celebrations—for example, the custom in **Skopje, Macedonia**, of going to a river and bringing back from it bottles of water.

ST. SARAH. *See* SAINTES MARIES DE LA MER.

SAINTES MARIES DE LA MER. A town in southern **France** where a pilgrimage of Gypsies occurs in May every year. The two saints of the town's name are Marie-Jacobé and Marie-Salomé, followers of Jesus who, according to legend, arrived by boat at the town after fleeing from Palestine after the crucifixion. They were accompanied by their Gypsy maid, Sarah, whose statue is in the church.

SAMPSON, JOHN **(1862–1931).** England. Librarian and scholar. He worked at Liverpool University from 1892 until 1928. With the help of **Dora Yates**, he compiled the comprehensive study *The Dialect of the Gypsies of Wales* (1926), the result of his collaboration with the family of **Abraham Wood**. In 1894, he had met Edward Wood, a harpist who spoke Romani fluently, and he extended his research during a stay at Abergynolwyn. Together with Yates, he recorded folktales and songs of the language and spent many hours with the descendants of Abraham Wood, specifically in the company of violinist Matthew Wood. He translated some 50 verses of the *Rubaiyat* of Omar Khayyam (a tentmaker who may well have been a Romany) into Welsh Romani, with the aid of D. Macalister. Many of his articles were published in the *Journal of the Gypsy Lore Society*.

SANDFORD, JEREMY **(1934–2003).** England. Writer and amateur **musician**. He became well known for his play *Cathy Come Home*, dealing with the issue of the homeless. He had many friends among the Gypsy and **New Traveler** communities and was for a short time editor of the periodical *Romano Drom*. His books include *The Gypsies*, reissued as *Rokkering to the Gorgios* (2002), and *Songs of the Road*, in addition to the music video *Spirit of the Gypsies*.

SAPERA. *See* KALBELIA.

SARAJEVO. Bosnia. In the years leading up to World War II, there were four distinct Romany **clans** in the city: A few Muslim Gypsies lived on the outskirts of the town, some assimilated Muslim Gypsies lived among non-Gypsies in Sarajevo itself, and a clan of non-Romani-speaking Christian Gypsies and some **Vlah** Gypsies were **nomadizing** in the region. Following the recent fighting, a small number still remain in the town. *See also* BOSNIA-HERZEGOVINA; SARAJEVO CONFERENCE; SARAJEVO PEACE CONFERENCES.

SARAJEVO CONFERENCE (1986). A scientific conference of Gypsy and non-Gypsy experts was held in what was then the peaceful town of **Sarajevo, Yugoslavia**. Speakers included the veteran scholar **Rade Uhlik**, who was living nearby. The conference was particularly remarkable in that Romani was used as a major language either as the language of papers or for translation. The papers of the conference were edited by Milan Šipka and have been published.

SARAJEVO PEACE CONFERENCES. The **International Romani Union** decided in 1994 to sponsor a conference for peace in the Balkans. At the time, it was thought that this conference could be held in **Sarajevo**. In the end, however, it was decided to hold it in May 1995 in Budapest, **Hungary**. The program covered issues pertaining to the Romanies and to international relations in general. Because of the success of this conference, a second one was held in 1996. Again it was felt premature to hold the conference in Sarajevo, so instead it was held in the town of Gasteiz (Vitoria) in the Basque country of **Spain**.

SARAY, JOZSI. Hungary. A Gypsy boy adopted by composer **Franz Liszt**. Liszt talks of him in his book *Des Bohémiens et de leur musique en Hongrie* (1859).

SARDINIA. The first record of Gypsies here stems from the records of the Sardinian Parliament in the middle of the 16th century (1553–1554) discussing the problem they are causing.

SARI, ANNELI. Finland. Contemporary singer. She is the sister of Feija and Taisto from the band **Hortto Kaalo**. Her repertoire is mainly light **music** by **Finnish** composers. She has performed in **France** and was one of the stars at the concert that took place in Geneva during the third **World Romany Congress**.

SASTIPEN NETWORK. Spain. European network for drug abuse and HIV/AIDS prevention in the Rom community.

SATKIEVICH, NIKOLAI (1917–1991). Union of Soviet Socialist Republics. **Poet** and civil rights activist. He was enthusiastic about **education** and went to great lengths to get Siberian Roma children to attend school, including using the police.

SATTLER, JAJA (?–1944). Germany. Missionary. While his family was living in a **caravan** in Berlin, he was sent by missionaries to study at a convent in Marburg. After this, he took up missionary activities himself. Sattler translated St. John's Gospel and some of the Psalms into the **Lovari dialect** of Romani. In 1944, he was deported to the concentration camp at **Auschwitz**, where he was killed.

SAVCHEV, SLAVCHO. Bulgaria. Contemporary journalist. He was the editor of *Andral* (Outwards), a literary periodical in Romani (Sliven **dialect**) and **Bulgarian**.

SCHNUCKENACH, REINHARDT (1921–). Germany. Violinist. His **musical** studies at Mainz Conservatoire were stopped when the Nazis deported him to **Poland**. With Reinhardt Daweli, he later formed the Schnuckenach-Reinhardt Quintet, which played Gypsy jazz in the style of **Django Reinhardt**. His recordings are included in the four-volume collection *Musik deutscher Zigeuner*.

SCOTLAND. Estimated population of Romanies, **Scottish Travelers**, and **Irish Travelers**: 4,000; on the basis of the 2003 census, it appears that some 560 families live year-round in **caravans**. In 1491 there is a record of "Spaniards" **dancing** before the Scottish king on the pavement at Edinburgh, although these may not have been Romanies. In 1505 a small party of Gypsies arrived—probably also from **Spain**— saying they were pilgrims and being given money by James IV. They were then sent to **Denmark** with a letter of recommendation. A second group of dancers from Spain in 1529 undoubtedly were Romanies. This group danced for James V. There is a record in 1540 of the king granting the Gypsies the right to their own laws and customs under **John Faa**, Duke of **Little Egypt**, in 1540. A year later, however, this decree was repealed and all Gypsies were ordered to leave Scotland, allegedly because James V—who had the custom of traveling in disguise around the country—had been in a fight with three Gypsies. He died in the following year, so this law was not carried out. In 1553 John Faa was again confirmed as officially being in charge of the Scottish Gypsies.

In 1573, a law was passed that Gypsies should either leave the country or settle down in paid work. If not, they would be imprisoned, publicly scourged, and removed from the realm. A year later, the law was strengthened: Gypsies were to be scourged and branded. Those who remained and did not settle down would be executed. In 1597 forced labor or banishment for life were added as punishments. The 17th century brought in heavy penalties against not only Gypsies but also anyone who aided them. In 1608 two Scots—David Gray and Alexander Aberdere—were fined for selling food and drink to Gypsies. Noblemen who protected Gypsies on their estates were fined as well. In 1611 three Gypsies were brought to trial and hanged. In 1624 eight more Gypsy men were hanged at Burgh Muir. Further executions took place, and then banishment became a regular treatment for Gypsies. In 1665 a Scottish company received permission to send Gypsies to Jamaica and Barbados.

The Scottish Parliament was dissolved in 1707, and all future legislation was made in London until devolution late in the 20th century. After 1707 the existing Acts against Gypsies of **England** (1530, 1554, and 1562) were applied in Scotland. In 1714 two female Gypsies were executed under the provisions of the 1554 Act, and 10 Gypsies were deported in 1715 from Scotland to Virginia in accordance with the English 1598 Act for the Punishment of Rogues, Vagabonds and Sturdy Beggars. The heavy pressure on Romanies in Scotland led to their virtual disappearance until the 20th century. They either moved to England or hid themselves among bands of native Scottish Travelers to escape arrest and punishment.

The Trespass (Scotland) Act of 1865 was introduced in the London Parliament to control the indigenous Scottish Travelers and has been used up to the present day to move Travelers and Gypsies on from stopping places. The British **Caravan Sites Act of 1968** did not apply to Scotland, although the 1994 **Criminal Justice and Public Order Act**—which further criminalizes trespass—does.

An **Advisory Committee on Travellers** was set up in 1971 and has produced several reports. Scottish local authorities have been encouraged to build caravan sites for the Scottish Travelers and the small numbers of Irish Travelers and Romanies from England who visit the country. A target of 941 plots was set, of which 742 had been provided by 1996. Authorities with insufficient campsites are asked to apply a toleration policy toward illegally parked caravans. The scheme by which the government gives grants was due to end in 1998 but was continued by the autonomous Scottish Parliament.

In 2001 the Scottish Parliament's Equal Opportunities Committee made a number of recommendations concerning **Travelers**, but these have not been put into practice. In October 2005 a committee of members of the Scottish Parliament led by Labour MP Cathy Peattie criticized the slow pace of progress on the earlier recommendations. The Scottish Travelers have, however, been given the status of a "racial group."

SCOTTISH GYPSY/TRAVELLER ASSOCIATION. Scotland. Est. 1993. Set up to unite Gypsies and **Scottish Travelers** to campaign for their rights. It has organized several conferences and occasionally published a magazine.

SCOTTISH TRAVELERS. It is likely that there were traveling **nomads** in **Scotland** before the arrival of the Romanies. Therefore, we cannot be sure whether records in the Middle Ages refer to indigenous Scottish Travelers or Romanies. Over the centuries, the two groups have mingled and intermarried, and the present-day population of Scottish Travelers is of mixed descent. They call themselves **Nawkins**. The Scottish Travelers have a rich tradition of singing and have preserved many ballads. Singers include the **Stewart family**, while contemporary folk-story tellers include Jimmy McBeath and **Duncan Williamson**. Most **Travelers** speak a variety of English known as **cant**, with an "exotic" vocabulary of words from a number of sources. In the northeast of Scotland, the cant is based on a Gaelic framework.

SCOTTISH TRAVELLERS' ACTION GROUP (STAG). Scotland. A civil rights group operating around 1970 and cooperating with the **Gypsy Council in England**.

SCOTTISH TRAVELLERS' COUNCIL. Scotland. Active around 1985. A civil rights group initiated by singers **Belle Stewart** and **Lizzie Higgins**.

SČUKA, EMIL. Czechoslovakia. Contemporary political and cultural activist. He was elected secretary of the **International Romani Union** at the fourth **World Romany Congress** and president at the fifth congress. He is also president of the **Rajko Djurić Foundation**.

SEFEROV, SULI (SAMUIL) **(1943–).** Bulgaria. **Artist**. He is a painter who was brought up in a district of Sofia inhabited by many Gypsies and who painted Romanies, among other subjects. He has exhibited in many countries.

SEJDIĆ, RASIM (1943–1980). Yugoslavia. **Poet**. He was also a collector of folktales from **Yugoslavia**. His poem "Gazisarde Romengi violina" [They Smashed the Romanies' Violin] commemorates the concentration camp at **Jasenovac**.

SEPEDJI. Turkish for "Basket Maker." The Basket Makers of the Shumen area in **Bulgaria** and those of **Turkey** and **Greece** speak different **dialects** of Romani and are not related.

SERBEZOVSKI, MUHAREM (1950–). Macedonia. **Musician**. He was one of the first Roma musicians to be a commercial success in **Yugoslavia** in the 1970s. As a professional vocalist, he sang in **Macedonian**, **Serbian**, and Romani. As well as being a musician, he is also known for writing short stories and **poems**, and in 1983 he published his first book, *Shareni Dijamanti*, in Serbo-Croatian.

SERBIA. Estimated population (including **Voivodina** and **Kosovo** but excluding **Montenegro**): 600,000. It is likely that the first Gypsies to reach Serbia were shoemakers who lived in Prizren some time around 1348. Under the **Ottoman Empire** (from 1459), the Gypsies were classed as one of the many ethnic groups in the country. No overall census figures are available for the Gypsy population at that time. The Viennese Gypsiologist Franz Miklosich reported that there were some 25,000 Gypsies in Serbia in the 1860s. At one time, the **Turkish** rulers of the country attempted to ban **nomadism**, but they were not successful. Many **Vlah** Gypsies came after the emancipation of the slaves in **Romania**, joining earlier immigrants from across the Danube who had by the end of the 18th century already become sedentary.

From 1878 Serbia was independent. In 1879 and 1884 the new state passed laws to prohibit Gypsies from nomadizing, and in 1891 there was an order that Gypsies who were not settled and without an **occupation** should be reported to the authorities. Foreign Gypsies were to be expelled. The censuses at the end of the 19th century showed around 50,000 Gypsies in Serbia. About half claimed Romani as the mother tongue, and 25 percent were Muslim.

In 1918 Serbia became part of **Yugoslavia**, until 1941 when it came under military rule by the **German** Army. Soon after the German conquest of Yugoslavia, regulations forbade Gypsies in Serbia to use public transport or cafés. They had to wear an armband with the letter Z on it. At first the Germans took Gypsy men to act as hostages and then shot them in reprisal for the deaths of German soldiers at the hands of Partisans. The **women** and children were placed in a concentration camp at Zemun (Semlin). Many were killed in gassing vans. Harald Turner—head of the German military administration—reported to Berlin that the "Gypsy problem had been solved," as he wanted to concentrate on the fight against the Partisans. However, large numbers were still living outside Belgrade. The German occupying forces began to round up Gypsies in Niš in eastern Serbia and imprison them at a concentration camp at Crveni Krst. Again many were shot in reprisals for attacks on German soldiers. During the German occupation of Serbia, some 30,000 Gypsies were killed.

In 1944 Yugoslavia was reestablished as a republic. The 1971 census recorded 49,894 Romanies for Serbia (including Voivodina and

Kosovo) and 396 for Montenegro, an unbelievably low figure, even allowing for the losses during the Nazi period.

In 1991–1992 Yugoslavia was split again. Only Serbia (including Voivodina and Kosovo) and Montenegro remained in the Yugoslav Republic, which was renamed Serbia and Montenegro. After 1993 the Serbian government made some efforts to get its Gypsy population to support the government. Government officials attended an official church service in Romani and subsidies were given to newspapers. **Poet Trifun Dimić** was able to publish the New Testament in Romani as well as a first reader for schools. One cloud in the picture was the harassment of **Rajko Djurić**, who was forced to flee the country because of his opposition to Serbia's support for the **Bosnian Serbs**.

The 1991 census gave a figure of 70,126 Roma in Serbia (excluding Kosovo and Voivodina). The figures were rising steadily, which reflected not merely the high birth rate of the population but also increasing self-confidence and willingness to be recognized as Roma at the start of the 1990s. However, there still remains some way to go before the recorded population reaches the estimated real figure of 600,000. Roma in Yugoslavia can be classified by **religion** (Orthodox, Catholic, or Muslim) or language (**Erlia** or a range of **dialects** used by previously nomadic groups such as the **Gurbet**). This applies equally to Serbia and **Montenegro**.

Before the breakup of the federal state, the Roma in Serbia had made attempts to get their status raised to that of a national minority, a desire that was voiced at academic conferences in Belgrade in 1976 as well as Novi Sad (Voivodina) in 1990 and 1997. In the terms of the 1991 Constitution of Serbia, the Roma had the lowest status, the third rank, as an "ethnic group."

The Romany Congress Party was founded at a meeting in Belgrade in 1997 on the symbolic date of 8 April (declared as **Roma Nation Day** at the first **World Romany Congress**) and soon had a membership of 2,000. One of its aims is for Roma to attain the status of a national minority. Its president, **Dragoljub Acković**, is editor of the magazine *Romano Lil*.

Yet, in spite of more overt Belgrade government support for Roma, police harassment is common and street traders are a prime target. There have been reports of isolated cases of racist attacks on Roma, though Romany leaders have said they hear of such attacks in Belgrade every two or three days. Skinheads are active. In one reported incident in September 1996, they assaulted Roma in Kraljevo. Graffiti saying "Death to Roma" have appeared in Kragujevac, while houses have been set on fire in some places. A Romany, Dragan Dimitrijević, insulted and beaten by police in Kragujevac in 1999, did not get justice until five years later, in November 2004, when the **United Nations** Committee against Torture gave the Serbian government 90 days to start the long delayed investigation of this attack.

Prejudice is widespread, and some villages will not allow the Roma to bury their dead in Orthodox cemeteries. There have been cases of discrimination in bars in Raska. In October 1997 the Serbian daily *Nedeljini Telegraf* published an article entitled "We Shall Expel the Roma, Negroes, Gays and Junkies and Create a Great White Serbia," quoting the words of skinheads from Novi Sad. In April 2001, the Roma cemetery in Niš was brutally violated, and the grave belonging to **Sait Balić**, a prominent Roma activist, was particularly badly damaged.

Even before the current economic depression, living conditions for Roma were inadequate, and in some parts of Serbia, life expectancy for Roma is only 29–33 years. Unemployment is high, and such work as the Roma have is usually of low status, such as day laborers, herdsmen, skinners, street sweepers, or cemetery workers. Meat is rarely on the menu in the Romany home and clothing is poor. Child allowances have not always been paid to Roma and **Albanians**.

The majority of Romany children do not complete primary **education** and the cultural association Matica Romska accepts that more than 80 percent of the Romani population is illiterate. One reason is that 30 percent of Romany children arrive at primary school with no knowledge of Serbian because of the isolation of their communities, and there is little preschool provision by which they could learn the language of the education system. Less than 1 percent of Roma have completed higher education. There is, however, a Romany Cultural Federation, whose members must have at least a college degree. Members of the federation were active in founding the Romany Congress Party. As elsewhere in eastern Europe, a number of Romany children are placed in special schools, not because of lack of intelligence but after failing tests designed for those living in a different culture.

Organizations having a responsibility other than culture and political activity include the [Romany] Committee for the Protection of **Human Rights** in Yugoslavia, founded in 1997 and based in Kragujevac, and the Society for the Improvement of Romany Settlements, established under the leadership of architect Vladmirt Macura and sociologist Aleksandrea Mitrović. *See also* CROATIA; MACEDONIA; MONTENEGRO; SLOVENIA.

SERBOIANU, POPP. Romania. Priest. He set up a nationwide Gypsy organization in 1933, the Asociatia Generala a Tiganilor din **Romania** (General Association of the Gypsies of Romania). One of his committee members, **Lazarescu Lazurica**, broke away and set up the rival General Union of the Gypsies of Romania. Popp continued to be active in the Oltenia region, together with **poet** Marin Simion. In 1933, he also set up a Chimney Sweeps Guild, which acted as a front for Gypsy civil rights activities. A conference was planned for the Romanies of Oltenia for late 1934, but before this took place, there was a further split, this time between Popp and Simion. The former's influence then waned. In 1934 Lazurica resigned from the presidency of the General Union and **Gheorghe Niculescu**, a flower dealer from Bucharest became president. Simion joined the Union and helped to set up their magazine *O Rom*. Lazurica then allied himself once more with Popp, but Niculescu remained the most powerful Gypsy leader, and his association continued work until 1940. The **nomadic** Gypsies did not take part in either of the two organizations but recognized as their leader the **Kalderash** Bulibaša Gheorghe Mihutescu.

SERGUNIN, IAKOV (IAN ALEKSANDROVICH RESHETNIKOV) (1954–2004). Union of Soviet Socialist Republics. Army officer and politician. He studied at the **Soviet** Military Academy and had a Ph.D. in law. He was at one time vice prime minister of Chechnya. After returning from Chechnya, he lived in Moscow and actively participated in the Roma movement. He published a book on the **human rights** of Roma, *Legal Self-Defence*, financed the creation of the Web page *Gypsies of Russia*, and created a fund for the support of minorities called Tolerance. Sergunin was murdered on 25 June 2004.

SEVILLE CONGRESS. *See* EUROPEAN CONGRESS.

SHAKESPEARE, WILLIAM **(1564–1616)**. England. Playwright. By Shakespeare's time, Gypsies were well known throughout **England** and the playwright could make references to them in his plays. He sometimes calls them "**Egyptians**" and sometimes Gypsies. In *Othello* (first performed in 1604), Desdemona talks of a handkerchief that "an Egyptian gave to my mother." It has been suggested that the name of the character Caliban in *The Tempest* comes from the Romani word *kaliben* meaning "blackness."

SHELTA. (1) The name used by scholars for **Irish Travelers' cant**. (2) A secret vocabulary from the Middle Ages formed by changing the first consonant of a word. An example is the word *feen* (man) from Irish *duine*. According to some scholars, it is one of the sources of vocabulary for **Travelers'** cant. The name *Shelta* itself is probably formed from the Irish word *béarla*, which originally meant "language."

SHERO (SZERO) ROM. Romany chief. The leader of the Lowland Gypsies in **Poland**. In 1890, Baso was elected to this office. He founded a hereditary dynasty that continued until at least 1976. In 1946 his grandson, Felus, was deposed for breaking the **Mageripen** code, but was purified in 1950 to take up leadership again, until 1975 when he was succeeded by his second cousin. *See also* KINGS.

SHUKAR COLLECTIVE. The name given to an ad hoc group of Romanian **musicians** whose playing was remixed for the CD *Urban Gypsy*. Not to be confused with the **Slovenian** group **Šukar**.

SHUTO (ŠUTO) ORIZARI. Popularly called Shutka. Shutka is a satellite town outside **Skopje** in **Macedonia**. It grew rapidly after the Skopje earthquake of 1963 when large numbers of Gypsies from the town were resettled there in houses donated by foreign governments. Numbers increased further as the result of a decision by Gypsies themselves to leave the old Gypsy quarter of Topana and move into the new town. By the mid-1970s Shuto Orizari had its own district council, offices, a cinema, and a soccer field. Some 5,000 more houses were subsequently built, assisted by the granting of free building land and flexible town planning regulations, and it became the only place in Europe where Gypsies were not a minority. The estimated population in 1977 was 40,000 and is now perhaps double this. The inhabitants are 90 percent Romany. However, facilities in Shutka are poor. There is one ambulance, and specialist medical care is lacking while the standard of **education** in the two primary schools is low.

SHUVANI ROMANI DANCE KUMPANIA. Australia. Coordinator: Margaret Cunningham. A mainly non-Romany **dance** ensemble that has tried to recreate the **music** and dances of 14th-century Romanies.

SICILY. The earliest definitive reference to Gypsies on the island dates from 1485 and refers to a horse dealer named Michele Petta. The first Gypsies had probably arrived some years earlier and from the Balkans by sea rather than from the mainland of **Italy**. In 1521 Duke Giovanni came with a group of followers and a safe conduct pass from Charles V. This party had previously been in **Spain** and passed down through Italy. For some time, the nomadic Gypsies enjoyed a limited form of self-government under their leaders. During the Fascist period, some Gypsy families from Italy were deported to Sicily. The island also has a population of non-Romany **Travelers** known as Camminanti.

SIM. A secret vocabulary based on Arabic used by the Helebi Gypsies of **Egypt**.

SIMFEROPOL. A town in the **Ukraine** where Gypsies settled after 1874. During the 1930s, there was a strong cultural life with a Gypsy Club—Ugolka Demirdji (Ironworkers Circle)—and a soccer team. However, the Romany population of some 800 was all massacred by the **German** occupiers in December 1941.

SINTE UNION. Freiburg, Germany. Under the leadership of Oskar Bierkenfelder, the Union operates independently of the **Verband der Deutschen Sinti und Roma**. It took part in the 1981 **World Romany Congress**.

SINTI (SINTE; *singular* SINTO). The term may originate with the **Indian** province of Sindh, or it may be an old Indian word meaning "community." It is a **clan** living mainly in **Germany** but with some families now established in **Belgium**, the **Netherlands**, northern **Italy**, **Poland**, and **Russia**. It is likely that the Sinti came to German-speaking lands during the 16th century and **nomadized** there until the 19th century when some families moved into other countries. The **dialect** contains a large number of loan words from German. The Sinti suffered huge losses during the Nazi period. The German organization **Verband der Deutschen Sinti und Roma** in Heidelberg (led by **Romani Rose**) is their main civil rights mouthpiece. Sinti organizations also operate in the Netherlands.

The term *Sinti* is additionally used by the Sinti themselves for some Gypsy clans which are not linguistically Sinti, for example, the Istriani Sinti from the Trieste region and the **Lalore Sinti** from Bohemia and Moravia.

SINTI ALLIANZ DEUTSCHLAND. Cologne, Germany. Chairperson: Natascha Winter. The organization operates independently of the **Verband der Deutschen Sinti und Roma**.

SKOKRA. A coalition of Romany groups from **South and Central America**, the **United States**, and **Canada**. *See also* QUITO CONFERENCE.

SKOPJE. Capital of the Republic of **Macedonia** with a large Gypsy population. The Folklore Institute in Skopje has set up a Romany section under the direction of Trajko Petrovski. **Radio** and **television** broadcasts are aired in Romani. *See also* SHUTO ORIZARI.

SKOU, MATHIASSEN. Norway. Author. He was of mixed Norwegian and **Traveler** descent and wrote a book about the traveling life, *Paa fantestien* [On the Gypsy Trail], published in 1893. He then married a **Norwegian Traveler** and returned with her to become a **nomad** himself.

SLOVAKIA. Slovakia became an independent state in 1993. In 1989, figures held locally gave the number of Gypsies for the region as

253,943, but this excluded many who were not in receipt of any welfare support. According to the 2001 census, Roma number only 90,000, but experts estimate the population to be some 400,000. Apart from a group passing through Spissky in 1423, the earliest record of Gypsies in the territory of present-day Slovakia is of an execution in Levoca in 1534. They were accused of starting fires there and in other towns. Slovakia was part of the Austro-Hungarian Empire until 1918. **Maria Theresa** tried her assimilationist policy of settling the Gypsies, with some success. By the end of the 19th century, it was estimated that around 90 percent of Slovak Romanies were settled. There were also several thousand **nomadic Vlah** Gypsies who had emigrated from **Romania**. The settled Gypsies in general lived in isolated settlements and pursued a range of **occupations**, from blacksmiths and bricklayers to **musicians**.

In 1918 Slovakia became part of an independent **Czechoslovakia**. From the 1920s a strong nationalistic movement arose in Slovakia, and there was a pogrom in Pobedim in 1928 in which six Gypsies were killed. The anti-Semitic Slovenska Narodná Strana (Slovak People's Party) saw Gypsies as "an ulcer which must be cured in a radical way." This party gained between 25 and 40 percent of the votes in elections in the years after 1918 and paved the way for the establishment of a puppet Slovak state following the **German** invasion of Czechoslovakia in 1938.

In 1940 the fascist government imposed compulsory labor on Gypsies, and they were forbidden to enter parks or cafés or use public transport. The following year, all Gypsies living among Slovaks were ordered to move and build themselves new isolated settlements. From many areas, male adults were sent to labor camps. In 1944, after the failure of a popular uprising against the fascist regime, Gypsies were accused—in some cases wrongly—of helping the resistance movement. Massacres of men, **women**, and children took place in Cierny Balog, Ilija, Kriz nad Hronom, Slatina, Tisovec, and elsewhere. Anton Facuna and Tomas Farkas had been active in the Partisan movement and were decorated after the war.

In Slovakia more Gypsies survived the war than did in the **Czech** lands (Bohemia and Moravia), but discrimination continued after 1945. They are still referred to as "blacks" (*cierny*) by the Slovaks. The Communist National Front government tried to eliminate the shantytowns (with little success) and force the Gypsies into paid employment. There was some voluntary movement in the first years of peace after 1945 to the Czech lands, where they took the place of ethnic Germans who had been expelled. In 1958 the Act for the Permanent Settlement of Nomadic Persons prohibited nomadism and ordered local councils to help the integration of the ex-nomads. The Czechoslovak government tried to introduce compulsory resettlement of Gypsies from Slovakia to the Czech lands to eliminate the high concentrations of Romanies in some areas.

Sterilization was also introduced as a means of controlling the Gypsies' population growth. Reports say that the operation was still being carried out without the women's consent in some hospitals as late as 2003. In 2005 the **United Nations** Committee on the Elimination of Discrimination against Women issued a mild statement condemning the past practice, but this has been misrepresented by the Slovak government and press who still deny that forced sterilization took place.

Romanies are classed as a national minority. As well as their own cultural organizations, there are consultative bodies such as the Council for the Affairs of Minorities and specialized advisory bodies concerned with **education** and other fields. The central control of solutions to "Romany problems" was abolished by the new state and the responsibility given to local councils. Nevertheless, the national Ministry of Labor, Social Affairs, and the Family issued a resolution in April 1996 on "Citizens in Need of Special Care." This saw Romanies as a problem and a burden to the state.

Discrimination and prejudice continue. Graffiti can be seen on the walls proclaiming "White Slovakia" or "Gypsies to the gas chambers." The Slovak National Party is openly anti-Gypsy. The sometime prime minister Vladimir Meciar said that social welfare payments should be cut to stop the Gypsies from having so many children, and the minister of labor accused them of not wanting to work. Vitazoslav Moric, former deputy of the nationalist political party SNS, stated at a press conference in August 2000 that the Roma should be rounded up and put on reservations the way Native Americans were. His immunity was lifted and he was due to be prosecuted for incitement to racial hatred, but in 2003, authorities closed the investigation with no criminal charges filed. Another controversial former leader of the SNS, Jan Slota, publicly stated that the government should offer Roma money to undergo sterilization. He also said in 2000 that what was required to deal with Slovakia's Roma population was "a small courtyard and a whip." Also in 2000, Michael Drobny of the Movement for Democratic Slovakia compared Roma to locusts and said that they "must be isolated because coexistence is impossible."

In this atmosphere, it is not surprising that racist attacks—mainly but not always by skinheads—have been reported regularly. In July 1995 Mario Goral was killed by skinheads in Ziar nad Hronom. In the same month, masked policemen beat up Gypsies in Jarovnice. Skinhead violence against Roma continues to be a serious problem in the 21st century, and police remain reluctant to take action. In August 2000, Anastazia Balazova, a Romany mother of eight, died from injuries sustained in a brutal attack on her family in Zilina, northwest Slovakia. In August 2001, 18-year-old Milan Daniel suffered permanent brain damage after a beating by three fascist skinheads, during which his assailants used baseball bats and iron bars. When the police asked them for a motive, they replied that he was a "Rom."

Mario Bango was imprisoned in 2001, awaiting trial after intervening to help his brother Edo, who was being attacked by a skinhead. The skinhead was wounded in the fight and died a few weeks later. Despite waiting on the spot after the fight and calling an ambulance, Mario was arrested and taken to prison. Reports in the Slovak press stated that he and his brother were thieves who had been stopped by the skinhead, who was a "brave citizen." Parliament observed a minute's silence for the dead skinhead. The case has been largely ignored except by left-wing groups. The Supreme Court sentenced Mario to 10 years in prison for attempted murder.

Although the constitution prohibits such practices, there are many examples of police beating Roma. They reportedly have used threats and pressure to discourage Roma from pressing charges of police brutality. In January 1999, two police officers in the eastern Slovak city of **Kosice** conducted a raid on Roma households at one o'clock in the morning. The officers harassed families in 14 apartments, shouting racial slurs and pointing revolvers at them. The three Berkova sisters, aged between 13 and 15, were made to strip to the waist.

Additionally, police have often been found to be unwilling to investigate thoroughly crimes against Roma. Lawyers, too, are often reluctant to represent Roma for fear it will have a negative effect on their legal practices. In February 2002 a new Police Code of Conduct was introduced. Also in 2002, a special police unit to monitor extremist activities began operating at the Police Praesidium.

The public perception of Roma remains very negative. According to a newspaper survey, 50 percent of those questioned did not want to have a Romany neighbor. A 2001 study by the Institute for Public Questions and United Nations Development Program reported that 71 percent of the majority Slovak population believed that relations with Roma were to some degree conflict-ridden or unpleasant, while only 31.5 percent of Roma held the same view.

In 2003, the national unemployment rate dropped to less than 15 percent, but was as high as 95 percent in Roma settlements in eastern Slovakia. Roma continue to face discrimination in housing. In 1989, members of seven Romany families who were permanent residents in the towns of Nagov and Rokytovce in Medzilaborce County in the northeast were forced from their homes when their employer, an agricultural cooperative, ceased operations. No village in the county would allow these Roma to settle within their territory. Their return to Medzilaborce in 1997 sparked a series of meetings by local political leaders, culminating in the banning of Roma from settlement in the two municipalities. The resolutions were revoked in April 1999, but the municipalities did not acknowledge that the resolutions were illegal or provide any form of compensation to the victims.

Although the law requires state administrators to register all citizens, some local officials have refused to give registration stamps to Roma citizens, which in turn prevents them from receiving social benefits and housing. However, in October 2001 the majority of 88 apartments built in Presov with funding from the **European Union** were allocated to Romany families.

Roma are discriminated against in the health care system and have unequal access to public services. The mortality rate for children is three times that of the majority population, and the life expectancy for Roma was lower by almost 17 years. At the end of 2003, the government reduced welfare payments to families with children, a move that has had a disproportionate effect on Roma families. In

February 2004 there were violent clashes with the police during protests against these cuts in welfare payments.

In February 1999, Parliament created a special Parliamentary Advisory Committee for Roma Issues. Many political parties promised to place Roma on their candidate lists; however, only five received positions on a total of three lists; and none was elected to Parliament. Some ethnic Romany parties were successful at winning representation at local level, though. In 2003 the village of Bystrany in the Spisska Nova Veš district elected a Rom, Frantisek Pacan, as mayor. Nine other Roma were also elected to the local board, which for the first time consists entirely of Roma deputies.

The government's special program for Roma has a budget of 50 million koruny ($1.5 million). Furthermore, there is a 10-year strategy for the development of Roma, which includes elements of positive discrimination or affirmative action. In 2004 the Parliament adopted a new law on Equal Treatment and Protection against Discrimination in the hope of improving the situation of the country's Roma. The country in 2001 ratified the European Charter on the Use of Minority Languages, which provides that in municipalities with a minority constituting at least 20 percent of the population, the minority language is an official language. In 2003, Romani was theoretically an official language in 53 towns. There is, however, little use of Romani in educational establishments.

A high percentage of Romany children do not attend school regularly. Some efforts have been made to establish a preschool year where the Romany children can improve their knowledge of Slovak or **Hungarian** (where that is the local language). In 1992–1993, some primary schools in Košice opened bilingual classes in Slovak and Romani. On the whole, however, little attention is paid to the fact that the Romany children come to school not knowing the language of instruction. In 1999, kindergarten attendance among Romany children was only 15 percent, lower than previously. Parents often do not have the money to cover expenses of kindergarten or extracurricular activities in schools. Many continue to be placed in special schools or in schools and classes where the majority of the pupils are Roma. Once placed in a special school, their future prospects are very limited, because they are not given the possibility of completing the primary education course required for entrance to secondary schools and university. The best they can hope for is to find themselves a place at a training school for blue-collar workers. In 2003, there were only three Romany students enrolled in colleges of higher education in eastern Slovakia.

The Act on Public Service was amended in June 2002 to introduce assistant teachers for primary and nursery schools. This step is intended to facilitate the integration of Roma children into the standard educational system. Educational specialists have shown that a preparatory program for five-year-olds has shown that they can succeed without the need for special schools.

The major associations that exist have received grants since the new state was formed. They include the Cultural Society of Citizens of Romany Origin, Romany Culture, the Association of Romany Intelligentsia, and the Cultural Union of the Romany Community. Seventeen Romany associations met in 1993 and formed the Council of Romanies in Slovakia. After an initial impetus, however, the council has not been very active. In 1995, therefore, six Romany parties formed a new umbrella organization, the Union of Roma Political Parties in the Slovak Republic. The **Romani Civic Initiative** had had one seat in the regional Slovak Parliament from 1990, but it was unsuccessful in the elections of 1992 and 1995 that followed independence.

A new Romany organization has been set up in Slovakia. The Council of Slovak Roma (RRS), which held its first conference in Košice in January 2003, is chaired by Frantisek Gulas and has 15,000 members. The RRS will cooperate with other Romany organizations and work with the Slovak government to improve the situation for the country's Roma population. In 1991, a Department of Romany Culture was established at the Pedagogical Faculty in Nitra. A Romany professional **theater**, **Romathan**, has existed since 1992 at Košice, and a specialist music school is based in the town. There is some broadcasting in Romani—within the Hungarian service—and six bilingual periodicals.

SLOVENIA. The 2002 census puts the Gypsy population figure at 3,246. The 1971 Yugoslav census recorded 977 Romanies, while in the 1991 census (the last in the **Yugoslav** Federation) 2,293 had declared themselves as Roma and, inexplicably, a larger number—2,847—said

Romani was their mother tongue. A report from the Institute for Nationality Questions in Ljubljana gave a figure of 5,300 for the Gypsy population for 1997. Experts estimate the Gypsy population as 10,000. Gypsies live in three regions: Prekmurje and near the borders of **Austria** and **Hungary**; Dolnesjska (southeast of Ljubljana); and Gorenjska-Alta Carniola near Bled.

The first report of Gypsies on the territory of present-day Slovenia dates from 1453 and refers to a smith. During World War II, part of Slovenia was annexed to **Germany** and the Gypsies living there were taken to concentration camps.

Slovenia became an independent state in 1991 after a brief skirmish with the Yugoslav Federation. Article 65 of the constitution of the new republic states: "The legal situation and particular rights of the Romany population living in Slovenia will be settled by the law." This vague statement has never been fully defined. The national law on local self-government stipulates that in areas where minorities live they should have members on councils, but in 1998 there was only one such Romany representative.

Although the Roma in Slovenia have escaped the miseries of the wars in the neighboring countries, their situation is unenviable. Most live in segregated settlements, are unemployed, and subsist on welfare payments, while the percentage in prison is much higher than for the Slovenian population as a whole. Only 509 were registered as having work, and only 25 percent of the children were at school. Roma children, as elsewhere in central and eastern Europe, have problems when they come to school because they do not know the majority language and lack social skills, while many schools try to avoid registering Romany children. Their lack of **education** leads the majority of Roma to depend on unskilled work, and they are the first to go when factory personnel are reduced. Such employment as there is includes cleaning, farmwork, road construction, stonemasonry, and horse trading. Even qualified Roma find it difficult to get work because of discrimination. The rate of mortality is higher than for the Slovenian population as a whole.

There have been some examples of extreme prejudice in housing, as in 1997 when the Slovene inhabitants of Malina prevented a Romany family from moving into a house in their village—a move designed as part of an integration program. Local authorities refuse planning permission for Roma to build houses, refuse to find accommodation for them, and then blame them for building houses illegally or for living in poor conditions.

The central government of Slovenia has set up an Inter-Departmental Commission for Roma Matters, which, aside from representatives of ministries, has members of the local authorities in areas where Roma live and from Romany organizations. Twenty distinct Romany communities are designated "autochthonous," that is, established in the country. They are entitled to a seat on their local municipal councils, and all but one council (Grosuplje) has complied.

In 1995 the government started a program to improve the lot of the Roma. Its aims included improving the living conditions in Romany settlements and increasing the educational opportunities for Romany children from nursery school to university. However, such official initiatives for Roma depend on local goodwill to carry them out. The Roma in Prekmurje are best organized and generally cooperate with the authorities, but in 1998 they organized a demonstration—blocking a highway—to press for the building of a road to the Romany village of Beltinci.

In the first seven years of the new state, seven Romany organizations were founded. They have now come together in one union, Zveza Romskih Drustev Slovenije (The Association of Romany Organizations in Slovenia), whose president is author Jozuek Horvat-Muc. These organizations are involved in the fields of culture, education, information, and sports, but not politics. **Radio** broadcasts in Romani come from Murska Sobota and Novo Mesto. In Murska Sobota, there is also a **theater** group that has been functioning since 1992. A magazine, *Romano Them* (Romany World), is published by a nongovernmental organization, while the Romanies in Murska Sobota produce their own bilingual paper, *Romske Novice*.

SMITH, CHARLES (1956–2005). England. **Poet**, local government politician, and civil rights worker. He was chairman of the **Gypsy Council for Education, Culture, Welfare and Civil Rights**. He served as a Labour Party councillor and mayor in Castle Point, Essex. Smith recently premiered a **film** he directed for the **Gypsy Council**, *Footprints in the Sand*, based on a visit to **Saintes Maries de la Mer**.

SMITH, CORNELIUS (1831–1922). England. Craftsman and evangelist. His parents were caners and basket makers. He was the father of **Rodney Smith** and grandfather of the Rev. **George Bramwell Evens**. He was converted to being an active Christian at a revivalist meeting in Notting Hill, London. He wrote a short autobiography, *The Life Story of Cornelius Smith*.

SMITH, ELEANOR (1845–1914). England. Writer and a champion of the Gypsy cause. Lady Smith's writings include *Red Wagon*, *Tzigane*, *Caravan*, and her autobiography *Life's a Circus*. She supported the right of the Gypsies to come to **Epsom Downs** for the **Derby** race week.

SMITH, GEORGE. England. 19th-century preacher. He wanted to settle the Gypsies and saw the Gypsy way of life as requiring reform through **education** and improved sanitary conditions. His books on the subject were *Gipsy Life: Being an Account of Our Gipsies and Their Children, with Suggestions for Their Improvement* (1880) and the antiromantic view of Gypsy life in *I've Been a-Gipsying*. The **Moveable Dwellings Bills**, which he tried to promote in Parliament, failed to be adopted.

SMITH, JASPER DERBY (1921–2003). England. Singer. He was born in a **caravan** on **Epsom Downs**, as was his father, born on **Derby** Day. Smith was a well-known folk singer who made recordings and sang on **radio** and **television**. He was a founder member of the **Gypsy Council** in the 1960s and campaigned for caravan sites in Kent and Surrey. After a 10-year battle, he persuaded the Epsom Council to reopen in 1983 the Cox's Lane site, of which he became the first warden. He is featured on the CD *My Father Is King of the Gypsies* (1999) and two Topic records—*Songs of the Open Road* (1975) and *The Travelling Songster* (1977).

SMITH, PHOEBE (1913–2001). England. Singer. She is from the south of England and had a large repertoire of English folk songs that were recorded by several collectors. Albums include *The Yellow Handkerchief* (1998).

SMITH, RODNEY (1860–1947). England. Evangelist. Son of **Cornelius Smith**. Born in East Anglia and known as "Gipsy" Smith, he was a Methodist preacher who could stir a crowd of 10,000 by his speechmaking and attracted popularity with his vocal recordings of hymns. He wrote many **religious** pamphlets and became a Member of the (Order of the) British Empire. His brother, Ezekiel, worked with the Railway Mission for many years and wrote hymns, and his son, Hanley, was a Methodist minister at Sutton Coldfield. His autobiography, written in 1902, *Gipsy Smith: His Life and Work*, was published by the Religious Tract Society.

SOCIETY FOR THE IMPROVEMENT OF LOCAL ROMA COMMUNITIES. Yugoslavia. Est. 1997. President: Aleksandra Mitrović. The society is a nongovernmental organization that brings together experts, scientists, and social activists to aid the development of Roma communities and improve their living conditions.

SOFIA CONGRESS (1905). This was not an international congress, as stated in some books, but a national gathering aimed at winning for **Bulgarian** Gypsies the right to vote.

SOLARIO, ANTONIO (1465–1530). Italy. Painter at the court of Naples. He was called "Lo Zingaro" (the Gypsy), a nickname given him either because his father was a Romany blacksmith or from the wandering life he himself led until he settled permanently in Naples. He is said to have worked at his father's trade until his love for the beautiful daughter of an artist led him to turn to **art**. His most important work is a series of 20 frescoes in the court of a monastery near San Severino. His "Carrying of the Cross" can be seen in the Church of San Domenico Maggiore in Naples.

SOLER, ANTONIO RUIZ (ANTONIO EL BAILARIN) (1921–1996). Seville, Spain. **Dancer.** He was known as **Spain**'s most famous and charismatic traditional dancer, possessing the quality of *duende*, the spirit of **flamenco**. He also included in his repertoire the stamping of feet, known as *taconeado*. Soler showed early promise by dancing publicly at the age of four, and by the time he was six, he had joined a dancing school. When he was eight years old, he had already started a partnership with another pupil, and in 1937 they left for a tour of North and **South America**, performing as "Antonio and Rosario." They performed in **films** with **Rita Hayworth** and Judy Garland before returning to Madrid, where Antonio made his debut in 1949. The duo danced together for 22 years before splitting in 1952. Soler also performed at Pablo Picasso's 80th birthday party in 1961 when the painter joined him in a rumba. He was director of the Spanish National Ballet from 1980 to 1983 and again for a short period in 1989.

SOROS, GEORGE (1930–). Hungary. Philanthropist. A financier of **Jewish-Hungarian** origin who has donated money to many Romany causes. *See also* OPEN SOCIETY INSTITUTE (OSI); SOROS FOUNDATION.

SOROS FOUNDATION (ROMA SOROS FOUNDATION). United States. Est. 1993 by **George Soros**. It has set up a number of cultural programs, in eastern Europe in particular. *See also* OPEN SOCIETY INSTITUTE (OSI).

SOTO, JOSE. *See* MERCE, JOSE.

SOUTH AFRICA. A small number of **Kalderash** families reside in and travel to South Africa.

SOUTH AND CENTRAL AMERICA. There could be more than a million Romanies in Latin America, the majority being descendants of **Kalderash** and other **Vlah** immigrants. Some writers give a figure as high as four million, with one million in **Brazil** alone. There are also descendants of Spanish and Portuguese Gypsies.

It is thought that Romanies began to arrive in the Americas from Europe during the late 15th and early 16th centuries. Many came during the period of colonization, with **transportation** to **Portugal**'s new colony bringing Portuguese Gypsies to Brazil. Aside from the forced deportations, many Romany families decided to come to the New World in order to seek new horizons and escape the persecution they were facing in their countries. **Spain**, however, discouraged Gypsies from crossing to its colonies in America.

In the early 20th century, many European Roma began to immigrate voluntarily to various destinations in Central and South America. These groups included Kalderash, **Machvaya**, **Bayash**, **Sinti**, and the Spanish and Portuguese **Caló**. More recently, due to the political events in eastern Europe and continued poverty and racism, many **Romanian**, **Serbian**, and **Bosnian** Roma have also arrived in South America. **Jorge Bernal** from Argentina is a poet and well-known figure at international conferences.

SOUZA, JOHN PHILIPS (1854–1932). United States. **Musician.** The composer of the song "Stars and Stripes Forever" and many other well-known marches. His ancestors were **Portuguese** Gypsies.

SOVIET UNION. Estimated Gypsy population in 1991: over 500,000. For a short time after the success of the 1917 Revolution, the Gypsies in the newly formed Soviet Union were given rights as an ethnic group in exchange for supporting communism. **Nomadism** was discouraged. In 1926, the Soviet Communist Party's Central Committee issued the decree "On Measures for Aiding the Transition of Nomadic Gypsies to a Working and Settled Way of Life." This encouraged Gypsies to adopt a settled life and accept land in each Union republic. By 1938 there were 52 Romany collective farms (*kolkhozi*). However, many Gypsies resisted land settlement, initiating a further settlement decree in 1928. The main factor in the resistance was caused by the change from the tradition of working in extended family groups and inexperience in farming. Large-scale workshops (*arteli*) were also created, such as the Natsmenbit metal workshop in Leningrad, which employed 200 people.

In 1925 the All-**Russian** Union of Gypsies was formed, headed by Andrei Taranov from Siberia, with **Ivan Rom-Lebedev** as its secretary. It pressed for Gypsies to be classed as a nation and achieved this status the same year. The authorities later took advantage of some irregularities in the accounts of the union to dissolve it. The Romani **dialect** of the **Haladitka** was approved as a language for official use within the USSR the following year. In 1927 the influential journal *Romani Zorya* (Romani Dawn) published its first issue. Wall posters in Romani were seen that year, and the All-Russian Union recorded 640 members. In 1929 a popular library series began publication,

Biblioteka Vaše Školi Nabut Siklyakirde Manušenge (Library for Schools for People with Little Education). The series included *Nevo dziben* [New Life], edited by **Aleksandr German**, and **Nikolai Pankov**'s *Buti i džinaiben* [Work and Knowledge]. The Romengiro Lav (Romani Word) writer's circle in Moscow had among its members Rom-Lebedev, poet Pankov, teacher **Nina Dudarova**, and G. Lebedev. Cultural clubs were set up in **Simferopol** and elsewhere. A first reader for schools *Džidi buti* [Living Things] by Pankov and Dudarova was published the following year, as was a story *Baxt* [Fortune] by Rom-Lebedev and *Nevo Gav* [New Village], an agricultural magazine edited by Alexandr Taranov. In 1930, too, four schools were opened using the **Romani language**.

In 1931 the Soviet policy promoted **dramas** in the languages of national minorities, but the **theaters** were not intended to promote separatism. A specially commissioned play with a message of integration *Romano Drom* [Romany Way], was a success and led to the creation of the Gypsy **Teatr Romen** later that year.

In the period 1928–1938, an **educational** program flourished, and in due course 86 Gypsy schools were opened and teacher-training colleges and courses established. There were more than 40 Romany medical students at Smolensk. Alongside these educational developments were more publications—for example, Maksim Sergievski's *Grammar of Romani* and his Romani–Russian dictionary written jointly with linguist Aleksei Barannikov.

In 1931 the first issue of a second journal, *Nevo Drom* (New Way) appeared with a 1,000-copy run and some 28 pages in size. Publication continued through the sixth issue, in June 1932, with political, literary, children's, and chess sections. Pankov translated a treatise on agricultural problems. In 1935 Aleksandr German published a collection of short stories and plays, *Ganka Chyamba, i vavre rosphenibena* [Ganka Chyamba and Other Stories]. Leo Tolstoy's children's stories about animals were translated into Romani as *Rosphenibena vaš životnonenge*.

All this activity came abruptly to a halt when, in January 1938, the Central Committee of the Communist Party ordered an end to all cultural activity in Romani and 15 other minority languages. The schools were closed and a number of intellectuals, such as **Averiand Voitiehovski**, were executed. Others were sent to labor camps in

Siberia. Only the Teatr Romen was to survive, with the Russian language playing a larger part in the performances. World War II and the **Holocaust** followed and not until 1970 was any further publication to appear in Romani.

Soon after the invasion of the Soviet Union in 1941 by Nazi Germany, the **Einsatzgruppen** (Task Forces) and other units set about killing **Jews** and Gypsies. Task Force B shot, and in some cases buried alive, 1,000 Gypsies at Rodnya near Smolensk, while Task Force D murdered more than 800 Gypsies in Simferopol in the Crimea in December 1941. Ivan Tokmakov, who had been in charge of the Communist Party's Gypsy program and who looked after the Gypsy collective farms, was executed by the Germans. Many Gypsies served in the Soviet armed forces, such as naval hero Ivan Kozlovski, while others joined the partisans. More than 30,000 Gypsies were murdered, representing about half of the population of the occupied territories.

After 1945, Josef Stalin's rule became even more despotic. The remaining Romany collective farms were abandoned, forcing Gypsies to move to non-Gypsy farms. A number of **Sinti** Gypsies were deported to the east, as were many Tatar-speaking Gypsies from the Crimea. After Stalin's death in 1953, Nikita Khrushchev, his successor, adopted policies in 1956 that aimed at finally destroying the nomadic traditions of the Romanies. In 1956 nomadism was forbidden by the law "On Reconciling Wandering Gypsies to Work." Some Gypsies resisted sedentarization by traveling around farms for seasonal labor or working as herdsmen moving from pasture to pasture.

The Gypsy Writers Club was set up for writers in the Russian language, but writing in Romani was still discouraged. The first census after World War II registered 130,000 Gypsies in the whole of the Soviet Union (including the Asian republics), but many Gypsies put themselves down as belonging to another nationality. Under Leonid Brezhnev after 1964, some liberalization occurred in the USSR. In 1970 the first publication in Romani since 1938 appeared when **Georgi Kantea** published in the Moldavian SSR a collection of **poems**, proverbs, and tales in the **Ursari** dialect. Prominent Gypsy writers in the Russian language included Kantea himself, **Karlis Rudjevics** in **Latvia, Aleksandr Belugins** (Leksa Manuš) in Moscow, and

Vano Romano in the Altai region. Nikolai Satkievitch published some of his own poetry and reopened Gypsy schools in Siberia.

Romanies began to outstrip the average of population growth in the 1980s, when the census recorded 210,000 Gypsies, with 74 percent claiming Romani as their mother tongue. With the advent in 1985 of a new national leader, Mikhail Gorbachev, freedom was in the air with *glasnost* (openness) and *perestroika* (restructuring). Gypsy culture thrived but was, until 1990, largely cut off from international contact. Then, government officials in 1990 allowed Gypsies to attend the fourth **World Romany Congress** near Warsaw, which heralded a growth in Soviet Romanies' participation in international Gypsy affairs. *See also* ARMENIA; BELARUS; ESTONIA; GEORGIA; LATVIA; LITHUANIA; MOLDOVA; UKRAINE.

SPAIN. Estimated Gypsy population (excluding the non-Romany **Quinquilleros**): 700,000. The first records of Gypsies in Spain date from the 15th century and refer to companies that crossed the border from **France**. However, some scholars think that Gypsies had entered Spain much earlier, accompanying the Muslims when they invaded from the south. The Egyptian writer Abdu-'l-Mulk, writing around 1200, advised Arabic poets in Spain (then under Arab rule) not to be "garrulous in the manner of the **Zott**" (the Arab term for Gypsies). Firmer evidence of their presence comes in 1425 when Don Johan of **Little Egypt** and Duke Thomas obtained letters of protection from King Alfonso V of Aragon. These leaders had certainly come via France.

From 1492 Spain was a federation under the joint monarchs Ferdinand and Isabella, and legislation (the Pragmatica) in 1499 ordered Gypsies nationwide to stop **nomadizing**, settle down, and find a trade within 60 days. If they continued to nomadize, they would be whipped, have a cut made in their ears (as an identification mark), and be forcibly bound to a master. Many did take up trades, replacing the expelled Moors as masons and bakers, for example. After 1539, Gypsies who continued to wander in groups were arrested, and males were used as galley slaves.

In 1633 Philip IV's government decreed that the Gypsies did not exist. They were not an ethnic group, he said, but Spanish people who had disguised themselves and made up a language. They were forbidden to speak any language other than Spanish or wear distinctive clothes. In 1695 they were, ineffectively, forbidden to have any employment other than farming. By 1746 a list of 75 towns had been drawn up, and Gypsies were—in theory—allowed to live only in the named towns.

Persecution continued. A roundup of all Gypsies was ordered in 1749. The aim was to eliminate the population completely by locking up the men and women separately and setting them to forced labor. Several hundred Gypsies were arrested and imprisoned in this campaign. Most of them were gradually released and allowed to return to their previous homes, however, after it was realized that they performed useful services in the villages, which found themselves suddenly without a blacksmith or a baker. The last of the arrested Gypsies were finally released in 1765, after 16 years of confinement. Repression ceased and was replaced by a firmer policy of assimilation with the enactment of a decree of Charles III in 1783, under which the Gypsies were granted equal citizenship. The use of the word *Gitano* (Gypsy) was to be banned. The Gypsies were again forbidden to speak Romani or wear distinctive dress. Many took the opportunity of free movement to migrate to the south of France. Largely as a result of the past penalties for speaking Romani in public, the language has died out, and Spanish Gypsies now speak a variety of Spanish with a few Romani words, known as **Caló**.

The Gypsies have continued to live in Spain on the edge of society, looked down upon by the majority population unless they are **musicians** or bullfighters. The Catholic Church took an interest in the Gypsies during the 20th century by organizing local missions and pilgrimages. Many Spanish Gypsies are now turning to **Pentecostalism**.

Since the fall of the Francisco Franco dictatorship in 1975, the Gypsies have been free to organize and publish magazines. However, latent anti-Gypsy racism has surfaced on many occasions. In one incident in 1984, a crowd of several hundred in Zaragoza demonstrated against the occupation of 36 prefabricated houses built for Gypsies in the Actur district. Slogans they carried included "Fight for your rights against Gypsies." In 1986 there were attacks on the Gypsy quarter of Martos when 30 houses were set on fire and the inhabitants fled to the nearby village of Torredonjimeno. The villagers there did not allow them to stop, though, and drove them out. The local authorities then tried to settle the evacuees in a third place, Monte Lope Alvarez, but the local population again protested, and the Gypsies had to sleep in tents provided by the Red Cross, protected by the police, until alternative accommodation was found. In the district of Otxarkoaga in Bilbao in 1996, Gypsy children were denied entry to the local school, and a special school was set up for them in a disused secondary school building. Some of the Gypsy parents then boycotted the new school, in a protest against segregation.

In 2004 a number of Gypsy organizations combined to hire the advertising company Saatchi and Saatchi to conduct a campaign to improve the standing of Gypsies among the general population. The slogan of the campaign was "Know them before judging them."

The number of Romany **women** in prison—4,000—is higher than one would expect in view of the size of the population. Project Barani has been set up to tackle this problem, which is largely the result of minor infringements of the law on narcotics. The economic situation has led to some young unemployed Gypsies trafficking in drugs and even beginning to experiment with the wares they sell. It is probably the only country in Europe where a serious drug problem exists among Gypsies.

Gypsies are among the best **dancers** and singers in Spain, and several of them have individual entries in this handbook, such as **Joaquín Cortés**, as does the soccer star **Jose Antonio Reyes**. A significant number of Romanies are going to college. **Juan de Dios Heredia Ramírez** was a lecturer and then member of Parliament for the Socialist Party in the Spanish and European Parliaments. The Spanish royal family supported the **European Congress** in Seville. Other positive features are the great interest in the revival of the **Romani language** and links with Gypsy organizations in other countries. The **Presencia Gitana** association in Madrid has a wide program of educational and cultural work. Many of the local groups are united in a network, the **Union Romani**, and their activities are reported in the journal *Nevipens Romani* (Romani News).

SPECIALIST GROUP ON ROMA/GYPSIES (MG-S-ROM). In 1995 the Committee of Ministers of the **Council of Europe** decided to set up this group to advise the council. The seven original members of the group were Outi Ojala (**Finland**), Carmen Santiago Reyes (**Spain**), Josephine Verspaget (**Netherlands**), Catalin Zamfir (**Romania**), Milcho Dimitrov (**Bulgaria**), Claudio Marta (**Italy**), and Andrzej Mirga (**Poland**). The first meeting of the group was held in Strasbourg, France, in March 1996. The second meeting, in October 1996, considered **human rights**, among other topics. Two members of the group took part in a fact-finding mission to **Bosnia** under the auspices of the Council of Europe. The group has met some 20 times with housing, **caravan** sites, and health high on the agenda.

SPINELLI, SANTINO (ALEXIAN) (1964–). Italy. Singer and cultural worker. He is the organizer of the annual **Them Romano** festival and editor of the journal of the same name.

SPITTA, MELANIE (1946–2005). Germany. Civil rights activist and filmmaker. A **Sinti** who, together with Katryn Seybold, made several documentary **films** about Sinti, including *Wir Sind Sintikinder und Keine Zigeuner* [We Are Sinti Children and Not Gypsies; 1981] and *Das Falsche Wort* [The False Word; 1987]. The latter deals with the question of the lack of **reparations** for Nazi crimes. In 1999 she was the first recipient of the **Otto Pankok** Prize for Romany cultural achievements.

STANDING CONFERENCE FOR COOPERATION AND COORDINATION OF ROMANI ASSOCIATIONS IN EUROPE. This body was founded in July 1994, in Strasbourg, **France**, and brings together representatives from some 40 Gypsy organizations. Meetings have been held at various locations, starting with Warsaw on 19–20 January 1996.

STANKIEWICZ, STANISLAW (1942–). Poland. **Television** producer and publisher. He is the editor of the journal *Rrom p-o Drom* [Romanies on the Road]. He was elected in 1990 as a vice president of the **International Romani Union** and became president in 2004.

STARKIE, WALTER (**1894–1976**). England. Author. He was an authority on Gypsy lore and **music**. He traveled widely in Europe between the two world wars with his violin and has described the Gypsies he met in several books.

STEINBACH, SETTALA (1935–1944). Netherlands. A Gypsy girl whose picture, peering through the door of a cattle wagon, has symbolized in many books the deportations to concentration camps during the Nazi period. Originally thought to be **Jewish**, she has recently been identified as a Romany. She was taken to **Auschwitz** on 19 May 1944 and gassed two months later. Dutch **television** made a **film** about her short life.

STENCL, A. N. **(1897–1983).** England. **Poet**. In 1962, he wrote a series of sonnets in Yiddish dedicated to the Gypsies that he published in the magazine he edited, *Loshn un Lebn* [Language and Life].

STENEGRY, ARCHANGE. France. Contemporary **musician** and political leader. A resistance leader during World War II, he later became the president of the Communauté Tzigane de France, which replaced the Organisation Nationale Gitane.

STEREOTYPES. We find in **literature** and in the popular mind many stereotypes of Gypsies. Miguel de Cervantes was one of the first to introduce the theme of Gypsies stealing a child, in his novel *La Gitanilla*. They teach her to **dance** and sing, but in her heart she remains a Spaniard. At the end of the novel, she is restored to her family and married to her Spanish lover. Beautiful and handsome Gypsies appear in plays, novels, and operas, for example, Georges Bizet's *Carmen* and D. H. Lawrence's *The Virgin and the Gypsy*.

STEWART, BELLE (1906–1997). Scotland. Singer. She was a **Scottish Traveler**. She, her husband Alex (singer and piper), and her daughters Sheila MacGregor (**Sheila Stewart**) and **Lizzie Higgins** became famous in folk clubs and concert halls throughout **Scotland** and **England**. Their many recordings include the CDs *The Travelling Stewarts* and *Festival at Blairgowrie*.

STEWART, DAVIE (1901–1972). Scotland. **Scottish Traveler**, singer, and **musician**. Stewart served as an underage soldier in World War I and became a piper with the Gordon Highlanders. He earned his living as a street busker in **Scotland** and **Ireland**, playing the accordion and the pipes. After his return to Scotland, he was a well-known figure in folk clubs and made several recordings.

STEWART, ELIZABETH (1939–). Scotland. **Traveler** from a branch of the **Stewart family**. Singer and pianist. CD: *Binnorrie*.

STEWART, SHEILA (SHEILA MacGREGOR) (1937–). Scotland. Folk singer. She is the daughter of **Belle Stewart** and sister of **Lizzie Higgins**, and her voice can be heard on recordings of the **Stewart family** as well as her own solo tape (reissued as a CD) *And Time Goes On*.

STEWART FAMILY. Most of the **musicians** among **Scottish Travelers** named Stewart are descended from the singer Jimmy Stewart of Struan. *See also* HIGGINS, LIZZIE; STEWART, BELLE; STEWART, ELIZABETH; STEWART, SHEILA.

STOJKA, CEIJA (1933–). Austria. A **Lovari** writer and singer. She has followed in her brother **Karl Stojka**'s footsteps and taken up painting. She is on the governing board of the **Romano Centro** in Vienna.

STOJKA, HARRI (1957–). Austria. **Musician.** Son of **Mongo Stojka** and nephew of **Ceija Stojka** and **Karl Stojka**. Harri is a guitarist in the rock, reggae, and heavy metal styles. His first LP record was *Off the Bone*, and after that he made about a dozen records. He has played in various rock bands, such as Gipsy Love and Harri-Stojka Express. His song "I Am So in Love with You" made the Austrian Hit Parade. Together with his father he made one CD, *Amari luma* [Our World; 1994], which is traditional and in quite a different style from his other recordings.

STOJKA, HOJDA. *See* AMENZA KETANE.

STOJKA, KARL (1931–). Austria. **Artist.** A brother of **Ceija Stojka**, he has had paintings exhibited in the **United States** and Europe.

STOJKA, MONGO (1929–). Austria. **Musician.** Based in Vienna, he produced the CD *Amari luma* [Our World] in 1994 with his son

Harri Stojka. The music is modern, but the lyrics are all in Romani. The original CD had five songs, but the second edition—from 1996—contains 10.

STOW-ON-THE-WOLD FAIR. Cotswolds region, England. A popular gathering for Gypsies. In 1476 a royal charter was granted by Edward IV for the fair. Gypsies have been attending it since about 1890. The fair takes place in May and October, and trading is on a Thursday. The Gypsies arrive in **caravans** on the preceding Sunday or Monday and leave on Friday. In May 1996, at its peak, there were some 400 caravans; in October, about 100. Numbers are slightly lower now. From 1990 the local authorities have been trying without success to stop Gypsies from attending the fair in their caravans. Councillor **Vera Norwood** has been instrumental in securing the continuation of the fair, though the lack of a field where the visiting caravans can legally stop has been a problem.

SUCURI, LJATIF (1915–1945). Yugoslavia. Civil rights activist. He was a prominent Gypsy in Kosovska-Mitrovica in **Kosovo** at the time of the occupation of the country by **Albanian** fascist forces during World War II. On several occasions, Sucuri intervened with the Albanian police chief to stop Gypsies from being killed. The police chief would tell the **German** authorities in **Yugoslavia** that there were no Gypsies in the town, only Muslims. At the end of the war, collaborators, trying to cover up their own activities, denounced him to the Partisans who took him away, without checking the allegations, and shot him.

ŠUKAR. A group based in **Slovenia** playing **music** in a Gypsy style. They appeared at the **Baxt** festival in Trondheim, **Norway**. CD: *Prvo iv* [First Snow].

SUMMER SCHOOLS. A **Romani-language** summer school (Nilajesqi Škola) has been organized by **Marcel Cortiade** and the **Rromani Baxt** organization. The first was held in Belgrade in 1989. It brings together young and not-so-young Romanies from different countries who wish to advance their knowledge of the language and **dialects**. Other language summer schools have been held in Scandinavia and the Balkans, principally for younger Romanies.

SUNDT, EILERT (1817–1875). Norway. Pastor and reformer. In 1848 he obtained a government grant to study the problem of **Travelers** in **Norway**. His **religious** beliefs led him to think that they would be better off in workhouses than traveling the roads. In 1863, Sundt reported that out of 425 Travelers who had been "reformed" (i.e., settled), approximately 100 had gone back to **nomadism**. In 1869, the work was taken from Sundt and given to a department of the church. *See also* NORWEGIAN TRAVELERS.

SVARTA PÄRLOR ("BLACK PEARLS"). A **musical** group formed by members of the Roma Ensemble of **Poland**, who immigrated to **Sweden** around the 1970s.

SVARTA SAFIRER ("BLACK SAPPHIRES"). Now based in **Sweden**, the members of this band are originally from **Yugoslavia**.

SVETSKY. In spite of occasional references found in books on Gypsies, these are circus families, not Gypsies or **Travelers**, in the **Czech** and **Slovak** republics.

SWANN REPORT. The 1985 report of a British committee investigating **education**, chaired by Lord Swann. It found that, although more Gypsy children were attending school, they were suffering discrimination and bullying from other pupils.

SWEDEN. Estimated Gypsy (Romany) population: 16,500 (not including **Travelers**). In 1512 Gypsies crossed from **Denmark** to Sweden, at a time when Swedish nationalists were fighting to free the country from Danish rule. In 1515 there were more immigrants, this time from **Estonia**. In 1523 Gustav Vasa became king of an independent Sweden, and two years later he wrote to the Gypsies, telling them to leave the country. During the second half of the 16th century, a number of Gypsies did leave and migrated to **Finland**. In 1560, the Lutheran Archbishop Petri told the priests not to baptize or bury Gypsies. This was changed in 1586 when priests were told they should baptize children, teach parents the Christian faith, and encourage them to settle down. However, eight years later, the Synod of Linköping reversed this again, and the previous policy was readopted.

In 1637 a new law was passed saying that all Gypsies must leave the country or else the men would be executed and the **women** expelled by force. In this law, the word *Zigenare* was used for the first time for Gypsies. Previously they had been called *Tattare* (in various spellings). In 1642 and 1662, the law was strengthened. However, no cases are known of Gypsies being executed in Sweden under these laws. Finally, in 1748 a new decree was published banishing Gypsies who had not been born in Sweden. It is thought that a substantial number of Romanies stayed in Sweden and merged with the local **nomadic** population, forming the group now called *Tattare* or *Resande*, the **Swedish Travelers**.

In 1860 entry restrictions in Sweden were lifted, resulting in a new immigration, principally of **Vlah** Gypsies. Under the 1914 Deportation Act, Gypsies could be deported or refused entry, but in fact, those already in the country were allowed to stay. The 1922 census in Sweden recorded 250 Gypsies and 1,500 Tattare. The wartime 1943 census listed 453 Gypsies. The government repealed the 1914 Deportation Act in 1954, and limited immigration began anew. In 1960 the state took responsibility for housing Gypsies, and nomadism for practical purposes ended. At the time, there were about 100 sedentary and 125 nomadic families. By 1965 only five families remained in **caravans**.

In 1963 **Katarina Taikon** published her first book, *Zigenarska*, the story of her childhood. She later took up the campaign for the admission of **Kalderash** Gypsies from **France** and **Spain**. The government decided to set up a policy of "organized importation" of Gypsies —a form of quota. In recent years, considerable numbers of Gypsies have arrived from eastern Europe and **Yugoslavia**, outnumbering the descendants of those Vlah Romanies who had arrived at the end of the 19th century. Many hundreds of Finnish Gypsies have also immigrated to Sweden. The **education** authorities have introduced mother-tongue teaching in Romani and special classes for adults to improve their education. A number of Gypsies take part in these programs as teachers or assistants. There is a steady stream of publications in Swedish and Romani by Roma writers, as well as translations of popular children's books into Romani.

Both the Romanies and the Travelers have set up self-help organizations: Romernas Riksforbund and Resande-romernas Riksforbund, respectively. Finnish Gypsies in Sweden are represented by the Finska Zigenarrådet—the oldest body, founded (originally as Stockholms Finska Zigenarförening) in 1972. An advisory council of Romanies was set up in 2003 to work with the government. The Gypsy **Pentecostal** church is also active.

SWEDISH TRAVELERS. The 1922 census in **Sweden** recorded 1,500 *Tattare*; since then, there has not been an official count. It is thought by some experts that a substantial number of Romanies stayed in Sweden after the expulsion order of 1748 and merged with the local nomadic population, forming the group now called *Tattare* (a pejorative term) or *Resande* (**Travelers**). The Swedish Travelers today speak a language with Swedish grammar and many words borrowed from Romani. They call this language Chivi or Rommani. In recent years, they have set up a self-help organization and many now call themselves "resande Romer" (traveling Romanies).

SWITZERLAND. Estimated Gypsy population: 32,500 (mainly **Jenisch**). Between 1418 and 1422 Gypsies came to Basel, Bern, and Zurich as pilgrims with letters of recommendation. They were given food and wine and then escorted out of the towns. In 1471, however, the Parliament of the Swiss Confederation, meeting in Lucerne, expelled Gypsies from the land. In 1510 the penalty of hanging was introduced for any Gypsies found in Switzerland. This edict was repeated six times in the years up to 1530. Nevertheless, in 1532, a company of 300 Gypsies appeared on the outskirts of Geneva. It evidently took some years before all the Gypsies were finally expelled, as is indicated by a decree in Graubünden in 1571 ordering any Gypsies who were captured to be sent to be galley slaves (one wonders whose galleys these would be). During the following centuries, very few Romanies came to Switzerland, and as late as the middle of the 20th century they were still being turned back at the borders—even Romanies in cars intending to pass through the country in transit. The second **World Romany Congress** was, nonetheless, held in Geneva.

For many years no Romanies lived in Switzerland, and there are very few even today. However, Switzerland has a large population of indigenous Jenisch **nomads** and seminomads. Early in the 20th century, the authorities began to take away the children of Jenisch

272 • SZÁSZCÁSVÁS BAND

families and bringing them up in orphanages or giving them to Swiss foster parents. Often the children were told their parents were dead and vice versa. When news of this program became public, there was great indignation. Many of the children who were taken away— now grown up—have rediscovered their Jenisch identity. An organization known as Scharotl (Caravan) published a magazine of the same name. Radgenossenschaft der Landstrasse, established in 1975, is the umbrella organization of the Jenisch. The foundation Naschet Jenische (est. 1986) and the association Children of the Highway (Kinder der Landstrasse; est. 1986) promote the rehabilitation of victims of the coercive measures, while the Travelling Gypsy Center (est. 1984) and the foundation A Future for Swiss Travelers (Zukunft für Schweizer Fahrende; est. 1997) are dedicated to the preservation and promotion of Jenisch culture. The Mission Tzigane is also engaged in furthering and protecting the rights of the **Travelers**.

SZÁSZCÁSVÁS BAND. Transylvania, Romania. A **musical** group from the ethnic **Hungarian** village of Kis-küküllő that plays in the Gypsy, Hungarian, **Romanian**, and Saxon (**German**) styles. Its singer, István Dumnezu Jámbor, leads the band, which has made several recordings. CD: *Folk Music from Transylvania: Szászcsávás Band*.

SZTOJKA, FERENCZ. Hungary. Writer. He was one of the first Gypsies to write **poetry** in Romani, toward the end of the 19th century.

– T –

TABOR. Romani word for **clan** or camp. It is of Slav origin.

TAIKON, FRED (1945–). Sweden. Political activist and editor. President of the Romany Culture Center in Stockholm, he is also the editor of the bilingual journal *Romani Glinda*.

TAIKON, JOHAN DIMITR (fl. 19th century). Sweden. Coppersmith and storyteller. He traveled in **Russia** and Scandinavia. Taikon's stories were recorded by the Gypsiologist Carl Herman Tillhagen and published as *Taikon berättar*. These and other materials he produced were the basis for the study of the Coppersmith (**Kalderash**) **dialect** of Romani by Olof Gjerdman and Erik Ljungberg.

TAIKON, KATARINA (1932–1995). Sweden. Writer and civil rights activist. Taikon's involvement in politics began when a group of Gypsies coming from **France** were interned at the border and refused entry to **Sweden**. After pressure, they were let in, and the Swedish government agreed to a program of organized immigration. Taikon edited the magazine *Zigenaren* together with her husband Björn Langhammer. She also became well known as a children's writer with her semiautobiographical books about a Gypsy girl, **Katitzi**. She is the sister of **Rosa Taikon**.

TAIKON, ROSA (1926–). Sweden. **Artist.** The sister of **Katarina Taikon**, her jewelry is typically crafted in metal. She has also written some **poetry**.

TARAF. The name—of Arabic origin—given to village bands in **Romania**. Many of the tarafs are Gypsies, such as Taraful Soporu de Cimple, Taraf de Carancebes (from Banat), and **Taraf de Haidouks**.

TARAF DE HAIDOUKS ("BAND OF BRIGANDS"). A Romanian Gypsy band from the village of Clejani that has toured widely across western Europe. After the fall of Nicolae Ceausescu in 1991, the band members were discovered by two Belgians who were in **Romania** searching for folk **musicians**. They found more than 200 during their trip, and it was out of these that the band developed. The ages of the players ranged from the youngest at 20 to their talented lead violinist Nicolae Neacu, who died recently at age 77. Taraf de Haidouks appeared in the **film** *The Man Who Cried* (starring their number-one fan **Johnny Depp**) and have modeled on the catwalks of Paris for designer Yohji Yamamoto. CDs: *Taraf de Haidouks, Musiques des Tsiganes de Roumanie, Dumbala Dumba*.

TARNÓW. A town in Poland where the **museum** has a strong Gypsy section, originating from an exhibition of 1979. It has been built up by the curator, Adam Bartosz. Nevertheless, there are right-wing elements in the town, and the 21st century has seen a serious attack on a Romany family and daubing of anti-Gypsy graffiti there.

TAROT CARDS. Tarot cards were invented in **Italy** in the 15th century and first used as a game. In the 18th century, they became popular for **fortune-telling** and have been adopted by some Gypsies.

TARTARS (TATARS). A **Turkic** people. Until the 16th century, a large independent Tartar state existed in western Asia that at one time reached into Europe as far as **Romania**. Some historians think that the Tartars had Gypsy slaves and brought them to Romania around the 13th century, where both they and some of their captors—after the defeat of the Tartars—became slaves of the Romanians.

TATERE. A pejorative term used for **Norwegian Travelers** and **Danish Travelers**, who prefer to be called *Reisende* (**Travelers**). The name *Tatere* was first used for both indigenous Travelers and Romanies in Norway and **Denmark** because of confusion with the **Tartars**, who made incursions into Europe in the Middle Ages.

TATTARE. A pejorative term used for **Swedish Travelers**, who prefer to be called *Resande* (**Travelers**). The name was first used for indigenous Travelers and Romanies because of confusion with the **Tartars**, who made incursions into Europe in the Middle Ages.

TCHATCHIPEN ("TRUTH"). France. President: Michel Zanko. An organization based in Toulon, **France**, working for the promotion of Romany culture.

TEATR ROMA. A **theater** in Sofia, **Bulgaria**, from 1947 to 1951, when it was closed by the government. Its director was **Mustafa Aliev** (Manush Romanov).

TEATR ROMEN. Moscow, Russia. Director: Aleksandr Kolpakov. The **theater** was founded in 1931 during the encouragement of Romany culture by Josef Stalin. Its aim was to replace the **stereotypical** romantic Gypsy figure by a new image of Gypsies taking part in the building of socialism. The theater was meant to help the sedentarization of the Gypsies. It officially opened in April 1931 and was assisted by the Moscow **Jewish** Theater and the actor Moshe I. Goldblatt, who became the first director. Popular songs and sketches were presented for censorship to the Commissariat of Enlightenment (Ministry of Culture) to convince them that Gypsies were following an appropriate political direction. Three Gypsy writers worked with the company: Michael Bezliudsky, **Aleksandr German**, and **Ivan Rom-Lebedev**. In 1933 a performance of *Carmen* was in the repertoire.

The Teatr Romen toured Siberia and the **Soviet** Far East after much of the western USSR was taken over by the **Germans** early in World War II. It returned to the west later with the advancing Soviet Army across the Caspian Sea and, with the Luftwaffe above, performed before soldiers at Rostov, showing its commitment to the combat. Two actors joined the armed forces and were decorated for bravery. The theater encountered accusations of "nationalistic deviation," but survived the later suppression of Gypsy culture.

The current repertoire varies from world classics to political plays, still encouraging Gypsies to give up the **nomadic** life and settle. Plays with songs and **dances** have always been a feature of the repertoire, and the artists have included many popular singers.

TEKAMELI ("A MESSAGE OF LOVE"). From Roussillon, **France**, the band plays the **music** of the **Gitanos** of southern France. CD: *Ida y Vuelta*.

TELEPHONE LEGAL ADVICE SERVICE FOR TRAVELLERS (T-LAST). Wales. Est. 1995. Operated by the Cardiff Law School as a three-year project, T-LAST aimed to provide not only a telephone legal advice service for Great Britain, as the name suggests, but also to develop a network of legal practitioners and to publish research about the needs of **Travelers** and Gypsies. Its first conference took place in March 1997. It began to publish a newsletter called *Travellers' Times*, which has outlasted the telephone service. There are currently other phone advice lines in **England** in Birmingham and Brighton.

TELEVISION. The first regular TV broadcasts in Romani were from Pristina, **Kosovo**, beginning around 1985; other **Yugoslav** stations

(Novi Sad and Prizren) followed later. In recent years, a number of TV stations have broadcast regularly in Romani or in the national language for Gypsy viewers. These include stations in Bratislava, Bucharest, Budapest, and **Skopje**.

TERESA, MOTHER. *See* BOJAXHIU, AGNES.

THEATER. Apart from the long-established **Teatr Romen** in Moscow, Romany **drama** companies are a phenomenon of the post-1945 years. Two major professional theater groups are now playing in or largely in the **Romani language**: **Romathan** and Teatr Romen.

THEATER ROMANCE. Kiev, Ukraine. The company performs in Russian and Romani. In November 1996 it made a guest visit to Vienna, **Austria**.

THEM ROMANO. Lanciano, Italy. An association that organizes an annual **music** festival and a literary competition (Amico Rom) and publishes a journal of the same name.

THESLEFF, ARTHUR **(1871–1920).** Finland. Diplomat and writer. He wrote a comprehensive survey of the situation of the Gypsies in Europe at the end of the 19th century. It was printed in 1901, and much of it was later reproduced in the *Journal of the Gypsy Lore Society*. Thesleff also compiled a Romani dictionary based on an earlier word list.

TINKER. (1) A worker with tin, often **nomadic**. The profession goes back many centuries in Europe. There are references to persons with the surname or trade of tinker in **England** from around 1175. In 1551–1552 the Act for Tinkers and Pedlars was passed in England. It is likely that the traveling tinkers in England were absorbed by the Romanies when they arrived in the country. **William Shakespeare** refers to Henry V being able to speak with every tinker in his tongue; some have seen this as a reference to the **cant** of **Irish Travelers**. (2) A pejorative name for **Travelers** in **Ireland** and **Scotland**.

TIPLER, DEREK (1940–1990). England. **Radio** and **television** journalist. While working for Radio Vatican, he decided that his mission was to translate the Bible for his own people. He then traveled with **Italian** Gypsies and set to work on the translation, earning money by playing in restaurants. He died of a heart attack after completing only one gospel (Mark), which has been published. He was an occasional contributor to the *Journal of the Gypsy Lore Society*.

TRANSNISTRIA (TRANSDNIESTRIA). During World War II, the **German** and **Romanian** armies conquered the **Ukraine** as far as the River Bug. Romanian troops were responsible for security up to the River Dnieper, and a new name was invented for the territory between the Dniester and Dnieper rivers—Transnistria. Some of this newly occupied area in the east was used by the Romanians as a dumping ground for Gypsies and **Jews**, as the Germans had used **Poland**. In 1941–1942 some 25,000 Gypsies were **transported** across to the other side of the Dniester. The government policy was to expel the Gypsies from the Romanian homeland to stop them mixing with the majority population and intermarrying. For those to whom the policy was applied, it brought disruption of family life, suffering, hardship, hunger, and sometimes death.

Between June and August 1942, more than 11,000 **nomads** were evacuated to the east. Although less danger to Romanian blood than the settled Roma—since they lived isolated socially from the townsfolk—their expulsion could be carried out with little effort. They had their own horses and wagons and just needed guards to accompany them on the journey east. In a few towns in Transylvania, the German-speaking villagers resisted attempts to deport the Gypsies. Clinic (Kelling) and Ungurei (Gergeschdorf) were among the villages where the Romanies remained unharmed. Policemen on horseback forced the Gypsy chiefs from Profa, Tirgu Jiu, and elsewhere to set off with their extended families eastward. Mihai Tonu and Stanescu Zdrelea each led 40 families.

A few leaders set off willingly, not knowing what awaited them. On arrival, they had to build huts for themselves. Some dug holes to sleep in and broke up their wagons to use as a roof and protection against the weather. The rest of the wagon was gradually burned as fuel to keep warm. The horses were eaten. Conditions were hard that first winter. At night, the temperatures dropped, and every morning frozen bodies were to be found. It is said that 1,500 died after one freezing night. The nomads had been able to take their gold with them. At night, they would creep out of the camp at night to exchange gold for food in the neighboring villages. Those who had no gold had to beg. Although some were surrounded with barbed wire, the camps were guarded ghettoes rather than labor camps, and for much of the time, the inmates could leave not only to shop but also to celebrate weddings and baptisms in Russian Orthodox churches nearby.

The deportation of settled Gypsies followed. In May 1942 the Ministry of Internal Affairs ordered that 12,500 settled Gypsies "dangerous to public order" should be deported across the Dniester, and this measure was carried out in September of that year. Gen. Constantin Vasiliu was in charge of the operation, with nine trains at his disposal. Dispatched from Bucharest in cattle trucks with only the possessions they could hold, the journey took weeks with stops and starts, and because of the cold nights, lack of blankets, and inadequate food supply, many died of hunger and exposure before arriving at the River Bug in the Ukraine. Those who had survived were lodged in huts and later made to work digging trenches. Those found with gold teeth had them pulled out. Anyone caught returning from Transdniestria to Romania was sent back and interned at Tiraspol.

The policy of transporting the Gypsies into the Ukraine aroused opposition among the local German officials. The Nazi governor of the Ukraine wrote on the subject to the minister for occupied Eastern territories in Berlin in August 1942. After this, a letter was sent from the minister to the Foreign Office in Berlin, dated 11 September 1942, pointing out the danger that these Gypsies would try to settle on the east bank of the Bug and would then be a bad influence on the Ukrainian population. The minister said the area set aside for Gypsies was in fact populated by ethnic Germans and asked the Foreign Office to persuade Romania to change its policy. During 1943, the deportations decreased in number. After this, the Gypsies in Romania remained comparatively free. As far as is known, no further large-scale activity against them took place, and many served in the army.

Toward the end of 1943, after the Germans and their Romanian allies had been driven back over the Bug, the guards fled, and Gypsies took the opportunity to try to return to Romania. Weakened by months of hunger and cold, many children and old people did not survive this return journey. The survivors eventually reached Dabuleni,

Profa, Tirgu Jiu, and the other towns from which they had been driven.

After the war, when the Romanian People's Court appointed an investigation committee to look into war crimes, it took a very unfavorable view of the treatment of the deportees. Ion Antonescu, the fascist dictator, said at his trial that the Gypsies had been deported because they had robbed people during the curfew and because the governor of Transnistria needed workers. The dictator was executed for war crimes.

It is thought that 19,000 Romanian Gypsies had perished in the east. **Luminita Cioaba** has recorded the memories of survivors in her **film** *Romane iasfa* [Romany Tears].

TRANS-EUROPEAN ROMA FEDERATION (TERF). United Kingdom. Est. 2002. Chairperson: Ladislav Balaz. London-based umbrella organization for Roma refugee groups in the United Kingdom. TERF has campaigned for an end to the detention and deportation of Roma asylum seekers in Britain.

TRANSPORTATION. Many European countries transported Gypsies to their colonies as one way of removing them from their territory. In 1648 **Sweden** proposed to deport the Gypsies to its colony in America, Delaware. This plan was not carried out, but Gypsies were transported from **England** and **Scotland** to North America and **Australia**, and from **Portugal** to Africa and **Brazil**. A magistrate is still sometimes called a *bitcherin' mush* in Romani English, from the phrase "*bitcherdi pawdal*" (sent overseas).

TRAVELER. A term used in this dictionary and elsewhere for industrial **nomadic** groups (**peripatetics**) who are not of **Indian origin**. In many countries, there are indigenous nomadic or semi-nomadic groups. In Europe, they include the Camminanti of **Sicily**; the **Jenisch** of **France**, **Germany**, and **Switzerland**; the **Karrner** of **Austria**; the **Quinquilleros** (or Merceros) of **Spain**; the Resande (or Reisande) of **Sweden** and **Norway**; and the Woonwagenbewoners of the **Netherlands**. They live very similar lives to the nomadic Romanies, and some intermarriage has occurred over the years.

In **Ireland** and **Scotland**, they have been called **Tinkers**, but they themselves prefer the name Travelers. The term *quinquis* or *quinquilleros* used in Spain is the equivalent of "Tinkers," and there they prefer the name *Merceros* (literally Haberdashers). **Norwegian Travelers** and **Swedish Travelers** became known as *Tattare* and now prefer terms meaning "Traveler"—*Reisande* and *Resande*, respectively. *See also* IRISH TRAVELERS; NEW TRAVELERS; SCOTTISH TRAVELERS.

TRAVELLER LAW REFORM BILL. United Kingdom. A proposal sponsored in the House of Commons during 2003 by MP David Atkinson.

TRAVELLER LAW REFORM COALITION. *See* GYPSY AND TRAVELLER LAW REFORM COALITION.

TRAVELLERS' AID TRUST. United Kingdom. Est. 1988. Coordinator: Susan Alexander. The Trust was founded in 1988 and has recently been revived. It is a charity and its objectives include the relief of hardship among **Travelers** and the advancement of the **education** of their children. It has launched a grants program, including the Small Grants Programme for Travellers, which offers grants to a maximum of £250 for a wide range of purposes that are of benefit to individual **Travelers** or the Traveler community.

TRAVELLERS' SCHOOL CHARITY. United Kingdom. Est. 1997. Founder: Alan Dearling. A charity that supports on-site **education** for **New Travelers'** children.

TRENT, COUNCIL OF. Conference of the Catholic Church, ending in 1563, which decreed, among other things, that persons without a fixed address could not become Catholic priests.

TROLLMANN, JOHANN (RUCKELLE) (?–1943). Germany. Boxer. He was the light-heavyweight boxing champion of **Germany**. In March 1933, the reigning champion, Erich Seeling, was deprived of his title because he was a **Jew**. On 9 June, Trollmann fought Adolf Wilt for the title and won on points. Eight days later, he in turn was deprived of his title on racial grounds because he was a Gypsy. In 1942, he was arrested and sent to Neuengamme concentration camp, where he was shot in February 1943.

TROSTANIETS. A concentration camp in the occupied **Soviet Union** during World War II, in which many Gypsies died.

TSIGAN (TSIGANE; TZIGANE). The Slav and French terms for Gypsy, derived (like the German *Zigeuner* and Italian *Zingaro*) from the Greek *atsingani* (heretics).

TURKEY. Estimated Gypsy population: 350,000, although some sources would say one million. An estimate for the years 1960–1970 gave a figure of 10,633 **nomads.**

When the Turks captured the land that forms present-day Turkey from the **Byzantine Greeks,** they found a substantial Gypsy population already there. Sultan Bayezid drove many Romanies out of the parts of Anatolia under his control, and they came into Europe (Thrace and **Serbia**). Only those who became Muslim were allowed to stay in Turkey. Later records show the Gypsies to have had an important role in the Turkish state as **musicians,** smiths, and entertainers. The report of a celebration organized by Sultan Murad III in Istanbul in honor of his newborn son talks of a procession including 60 Gypsy smiths, pulling a cart in which three smiths were working. In a second procession the following month, 400 Romany smiths took part, as well as broom makers, bear trainers, chimney sweeps, musicians, acrobats, and **dancers.**

In the Turkish **Ottoman Empire,** the Gypsies were generally treated as a slightly lower rank of Muslims. They paid higher taxes and were exempt from military service. In 1874 Muslim Gypsies gained equality with other Muslims in the empire. They were called up for military service and ceased paying the special tax.

After World War II, many Muslim Gypsies moved from Greece to Turkey. Gypsies are referred to in Turkish by the pejorative term *Cingene* and also *Kipti.* Apart from the Romanies, there are also **Lom** (Bosha) and Dom (**Nawwar**) **clans,** in particular in the eastern regions. The nomads practice **fortune-telling,** sell crafts, or work with metals. The **occupations** of the settled Gypsies include musicians, flower sellers, or porters.

During the 20th century, the Gypsies played a substantial role in creating music in the regions of Edirne, Istanbul, and Izmir. Since strict Islam forbade the playing of music, Greek, **Jewish**, and Gypsy musicians filled this gap. The most important instruments they played were the *darabuka* (drum), tambourine, *qanun* (zither), *oud* (lute), clarinet, and *kemam* (violin). Kibariye is a well-known singer of popular melodies.

There is much prejudice against Gypsies, and there have been some incidents of conflict with the local population. In 1995 Zehala Baysal died in police custody in Istanbul. In 1996, 5,000 Gypsies were evicted from the Selamsiz quarter of Istanbul.

Ali Celikbilek was Turkey's representative on the **Comité International Tzigane** until his death in 2001. One of his ideas was for Imrali Island to become a home for all the Gypsies in Turkey. Academic conferences held in Istanbul since 2003 have awakened local interest in the history and culture of the Gypsies as well as encouraging the Roma themselves to organize. Local organizations are linked by TROMDEF (Federation of Turkish Roma Associations), whose president is Erdinc Cekic.

TZIGANE. (1) A composition for piano and violin by 20th-century French composer Maurice Ravel. (2) *See* TSIGAN.

– U –

UHLIK, RADE **(1899–1991).** Yugoslavia. Academic. He published a number of articles on the **Romani language** and compiled a dictionary. Many of the folktales he collected are printed in the *Journal of the Gypsy Lore Society*.

UKRAINE. Estimated Gypsy population: 75,000. Since the end of the **Soviet Union** in 1991, Ukraine has been an independent state. The first Gypsies arrived in what is now the territory of Ukraine as early as 1427 and a substantial Gypsy population has lived there ever since.

During World War II, the Ukraine was conquered by the **Germans** and many Gypsies were killed by the **Einsatzgruppen** in Duma-Eli, Krasnye Yerchi, Staryi Krum, Ungut, and elsewhere. A delegation of three older Crimean **Tatars** in the village of Asan-Bey asked the German commander to spare the Gypsies there, but the officer said he would free them only if the Tatars were willing to die in their place. The Gypsies were locked in a storehouse and shot.

There have been some anti-Gypsy pogroms since the political changes in 1991. An entire Romany family was burned to death after an arson attack on their home in the village of Malaya Kahnivka in central Ukraine. According to a relative who witnessed the attack, one of the three men responsible for setting the house on fire was a police officer. There have been other reports of Roma being harassed by the police.

The Ukrainian Association of Roma, formed in 2002, is based in Kiev. In June 2003, a conference entitled "Roma **Women**: Double Discrimination" took place in Kiev, organized by the Chirikli Romany Women's Charity Foundation and the Roma of Ukraine Program of the International Renaissance Foundation.

In Ukraine, generally three **dialects** of Romani are spoken: Carpathian, Ukrainian (or Servi), and **Haladitko**. The **poet** Kazimierenka writes in the Haladitko dialect, as did Djura Makhotin. In addition, in the Crimea the local Gypsies speak their own (Krimitka) dialect—which is close to Balkan Romani—or a dialect known as Ursari (which is not the same as the **Ursari** of **Romania**).

UNIFIED NOMADIC AND INDEPENDENT TRANSNATIONAL EDUCATION (UNITE). United Kingdom. Coordinator: Barrie Taylor. A site in Essex has been found to develop a **Holocaust** and Cultural Heritage Center. The center will also provide supplementary **education** and advice to Gypsies.

UNION ROMANI. Spain. Est. 1986. President: **Juan de Dios Ramírez-Heredia**. An umbrella organization linking the majority of the local and national associations in **Spain**.

UNITED KINGDOM. *See* ENGLAND; NORTHERN IRELAND; SCOTLAND; WALES.

UNITED KINGDOM ASSOCIATION OF GYPSY WOMEN. Founded in 1994 as the National Association of Gypsy Women.

Chair: Kay Beard. Its aim has been to give more voice to Gypsy **women**. It holds traditional rather than feminist values.

UNITED NATIONS (UN). The first time the United Nations paid attention to Gypsies was in 1977, when the Subcommission on the Prevention of Discrimination and Protection of Minorities of the **Economic and Social Council**'s Commission on Human Rights adopted a resolution on the protection of the Gypsies asking all states to accord equal rights to Roma (Gypsies). In 1991 the same subcommission noted that there was still discrimination against Gypsies, and so in 1992 the main Commission on Human Rights passed Resolution 65 on the Protection of Roma (Gypsies). This measure "invites States to adopt all appropriate measures in order to eliminate any form of discrimination against Roma (Gypsies)."

Following the publication of its report *Avoiding the Dependency Trap* (2003), the UN has launched a new development program, under the directorship of Kalman Miszei, which aims to empower Roma in central and eastern Europe. The report underlined the fact that unemployment among Roma in eastern Europe averaged 40 percent and that it was 90 percent in some areas.

UNITED STATES. Estimated Gypsy population: over two million, the majority being descendants of the **Kalderash** and other **Vlah** immigrants. **English** Romanies and **Irish Travelers** are also found in North America.

It is thought that Romanies began to arrive in the Americas during the late 15th or early 16th century from Europe. Many came during the period of colonization. **Transportation** from **England** to North America began in 1614. Aside from the forced deportations, many Romany families decided to come to the New World in order to seek new horizons and escape the persecution they were facing in their countries.

In 1908 the Machvano Adams family founded the National Gypsy Association of America, and in 1928 Steve Kaslov, a Kalderash, set up the Red Dress Gypsies' Association. Attempts to set up a national organization in the United States have been hampered by the vast geographical distances between centers. However, more recently the American Romani Alliance was established by **Ian Hancock** and

John Nickels. Among its activities is a family counseling center in New York for newly arrived Roma. *See also* CANADA; SOUTH AND CENTRAL AMERICA.

URSARI. Bear trainers. The word is derived from **Romanian** *urs*. It is the name of several **clans** of Gypsies who traditionally trained bears and of at least two distinct **dialects** of Romani.

URSITORY. In **Kalderash** tradition, female spirits who appear at the **birth** of a baby to name the child. **Matéo Maximoff** wrote a novel *Ursitory* in which these spirits appear.

USTI NAD LABEM. In October 1999, a wall measuring 2 meters (6 feet) high and 65 meters (213 feet) long was erected on Maticni Street in the northern **Czech** town of Usti Nad Labem to separate Gypsies from their non-Gypsy neighbors. Romany activists from around the Czech Republic went there to try to prevent the wall's construction, but it was finally completed under police guard. Dubbed the "wall of shame," it was erected at the request of non-Gypsy homeowners who complained of noise and disorder from nearby Gypsy flats. Although legally empowered to do so, central Czech authorities failed to prevent the wall's construction, and only annulled the municipal resolution to build the wall after it had been completed. The wall has since been removed.

USTIBEN ("RISING UP"). United Kingdom. Est. 2001. President: Ladislav Balaz. Organization created to coordinate political activity on behalf of the Roma.

– V –

VAGHRI. It has been suggested that, at the same time as the ancestors of the European Gypsies moved west from **India**, a small group of nomads, the Narikuravar or Vaghri, migrated south. The Vaghri speak a North Indian language and their traditional **occupation** is catching birds—which is the meaning of their name in Tamil. They call themselves Vaghri. Since the enforcement of the Wild Life Protection Act of 1972, many have switched to selling beads and other trinkets. Making plaits of false hair is another new occupation.

In 1961 a Tamil named K. Raghupathi gave up his work with a bus company and started a day school for Vaghri in Trichi. Six years later, he set up a meeting of 67 leaders of the community to form the Nadodi Nalvazue Sangam. Raghupathi married a woman from the tribe, Jnasundari, which made him more accepted by the people he was working with. In 1972 he opened a boarding school in Madras against much initial opposition from the parents of the children; since then, further school projects have been initiated.

The Vaghri have not reached the political maturity of the **Banjara** and **Kalbelia**, and links between them and European Romanies have been solely through **Pentecostal** missionaries.

VAIDA VOEVOD III (IONEL ROTARU). France. Political activist. In 1959, he was elected to the title Voevod by members of the **Romanian Ursari** tribe. In 1960, he founded the **Communauté Mondiale Gitane (CMG).** His aims included setting up an independent state, **Romanestan.** After the French government banned the CMG, he became less active.

VANNER. United Kingdom. A breed of horse developed by the Romanies of Great Britain to pull their traditional **caravans,** whence the name. They are a combination of Clydesdale, Dales, Friesian, and Shire breeds and are considered to be docile and intelligent. The first Vanner horse was imported to the **United States** in 1996 by Dennis and Cindy Thompson.

VERBAND DER DEUTSCHEN SINTI UND ROMA. Germany. The main organization of **Sinti,** based in Heidelberg and run by **Romani Rose.** It represents the Sinti in consultations with the **German** government, has a documentation center, and intervenes on behalf of the rights of the Sinti and Romanies.

VERBUNKOS. A **dance** used by recruiting units in **Hungary** in the 18th and 19th centuries. It was adopted and adapted by Gypsies and, later, by the composer **Franz Liszt.**

VIG, RUDOLF **(1929–1983).** Hungary. Musicologist. He collected more than 3,000 Gypsy songs. Some have been issued as recordings, for example, those from Szabolcs-Szatmar County.

VLAH (VLACH; VLAX; OLAH). "Ch" as in Scottish *loch*. The description *Vlah* should strictly be applied only to Gypsy **clans** and **dialects** of Romani that originate from **Wallachia**, but it is used more generally in **Gypsy studies** for those clans that come from, or are still on, any **Romanian**-speaking territory (Banat, Moldavia, Transylvania, or Wallachia). The Vlah dialects are divided by linguists into two groups. Those of the earliest clans to leave Romania have not palatalized the sounds *ch* and *sh*. The second group includes the **Kalderash** and **Lovari**.

VOICE OF ROMA (VOR). United States. President: Sani Rifati. The organization promotes **educational** and charitable projects for and about Roma. In recent years, VOR has conducted humanitarian aid projects for Roma in and from **Kosovo**. In addition to these projects, it has acted as an advocate for Romany refugees from Kosovo.

VOITIEHOVSKI, AVERIAND (?–1938). Union of Soviet Socialist Republics. Teacher. He was headmaster of the Gypsy school in Leningrad during the period when Romany culture was encouraged by the **Soviet** authorities. In 1938, he was executed for "antigovernment activities."

VOIVODINA. Estimated Roma population: 65,000, including recent immigration from **Kosovo**; the official returns in the 1971 census showed 7,760 Roma, but by 1991 the figure had reached the more realistic total of 24,895. A province formerly of **Yugoslavia** and now of **Serbia**, Voivodina remains part of Serbia, its autonomy having been suspended in 1990 at the same time as a similar proclamation in the province of Kosovo. During World War II, it was occupied by **Hungary**, which tried to deport many of the Romany population into Serbia proper. Nevertheless, many Roma remained there throughout the wartime period. When Voivodina was reoccupied by Yugoslav forces after the war, the population was manipulated in various ways until the ethnic Hungarian majority became a minority.

A number of **dialects** are spoken, in particular **Vlah** and **Gurbet**, though many Roma have Hungarian or Romanian as their mother tongue. The frontier town of Sremska Mitrovica saw an influx of Muslim refugees from **Bosnia** after 1992, bringing its Romany population up to some 8,000. Further refugees have arrived from Kosovo in later years.

In Voivodina, the Roma are not integrated, and most still live in settlements on the outskirts of towns and villages. Anti-Roma graffiti have appeared here, and instances of police brutality have been reported. In November 2005 the **United Nations** Committee against Torture determined that the Serbian government had violated the International Convention against Torture in the treatment by the Novi Sad police of Danilo Dimitrijević in 1997. Among other violations, he had been tied to a metal post for three days.

Educational levels for Roma are low, as elsewhere in Yugoslavia. In 1996 the cultural organization Matrica Romska was set up in Novi Sad but with a remit to cover all Serbia. Its first president was writer **Trifun Dimić**. The following year a roundtable on the Standardization of the **Romani Language** in Yugoslavia was organized in Novi Sad by the Matrica Romska and the Voivodina Society for the Romani Language, one of many attempts in recent years to standardize Romani. The organization Drustvo Voivodina (Voivodina Association) is also working for the advancement of the language, while optional instruction in Romani has been introduced in primary schools in Obrovac and Tovarisevo.

Band leader and fiddler Pera Petrović and his group **Rromano Centar** live now in **Austria**, but all come originally from Voivodina.

VRANCKX, AGNES (BIBI ANISHA). France. Contemporary political activist. She became secretary of a Gypsy organization in **Belgium** and then helped to set up the Common Market Gypsy Committee of the **International Romani Union** and, later, the **West European Gypsy Council**. She later moved to Rajasthan.

– W –

WAJS, BRONISLAWA (PAPUSZA) (1910–1987). Poland. **Poet.** During World War II, she survived by hiding in the forests, an experience described in her lyrics, written in Romani, such as "Ratvale jasva" [Tears of Blood]. Her verse was brought to the public by **Jerzy Ficowski**. Her family and many Gypsies were against this publication, as they felt Wajs was collaborating with a society intent on destroying their traditional way of life.

WALES. Estimated Gypsy population: 3,000. In 1996—the date of the last formal count—there were 489 **caravans** recorded (a drop from earlier figures), of which 36 were on unauthorized encampments. For most legislative purposes, Wales is part of the United Kingdom, while the Welsh Assembly in Cardiff has only limited powers. Legislation passed in the London Parliament generally applies in Wales.

Gypsies probably arrived in Wales for the first time during the 16th century. The first use of the Welsh term *Sipsiwn* (Gypsies) can be found in a **poem** composed by Morris Kyffin at the end of that century. The first official record of Gypsies recorded in Wales dates from 1579 and refers to the arrest of Gypsies in the then county of Radnor. A Romany named **Abraham Wood** arrived in Wales around 1730. He is said to have brought the violin to Wales, and his descendants included many well-known **musicians**. Other families that came to Wales and have spent a long time there include the Ingrams and some of the Lees and Prices. They are classed as Welsh Gypsies even when they nomadize outside the country.

Gypsies from Europe arrived in Wales in 1906, but they were kept under strict police supervision, before being escorted back into **England** and deported from Hull.

The last known speaker of Romani in Wales, Manfri Wood, died around 1968. **Derek Tipler** met a group of Romani-speaking Welsh Gypsies in Caernarvonshire in 1950, but it is not known whether any of them are still alive. The dialect was recorded by **John Sampson**. Many of the Welsh Gypsies have moved into houses. Others continue to travel in caravans and visit England and **Scotland**. The caravan-dwelling population of Wales today includes **Irish Travelers** and, in south Wales, descendants of marriages between English and Welsh Gypsies. The Welsh Assembly commissioned a Review of Service Provision for Gypsies, which was published in April 2003. It made 52 recommendations including reestablishing the twice yearly counts and making local authorities responsible to provide or facilitate sites. In October 2005, the Cardiff city council organized a Gypsy and Traveller Awareness Day to help "dispel **stereotypes** and myths" about the community.

WALLACHIA. A province of **Romania**. The first record of Gypsies in Wallachia dates from around 1360 when a document records the transfer of slaves. Gypsies were among those who later suffered the cruelties of Vlad IV, Prince of Wallachia, better known today as Dracula. It is said that he had many of them boiled alive, burned, or hanged. Slavery was abolished in Wallachia in 1856. *See also* VLAH.

WARD, BERNIE. Ireland. Boxer. Known in **Ireland** as the "King of Travellers," he was crowned at the Connemara pony fair. It is said that he beat a number of **Travelers** from the Sweeney clan in a bareknuckle fistfight in a bid to settle an ongoing feud.

WASO. Belgium. A group that plays Gypsy **music** from many countries. **Fapy Lafertin** can be heard on some of their recordings.

WEISS, HÄNSCHE. Germany. Contemporary **musician**. Though leader of a jazz sextet, it was with a quintet that he recorded volumes 5 and 6 of the compilation *Musik Deutscher Zigeuner* [Music of German Gypsies]. *See also* WEISS, KUSSI.

WEISS, KOKALO, AND MEISEL WEISS. *See* MIRANDO, TATA, JR., AND TATA MIRANDO SR.

WEISS, KUSSI. Germany. Contemporary **musician**. A guitarist and nephew of **Hänsche Weiss**, he plays Gypsy style and popular jazz.

WEISS, LALLA. The Netherlands. Contemporary civil rights activist. She is a spokesperson for the **Sinti**.

WELT-ZIGLER, STERNA. France. Contemporary **poet**. She writes in French and **Sinti dialect**.

WEST EUROPEAN GYPSY COUNCIL. 1981. A relaunch of the earlier Common Market Gypsy Council. It is no longer active. **Agnes Vranckx** and **Giles Eynard** were the first secretaries.

WIESENTHAL, SIMON (1908–2005). Galicia. **Jewish** "Nazi hunter." He was active in seeing that the fate of the Gypsies during the **Holocaust** was not forgotten.

WILLIAMSON, DUNCAN (1928–). Scotland. **Scottish Traveler**, storyteller, and singer. His tales have been published in many books. He has also recorded a cassette, *Put Another Log on the Fire*, on which he recites, sings, and plays the mouth organ and Jew's-harp. He is now settled in a house in Fife, but tours widely in Great Britain, entertaining in schools and at festivals.

WINTERSTEIN, TITI. Germany. A contemporary **Sinti** violinist and singer. Since 1978, his quintet has played a variety of jazz and Gypsy music in the **Hungarian** style. His recordings include *Djinee tu kowa ziro* [Do You Know This Time], *Saitenstrassen* [String Streets—a pun on *Seitenstrassen*, side streets], and the compilation *Best of Titi Winterstein.*

WLISLOCKI, HENRICH. Transylvania. Scholar. He studied the Gypsies in the 19th century and published a number of important books, including *Vom wanderenden Zigeunervolke* [About the Roaming Gypsy People; 1890] and *Die Sprache der Transilvanischen Zigeuner* [The Language of the Transylvanian Gypsies; 1884].

WOMEN. In general, **women** have held a subsidiary position in Romany society while often being the decision-making partner within a marriage. The **mockerdi** rules of hygiene mean women are seen as unclean after childbirth and during the monthly period. Their clothes always have to be washed separately from those of men. In recent years, a number of women have come to the fore as writers and political activists, including **Katarina Taikon** and the European MP **Livia Jaroka**.

WOOD, ABRAHAM (ABRAM) (?–1799). England. Violinist. He came to **Wales** from the west of **England** around 1730 with his wife Sarah and children and set up a base near Monmouth. He is said to have been the first person to play the violin in Wales. Wood had four children: Valentine (John), William, Solomon, and Damaris. They married into other Gypsy families—the Stanleys, Ingrams, and Boswells—and the eldest son, Valentine, was the grandfather of the famous harpist **John Wood Jones.** Other harpist descendants of Abraham Wood include John Roberts and William Lewis. The former performed before Grand Duke Constantine of **Russia** at Aberystwyth in 1847 and the king of the Belgians the following year, while the latter played at a Royal Command concert in London in 1932 and later gave performances at the Phoenix Theatre.

John Sampson, the great scholar of the **Romani language**, recorded the **dialect**, folktales, and songs of the **Wood** family and identified their dialect as distinct from that of the English Gypsies recorded by Leland, Smart, and Crofton during the 19th century. Sampson learned Romani from harpist Edward Wood, a descendant of Abraham Wood, and other members of the family.

WOOD, FRED (MANFRI). England. Contemporary political activist. First president of the **Gypsy Council** in December 1966. A skilled woodcarver and performer on the Jew's-harp, his biography is called *In the Life of a Romany Gypsy.*

WOONWAGENBEWONERS ("CARAVAN DWELLERS"). Indigenous **Travelers** in the **Netherlands**. They number some 20,000 and form a separate community with their own customs. Some speak a variety of Dutch known as **Bargoens**. After 1945 the official policy was to build **caravan** camps and get them to stop traveling. These camps were at first very large, with a school, shop, and church. But it soon became evident that these large camps caused problems, for example, too much competition for the same sort of work. Policy then switched to building smaller camps and breaking up the large ones.

WORLD BANK. As the countries of eastern Europe were moving toward accession to the **European Union**, the World Bank organized a conference in Budapest, **Hungary**, in 2003 under the title "Roma in an Expanding Europe: Challenges for the Future." The report *Breaking the Poverty Cycle for the Roma* was presented at the conference. James Wolfensohn, president of the World Bank, said, "Europe must not leave the Roma behind." *See also* DECADE OF ROMA INCLUSION.

WORLD ROMANY CONGRESS. There have been six congresses organized by the **International Romani Union (IRU)** and its predecessors in the years since the end of World War II.

The first World Romany Congress in 1971, with delegates attending from 14 countries, was held near London under the auspices of the **Comité International Tzigane**. It was originally intended to be a preparatory meeting to plan the first congress. However, because of the number of delegates coming and the number of countries represented, it was decided to make this meeting the first congress itself. **Grattan Puxon** was elected secretary and **Slobodan Berberski**, from Belgrade, president. During the congress, work was divided among five specialized commissions dealing with **education**, social problems, war crimes **reparations**, culture, and language. It was agreed to campaign against illiteracy and that the use of Romani in schools should be officially recognized. The language commission agreed that there should be a move toward unifying the language. The opening day of the conference, 8 April, was proclaimed the national day (**Roma Nation Day**) to be celebrated every year. A **national anthem** and a **flag** were adopted.

The second World Romany Congress was held in April 1978 in Geneva, **Switzerland**, and was attended by 120 delegates from 26 countries. The **United Nations**, the Human Rights Commission, and the United Nations Educational, Social, and Cultural Commission had representatives at the Congress who put the case for future cooperation. **Jan Cibula** was elected president replacing Berberski and **Shaip Jusuf** was elected vice president. **Yul Brynner** was chosen as the honorary president and took part in the final press conference. During the congress, the IRU was established.

The work of organizing further congresses was carried out by the IRU. The third World Romany Congress was held in Göttingen, **Germany**, in May 1981, with 300 representatives from 22 countries and the support of the **Gesellschaft für Bedrohte Völker**. The history of the Gypsy people under the Nazis was confronted on the first day. **Simon Wiesenthal** and **Miriam Novitch** were among the speakers. At this congress, Puxon was replaced as secretary by **Rajko Djurić**, and **Sait Balić** replaced Cibula as president.

The fourth World Romany Congress, organized by the IRU, was held in April 1990 near Warsaw, **Poland**. More than 200 delegates from 18 countries were present, with a higher number of delegates from eastern Europe than any of the previous three. It was preceded by a Language Conference on the Standardization of the **Romani Language**. After the formal opening ceremony on 8 April, the next day was devoted to reports from different countries. Language was an important item on the agenda of the congress itself, and a proposal was accepted for a new common **alphabet**. A highlight of the congress was a televised concert in which many well-known groups took part, including **Esma Redjepova**'s ensemble. Djurić replaced Balic as president and **Emil Sćuka** was elected general secretary. The membership of the commissions was fixed by elections. The following commissions were set up: Cultural, Encyclopedia, Language, **Holocaust** and Reparations, and Education and Information. Because of lack of funds, however, these commissions were not particularly active.

The fifth World Romany Congress, again organized by the IRU, was held in Prague, **Czech Republic**, in July 2000 in the headquarters of Radio Free Europe, and 122 delegates from 38 different countries attended in order to approve a new program, statutes, and elect a new leadership of the IRU. The first day was spent electing a committee to oversee the congress and forming working groups. On the following day, topics were agreed upon for the agenda, including the situation of Roma in **Kosovo**, reparations for Romani Holocaust victims, the migration of Roma from central and eastern Europe, and the standardization of the Romani language. Out of these discussions in the working groups, it was agreed that a new statute for the IRU be created, declaring that the Roma want to be recognized as a nation. There were also calls for Germany to apologize for what has become known as the Roma Holocaust, in which up to half a million Roma were killed by the Nazis. The culmination of the congress was the election of a new president for the IRU. The successful candidate was

Scuka, from the Czech Republic, previously the general secretary. **Hristo Kyuchukov** from **Bulgaria** was elected as the new general secretary. The sixth World Romany Congress was held in Lanciano, **Italy**, in 2004. In spite of the late announcement of the date and venue, a representative number of Roma attended. Sćuka, the outgoing president, was unable to be present due to illness. **Stanislaw Stankiewicz** was elected president. The vice presidents are **Nadezhda Demeter**, **Victor Famulson**, and **Normundus Rudjevics**. **Zoran Dimov** was elected secretary of the IRU and **Dragan Jevremović** was reelected as chairman of the IRU Parliament. *See also* INTERNATIONAL MEETINGS; LODZ CONGRESS.

– X –

X. In the international phonetic **alphabet** and in most systems of writing Romani, the letter *x* represents the sound in Scottish *loch* or German *doch*.

– Y –

YATES, DORA **(1879–1974).** England. Scholar. From a **Jewish** background, she was for many years secretary of the **Gypsy Lore Society** and editor of its journal.

YUGOSLAVIA. Estimated Gypsy population of Yugoslavia in 1992 (before the breakup of the republic): one million. More than 50,000 Yugoslav Gypsies had perished during the Nazi **Holocaust**, leaving a population of perhaps 600,000 in 1945. In 1981 a census gave the figure of 850,000 Gypsies for the whole of Yugoslavia. This showed a rise throughout the country compared to previous censuses, as Gypsies felt encouraged to declare their ethnicity. Only in **Macedonia** and **Kosovo** were there demands on them to declare themselves otherwise—as **Albanians**, pressured by that community. The reduced Yugoslav state after 1992 (comprising only **Serbia** and **Montenegro**) had a population of some 150,000–200,000 Gypsies.

The first Gypsies appeared on the territory of modern Yugoslavia in the 14th century. After having been part of the **Byzantine, Ottoman,** and **Habsburg** Austro-Hungarian empires, Yugoslavia became an independent country in 1918. At that time, the Gypsy population was for the most part settled or seminomadic and had Catholic, Muslim, and Orthodox Christian members. Only in Montenegro was there a large **nomadic** population. Some cultural activity took place in Belgrade, where there was a settled community, mostly living in separate Gypsy quarters. Three issues of a bilingual magazine *Romano Lil* (Romani Paper), edited by Svetozar Simić, were published in 1935.

In 1941 the **German** Army invaded Yugoslavia, which was split into separate parts. After the liberation in 1945, the Yugoslav Federation was reestablished as a republic. It is said that Marshal Tito (the Partisan leader and president of the new republic) had promised the Gypsies who fought with the Partisans that they would have their own state after the war. It was likely that this would have been carved out of Macedonia. However, this plan was dropped, probably because Tito did not wish to reduce Macedonia in size in case it became the object of territorial demands by **Greece** or Albania. It was the Romanies of Macedonia, however, who developed the largest Gypsy community called **Shuto Orizari** on the outskirts of **Skopje.**

The economic restructuring of Yugoslavia during the 1960s also saw a wave of mass migration of many Gypsies to the West as the restrictions on emigration were eased. Predominantly from **Bosnia-Herzegovina,** Montenegro, and Kosovo, the migrants moved to Germany, **France,** and other countries. Many took jobs in factories; others nomadized in **caravans.**

The antagonisms among nationalities in the country intensified, which led Tito and the Yugoslav government to hold back the official recognition of Gypsies as a nationality (as opposed to the lower status of "ethnic group") across Yugoslavia. In 1971, however, **Faik Abdi,** the representative from Shuto Orizari in the Macedonian Parliament, was able to upgrade the status of Romanies to an officially recognized nationality in Macedonia. This allowed the use of the Romany **flag** and language, as well as time on

radio and **television**. In 1981 Roma were recognized as a national minority across Yugoslavia.

The press began to refer to "Roma" instead of the pejorative word *Tsigani*. Publications in Romani included local periodicals and a biography of Tito translated into Romani in 1978 by **Shaip Jusuf**. In 1981 Radio Tetovo began a half-hour program in Romani. Eighty local Romany associations also sprang up during this period, many focusing on cultural activities and calling themselves **Phralipe** (Brotherhood).

There was still discrimination and prejudice. In 1986 Muslim Gypsies were prevented from burying their dead in a Muslim cemetery in Bosnia and officials in **Slovenia** tried to stop Gypsies from voting in local elections. In Kuršumlija, a Gypsy woman was doused with gasoline and burned. The greatest barrier for the Gypsies remained illiteracy, as most children did not complete secondary **education**.

Bilingual magazines have appeared sporadically in Serbia and Macedonia. The editor of one (*Romano Lil*), Dragomir Asković, is also active in the radio broadcasts in Romani from Radio Belgrade. The government of the new smaller Yugoslavia—consisting of Serbia (incorporating **Voivodina** and Kosovo) only—has made some attempt to gain the allegiance of the Gypsies, for example, by holding a ceremonial Orthodox service with prayers in Romani that was attended by government figures. *See also* BANAT; CROATIA.

– Z –

ZAMOLY ROMA. On 2 July 2000, 12 Roma families from the **Hungarian** village of Zamoly traveled to Strasbourg, **France**, where they demanded political asylum and protection from racial persecution after their houses had been destroyed. In 2001, 37 out of the original 46 Roma were declared to be refugees by the **European Court of Human Rights** in Strasbourg. It has been suggested that the Roma had been manipulated by the **Russian** secret service as part of a master plan to darken Hungary's **human rights** record and keep the **European Union** from expanding eastward.

ZANKO. France. 20th-century chief of the **Kalderash** of southern **France**. His account of the traditions of his **clan** were recorded by Père Chatard in the book *Zanko: Chef Tribal* (1959).

ZIGENARE. *See* ZIGEUNER.

ZIGEUNER. The old **German** word for Gypsies, derived from the **Greek** *atsingani*, as are its Scandinavian equivalents (*Zigenare*, etc.). Because of the association of the term *Zigeuner* with the Nazi period, books and the press in Germany now often use the term "*Rom und Sinti*" to refer to all Gypsies, regardless of whether they are in fact Roma or **Sinti**.

ZIGEUNERLEBEN ("GYPSY LIFE"). The title of the writers' conference Biennale Kleinere Sprachen (Biennial for Minor Languages) held in Berlin in October 1991, which was devoted to Gypsy writers. Among those taking part were **Rajko Djurić**, **Margita Reiznerová**, and **Philomena Franz**, as well as Jovan Nicolić from Belgrade.

ZINGARI. The common **Italian** name for Gypsies, derived from the **Greek** *atsingani*. *Gitano* is also used.

ZOLTAN, FLORINA (1964–). Romania. Civil rights activist. She is now living in **England** and has set up the **Romani Resource Centre**.

ZOTT. An old Arabic word used for all **Indians**, not just the Jats. It was used to refer to the many people of **Indian origin** in the Middle East in the times of the great Arab Caliphate and is still used as another name for the **Nawwar**, a Gypsy **clan**. *See also* AFGHANISTAN.

ZSIGO, JENO (1951–2000). Hungary. Youth leader and **musician**. He played with the band **Ando Drom**.

Bibliography

CONTENTS

I. INTRODUCTION

The bibliography is arranged by classes and subclasses. With very few exceptions, only works published after 1945 have been included. For historical works, one should consult George Black's *A Gypsy Bibliography* (Edinburgh: Gypsy Lore Society, 1914). A supplementary list was published in 1940 in the *Journal of the Gypsy Lore Society* (3rd series) 19, nos. 1–2: 20–33. Translations are given for titles in Russian and less common languages. Books are normally listed only once, in the most appropriate section. A book dealing with the history or present-day situation of a single country will be found under that country's heading, not in the History section. Many other titles are listed by subject (e.g., health, music). Books and articles dealing with more than one of the countries that make up the United Kingdom will be found under the United Kingdom heading. There are separate headings, however, for England, Scotland, and Wales where titles deal only with that part of the United Kingdom; Northern Ireland will be found under Ireland.

Apart from Black for the classical literature, Diane Tong's *Gypsies: A Multidisciplinary Annotated Bibliography* (New York: Garland, 1995) gives good coverage of material in English, though it is not comprehensive on works in other languages. A good overall introduction is Angus Fraser's *The Gypsies* (Oxford: Blackwell, 1992). For the modern period, the various works by Jean-Pierre Liégeois should be consulted. Isabel Fonseca's account of her travels through eastern Europe—although criticized—is an easy-to-read introduction to the world of the Gypsies *(Bury Me Standing*, New York: Knopf, 1995).

Nearly all works written up to 1939 deal with Gypsies as an exotic race. An exception was the substantial number of books written in Romani in the early years of the Soviet Union. After 1945, there is a wider coverage of themes and an increase in books written by Romanies themselves. Again, until the end of World War II, the *Journal of the Gypsy Lore Society (JGLS)*, is the only serious publication and is a rich source of information. Anyone embarking on a study of Gypsies should first leaf through the *JGLS* to see what has been written on the themes that interest them. After 1945, more learned journals appear, in particular *Études Tsiganes* and *Lacio Drom*, the latter no longer published. They, too, are a valuable source of information on a variety of topics. A selection of recent articles from all three journals has been included. As regards the different clans, the Kalderash and Manouche are those that have the best descriptions. In fact, many books and articles about Gypsies write only about the Kalderash clan.

The section on the Holocaust contains many titles and is one of the largest. Although in the first years after 1945 very little was written about the fate of the Gypsies, this lapse has been remedied recently, particularly with books dealing with individual towns in Germany. An overall picture of the Holocaust period will be found in Donald Kenrick and Grattan Puxon's *Destiny of Europe's Gypsies* (London: Heinemann, 1972). This has an index and detailed references. The updated edition under the title *Gypsies under the Swastika* (Hatfield: University of Hertfordshire Press, 1995) is more for the general reader and has no references. A three-volume work on the Holocaust entitled *The Gypsies during the Second World War*, originally prepared in Paris by the Centre de Recherches Tsiganes, has now been published in parts (University of Hertfordshire Press, 1997–2006). Guenter Lewy's *The Nazi Persecution of the Gypsies* (Oxford University Press, 2000) has been criticized for playing down the magnitude of the genocide. Michael Zimmermann's *Rasseutopia und Genozid* (Hamburg: Christians,1996) is a comprehensive work with more than 100 pages of notes alone.

Rajklo Djurić's *Die Literatur der Roma und Sinti* (Berlin: Parabolis, 2002) is a survey of Roma writers in many lands.

Two recent works will interest the general reader. The first is Ian Hancock's *We Are the Romani People* (Hatfield: University of Hertfordshire Press, 2002), which is designed as a textbook for first-year undergraduates. Second, Peter Bakker has edited a collection of articles under the title *What Is the Romami Language?* (Hatfield: University of Hertfordshire Press, 2000).

There is now for the first time a textbook for Romani that teaches the language in a traditional way rather than just describing it for scholars: Ronald Lee's *Learn Romani* (Hatfield: University of Hertfordshire Press, 2005). It deals with the widely spoken Kalderash dialect. The same publisher promises a guide to learning other dialects.

Currently a large number of bilingual periodicals are being published in eastern Europe. However, many of them are irregular, and sometimes financial difficulties have led to a gap in their appearance. Addresses are provided for a number of publications that are informative, rather than literary, and that have a track record of reliability. This listing should not be seen as reflecting in any way on the quality of those for which no address is given.

II. GENERAL

1. Overall Studies

Acton, T. A., ed. *Gypsy Politics and Traveller Identity*. Proceedings of the ESRC Romany Studies Seminar Series, vol. 1. Hatfield: University of Hertfordshire Press, 1997.

Acton, T. A., and G. J. Mundy, eds. *Romani Culture and Gypsy Identity*. Proceedings of the ESRC Romany Studies Seminar Series, vol. 2. Hatfield: University of Hertfordshire Press, 1997.

Andersen, Kirsten. *Sigøjnere*. Copenhagen: Munksgaard, 1971.

Asséo, Henriette. *Les Tsiganes, une destinée européenne*. Paris: Gallimard, 1994.

Bancroft, Angus. *Roma and Gypsy-Travellers in Europe: Modernity, Race, Space and Exclusion*. Burlington, Vt.: Ashgate, 2005.

Block, Martin. *Die Zigeuner: Ihr Leben und ihre Seele*. New ed. Frankfurt am Main: Lang, 1997.

Bodi, Zsuzsanna, ed. *Readings of the 1st International Conference on Gypsy Ethnography (Budapest 1993)*. Studies in Roma (Gypsy) Ethnography, vol. 2. Budapest: Mikszáth Kiadó, 1994. [In English and Hungarian.]

Bogaart, Nico, et al. *Zigeuners*. Amsterdam: El Sevier, 1980.

Djurić, Rajko. *Seobe Roma* (Romany Migrations). Belgrade: BIGZ, 1987.

Earle, Fiona, et al. *A Time to Travel? An Introduction to Britain's Newest Travellers*. Lyme Regis, UK: Enabler, 1994.

Gronemeyer, Reimer, and Georgia Rakelmann. *Die Zigeuner, Reisende in Europa*. Cologne: Dumont, 1988.

Hemetek, Ursula, and Mozes Heinschink, eds. *Roma: Das unbekannte Volk.* Munich: Boehlau, 1994.

Hohmann, Joachim, ed. *Handbuch zur Tsiganologie.* Frankfurt am Main: Lang, 1996.

Hund, Wulf, ed. *Zigeuner: Geschichte und Struktur einer rassistischen Konstruktion.* Duisburg: DISS, 1996.

Hundsalz, Andreas. *Stand der Forschung über Zigeuner und Landfahrer.* Stuttgart: Kohlhammer, 1978.

Karpati, Mirella, ed. *Zingari, ieri e oggi.* Rome: Centro Studi Zingari, n.d. [Also in German as *Sinti und Roma: Heute und Gestern.*]

Klein, N. *Sinti und Roma.* Stuttgart: Institut für Auslandsbeziehungen, 1981.

Liégeois, Jean-Pierre. *Roma, Gypsies and Travellers.* Rev. ed. Strasbourg: Council of Europe Press, 1994. [Also in French as *Roma, Tsiganes, Voyageurs.*]

Lo-Johansson, Ivar. *Zigenare.* Stockholm: Prisma, 1963.

Lucassen, Leo, et al., eds. *Gypsies and Other Itinerant Groups.* Basingstoke, UK: Macmillan, 1998.

Marsh, Adrian, and Elin Strand. *Contextual, Constructed and Contested: Gypsies and the Problem of Identities.* Istanbul: Swedish Research Institute, 2005. [Proceedings of the 1st Istanbul International Romani Studies Conference.]

Maur, Wolf in der. *Die Zigeuner: Wanderer zwischen den Welten.* Vienna: Molden, 1969.

Mayall, David, ed. "Gypsies: The Forming of Identities and Official Responses." *Immigrants and Minorities* 2, no. 1 (March 1992). [Special edition.]

Mercier, Denis. *Latcho drom: Un film de Tony Gatlif.* Paris: K.G. Productions, 1993.

Mroz, Lech. *Cyganie.* Warsaw: Ksiazka i Wiedza, 1971.

Nordström-Holm, Gunni, and Armas Lind. *Om zigenare.* Stockholm: SI Pocket, 1982.

Nordström-Holm, Gunni, and Björn Myrman. *Vi kallar dem Zigenare.* Stockholm: Alfabeta, 1991.

Osella, Carla. *Zingari: Storie di un popolo sconosciuto.* Turin: N.p., 1985.

Rehfisch, F., ed. *Gypsies, Tinkers and Other Travellers.* London: Academic Press, 1975.

Rostás-Farkas, György. *Cigányságom vállalom.* Budapest: TIT, 1992. [Essays on Romani culture in Hungarian.]

Salo, Matt, ed. *100 Years of Gypsy Studies.* Cheverly, Md.: Gypsy Lore Society, 1990. [Papers from the 10th Annual Meeting of the Gypsy Lore Society, 1988.]

Saul, Nicholas, and Susan Tebbutt, eds. *The Role of the Romanies*. Liverpool: Liverpool University Press, 2004. [Papers from the 2000 Liverpool Conference.]

Šipka, Milan, ed. *International Symposium: Romani Language and Culture*. Sarajevo: Institut za Proućavanje Nacionalnih Odnosa, 1989. [Papers of the 1986 Sarajevo Seminar.]

Thesleff, Arthur. *Report on the Gypsy Question*. 1901. [Reprinted in *JGLS* new series.]

Tong, Diana. *Gypsies: An Interdisciplinary Reader*. New York: Garland, 1998.

Vossen, Rüdiger, ed. *Zigeuner*. Frankfurt am Main: Ullstein, 1983.

Wedeck, H. E., and Wade Baskin. *Dictionary of Gipsy Life and Lore*. London: Owen, 1973.

Willems, Wim. *In Search of the True Gypsy*. London: Cass, 1997. [trans.]

——. *Op zoek naar de ware Zigeuner* (Looking for the Real Gypsies). Utrecht: van Arkel, 1995.

Zatta, Jane. *Gli Zingari i Roma: Una cultura ai confini*. Padua: Centro di Initiativa Democratica degli Insegnanti, 1988.

Zoon, Ina. *On the Margins: Roma and Public Services in Romania, Bulgaria and Macedonia*. New York: Open Society, 2001.

2. Bibliography

Binns, Dennis. *A Gypsy Bibliography*. Manchester, UK: Dennis Binns, 1982 [with later supplements].

Black, G. F. *A Gypsy Bibliography*. London: Constable, 1913.

Collie, Michael, and Angus Fraser. *George Borrow: A Bibliographical Study*. Winchester, UK: St. Paul's Bibliographies, 1984.

da Costa, Elisa Maria Lopes. *Os Ciganos: Fontes bibliograficas em Portugal*. Madrid: Presencia Gitana, 1995.

Franzese, Sergio. "Internet e gli Zingari." *Lacio Drom* 33, nos. 3–4 (1997): 40–45.

Gmelch, G., and S. B. Gmelch. "Ireland's Travelling People: A Comprehensive Bibliography." *JGLS* (3rd series) 3 (1978): 159–69.

Gronemeyer, Reimer. *Zigeuner in Osteuropa: Eine Bibliographie zu den Ländern Polen, Tschechoslowakei und Ungarn, mit einem Anhang über ältere Sowjetische Literatur*. Munich: Saur, 1983.

Hohmann, Joachim S. *Neue deutsche Zigeunerbibliographie: Unter Berücksichtigung aller Jahrgänge des "Journal of the Gypsy Lore Society."* Frankfurt am Main: Lang, 1992.

Hovens, Pieter, and Jeanne Hovens. *Zigeuners, Woonwagenbewoners en reizenden: Een bibliografie* (Gypsies, Caravan-Dwellers and Travellers: A

Bibliography). Rijswijk: Ministry of Cultural Affairs, Recreation and Social Welfare, 1982.

Leeds University. *Catalogue of the Romany Collection*. Edinburgh: Nelson, 1962.

Neacsu, Dana. *Roma and Forced Migration: An Annotated Bibliography*. New York: Open Society Institute, 1997.

Ortega, José. *Los Gitanos: Guia bibliográfica y estudio preliminar*. Manchester: Binns, 1987.

Tong, Diane. *Gypsies: A Multidisciplinary Annotated Bibliography*. New York: Garland, 1995.

Tyrnauer, Gabrielle. *Gypsies and the Holocaust: A Bibliography and Introductory Essay*. 2nd ed. Montreal: Institute for Genocide Studies, 1991. [A version of this work appears in *Genocide: A Critical Bibliographic Review*, ed. Israel W. Charny, vol. 3, *The Widening Circle of Genocide*. New Brunswick, N.J.: Transaction, 1994.]

University of Liverpool. *A Catalogue of the Gypsy Books Collected by the Late Robert Andrews Scott Macfie, Sometime Editor and Secretary of the Gypsy Lore Society*. Liverpool: University of Liverpool Press, 1936.

3. Demography

Arnold, Hermann. *Fahrendes Volk*. Neustadt: Pfälzische Verlaganstalt, 1980. [Revised edition of his *Randgruppen des Zigeunervolkes*, 1975.]

Brown, Marilyn R. *Gypsies and Other Bohemians: The Myths of the Artist in Nineteenth-Century France*. Ann Arbor, Mich.: UMI Research Press, 1985.

Charlemagne, Jacqueline. *Populations nomades et pauvreté*. Paris: Presses Universitaires de France, 1983.

Liégeois, Jean-Pierre, and Nicolae Gheorghe. *Roma/Gypsies: A European Minority*. London: Minority Rights Group, 1995.

Vaux de Foletier, François de. *Le monde des Tsiganes*. Paris: Berger-Levrault, 1983.

Webb, G. E. C. *Gypsies: The Secret People*. London: Barrie Jenkins, 1960. [Reprint, Greenwood Press, 1974.]

Wilson, Nerissa. *Gypsies and Gentlemen: The Life and Times of the Leisure Caravan*. London: Columbus Books, 1986.

4. Travel and Description

Croft-Cooke, Rupert. *The Moon in My Pocket: Life with the Romanies*. London: S. Low, Marston, 1984.

Fonseca, Isabel. *Bury Me Standing*. London: Chatto Windus, 1995. [Also in German as *Begrabt mich Aufrecht*.]

Harvey, Denis. *The Gypsies: Waggon-time and After*. London: Batsford, 1979.

McDowell, Bart. *Gypsies, Wanderers of the World*. Washington, D.C.: National Geographic Society, 1970.

Tomasević, Nebojsa, and Rajko Djurić. *Gypsies of the World*. London: Flint River Press, 1988.

Ward-Jackson C. H., and Denis E. Harvey. *The English Gypsy Caravan: Its Origins, Builders, Technology, and Conservation*. 2nd ed. Newton Abbot, UK: David & Charles, 1986.

III. HISTORY

1. General

Barany, Zoltan. *The East European Gypsies: Regime Change, Marginality and Ethnopolitics*. Cambridge: Cambridge University Press, 2002.

Bartolomej, Daniel. *Dejiny Romu* (History of the Gypsies). Olomouc, Czech Republic: Univerzita Palackéhou, 1994.

Crowe, David. *A History of the Gypsies of Eastern Europe and Russia*. New York: St. Martin's, 1994.

Crowe, David, and John Kolsti, eds. *The Gypsies of Eastern Europe*. Armonk, N.Y.: Sharpe, 1991.

Djurić, Rajko. *Seobe Roma* (History of the Romanies). Belgrade: BIGZ, 1985.

Fraser, Angus. *The Gypsies*. Oxford: Blackwell, 1992.

Gilsenbach, Reimar. *Weltchronik der Zigeuner. Pt. 1*. Frankfurt am Main: Lang, 1994.

Hancock, Ian. *We Are the Romani People*. Hatfield: University of Hertfordshire Press, 2002.

Liégeois, Jean-Pierre. *Gypsies: An Illustrated History*, trans. Tony Berrett. London: Al Saqi Books, 1985. [Translation in part of Liégeois's *Tsiganes*.]

———. *Tsiganes*. Paris: Découverte, 1983.

Nicolini, Bruno. "La chiesa cattolica e gli Zingari." In *Zingari, ieri e oggi*, ed. M. Karpati. Rome: Centro Studi Zingari, n.d.

Vaux de Foletier, François de. *Mille ans d'histoire des Tsiganes*. Paris: Fayard, 1970.

2. Early Migration and Indian Origins

Hancock, Ian. *The Indian Origins and Westward Migration of the Roma*. Manchaca, Texas: Romany Union, 1997.

Kenrick, Donald. *Gypsies, from the Ganges to the Thames*. Hatfield: University of Hertfordshire Press, 2004. [Also available in other languages.]

Lal, C. *Gipsies, Forgotten Children of India*. Delhi: Ministry of Information, 1962.

Moreau, Roger. *The Rom: Walking in the Paths of the Gypsies*. Toronto: Key Porter, 1995.

Rishi, W. R. *Roma: The Panjabi Emigrants in Europe, Central and Middle Asia, the USSR, and the Americas*. Patiala, India: Punjabi University, 1976.

Singhal, D. P. *Gypsies: Indians in Exile*. Meerut, India: Archana, 1982.

Soulis, G. "The Gypsies in the Byzantine Empire and the Balkans in the Late Middle Ages." *Dumbarton Oaks Papers* 15 (1961).

3. History to 1939 (Excluding the Holocaust)

Daniel, Bartolomej. *Geschichte der Roma in Böhmen, Mähren and der Slowakei*. Frankfurt am Main: Lang, 1998.

Haley W. "The Gypsy Conference at Bucharest." *JGLS* (3rd series) 13 (1934).

Opfermann, Ulrich. *Dass sie den Zigeuner-Habit ablegen: Die Geschichte der Zigeuner-Kolonien*. Frankfurt am Main: Lang, 1996.

4. The Holocaust (1933–1945)

Acković, Dragoljub. *Roma Suffering in Jasenovac Camp*. Belgrade: Strucna Kniga, 1995. [Original-language version, *Stradanja Roma u Jasenovcu*. Belgrade: NIGP "ABC GLAS" DD, 1994.]

Alt, Betty, and Silvia Folts. *Weeping Violins*. Kirksville, Mo.: Thomas Jefferson University Press, 1996.

Ayass W., et al. *Feinderklärung und Prävention*. Berlin: Rotbuch, 1988.

Beckers, Jan, ed. *Me hum Sinthu / Ik ben Zigeuner* (I Am a Gypsy). The Hague: Horus, 1980.

Berenbaum, M., ed. *A Mosaic of Victims*. New York: New York University Press, 1989; London: Tauris, 1990.

Bernadac, Christian. *L'Holocauste oublié: Le massacre des Tsiganes*. Paris: France-Empire, 1979.

Bulajić, Milan. *Ustaški zlocini genocida* (Ustashe Criminal Genocide). Belgrade: RAD, 1988.

Dlugoborski, Waclaw, ed. *50-lecie zaglady Romów w KL Auschwitz-Birkenau* (50th Anniversary of the Massacre in Auschwitz-Birkenau Concentration Camp). Oswiecim: Stowarzyszenie Romów w Polsce, 1994. [In Polish and German.]

Dokumentationzentrum Deutscher Sinti und Roma. *Kinder und Jugendliche als Opfer des Holocausts.* Heidelberg: Dokumentationzentrum, 1995.

Duna, William A. *Gypsies: A Persecuted Race.* Minneapolis, Minn.: Duna Studios, 1984.

Fings, Karola, and Frank Sparing. *"Zt. Zigeunerlager": Die Verfolgung der Düsseldorfer Sinti und Roma im Nationalsozialismus.* Cologne: Volksblatt, 1992.

Fings, Karola, et al. *Einziges Land, in dem Judenfrage und Zigeunerfrage gelöst: Die Verfolgung der Roma im faschistisch besetzten Jugoslawien, 1941–1945.* Cologne: Rom, n.d.

Friedman, Ina. "Bubili: A Young Gypsy's Fight for Survival." In *The Other Victims: First-Person Stories of Non-Jews Persecuted by the Nazis.* Boston: Houghton Mifflin, 1990.

Gilsenbach, Reimar. *Oh Django, sing deinen Zorn.* Berlin: BasisDruck, 1993.

Günther, Wolfgang. *Ach Schwester, ich kann nicht mehr tanzen: Sinti und Roma im KZ Bergen Belsen.* Hanover: SOAK, 1990.

———. *Zur preussischen Zigeunerpolitik seit 1871.* Hanover: ANS, 1985.

Hancock, Ian. *The Pariah Syndrome.* Ann Arbor, Mich.: Karoma, 1987.

———. "Responses to the Porrajmos: The Romani Holocaust." In *Is the Holocaust Unique? Perspectives on Comparative Genocide,* ed. Alan Rosenbaum. Boulder, Colo.: Westview Press, 1996.

Heuss, Herbert. *Darmstadt, Auschwitz: Die Verfolgung der Sinti in Darmstadt.* Darmstadt: Verband deutscher Sinti und Roma, 1995.

Heuss, Herbert, Karola Fings, and Frank Sparing. *The Gypsies during the Second World War,* vol. 1: *From Race Science to the Camps.* Hatfield: University of Hertfordshire Press, 1997. [Also available in French and German.]

Hohmann, Joachim. *Robert Ritter und die Erbe der Kriminalbiologie.* Frankfurt am Main: Lang, 1991.

———. *Zigeuner und Zigeunerwissenschaft: Ein Beitrag zur Grundlagenforschung und Dokumentation des Völkermords im "Dritten Reich."* Marburg: Guttandin Hoppe, 1980.

Holy, Dusan, and Ctibor Nečas. *Zalujici pisen.* Straznica: Ustav Lidové Kultury, 1993.

Ioanid, Radu. *The Holocaust in Romania: The Destruction of Jews and Gypsies under the Antonescu Regime, 1940–1944.* Chicago: Ivan Dee, 2000.

Johansen, Jahn Otto. *Sigøynernes Holocaust.* Oslo: Cappelen. 1989. [Original Norwegian edition.] Swedish edition, *Zigenarnas Holocaust.* Stockholm: Symposion, 1990.

Kenrick, Donald, and Gratton Puxon. *The Destiny of Europe's Gypsies.* London: Heinemann Educational, 1972. [Also available in French, German, Italian, and Japanese. For two editions in Romani, see Puxon and Kenrick below.]

——. *Gypsies under the Swastika.* Hatfield: University of Hertfordshire Press, 1995. [A revised edition of *Destiny of Europe's Gypsies*, also available in French, Spanish, and other languages.]

Kladivová, V. *Konečná Stanice Auschwitz-Birkenau.* Olomouc, Czech Republic: Univerzita Palackého, 1994.

Krausnick, M. *Wo sind sie hingekommen?* Stuttgart: Bleicher, 1995.

Lessing, A. *Mein Leben in Versteck.* Düsseldorf: Zebulon, 1993.

Lifton, Robert Jay. *The Nazi Doctors: Medical Killing and the Psychology of Genocide.* New York: Basic Books, 1986.

Lipa, Jiri. "The Fate of Gypsies in Czechoslovakia under Nazi Domination." In *A Mosaic of Victims*, ed. M. Berenbaum. New York: New York University Press, 1990.

Müller-Hill, Benno. *Murderous Science: Elimination by Scientific Selection of Jews, Gypsies, et al., Germany, 1933–1945*, trans. George R. Fraser. New York: Oxford University Press, 1988.

Nazi Genocide in Poland Seminar. Papers by Ciechanowski, Galinski, Wilczur, and Zabierowski, translated and reprinted in *Lacio Drom* 20, nos. 2–3 (May–June 1984).

Nečas, Ctibor. *Ceskoslovenstí Romové v letech 1939–1945* (Czechoslovak Gypsies in the Years 1939–1945). Brno: Masaryková Univerzita, 1994.

——. *Nad osudem českych Cikánu a slovenskych cikánu v letech 1939–1945* (On the Fate of the Czech and Slovak Gypsies). Brno: Univerzita J. S. Purkyne, 1981.

——. *Nemužeme zapomenout: Našti bisteras* (We Cannot Forget). Olomouc, Czech Republic: Univerzita Palackého, 1994.

Pape, Marcus. *A Nikdo vám Nebude Verit: Dokument o koncentracním tábore Lety u Písku* (Nobody Will Believe You: Documents about the Lety Concentration Camp). Prague: GplusG, 1997.

Parcer J., ed. *Los Cyganów w KL Auschwitz-Birkenau: Das Schicksal der Sinti und Roma im KL Auschwitz-Birkenau.* Oswiecim: Stowarzyszenie Romów w Polsce, 1994.

——, ed. *Memorial Book. The Gypsies at Auschwitz-Birkenau.* Munich: Saur, 1993.

Pedersen, F. *Skyd Zigeunerne.* Copenhagen: Carnet, 1990.

Peschanski, Denis. *Les Tsiganes en France, 1939–1946.* Paris: CNRS, 1994.

Puxon, Grattan, and Donald Kenrick. *Bibahtale berša* (Unhappy Years). London: Romanestan, 1990. New ed., Madrid: Presencia Gitana, 1996.

Rose, Romani, and Walter Weiss. *Sinti und Roma im "Dritten Reich": Das Programm der Vernichtung durch Arbeit.* Göttingen: Lamuv, 1991.

Sigot, Jacques. *Ces Barbelés oubliés par l'histoire.* Bordeaux: Wallada, 1994.

Sijes, B. A. *Vervolging van Zigeuners in Nederland, 1940–1945.* The Hague: Martinus Nijhoff, 1979.

Sonneman,Toby. *Shared Sorrows: A Gypsy Family Remembers the Holocaust*. Hatfield: University of Hertfordshire Press, 2002.

Thurner, E. *Nationalsozialismus und Zigeuner in Osterreich*. Vienna: Geyer, 1983. English edition, *National Socialism and Gypsies in Austria*. Tuscaloosa: University of Alabama Press, 1998.

Tyrnauer, G. "A Sinto Survivor Speaks." In *Papers from the 6th and 7th Annual Meetings of the Gypsy Lore Society*. New York: Gypsy Lore Society, 1986. [Also in *Social Education* 55, no. 2 (February 1991).]

Vexler, Y. "J'étais médecin des Tsiganes à Auschwitz." *Monde Gitan* 27 (1973): 1–10.

Wagenbaar, Aad. *Settela*. Amsterdam: Arbeiderpres, 1996.

Wippermann, W. *Das Leben in Frankfurt zur NS Zeit*. Frankfurt am Main: Kramer, 1986.

Zimmermann, M. *Rassenutopie und Genozid: Die nationalsozialistische "Lösung der Zigeunerfrage."* Hamburg: Christiansverlag, 1996.

———. *Verfolgt, vertrieben, vernichtet: Die nationalsozialistische Vernichtung gegen Sinti und Roma*. Essen: Klartext, 1989.

5. History from 1945, General

Auzias, Claire, ed. *Les familles Rom d'Europe de l'Est*. Paris: ALIZE, n.d.

Braham, Mark. *The Untouchables: A Survey of the Roma People of Central and Eastern Europe*. Geneva: United Nations High Commissioner for Refugees, 1993.

Brearley, Margaret. *The Roma/Gypsies of Europe: A Persecuted People*. London: Institute for Jewish Policy Research, 1996.

Kocze, Angela. *The Roma of Central and Eastern Europe: Legal Remedies or Invisibility?* Warsaw: OSCE, 1996.

Margalit, Gilad. *Germany and Its Gypsies: A Post-Auschwitz Ordeal*. Madison: University of Wisconsin, 2002.

Pogács, István. *The Roma Café: Human Rights and the Plight of the Romani People*. London: Pluto Press, 2004.

Schenk, Michael. *Rassismus gegen Sinti und Roma*. Frankfurt am Main: Lang, 1994.

Svanberg, Frederik Folkeryd-Ingvar. *Gypsies (Roma) in the Post-Totalitarian States*. Stockholm: Olof Palme International Center, 1995.

6. History, 1945–1990: Eastern Europe under Communism

Destroying Ethnic Identity: The Gypsies of Bulgaria. New York: Human Rights Watch, 1991.

McCagg, W. "Gypsy Policy in Socialist Hungary and Czechoslovakia, 1945–1989." *Nationalities Papers* 19, no. 3 (1991): 313–36.

Silverman, Carol. "Bulgarian Gypsies: Adaptation in a Socialist Context." *Nomadic Peoples*, nos. 21–22 (December 1986): 51–62.

Sus, Jaroslav. *Cikánská otázka v CSSR*. Prague: N.p., 1961.

7. History, 1990–2006: Eastern Europe after Communism

Barany, Zoltan. *The East European Gypsies: Regime Change, Marginality and Ethnopolitics*. Cambridge: Cambridge University Press, 2002.

Guy, Will, ed. *Between Past and Future: The Roma of Central and Eastern Europe*. Hatfield: University of Hertfordshire Press, 2001.

Johansen, Jahn Otto. *Folket som ingen vil ha*. Oslo: Aschehoug, 1995.

Mihok, Brigitte. *Vergleichende Studie zur Situation der Minderheiten in Ungarn und Rumänien (1989–1996) unter besonderer Berücksichtigung der Roma*. Frankfurt am Main: Lang, 1999.

IV. POLITICS

1. General

Acton, Thomas. *Gypsy Politics and Social Change: The Development of Ethnic Ideology and Pressure Politics among British Gypsies from Victorian Reformism to Romany Nationalism*. London: Routledge & Kegan Paul, 1974.

Adams, Barbara, Judith Okely, David Morgan, and David Smith. *Gypsies and Government Policy in England: A Study of the Travellers' Way of Life in Relation to the Policies and Practices of Central and Local Government*. London: Heinemann, 1975.

Bauer, Rudolph, Josef Bura, and Klaus Lang, eds. *Sinti in der Bundesrepublik: Beiträge zur sozialen Lage einer verfolgten Minderheit*. Bremen: Universität Bremen, 1984.

Fienborg, Gunoula, et al. *Die Roma: Hoffen auf ein Leben ohne Angst*. Hamburg: Rowohlt, 1992.

Geigges, Anita, and Bernhard W. Wette. *Zigeuner Heute: Verfolgung und Diskriminierung in der BRD*. Bornheim-Merten: Lamuv, 1979.

Klímová-Alexander, Ilona. *The Romani Voice in World Politics: The United Nations and Non-State Actors*. Burlington, Vt.: Ashgate, 2005.

Liégeois, Jean-Pierre, et al. *Gypsies and Travellers: Socio-Cultural Data, Socio-Political Data*. Strasbourg, France: Council for Cultural Co-operation, 1987.

Matras, Yaron, and Ian Hancock. *Rezoluciji e EUROM-eske*. Hamburg: Rom Cinti Union, 1990.

Soest, George von. *Zigeuner zwischen Verfolgung und Integration: Geschichte, Lebensbedingungen und Eingliederungsversuche*. Weinheim: Beltz, 1979.

Zürcher-Berther, Maria-Luisa. *Nomades parmi les sédentaires: Problèmes posés par un autre mode de vie*. Basel: Helbing Lichtenhahn, 1989.

2. Civil Rights Movements

Acton, Thomas. "IV Congresso Mondiale dei Rom." *Lacio Drom* 26, no. 5 (1990).

Gesellschaft für bedrohte Völker. *III. Welt-Roma-Kongress 1981. Pogrom*, nos. 80–81 (1981).

Liégeois, Jean-Pierre. *Mutation tsigane*. Brussels: Complexe, 1976.

Lopez, Sergio Rodriguez, ed. *I Congreso Gitano de la Unión Europea*. Barcelona: Instituto Romanó, 1995.

Puxon, Grattan. "The First World Romani Congress." *Race Today* (June 1971).

Rishi W. R., ed. "IV World Romani Congress." *Roma*, nos. 33–34 (July 1990/January 1991). [Special issue.]

3. Law

American Journal of Comparative Law 46, no. 2 (Spring 1997). [Special issue on Gypsy law.]

Bergen-Schuijt, Ada van. "Buitenlandse zigeuners en de Nederlandse wetgeving . . . in 1977 en 1978." In *Zigeuners in Nederland*, ed. Peter Hovens and Rob Dahler, 229–56. Nijmegen: Instituut voor Culturele en Sociale Antropologie, 1988.

Danbakli, Marielle, ed. *On Gypsies: Texts Issued by International Institutions*. Toulouse, France: CRDP, 1994. [Also in Bulgarian and French.]

Doering, Hans-Joachim. *Die Zigeuner in Nationalsozialistischen Staat*. Hamburg: Kriminalistik, 1964.

Helsinki Foundation for Human Rights. *Try to Use It, It Is Your Right! A Practical Guide on the Rights of Romanies*. Warsaw: Helsinki Foundation, 1997.

Johnson, Chris, and Marc Willers, eds. *Gypsy and Traveller Law*. London: Legal Action Group, 2004.

Mroz, Lech. "Gypsies and the Law." *Ethnologia Polona* 3 (1977): 175–83.

Wolfrum, Rüdiger. "The Legal Status of Sinti and Roma in Europe: A Case Study Concerning the Shortcomings of the Protection of Minorities." *Annuaire Européen / European Yearbook* 33 (1986): 75–91.

V. ECONOMY

Chignard, Louis. "Le système économique du voyage." *Hommes et Migrations* (June/July 1995).

VI. SOCIETY

1. Anthropology/Ethnology

Belton, Brian. *Gypsy and Traveller Ethnicity: The Social Generation of an Ethnic Phenomena*. London: Routledge, 2005.

———. *Questioning Gypsy Identity: Ethnic Narratives in Britain and America*. Walnut Creek, Calif.: AltaMira, 2005.

Clébert, Jean-Paul. *The Gypsies*, trans. Charles Duff. London: Vista, 1963.

Csaba, Pronai. *Ciganykutatas es Kulturalis Antropologia*. Budapest: Kaposvar, 1995.

Dollé, Marie-Paul. *Les Tsiganes Manouches*. Sand: Dollé, 1980.

Giere, Jacqueline, ed. *Die gesellschaftiche Konstruktion des Zigeuners*. Frankfurt am Main: Campus, 1996.

Graham-Yooll, Andrew. "In Search of Saint George." *London* (August/September 1990): 754–88.

Gresham, David, et al. "Origins and Divergence of the Roma." *American Journal of Humam Genetics*, no. 96 (2001): 1314–31.

Okely, Judith. "Some Political Consequences of Theories of Gypsy Ethnicity." In *After Writing Culture*, ed. Alison James et al. ASA Monographs 34. London: Routledge, 1997.

Rao, Aparna, ed. *The Other Nomads*. Cologne: Böhlau, 1987.

The State of Ambiguity: Studies of Gypsy Refugees. Anthropological Research Series. Gothenburg: University of Gothenburg, n.d.

Stewart, Michael. *The Time of the Gypsies*. Oxford: Westview, 1997.

Williams, Patrick. *Mariage tsigane*. Paris: L'Harmattan, 1984.

———. *Nous, on n'en parle pas: Les vivants et les morts chez les Manouches*. Paris: Maison des Sciences de l'Homme, 1993.

———, ed. *Tsiganes: Identité, évolution*. Paris: Syros Alternatives, 1989. [Papers of the 1986 Etudes Tsiganes conference.]

2. Children

Réger, Zita. "Bilingual Gypsy Children in Hungary: Explorations in 'Natural' Second-Language Acquisition at an Early Age." *International Jour-*

nal of the Sociology of Language 19 (1979). [Special issue on Romani sociolinguistics.]

3. Education

Acton, Thomas, and Morgan Delphinis. *Languages, Blacks and Gypsies*. London: Whiting and Burch, 2000.

Acton, Thomas, and Donald Kenrick. "From Summer Voluntary Schemes to European Community Bureaucracy: The Development of Special Provisions for Traveller Education in the United Kingdom since 1967." *European Journal of Intercultural Studies* 1, no. 3 (March 1991): 47–62.

Binns, Dennis. "History and Growth of Traveller Education." *British Journal of Educational Studies* 38, no. 3 (August 1990): 251–58.

Conway, Laura. *On the Status of Romani Education in the Czech Republic*. Prague: HOST, 1996. [Also available in Czech.]

Csapo, Marg. "Concerns Related to the Education of Romany Students in Hungary, Austria and Finland." *Comparative Education* 18, no. 2 (1982): 205–19.

Derrington, C., and S. Klendall. *Gypsy Traveller Students in Secondary Schools*. Stoke on Trent, UK: Trentham, 2004.

Donzello, G., and Mirella Karpati. *Un ragazzo zingaro nella mia classe*. Rome: ANICIA, 1998.

Dowber, Hilary. *Travellers and School: Travellers in Lewisham Talk of Their Experiences of School*. London: Lewisham Bridge, 1991.

Gustafsson, Inga. *Studies of a Minority Group's Efforts to Preserve Its Cultural Autonomy*. Stockholm: IMFO-GROUP, Institute of Education, University of Stockholm, 1973.

Hermann Dyba. "The Gandhi School: Seeds of Cross-cultural Conflict." *JGLS* (5th series) 8, no. 2 (August 1998): 133–44.

Krause, Mareile. *Verfolgung durch Erziehung: Eine Untersuchung über die jahrhundertelange Kontinuität staatlicher Erziehungsmassnahmen im Dienste der Vernichtung kultureller Identität von Roma und Sinti*. Hamburg: An der Lottbek, 1989.

Kyuchukov, Hristo. *Romany Children and Their Preparation for Literacy: A Case Study*. Tilburg, The Netherlands: Tilburg University Press, 1995.

Lee, Ken, and W. Warren. "Alternative Education: Lessons from Gypsy Thought and Practice." *British Journal of Educational Studies* (1991).

Liégeois, Jean-Pierre. *School Provision for Ethnic Minorities: The Gypsy Paradigm*. Hatfield, University of Hertfordshire Press, 1998. [An updated version of *School Provision for Gypsy and Traveller Children: A Synthesis*

Report, Luxembourg: Commission of the European Communities, 1987.]
French edition, *Minorité et scolarité: Le parcours tsigane*. Toulouse: CRDP, 1998.

Reiss, Christopher. *Education of Travelling Children*. London: Macmillan, 1975.

Sangan, Jean-Claude. *Une école chez les Tziganes*. Paris: Droit et Liberté, 1974.

School Provision for Gypsy and Traveller Children. Brussels: European Communities, 1996. [Not a new edition of Liégeois's study of the same title.]

Stigmata: Segregated Schooling of Roma in Central and Eastern Europe. Budapest: European Roma Rights Center, 2004.

4. Religion

Ridholls, Joe. *Travelling Home: God's Work of Revival among Gypsy Folk*. Basingstoke, UK: Marshall Pickering, 1986.

Trigg, E. B. *Gypsy Demons and Divinities: The Magical and Supernatural Practices of Gypsies*. Secaucus, N.J.: Citadel, 1973.

5. Sociology

Falque, Edith. *Voyage et tradition: Approche Sociologique d'un sous-groupe Tsigane—Les Manouches*. Paris: Payot, 1971.

Lucassen, Leo. "Under the Cloak of Begging? Gypsy Occupations in Western Europe in the 19th and 20th Century." *Ethnologia Europaea* 23 (1993): 75–94.

Marushiakova, Elena, and Veselin Popov. "The Gypsy Court as a Concept of Consensus among Service Nomads in the Northern Black Sea Area." In *Shifts and Drifts in Nomad-Sedentary Relations*, ed. S. Leder and B. Streck. Wiesbaden: Reichert, 2005.

Rakelmann, Georgia. *Interethnik: Beziehungen von Zigeunern und Nichtzigeunern*. Münster: Literatur, 1988.

Reyniers, Alain. "Le rôle de la parenté dans la formation d'une communauté manouche." *Études Tsiganes* (n.s.) 6, no. 2 (1994).

San Roman., Teresa. *La diferencia inquietante: Viejas y nuevas estrategias culturales de los Gitanos*. Madrid: Siglo XXI, 1997.

Tauber, E. "Studi sugli Zingari: Recensione critica secondo la teoria di Gerarchia di Dumont." *Lacio Drom* 30, no. 5 (September–October 1994): 4–55.

Ward-Jackson, C. H., and Denis E. Harvey. *The English Gypsy Caravan: Its Origins, Builders, Technology, and Conservation*. 2nd ed. Newton Abbot, UK: David & Charles, 1986.

Weyrauch, Walter. *Gypsy Law: Romani Legal Traditions and Culture.* Berkeley: University of California Press, 2001.

Wippermann, Wolfgang. *Wie die Zigeuner: Antisemitismus und Antiziganismus im Vergleich.* Berlin: Elefantenpress, 1997.

6. Women

Equipo de Estudios de Presencia Gitana. *Mujeres gitanas ante el futuro.* Madrid: Presencia Gitana, 1990.

Chaderat, Sarge. *Variations gitanes.* Paris: Flammarion, 1992.

Cipollini, Roberta, Franca Faccioli, and Tamar Pitch. "Gypsy Girls in an Italian Juvenile Court." In *Growing Up Good: Policing the Behaviour of Girls in Europe,* ed. Maureen Cain. London: Sage, 1989.

Fernández, Maria Dolores, and Carmen Bajo. *Jornadas sobre la situación de la mujer gitana.* Granada, Spain: Asociación de Mujeres Gitanas de Granada "Romi," 1990.

Mossa. *La Gitane et son destin: Témoignages d'une jeune Gitane sur la condition féminine et l'évolution du monde gitan.* Textes présentés par Bernard Leblon. Paris: L'Harmattan, 1992.

Okely, Judith. "Gypsy Women: Models in Conflict." In *Perceiving Women,* ed. Shirley Ardener. London: Malaby, 1975.

Wang, Kirsten, ed. *Mujeres gitanas ante el futuro.* Madrid: Editorial Presencia Gitana, 1990.

VII. CULTURAL

1. Dance

Balázs, Gusztáv. *A nagyecsedi oláh cigányok tánchagyománya* (The Dance Tradition of Vlach Gypsies in Nagyecsed). Studies in Roma (Gypsy) Ethnography, vol. 3. Budapest: Magyar Néprajzi Társaság, 1995.

Dunin, Elsie. "Dance Change in the Context of the Gypsy St. George's Day, Skopje, Yugoslavia, 1967–1977." In *Papers from the 4th and 5th Annual Meetings of the Gypsy Lore Society,* ed. Joanne Grumet, 110–20. New York: Gypsy Lore Society, 1982.

2. Folk Arts

Dummett, Michael. "The Gypsies and the Tarot." In *Traveller Education* 17 (1982). [Reprinted from M. Dummett, *The Game of Tarot from Ferrara to Salt Lake City* (London: Duckworth, 1980).]

3. Linguistics

a. General

Bakker, Peter, ed. *What Is the Romami Language?* Hatfield: University of Hertfordshire Press, 2000.

Bakker, Peter, and Marcel Cortiade, eds. *In the Margin of Romani: Gypsy Languages in Contact.* Amsterdam: Institute for General Linguistics, 1991.

Bakker, Peter, and Yaron Matras. *Bibliography of Modern Romani Linguistics.* Amsterdam: Benjamin, 2003.

Bakker, Peter, and Hein Van der Voort. "Para-Romani Languages: An Overview and Some Speculations on Their Genesis." In Bakker and Cortiade, *In the Margin of Romani*, 16–44.

Boretzky, Norbert. "Sind Zigeunersprachen Kreols?" In *Akten des 1. Essener Kolloqiums über Kreolsprachen und Sprachkontakte (1985)*, ed. Boretzky, Enninger, and Stolz, 43–70. Bochum: Brockmeyer, 1985.

Boretzky, Norbert, and Birgit Igla. "Romani Mixed Dialects." In *Mixed Languages*, ed. Peter Bakker and Maarten Mous. Amsterdam: Amsterdam University. 1998.

Halwachs, Dieter, and Florian Menz, eds. *Die sprache der Roma.* Klagenfurt, Austria: Drava, 1999.

Hancock, Ian. "The Development of Romani Linguistics." In *Languages and Cultures: Studies in Honor of Edgar C. Polomé*, ed. M. Jazayery and W. Winter. Amsterdam: Mouton, 1988.

——. *Handbook of Vlax Romani.* Columbus, Ohio: Slavica, 1995.

Hübschmannová, Milena. "Bilingualism among the Slovak Rom." *International Journal of the Sociology of Language* 19 (1979).

Kenrick, D. S. "Report on the Warsaw Linguistics Conference." *Roma* 33/34 (2000): 180.

Kirk, John, and Donall O Baoill. *Travellers and Their Language.* Belfast: Queens University Press, 2002.

Matras, Yaron. *Romani: A Linguistic Introduction.* Cambridge: Cambridge University Press, 2002.

——, ed. *Romani in Contact.* Amsterdam: Benjamin, 1995.

——. *Untersuchungen zur Grammatik und Diskurs des Romanes.* Wiesbaden: Harrassowitz, 1994.

Matras, Yaron, et al., eds. *The Typology and Dialectology of Romani.* Amsterdam: Benjamin, 1997.

McLane, M. "The Calo of Guadix." *Anthropological Linguistics* 19 (1997).

Schrammel, Barbara, et al. *General and Applied Romani Linguistics: Proceedings from the 6th International Conference (Graz 2002).* Munich: Lincom, 2005.

b. Grammars and Description

Acton, Thomas, and Donald Kenrick, eds. *Romani rokkeripen to-divvus* (The Contemporary English Romani Dialect). London: Romanestan, 1984. [In English.]

Bakker, Peter. "Basque Romani: A Prelimary Grammatical Sketch of a Mixed Language." In *The Margin of Romani: Gypsy Languages in Contact*, ed. Peter Bakker and Marcel Cortiade, 56–90. Amsterdam: Institute for General Linguistics, 1991.

Boretzky, Norbert. *Burgudži*. Wiesbaden: Harrassowitz, 1993.

——. *Die Vlach-Dialekte des Romani*. Wiesbaden: Harassowitz, 2003.

——. *Romani: Grammatik des Kalderaš-Dialekts mit Texten und Glossar*. Wiesbaden: Harrassowitz, 1994.

Boretzky, Norbert, and Birgit Igla. *Kommentierter Dialektatlas des Romani*. Wiesbaden: Harrowitz, 2004.

Borrow, George. *Romano lavo lil* (Romani Wordbook). London: Murray, 1874. [Many reprints since.]

Cech, Petra, and Mozes Heinschink. *Sepečides (Romani)*. Munich: Lincom Europa, 1996.

Daroczi, Jószef Choli, and Feyer Levente. *Zhanes Romanes?* (Do You Know Romani?). Budapest: Cigany Nielkónvy, 1988.

Endt, Enno. *Een taal van horen zeggen: Bargoens*. Amsterdam: Scheltema Holkema, 1969.

Friedman, Victor. "Problems in the Codification of a Standard Romani Literary Language." In *Papers from the 4th and 5th Annual Meetings of the Gypsy Lore Society*, ed. Joanne Grumet. New York: Gypsy Lore Society, 1985.

Gjerdman, Olof, and Erik Ljungberg. *The Language of the Swedish Coppersmith Gipsy Johan Dimitri Taikon*. Uppsala, Sweden: Lundequist, 1963.

Haarmann, Harald. *Spracherhaltung und Sprachwechsel als Probleme der interlingualen Soziolinguistik: Studien zur Gruppenmehrsprachigkeit der Zigeuner in der Sowjetunion*. Hamburg: Busje, 1980.

Halwachs, Dieter. *Amaro vakeripe Roman hi: Unsere Sprache ist Roman*. Klagenfurt, Austria: Drava, 1998.

Halwachs, Dieter, et al. *Roman: The Dialect of the Burgenland Romanies*. Munich: Lincom Europa, 1997.

Hancock, Ian. *Grammar and Dictionary of the Hungarian-Slovak Romani Language*. Manchaca, Texas: Romany Union, 1990.

——. *Handbook of Vlax-Romani*. Columbus, Ohio: Slavica, 1985.

Holzinger, Daniel. *Romanes (Sinti)*. Munich: Lincom Europa, 1997.

Igla, Birgit. *Das Romani von Ajia Varvara*. Wiesbaden: Harrassowitz, 1996.

Iversen, R. *Secret Languages in Norway*. 2 parts. Oslo: Norske Videnskapsakademi, 1944, 1945.

Kepeski, Krume, and Šaip Jusuf. *Romani Gramatika / Romska Gramatika*. Skopje: Naša Kniga, 1980. [Bilingual, Macedonian and Romani.]

Kochanowski, Vanja [Jan]. *Gypsy Studies*. 2 vols. New Delhi: International Academy of Indian Culture, 1963.

——. *Parlons Romanes*. Bordeaux: Wallada, 1995.

Lee, Ronald. *Learn Romani*. Hatfield: Univerity of Hertfordshire Press, 2005.

Macalister, R. A. S. *The Secret Languages of Ireland*. Cambridge: Cambridge University Press, 1937.

Pobozniak, T. *Grammar of the Lovari Dialect*. Krakow: Polska Akademia Nauk, 1964.

Russell, A. "Scoto-Romani and Tinkers' Cant." *JGLS* (n.s.) 8 (1914–1915): 11–79.

Sampson, John. *The Dialect of the Gypsies in Wales, Being the Older Form of British Romani Preserved in the Speech of the Clan of Abram Wood*. Reprint. Oxford: Clarendon, 1992.

Sarau, Gheorghe. *Limba Romani*. Bucharest: Ministerul Invatamantului, 1992.

Smart, Bath Charles, and Henry Thomas Crofton. *The Dialect of the English Gypsies*. London: Asher, 1875.

Soravia, Giulio. *Dialetti degli Zingari italiani*. Pisa: Pacini, 1977.

Tcherenkow [Cherenkov], Lev, and Mozes Heinschink. *Kalderaš*. Munich: Lincom Europa, 1996.

Toro, Rita Paola. "Il gergo dei Camminanti." *Lacio Drom* 27, nos. 3–4 (1991).

Ventzel, T. V. *The Gypsy Language*, trans. S. S. Gitman. Moscow: Nauka, 1983. [Also available in German as *Die Zigeunersprache* (Leipzig: Enzyklopädie, 1980).]

Windolph, Wolfram. *Nerother Jenisch*. Wiesbaden: Harrassowitz, 1998.

c. Dictionaries

Barthelemy, André. *Dictionnaire du Tsigane Kalderash*. Paris: Barthelemy, n.d.

Boretzky, Norbert, and Birgit Igla. *Wörterbuch Romani–Deutsch–Englisch für den südosteuropäischen Raum*. Wiesbaden: Harrassowitz, 1994.

Calvet, Georges. *Dictionnaire Tsigane–Français, dialecte Kalderash*. Paris: L'Asiathèque, 1993.

Demeter, R. S., and P. S. Demeter. *Gypsy–Russian and Russian–Gypsy Dictionary (Kalderash dialect)*. Moscow: Russky Yazyk, 1990.

Hübschmannová, Milena, et al. *Romsko–Česky a Česko–Romsky kapesní slovník* (Czech–Romani Pocket Dictionary). Prague: Státní Pedagogické Nakladatelství, 1991.

Koivisto, Viljo. *Romano–Finitiko–Angliko laavesko liin* (Romani–Finnish–English Dictionary). Helsinki: Painatuskeskus, 1994.

Messing, G. *A Greek–Romany Glossary.* Columbus: Slavica, 1988.

Mija, J. *Romcina do vrecka.* Košice: 1995. [Slovak–Romani Pocket Dictionary.]

Rishi, W. R. *Multilingual Romani Dictionary.* Chandigarh, India: Roma, 1974.

——. *Romani–Punjabi–English Dictionary.* Patiala, India: Punjabi University, Language Department, 1981.

Rostas-Farkas, György, and Ervin Karsai. *Cigány–Magyar, Magyar–Cigány szótár* (Romani–Hungarian, Hungarian–Romani Dictionary). Budapest: Kossuth Könyvkiadó, 1991.

Sarau, Gheorghe. *Mic dictionar Rom–Roman* (Small Romani–Romanian Dictionary). Bucharest: Kriterion, 1992.

Uhlik, Rade. *Srpskohrvatsko–Romsko–Engleski rječnik* (Serbocroat–Romani–English Dictionary). Sarajevo: Svjetlost, 1983.

Valtone, Pertti. *Suomen Mustalaiskielen etymologinen sanakirja* (Romani–Finnish–English Etymological Dictionary). Helsinki: Suomalaisen Kirjallisuuden Seura, 1972.

Wolf, S. *Grosses Wörterbuch der Zigeunersprache.* Hamburg: Helmut Buske, 1993.

4. Literary Criticism

Ackovic, D. "Le journal *Romano Lil.*" *Études Tsiganes* (n.s.) 7, no. 1 (1995): 123–32.

Binns, Dennis. *Children's Literature and the Role of the Gypsy.* Manchester, UK: Travellers' School, 1984.

Courthiade [Cortiade], M. "Jeunes poètes roms de Cassove." In *Études Tsiganes* 28, no. 3 (1982), and 29, no. 1 (1983).

Djurić, Rajko. *Die Literatur der Roma und Sinti.* Berlin: Parabolis, 2002.

——. *Roma und Sinti im Spiegel der deutschen Literatur.* Frankfurt am Main: Lang, 1995.

Djurić, Rajko, and Marcel Courthiade [Cortiade]. *Les Rroms dans les Belles-lettres européennes.* Paris: L'Harmattan, 2004.

Eder, Beate. *Geboren bin ich vor Jahrtausenden.* Klagenfurt, Austria: N.p., 1993.

Gröndahl, Satu. "Stay Silent No Longer: Romanies, Travellers and Literature." In *Nordic Voices,* ed. Jenny Fossum Grön. Oslo: ABM-Utvikling, 2005.

Kenrick, Donald, and Gillian Taylor. "The Portrayal of the Gypsy in English Schoolbooks." *Internazionale Schulbuchforschung* 6, no. 1: 38–47.

Kommers, Jean. *Kinderroof of Zigeunerroof* (Stealing Children or Stealing Gypsies). Amsterdam: Van Arkel, 1993.

Leblon, Bernard. *Les Gitans dans la littérature espagnole.* Toulouse: France-Ibérie Recherche, 1982.

Lundgren, Gunilla. *Svarta Rosor, Kale Ruze: Romsk litteratur, kultur och historia* (Black Roses). Stockholm: Tranan, 2003.

Niemandt, Hans-Dieter. *Die Zigeunerin in den Romanischen Literaturen.* Frankfurt am Main: Lang, 1992.

Panebianco, Candido. *Lorca e i Gitani.* Rome: Bulzoni, 1984.

Reyniers A. "Quelques élements pour une histoire des médias Tsiganes." *Études Tsiganes* (n.s.) 7, no. 1 (1995): 141–46.

5. Literature

a. Anthologies

Balić, Sait, et al. *Jaga / Vatre* (Fires). Leskovac: Napredak, 1984. [Poetry in Romani and Serbian.]

Bari, Karoly, ed. *Le vešeski dej* (The Forest Mother). Budapest: Országos Közmövelödési Központ, 1990. [Folktales and poetry in Romani and Hungarian.]

———, ed. *Tüzpiros Kígyócska / Feurige kleine rote Schlange.* Debrecen: Gondolat, 1985. [Romani and German editions.]

Coughlan, Tim. *Now Shoon the Romano Gillie.* Cardiff: University of Wales Press, 2001.

Daróczi, Jószef Choli. "Mashkar Le Shiba Dukhades." *Roma Módszertani Kiadványok* 1 (1994).

———. *Romane Poetongi Antologia.* Budapest: Ariadne Foundation, 1995. [Poetry in Romani, English, and Hungarian.]

Djuric, Rajko. *Märchen und Lieder europäischer Sinti und Roma.* Frankfurt am Main: Lang, 1997.

Hancock, Ian, et al. *The Roads of the Roma: A PEN Anthology of Gypsy Writers.* Hatfield: University of Hertfordshire Press, 1998.

Rostás-Farkas, György, ed. *Maladyipe / Találkozás* (Meeting). Budapest: Müfordítások, 1993. [Poetry in Romani and Hungarian.]

b. Autobiography and Biography

Boswell, Silvester Gordon. *The Book of Boswell: Autobiography of a Gypsy,* ed. John Seymour. London: Gollancz, 1970.

Caldaras, Hans. *I betraktarens ögon* (In the Eye of the Beholder). Stockholm: Prisma, 2002.

Cannon, Jon, and the Travellers of Thistlebrook. *Travellers: An Introduction.* London: Emergency Exit Arts/Interchange Books, 1989.

Delaunay, C. *Django Reinhardt.* London: Cassell, 1961.

Dybing, Svein, and Terje Gammelsrud. *Raya*. Oslo: Tiden, 1983.

Franz, Philomena. *Zwischen Liebe und Hass: Ein Zigeunerleben*. Freiburg: Herder, 1985.

Joyce, Nan. *Traveller: An Autobiography*, ed. Anna Farmar. Dublin: Gill Macmillan, 1985.

Lacková, Elena. *Narodila jsem pod st'asnou hvezdou* (I Was Born under a Lucky Star). Prague: Triada, 1997. English edition, *A False Dawn: My Life as a Gypsy Woman in Slovakia*. Hatfield: University of Hertfordshire Press, 2000.

Lazell, David. *Gypsy from the Forest*. Pen y Bont, Wales: Bryn Tyrion, 1997. [Biography of Gypsy Smith.]

Loveridge, Guy. *Biography of Bramwell "Romany" Evens*. Huddersfield, UK: Loveridge, 1995.

Lowe, Richard, and William Shaw, eds. *Travellers: Voices of the New Age Nomads*. London: Fourth Estate, 1993.

Lundgren, Gunilla, and Aljosha Taikon. *Aljosha: Zigernarhövdingens pojke* (Aljosha: The Gypsy Chief's Son). Stockholm: Bonnier Carlsen, 1998. English/Romani translation, *Alyosha: From Coppersmith to Nurse*. Hatfield: University of Hertfordshire Press, 2004.

Lundgren, Gunilla, and Sofia Taikon. *Sofia Z-4515*. Stockholm: Tranan/Podium, 2005. [Romani and Swedish.]

Maximoff, Matéo. *Ce monde qui n'est pas le mien*. Paris: Concordia, 1992.

——. *Dites-le avec des pleurs*. Paris: Concordia, 1990.

——. *Routes sans Roulottes*. Paris: Maximoff, 1993.

Nikolic, Miso. *Und dann Zogen wir weiter*. Klagenfurt, Austria: Drava, 1997.

Nussbaumer-Moser, Jeanette. *Die Kellerkinder von Nivagl*. Basel, Switzerland: Friedrich-Reinhardt, 1995.

Reeve, Dominic. *No Place Like Home*. London: Phoenix House, 1960.

——. *Smoke in the Lanes*. London: Constable, 1958.

Rosenberg, Otto. *Das Brennglas*. Berlin: Eichhorn,1998. English translation, *A Gypsy in Auschwitz*. London: London House, 1999.

Sampson, Anthony. *The Scholar Gypsy*. London: Murray, 1997.

Sandford, Jeremy. *Gypsies*. London: Secker and Warburg, 1973.

Sebková, Hana, Edita Zlanayová, and Milena Hübschmannová. *Fragments tsiganes: Comme en haut, ainsi en bas*. Paris: Lierre Coudrier, 1991.

Skogholt, P., and K. Lilleholt. *En for hverandre: Sigøynere Milos Karol og Frans Josef forteller* (One for All: Gypsies Milos Karol and Frans Josef Relate). Oslo: Gyldendal, 1978.

Slee, Yvonne. *Torn Away Forever*. Queensland, Australia: Amber Press, 2005.

Stancu, Z. *The Gypsy Tribe*, trans. R. MacGregor-Hastie [from the original Romanian title *Satra*]. London: Abelard, 1973.

Stockin, Jimmy, et al. *On the Cobbles: The Life of a Bare-Knuckled Gypsy Warrior*. Edinburgh: Mainstream, 2001.

Stojka, C. *Reisende auf dieser Welt*. Vienna: Picus, 1992.

———. *Wir leben im Verborgenen*. Vienna: Picus, 1988.

Tremlett, G. *The David Essex Story*. London, 1974.

Tschawo, Latscho. *Die Befreiung des Latscho Tschawo: Ein Sinto-Leben in Deutschland*. Bornheim-Merten: Lamuv, 1984.

Wang, Kirsten. *The Story of Tío Carlos*. Frankfurt am Main: Lang, 1996.

Whyte, Betsy. *The Yellow on the Broom: The Early Days of a Traveller Woman*. Edinburgh: Chambers, 1979.

Williamson, Duncan. *The Horsieman: Memories of a Traveller, 1928–1958*. Edinburgh: Canongate, 1994.

Winter, Walter. *Winter Time*. Hatfield: University of Hertforshire Press, 1999. [Translation of *WinterZeit* (Hamburg: Ergebnisse, 1999).]

Winterstein, Adolf Boko. *Zigeunerleben: Der Lebensbericht des Sinti-Musikers und Geigenbauers*, ed. Erich Renner. Frankfurt am Main: Büchergilde Gutenberg, 1988.

Wood, Manfri Frederick. *In the Life of a Romany Gypsy*. London: Routledge & Kegan Paul, 1979.

Yates, Dora. *My Gypsy Days: Recollections of a Romany Rawnie*. London: Phoenix House, 1953.

Yoors, Jan. *Crossing: A Journal of Survival and Resistance in World War II*. New York: Simon & Schuster, 1971.

———. *The Heroic Present. Life among the Gypsies*. New York: Monacelli Press, 2004.

c. Folktales and Folk Poetry

Berki, János. *Tales of János Berki Told in Gypsy and Hungarian*, ed. Veronika Görög-Karády. Budapest: MTA Néprajzi Kutató Csoport, 1985.

Copoiu, Petre. *Povesti Tiganesti / Romane Paramica* (Romany Tales), ed. Gheorghe Sarau. Bucharest: Kriterion, 1996.

Court, Artelia. *Puck of the Droms: The Lives and Literature of the Irish Tinkers*. Berkeley: University of California Press, 1986.

Demeter, R. *Obrazoy folklora cygan-kelderarej* (Collection of Kalderash Gypsy Folklore). Moscow: Nauka, 1981.

Druts, Yefim, and Aleksei Gessler. *Russian Gypsy Tales*. Edinburgh: Canongate, n.d.

Fennesz-Juhasz, C., et al. *Die schlaue Romni*. Klagenfurt, Austria: Drava, 2003.

Gjerde, Lars, and Knut Kristiansen. *The Orange of Love, and Other Stories: The Rom-Gypsy Language in Norway*. Oslo: Scandinavian University Press, 1994.

Grabócz, Gábor, and Katalin Kovalcsik. *A Mesemondo Rostás Mihály/Mihály Rostás: A Gypsy Story Teller.* Budapest: MTA Néprajzi Kutató Csoport, 1988.

Groome, Thomas E. *Gypsy Folk-tales*. London: Hurst Blackett, 1899.

Hübschmannová, Milena, ed. *Romske pohádky* (Romany Tales). Prague: Odeon, 1973.

Jagendorf, M. A., and C. H. Tillhagen. *The Gypsies' Fiddle, and Other Gypsy Tales*. New York: Vanguard, 1956.

MacColl, Ewan, and Peggy Seeger. *Till Doomsday in the Afternoon: The Folklore of a Family of Scots Travellers, the Stewarts of Blairgowrie*. Manchester, UK: Manchester University Press, 1986.

———. *Travellers' Songs from England and Scotland*. London: Routledge & Kegan Paul, 1977.

Mode, Heinz, and Milena Hübschmannová, eds. *Zigeunermärchen aus Aller Welt*. Leipzig: Insel, 1983.

Nagy, Olga. *A havasi sátaro: David Gyula mesel* (The Ten [Fingers] of a Gypsy of the Alps: Tales Told by Gyula David). Budapest: MTA Néprajzi Kutató Csoport, 1988.

Osella, Carla. *Racconti zingari*. Turin: N.p., 1978.

Sampson, John, ed. *Gypsy Folk Tales*. London: Robinson, 1984. [Reprint from 1933 edition.]

Serra, Maria João Pavao. *Filhos da Estrada e do vento: Contos e fotografias de Ciganos Portugueses*. Lisbon: Assirio Alvim, 1986.

Solet, Bertrand. *Mille ans de contes tsiganes*. Toulouse: Editions Milan, 1998.

Szegö, László. *Cigány bölcsödal* (Gypsy Lullaby). Budapest: Móra, 1980. [Songs in Romani with Hungarian translations.]

———. *Csikóink kényesek*. Budapest: Europa Könyvkiadó, 1977. [Songs in Romani with Hungarian translations.]

Taikon, Katerina, ed. *Zigenerdikter* (Gypsy Poems). Stockholm: FIB's Lyrikklubb, 1964.

Tillhagen, Carl Herman. *Taikon erzählt Zigeunermärchen*. Zurich: Artemis, 1948. [Translation of *Taikon Berättar* (Stockholm: Norstedt, 1946).]

Tong, Diane. *Gypsy Folk Tales*. San Diego: Harcourt Brace Jovanovich, 1989.

Valet, Joseph. *Contes manouches*. 2 vols. Paris: Études Tsiganes, 1988, 1991.

Williamson, Duncan. *May the Devil Walk behind Ye*. Edinburgh: Canongate, 1989.

Williamson, Duncan, and Linda Williamson. *A Thorn in the King's Foot: Folktales of the Scottish Travelling People*. Harmondsworth, UK: Penguin, 1987.

d. Literature in Romani

Balić, Sait, ed. *Po Tito* (About Tito). Niš, Yugoslavia: Prosveta, 1980. [Essays.]

Cioaba, Luminita. *The Rain Merchant*. Sibiu, Romania: Neo Drom, 1997. [Poems in Romani with translation.]

Dimić, Trifun, trans. *Nevo Sovlahardo Cidipe* (New Testament). Novi Sad, Yugoslavia: Dobri Vest, 1990.

Djurić, Rajko. *A i U / A thaj U.* Belgrade: Narodna Knjiga, 1982. [Poems in Romani and Serbian.]

———. *Bi kheresko, bi limoresko / Bez doma, bez groba* (Without a House, without a Grave). Belgrade: Nolit, 1979. [Poems in Romani and Serbian. Also in French as *Sans maison, sans tombe* (Paris: L'Harmattan, 1990).]

———. *Les disciples d'Héphaistos*. Troyes: Librairie Bleue, 1994. [Selected poems in French.]

———. *Zigeunerische Elegien*. Hamburg: Helmut Buske, 1989. [Poems in German and Romani.]

Gjunler, Abdula. *Bizoagor / Eindeloos* (Without End). Oss, the Netherlands: Gjunler, 1995. [Bilingual, Dutch and Romani.]

Jusuf, Šaip, trans. *Amen sam e Titoske, O Tito si amaro* (We Are Tito's, Tito Is Ours). Ljubljana: Univerzum, 1978. [Translation from Slovenian original *Mi smo Titoske, Tito je naš* (Ljubljana: Partizanska knjiga, 1995).]

Kalinino, Valdemaro. *Romane Sune / Romani Dreams*. Vitebsk, Belarus: Ablasnaya Drukarna, 2005.

Manuš, Leksa [Aleksis Belugins], trans. "Ramayana." *Roma*, nos. 31–32 (July 1989/January 1990).

Maximoff, Matéo, trans. *E Nevi Vastia* (New Testament). Paris: Societé Biblique Française, 1995.

Metkov, Sulyo, trans. *Neevo Zakon* (New Testament). Sofia: Adventist, 1995.

Olah, Vlado. *Khamori luludi / Slunecnice* (Sunflower). Prague: MMM, 1996. [Bilingual, Romani and Czech.]

Papusza [pseud., Bronislawa Weiss]. *Piesni Papuszy* (Songs of Papusza). Wroclaw, Poland: Ossolinski, 1956. [In Romani and Polish.]

Wlislocky, H., ed. *Volksdichtungen der siebenbürgischen und südungarischen Zigeuner*. Vienna: Graeser, 1890. [In Romani and German.]

e. Literature in Other Languages by Gypsy Authors

Baltzar, Veijo. *Brännande väg* (Burning Road). Borgå, Finland: Norstedt, 1969. [Translated from the Finnish original *Polttava tie*.]

Binns, Dennis, ed. *Gavvered All Around*. Manchester, UK: Manchester Travellers' Education Service, 1987. [Anthology of poetry.]

Doughty, Louise. *Fires in the Dark*. London: Simon & Schuster, 2003. [Novel.]

Jayat, Sandra. *Nomad Moons*, trans. Ruth Partington. St. Albans, UK: Brentham Press, 1995. [A selection from *Lunes nomades* and other collections.]

Kieffer, Jane. *Cette sauvage lumière*. Paris: Gallimard, 1961.

Lakatos, Menyhért. *Bitterer Rauch*. Stuttgart: Deutsche Verlags-Anstalt, 1979. [German translation of *Füstös Képek* (Budapest: Könyvkiadó).]

Maximoff, Matéo. *Condamné à survivre*. Paris: Concordia, 1984.

———. *La poupée de mamaliga*. Paris: Concordia, 1986.

———. *Prix de la liberté*. Paris: Concordia, 1981.

———. *Savina*. Bordeaux: Wallada, 1986.

———. *Septième fille*. New ed. Paris: Concordia. 1982.

———. *The Ursitory*, trans. Brian Vesey-FitzGerald [from the French original *Les Ursitory*]. London: Chapman Hall, 1949.

———. *Vinguerka*. Paris: Concordia, 1987.

Smith, Charles [Charlie]. *Not All Wagons and Lanes*. Aveley, UK: Smith, 1996. [Poems.]

———. *The Spirit of the Flame: Poems by Charlie Smith*. Manchester, UK: Travellers Education Service, 1990.

Spinelli, Santino, ed. *Baxtalo drom / Felice cammino* (Happy Road). Lanciano, Italy: Them Romano/Tracce, 1995. [Anthology in Italian and Romani.]

f. The Holocaust in Fiction

De Lint, Charles. *Mulengro: A Romany Novel*. New York: Ace Fantasy, 1985.

Florence, Ronald. *The Gypsy Man*. New York: Villard, 1985.

Hackl, Erich. *Abschied von Sidonie*. Zurich: Diogenes, 1989/1991. [Based on a true story.]

Kanfer, Stefan. *The Eighth Sin*. New York: Random House, 1978.

Kosinski, Jerzy. *The Painted Bird*. New York: Bantam, 1965.

Ramati, Alexander. *And the Violins Stopped Playing*. New York: Franklin Watts, 1986.

Sagan, Francoise. *Painting in Blood*, trans. Anthea Bell. Henley-on-Thames, UK: Aidan Ellis, 1988.

Stancu, Zaharia. *The Gypsy Tribe*, trans. Roy MacGregor-Hastie. London: Abelard-Schuman, 1973.

g. The Gypsy in World Literature

Cervantes, Miguel de. *The Gipsy Maid: Six Exemplary Novels*, trans. Harriet de Onis. Woodbury, N.Y.: Barron's Educational, 1961.

Christie, Agatha. *Endless Night*. New York: Pocket Books, 1969.

Eliot, George. "The Spanish Gypsy." In *The Writings of George Eliot*, vol. 18. Boston: Houghton Mifflin, 1908.

Freud, Jonathan. *Uppbrott.* Stockholm: Carlssons, 1993.

Garcia Lorca, Federico. "Gypsy Ballads," trans. Langston Hughes. *Beloit Poetry Journal,* chapbook no. 1 (Fall 1951). Beloit, Wis.: Beloit College, 1951.

Hugo, Victor. *Notre-Dame de Paris.* Various editions. [In English as *The Hunchback of Notre Dame.*]

Kaygili, Osman. *Cingeneler.* Istanbul: Etiman Kitabevi, 1939.

Lawrence, D. H. *The Virgin and the Gipsy.* 1925. Reprint, New York: Bantam, 1970.

Márquez, Gabriel Garcia. *One Hundred Years of Solitude.* New York: Avon, 1971.

Mérimée, Prosper. *Carmen, and Other Stories,* trans. Nicholas Jotcham. Oxford: Oxford University Press, 1989.

Podgorets, Vidoe. *Beloto Tsiganche* (The White Gypsy). Skopje: Naša Kniga, 1988.

Pushkin, Alexandr. "Gypsies." In *The Bronze Horseman: Selected Poems of Alexander Pushkin,* trans. D. M. Thomas. New York: Viking, 1982. [Also in *Selected Verse,* trans. John Fennell (London: Penguin, 1994; reprint, Bristol: Classical Press, 1991) and *Selected Works in Two Volumes,* vol. 1: *Poetry* (Moscow: Progress Publishers, n.d.).]

Scott, Walter. *Guy Mannering; or, The Astrologer.* 1815. Reprint, London: Soho, 1987.

h. Music and Theater

Acton, Thomas, Rosy Denaro, and Bernard Hurley, eds. *The Romano Drom Song Book.* Oxford: Romanestan, 1971.

Barrios, Manuel. *Gitanos, Moriscos y cante flamenco.* Seville: Rodríguez Castillejo, 1989.

Beissinger, Margaret. *The Art of the Lautar: The Epic Tradition of Romania.* New York: Garland, 1991.

Billard, Francois, and Alain Antonietto. *Django Reinhardt: Un géant sur son nuage.* Paris: Lieu Commun, 1993.

Blau, Dick, et al. *Bright Balkan Morning: Romani Lives and the Power of Music in Greek Macedonia.* Middletown, Conn.: Wesleyan University, 2002.

Bobri, Vladimir. "Gypsies and Gypsy Choruses of Old Russia." *JGLS* (3rd series) 40, nos. 3–4 (1961): 112–20.

Brune, John. "Songs of the Travelling People." In *Folksongs of Britain and Ireland,* ed. Peter Kennedy. London: Cassell, 1975.

Cartwright, Garth. *Princes among Men: Journeys with Gypsy Musicians.* London: Serpent's Tail, 2005.

Davanellos, Nick. "Les Tsiganes et la musique démotique grècque." In *Tsiganes: Identité, Evolution*, ed. Patrick Williams. Paris: Études Tsiganes, 1989.

Davidová, Eva, and Jan Zizka. *Folk Music of the Sedentary Gypsies of Czechoslovakia*. Budapest: Magyar Tudományos Akadémia, 1991.

Equipo, Alfredo. *El flamenco y los Gitanos: Una aproximación cultural*. Granada: Universidad de Granada, 1978.

Haederli, Freddy. *Django Reinhardt: Discography*. Geneva: Haederli, 1996.

Hemetek, Ursula, et al. *Romane Gila: Lieder und Tänze der Roma in Österreich*. Vienna: Institut für Volksmusikforschung an der Hochschule für Musik und darstellende Kunst, 1992.

Kertesz-Wilkinson, Irén. "The Fair Is Ahead of Me." Budapest: Magyar Tudományos Akadémia, 1997. [A Hungarian Vlach Gypsy song.]

Kovalcsik, Katalin, ed. *Ernö Király's Collection of Gypsy Folk Music from Voivodina*. Budapest: Magyar Tudományos Akadémia, 1992.

———. *Vlach Gypsy Folk Songs in Slovakia*. Budapest: Magyar Tudományos Akadémia, 1985.

Lajtha, Lázsló. *Instrumental Music from Western Hungary: From the Repertoire of an Urban Gipsy Band*, ed. Bálint Sárosi, trans. Katalin Halácsy. Budapest: Akadémiai Kiadó, 1988.

Leblon, Bernard. *El cante flamenco, entre las músicas gitanas y las tradiciones andaluzas*. Madrid: Cinterco, 1991.

———. *Gypsies and Flamenco*. Hatfield: University of Hertfordshire Press, 1995. [Also available in French, German, and Italian.]

———. *Musiques tsiganes et flamenco*. Paris: L'Harmattan, 1990.

Lefranc, Pierre. *Le cante jondo*. Nice: Faculté des Lettres, 1998.

Lemon A. "Roma (Gypsies) in the USSR and the Moscow Teatr Romen." *Nationalities Papers* 14, no. 3 (1991). Also in Diane Tong, *Gypsies: An Interdisciplinary Reader*. New York: Garland, 1998.

Liszt, Franz. *The Gypsy in Music*. 1926. [English translation of *A cziganyokrol és a cigány zenérol Magyarországon* (Pest: Heckenast, 1861).]

Mitchell, T. *Flamenco Deep Song*. New Haven, Conn.: Yale University Press, 1995.

Rasmussen, Ljerka Vidic. "Gypsy Music in Yugoslavia: Inside the Popular Culture Tradition." *JGLS* (5th series) 1, no. 2 (August 1991).

Sárosi, Bálint. *Cigányzene*. Budapest: Gondolat, 1971. [German translation, Zurich: Musikbuch, 1977. English translation, *Gypsy Music* (Budapest: Corvina, 1978).]

———. "Gypsy Music." In *The New Grove Dictionary of Music and Musicians*, ed. S. Sadie. London: Macmillan, 1980.

Seton, Marie. "The Evolution of the Gypsy Theatre in the USSR." *JGLS* (3rd series) 14: 66–72.

Stanley, Denise, and Rosy Burke. *The Romano Drom Song Book*. Warley, UK: Romanestan, 1986.

Uffreduzzi, Marcella, ed. *Canti zigani*. 2nd ed. Genoa: Sabatelli Editore, 1973.

Van de Port, Mattijs. *Gypsies, Wars and Other Instances of the Wild*. Amsterdam: Amsterdam University Press, 1998.

Williams, Patrick. *Django*. Paris: Parentheses, 1998.

i. Painting

Balázs, János. *A Hungarian Gipsy Artist*. Budapest: Corvina, 1977.

Dzurko, Ruda. *Ich bin wieder Mensch geworden*, ed. Milena Hübschmannová. Leipzig: Stiepenheuer, 1990.

Stojka, Karl. *Ein Kind in Birkenau*. Vienna: Stojka, 1990. English edition, *The Story of Karl Stojka: A Childhood in Birkenau*, ed. Sybil Milton. Washington, D.C.: U.S. Holocaust Memorial Council, 1992.

j. Photography and Film

Carret, Marie-Jose, and Claude Carret. *Les anges du destin*. Trézélan, Paris: Filigranes, 1996.

Iordanova, Dina, ed. "Cinematic Images of Romanies." *Framework* 44, no. 2 (Fall 2003).

Koudelka, Josef. *Gypsies*. London: Hale, 1975.

Kuznetsova, Ljalja. *Gypsies: Free Spirits of the Open Steppe*. London: Thames & Hudson, 1998.

Szuhay, Péter, and Antónia Barati. *Pictures of the History of the Gipsies in Hungary in the 20th Century*. Budapest: Néprajzi Museum, 1993.

VIII. HEALTH

Smith, Tracy. "Romani (Gypsy) Women and Mainstream Health Services." *European Journal of Women's Studies* 4, no. 2 (May 1997): 183–96.

Takman, John. *The Gypsies in Sweden: A Socio-Medical Study*. Stockholm: LiberFörlag, 1976.

IX. LISTING BY COUNTRY

1. Albania

Hasluck, Margaret. "The Gypsies of Albania." *JGLS* (3rd series) 17, nos. 2–4 (1938).

No Record of the Case: Roma in Albania. Budapest: European Roma Rights Center, 1997.

2. Angola

Lopes Da Costa, Elisa Maria. *El Pueblo Gitano y el espacio de de la colonalizacion portuguesa.* In *Deportaciones de Gitanos*, ed. A. Alfaro et al. Madrid: Presencia Gitana, 1999.

3. Austria

Cahn, Claude. *Divide and Deport: Roma and Sinti in Austria.* Budapest: European Roma Rights Center, 1996.

Fennesz-Juhasz, Christiane, et al. "Sprache und Musik der Osterreichischen Roma und Sinti." *Grazer Linguistische Studien* 46 (1996): 61–110.

Mayerhofer, Claudia. *Dorfzigeuner.* 2nd ed. Vienna: Picus, 1988.

———. "Gli ungrika Roma del Burgenland." *Lacio Drom* 21, no. 6 (1985).

4. Belgium

Cuijle, J. H. *Zigeuners in Vlaanderen.* Antwerp: Ecclesiola, n.d.

Mijs, J. "Een bank vooruit: Onderwijs in Belgie." *Drom* 10, no. 4 (December 1995).

Tambour L. "Roma in Belgium: Past and Present." *Roma* 3, no. 1 (January 1977).

5. Bosnia

The Non-Constituents: Rights Deprivation of Roma in Post-Genocide Bosnia and Herzegovina. Budapest: ERRC, 2004.

6. Bulgaria

Children of Bulgaria: Police Violence and Arbitrary Confinement. New York: Human Rights Watch, 1996.

"Increasing Violence against Roma in Bulgaria." New York: Human Rights Watch, 1994. [Pamphlet.]

Marushiakova, Elena, and Veselin Popov. *Tsiganite v Balgaria.* Sofia: Klub 90, 1993. English translation, *Gypsies (Roma) in Bulgaria.* Frankfurt am Main: Lang, 1997.

"Police Violence against Gypsies." New York: Human Rights Watch, 1993. [Pamphlet.]

Silverman, Carol. "Bulgarian Gypsies: Adaptation in a Socialist Context." *Nomadic Peoples* 21–22 (1986): 51–62.

Tomova, Ilona. *The Gypsies in the Transition Period.* Sofia: International Center for Minority Studies, 1995.

7. Croatia

Hrvatic, N., ed. "Education and Upbringing of Romany Children in Croatia." *Romano Akharipe* [Special edition, 1994].

8. Cyprus

Kenrick, Donald, and Gillian Taylor. "Gypsies of Cyprus." *Roma* 24 (January 1986).

Mene, Asik. "Interview." Translation from *Kibris* in *Drom* 10, no. 4 (1995).

9. Czech Republic

Conway, Laura. *Report on the Status of Romani Education in the Czech Republic.* Prague: HOST, 1996.

Roma in the Czech Republic: Foreigners in Their Own Land. New York: Human Rights Watch, 1996.

10. Czechoslovakia

Davidová, Eva. "The Gypsies in Czechoslovakia." *JGLS* (3rd series) 69, nos. 3–4 (1970): 84–97, and 70, nos. 1–2 (1971): 39–54.

———. *Romano drom: Cesty romu, 1945–1990.* Olomouc, Czech Republic: Centre de Recherches Tsiganes, 2004.

Guy, Will. "Ways of Looking at Roma: The Case of Czechoslovakia." In *Gypsies: An Interdisciplinary Reader*, ed. Diane Tong. New York: Garland, 1998.

Hübschmannová, M. "Birth of Romani Literature in Czechoslovakia." *Cahiers de Littérature Orale* 30 (1991): 91–98.

Kostelancik, David. "The Gypsies of Czechoslovakia: Political and Ideological Considerations in the Development of Policy." *Studies in Comparative Communism* 22, no. 4 (1989): 307–21.

Struggling for Ethnic Identity: Czechoslovakia's Endangered Gypsies. New York: Human Rights Watch, 1992.

Ulc, Otto. "Communist National Minority Policy: The Case of the Gypsies in Czechoslovakia." *Soviet Studies* 20, no. 4 (April 1969): 421–43.

———. "Integration of the Gypsies in Czechoslovakia." *Ethnic Groups* 9, no. 2 (1991): 107–17.

11. Denmark

Albert, Jorn. *Sigøjnere er et folk* (Gypsies Are a People). Copenhagen: Forum, 1983.

Anderson, K. *Sigøjnere*. Copenhagen: Beta Bog Munksgaard, 1971.

Bartels, E., and B. Brun. *Gypsies in Denmark*. Copenhagen: Munksgaard, 1943.

Enevig, Anders. *Sigøjnere i Danmark*. Copenhagen: Fremad, 1969.

———. *Tatere og rejsende* (Nomads and Travelers). Copenhagen: Fremad, 1965.

12. Egypt

Nabil, Hannah. *Die Ghajar*. Munich: Trickster, 1993.

13. England

Birtill, Angie. *Rights for Travellers*. London: Irish Women's Centre, 1995.

Daley, Ian, and Jo Henderson. *Static: Life on the Site*. Castleford, UK: Yorkshire Art Circus, 1998.

Dodds, Norman N. *Gypsies, Didikois and Other Travellers*. London: Johnson, 1966.

Kenrick, Donald, and Sian Blakewell. *On the Verge: The Gypsies of England*. Hatfield: University of Hertfordshire Press, 1995.

Kenrick, Donald and Colin Clark. *Moving On: The Gypsies and Travellers of Britain*. New expanded ed. Hatfield: University of Hertfordshire Press, 1998.

Mayall, David. *English Gypsies and State Policies.* Hatfield: University of Hertfordshire, 1996.

——. *Gypsies-Travellers in Nineteenth-Century Society.* Cambridge: Cambridge University Press, 1988.

——. *Gypsy Identities, 1500–2000.* London: Routledge, 2004.

Morris, Rachel, and Luke Clements. *At What Cost? The Economics of Gypsy and Traveller Encampments.* Bristol: Policy Press, 2002.

Sibley, David. *Outsiders in Urban Society.* Oxford: Blackwell, 1981.

Smith, Len. *Romany Nevi-Wesh: New Forest Gypsies.* Lyndhurst, Hants, UK: 2004.

14. Finland

Grönfors, Martti. *Blood Feuding among Finnish Gypsies.* Helsinki: University of Helsinki, Department of Sociology, 1977.

15. France

Always Somewhere Else: Anti-Gypsyism in France. Budapest: European Roma Rights Center, 2005.

Filhol, Emanuel. *L'histoire et l'oubli: L'internement des Tsiganes en France.* Paris: L'Harmattan, 2004.

Vaux de Foletier, François de. *Les bohémiens en France au 19e siècle.* Paris: Lattès, 1981.

——. *Les Tsiganes dans l'Ancienne France.* Paris: Connaissance du Monde, 1981.

16. Germany

Geigges, A., and B. Wette. *Zigeuner heute.* Bornheim-Merten: Lamuv, 1979.

Hohmann, Joachim, ed. *Sinti und Roma in Deutschland.* Frankfurt am Main: Lang, 1995.

——. *Verfolgte ohne Heimat: Geschichte der Zigeuner in Deutschland.* Frankfurt am Main: Lang, 1990.

Lucassen, Leo. *Die Zigeuner: Die Geschichte eines polizeilichen Ordnungsbegriff in Deutschland, 1700–1945.* Vienna: Böhlau, 1996.

Margalit, Gilad. *Antigypsyism in the Political Culture of the Federal Republic of Germany.* Jerusalem: Hebrew University Vidal Sassoon Center for the Study of Antisemitism, 1996.

——. *Germany and Its Gypsies: A Post-Auschwitz Ordeal.* Madison: University of Wisconsin Press, 2002.

Martins-Heuss, Kirsten. *Zur mythischen Figur des Zigeuners in der Deutschen Zigeunerforschung.* Frankfurt am Main: Hagg Herchen, 1983.

Opfermann, Ulrich. *Dass sie den Zigeuner-Habit ablegen.* Frankfurt am Main: Lang, 1996.

Rinser, Luise. *Wer Wirft den Stein? Zigeuner sein in Deutschland: Eine Anklage.* Stuttgart: Weitbrecht, 1985.

Schenk, Michael. *Rassismus gegen Sinti und Roma.* Frankfurt am Main: Lang, 1994.

Tebbutt, Susan, ed. *Gypsies in German-Speaking Society and Literature.* New York: Berghahn Books, 1998.

17. Greece

Bereris, Petros. "Information File: Greece." *Interface* 13 (February 1994).

18. Hungary

Hajdu, Mihaly. "Gypsies, 1980." *Hungarian Digest* 6 (1980): 28–34.

Karsai, Lászó. *A Cigánykérdés Magyarorzágon, 1919–1945: Út a Cigány holocausthoz.* Budapest: Scientia Hungariae, 1992.

Kovats, Andras. *Roma Migration.* Budapest: Hungarian Academy of Sciences, 2002.

Kovats, Martin. "The Roma and Minority Self-Governments in Hungary." *Immigrants and Minorities* 15, no. 1 (March 1996).

Pradka, Peter. *Self-Government in Hungary: The Gypsy/Romani Experience.* Princeton, N.J.: PER, 1998.

Rights Denied: The Roma of Hungary. New York: Human Rights Watch, 1966.

Struggling for Ethnic Identity: The Gypsies of Hungary. New York: Human Rights Watch, 1993.

Szabó, György. *Die Roma in Ungarn.* Frankfurt am Main: Lang, 1991.

Szuhay, Peter, et al., eds. *Pictures of the Gypsies in Hungary in the 20th Century.* Budapest: Hofer Tamas, 1993.

Vekerdi, Jozef. "The Gypsies and the Gypsy Problem in Hungary." *Hungarian Studies Review* 15, no. 2 (1988): 13–26.

Wagner, Francis. "The Gypsy Problem in Postwar Hungary." *Hungarian Studies Review* 14, no. 1 (1987): 33–43.

19. India

Iwatani, Ayako. "Strategic Otherness: A Case of the Vaghri in South India." *Journal of the Japanese Association for South Asian Studies* 14 (2002).

Olsson, Torvald, and Lukas Werth. *Sjakalerna: Nomader i kastsamhällets utkant* (Nomads on the Edge of the Caste System). Stockholm: Fjärde Varlden, 1990.

Robertson, Miriam. *Snake Charmers.* Jaipur, India: Illustrated Book Publishers, 1998.

20. Iran

Sistani, Afhshar, and Iraj Rozaneh. *Gypsies: A Research into Lives of Gypsies in Iran and the World.* Tehran: N.p., 1998.

21. Ireland

Gmelch, George. *The Irish Tinkers: The Urbanization of an Itinerant People.* Menlo Park, Calif.: Cummings, 1977.

McCann, May, et al., eds. *Irish Travellers: Culture and Ethnicity.* Belfast: Institute of Irish Studies, 1994. [Papers from a conference in 1991.]

Paris, C., et al. *A Review of Policies Affecting Travellers in Northern Ireland.* Coleraine: Magee College, 1995.

22. Israel

Williams, Allan, ed. *The Dom of Jerusalem.* Larnaca, Cyprus: Dom Research Center, 2001.

23. Italy

Luciani, A. "Zingari a Roma nel 1700." *Lacio Drom* 31, no. 6. (November–December 1995).

Martelli, Vladimyr. "Gli Zingari a Roma dal 1525 al 1680." *Lacio Drom* 32, nos. 4–5 (August–October 1996).

Piasere, Leonardo, ed. *Italia Romaní.* Rome: CISU di Colamartini Enzo, 1996.

Viaggio, Giorgio. *Storia degli Zingari in Italia.* Rome: Anicia, 1998.

24. Luxembourg

Reynier, Alain. "Luxembourg: The Presence of an Invisible Population." *Interface* 29 (February 1998).

25. Macedonia, Republic of

Barany, Zoltan. "The Romas in Macedonia." *Ethnic and Racial Studies* 18 (1995): 515–31.

Friedman, Victor. "Language Policy and Language Behaviour in Macedonia: Background and Current Events." In *Language Contact, Language Conflict*, ed. Eran Fraenkel and Christina Kremer, 73–99. New York: Peter Lang, 1993.

A Pleasant Fiction: The Human Rights Situation of Roma in Macedonia. Budapest: European Roma Rights Center, 1998.

26. Middle East

Berland, Joseph C., and Aparna Rao. *Customary Strangers: New Perspectives on Peripatetic Peoples in the Middle East, Africa, and Asia.* Westport, Conn.: Praeger, 2004.

27. Netherlands

Buis, Hans. "Zigeuners gezien? Haal dan de was binnen!" In *Vreemd Gespuis*, ed. Jan Dubleman et al. Amsterdam: Anne Frank Stichting, 1987.

Cottaar, Annemarie. *Kooplui, Kermisklanten en ander Woonwagenbewoners.* Amsterdam: Het Spinhuis, 1996.

Cottaar, Annemarie, et al. "The Image of Holland: Caravan Dwellers and Other Minorities in Dutch Society." *Immigrants and Minorities* 2, no. 1 (March 1992).

———. *Mensen van de Reis, Woonwagenbewoners en Zigeuners in Nederland, 1868–1995.* Zwolle: Waanders, 1995.

Hovens, P., and R. Dahler, eds. *Zigeuners in Nederland.* Nijmegen: Instituut voor Culturele en Sociale Antropologie, 1988.

Lucassen, Leo. *En Men noemde hen Zigeuners.* Amsterdam: Stichting IISG/SDU, 1990.

Schaap, Dick, and Wim Bont. *Het volk van Koka Petalo.* Amsterdam: ABC, 1965.

Tanja, Jaap. "Een zeldzaam volk geneegen om te dwaalen." In *Vreemd Gespuis*, ed. Jan Dubleman et al. Amsterdam: Anne Frank Stichting, 1987.

Van Kappen, O. *Geschiedenis der Zigeuner in Nederland.* Assen: Van Gorcum, 1965.

Willems, Wim, and Leo Lucassen. "A Silent War: Foreign Gypsies and Dutch Government Policy, 1969–1989." *Immigrants and Minorities* 2, no. 1 (March 1992).

28. Norway

Flekstad, K. *Omstreifere og sigøynere* (Travelers and Gypsies). Oslo: Aschehoug, 1949.

Hanisch, Ted. *Om sigøynersporsmalet* (On the Gypsy Question). Oslo: Institutt for Samfunnsforskning, 1973.

Midboe, O. *Eilert Sundt og fantesaken* (Eilert Sundt and the Nomad Question). Oslo: Universitets Forlaget, 1968.

Schlüter, Ragnhild. *De Reisende* (The Travelers). Oslo: Gyldendal, 1993.

29. Poland

Ficowski, Jerzy. *Cyganie na polskich drogach*. Krakow: Wydawnictwo Literackie, 1985.

———. *Gypsies in Poland: History and Customs*. Warsaw: Interpress, 1991. [Also in German and Polish.]

———. *Wieviel Trauer und Wege*. Frankfurt am Main: Lang, 1992.

Postolle, Angele. "Who Are the Romanian Roma Living in Poland?" *CPRSI Newsletter* 3, no. 3 (1997).

30. Portugal

Coelho, Francis Adolpho. *Os Ciganos de Portugal: Com um estudo sobre o calao*. Lisbon: Imprensa Nacional, 1892. [Reprinted 1995.]

Nunes, Olimpio. *O Povo Cigano*. Porto: Livrari Apostolado da Imprensa, 1981.

Serra, Maria João Pavao. *Filhos da Estrada e do vento: Contos e fotografias de Ciganos Portugueses*. Lisbon: Assirio Alvim, 1986.

31. Romania

Achim, V. *Tigani in istoreia Romaniei*. Bucharest: Editura Enciclopedica, 1998.

Beck, Sam. "Ethnicity, Class and Public Policy: Tiganii/Gypsies in Socialist Romania." In *Papers from the Vth Congress of Southeastern European Studies, Belgrade*, ed. K. K. Shangriladze and E. Townsend, 19–38. Columbus, Ohio: Slavica, 1984.

———. "The Origins of Gypsy Slavery in Romania." *Dialectical Anthropology*, no. 14 (April 1989): 53–61.

———. "Racism and the Formation of a Romani Ethnic Leader (Gheorghe Nicolae)." In *Perilous States*, ed. G. Marcus, 165–91. Chicago: University of Chicago Press, 1993.

Block, Martin. *Die materielle Kultur der rumänischen Zigeuner.* Revised by J. Hohmann. Frankfurt am Main: Lang, 1991.

Destroying Ethnic Identity: The Persecution of the Gypsies in Romania. New York: Human Rights Watch, 1991.

Lynch Law: Violence against Roma in Romania. New York: Human Rights Watch, 1994.

Nicolae, Gheorghe. "Origin of Roma's Slavery in the Romanian Principalities." *Roma* 7, no. 1 (1983): 12–27.

Potra, George. *Contributiuni la istoricul tiganilor din Romania.* Bucharest: Fundatia Regele Carol I., 1939.

Remmel, Franz. *Die Roma Rumäniens.* Vienna: Picus, 1993.

Sudden Rage at Dawn: Violence against Roma in Romania. Budapest: European Roma Rights Center, 1996.

32. Russia

Demeter, Nadezhda, et al. *Istoriya tsigan.* Voronezh: Russian Academy of Science, 2000.

Gilsenbach, Reimar. "Roma in Russia: A Community Divided." *Transition: Open Media Research Institute Reports* 1, no. 4 (March 1995).

Gilsenbach, Reimar, with Ljalja Kuznetsova [photographs]. *Russlands Zigeuner.* Berlin: BasisDruck, 1994.

In Search of Happy Gypsies. Budapest: ERRC, 2005.

Lemon, Alaina. *Between Two Fires: Gypsy Performance and Romani Memory from Pushkin to Postsocialism.* Durham, N.C.: Duke University Press, 2000.

33. Scotland

Braid, Donald. *Scottish Traveller Tales: Lives Shaped through Stories.* Jackson: University of Mississippi Press, 2002.

Duncan, Tom. *Neighbours' Views on Official Sites for Travelling People.* Glasgow: Planning Exchange, 1996.

Gentleman, Hugh, and Susan Smith. *Scotland's Travelling People: Problems and Solutions.* Edinburgh: HMSO, 1971.

MacRitchie, D. *Scottish Gypsies under the Stewarts.* Edinburgh: Douglas, 1894.

Neat, Timothy. *The Summer-Walkers: Travelling People and Pearl Fishers of the Highlands of Scotland.* Edinburgh: Canongate, 1996.

Secretary of State's Advisory Committee. *Scotland's Travelling People: Reports.* Edinburgh: HMSO, 1974–1998.

34. Serbia

Vojvodanska Muzej. *Etnoloska Grada o Romima: Ciganima i Vojvodine* (Gypsies: Roms in Vojvodina). Novi Sad: Vojvodanska Muzej, 1979.

35. Slovakia

Horváthová, Emilia. *Cigáni na Slovensku* (Gypsies in Slovakia). Bratislava: Vydavatelstvo Slovenskej Akadémie Vied, 1964.

Mann, Arne. *Neznami Romovia* (The Unknown Romany Story). Bratislava: Ister Science Press, 1992.

Time of the Skinheads: Denial and Exclusion of Roma in Slovakia. Budapest: European Roma Rights Center, 1997.

Vasecka, Michal, et al., eds. *Cacipen pal o Roma* (Truth about the Roma): *A Global Report on Roma in Slovakia*. Bratislava: Institute of Public Affairs, 2003.

36. Slovenia

Strukelj, Paula. *Romi na Slovenskem*. Ljubljana: Cankarjeva Zalozba, 1980.

37. Spain

Alfáro, Antonio. *The Great Gypsy Round-Up*. Madrid: Presencia Gitana, 1993. [Also available in French, Italian, Romanian, and Spanish.]

Calvo Buezas, Tomás. *España racista? Voces payas sobre los Gitanos*. Barcelona: Anthropos, 1990.

Chamon-Deutsch, Lou. *The Spanish Gypsy: The History of a European Obsession*. University Park: Pennsylvania State University Press, 2004.

Garcia, José Manuel Fresno. "La situation sociale de la communauté gitane d'Espagne." *Ethnies* 8, no. 15 (1993).

Leblon, Bernard. *Les Gitans d'Espagne: Prix de la différence*. Paris: Presses Universitaires de France, 1985. Spanish translation, *Los gitanos de España: El precio y el valor de la diferencia*. Barcelona: Gedisa, 1987.

Leon-Ignacio. *Los Quinquis*. Barcelona: Ediciones 29, 1974.

Lopez de Menses, A. *La immigración gitana en España en el siglo XV*. Madrid: Martinez Ferrandi Archivero, 1968.

Luna, José Carlos de. *Gitanos de la Bética*. Madrid: EPESA, 1951.

McLane, M. *Los Gitanos españoles*. Madrid: Castellote, 1977.

———. *Proud Outcasts*. Cabin John, Md.: Carderock, 1987.

Ramírez Heredia, Juan de Dios. *En Defensa de los Míos: Qué sabe Vd. de los Gitanos?* Barcelona: Ediciones 29, 1985.
———. *Nosotros los Gitanos.* Barcelona: Ediciones 29, 1972.
———. *Vida gitana.* Barcelona: Ediciones 29, 1985.
Sanchez Ortega, Maria Helena. *Dieser wichtige Zweig der Landesordnung: Zur Geschichte der Zigeuner in Spanien.* Frankfurt am Main: Lang, 1998.
———. *La Inquisición y los Gitanos.* Madrid: Taurus, 1988.
Wang, Kirsten, ed. *Mujeras gitanas ante el futuro.* Madrid: Presencia Gitana, 1990.
Yoors, Jan. *The Gypsies of Spain.* New York: Macmillan, 1974.

38. Sweden

Heymowski, A. *Swedish Travellers and Their Ancestry.* Uppsala: Almquist Wiksell, 1969.
Marta, C. *A Group of Lovara Gypsies Settle Down in Sweden.* Stockholm: MFO-Gruppen. 1979.
Taikon, Katerina. *Förlat att vi stör* (Excuse the Disturbance). Stockholm: N.p., 1970.
Tillhagen, Carl-Hermann. *Zigenarna i Sverige.* Stockholm: Natur Kultur, 1965.
Trankell, A. *Kvarteret Flisan* (The Flisan District). Stockholm: Nordstedt Soner, 1973.

39. Switzerland

Thodé-Studer, Sylvia. *Les Tsiganes suisses: La marche vers la reconnaissance.* Lausanne: Réalités Sociales, 1987.

40. Turkey

Rooker, Marcia. "Field Report from Turkey." *Roma Rights* (Spring 1997): 33–35.

41. Ukraine

The Misery of Law: The Rights of Roma in the Transcarpathian Region of Ukraine. Budapest: European Roma Rights Center, 1997.

42. United Kingdom

Acton, Thomas, and David Gallant. *Romanichal Gypsies*. Hove, UK: Wayland, 1997.
Hawes, Derek, and Barbara Perez. *The Gypsy and the State*. 2nd ed. Bristol: Policy Press, 1996.
Ministry of Housing and Local Government. *Gypsies and Other Travellers*. London: HMSO, 1967.
Okely, Judith. *The Traveller-Gypsies*. Cambridge: Cambridge University Press, 1983.
Vesey-Fitzgerald, Brian. *The Gypsies of Britain*. Newton Abbot: David & Charles, 1973.

43. United States

Gropper, C. *Gypsies in the City*. Princeton, N.J.: Darwin, 1975.
Nemeth, David. *The Gypsy-American: An Ethnographic Study*. Lewiston, Maine: Edwin Mellen, 2002.
Sutherland, Anne. *Gypsies: The Hidden Americans*. Long Grove, Ill.: Waveland, 1986.

44. Wales

Davies, J. Glyn. "Welsh Sources for Gypsy History." *JGLS* (3rd series) 9: 64–86.
Jarman, A. O. H., and Eldra Jarman. *Y Sipsiwn Cymreig*. Cardiff: University of Wales Press, 1979. Rev. English edition, *The Welsh Gypsies*. Cardiff: University of Wales Press, 1991.

45. Yugoslavia

Vukanović, Tatomir. *Romi (Tsigani) u Jugoslaviji*. Vranje, Yugoslavia: Nova Jugoslavia, 1983.

X. PRESS

The list below includes current journals of Gypsy studies and others which, although no longer published, had long runs and can be found in major libraries.

Drom, O (Dutch). No longer published.
Études Tsiganes (French). 59 Rue d'Ourcq, 75019 Paris, France.

Interface (English and French). Centre de Recherches Tsiganes; no longer published.

Journal of the Gypsy Lore Society (JGLS). There have been five series. The second is known as the New Series (n.s.). The third series was the longest, with 52 volumes. The fifth series is published in the United States (5607 Greenleaf Rd., Cheverly, MD 20785) with the new title *Romani Studies*.

Lacio Drom (Italian). Centro Studi Zingari; no longer published.

Roma (English). 3290/15-D, Chandigarh 160 015, India; publication suspended.

Romani Studies. Fifth series of the *Journal of the Gypsy Lore Society* (see above).

Romano Džaniben (Czech and Romani). Prague.

Romnews (English). Roma National Congress, Simon-von-Utrecht Str. 85, Hamburg, D-20359, Germany.

Studii Romani (bilingual, Bulgarian and English). Sofia, Bulgaria.

XI. WEBSITES

Association of Gypsies/Romani International, http://www.christusrex.org/www2/gypsies.net

European Roma and Travellers Forum, http://www.ERTF.org

European Roma Rights Center, http://www.errc.org

Gypsy Lore Society, http://www.gypsyloresociety.org

Patrin, http://www.geocities.com/~patrin/patrin.htm

Romnews Society, http://www.romnews.com

XII. DISCOGRAPHIES

A first step into the rich world of recorded Gypsy music can be made by consulting the review pages of the British magazines *Folk Roots* and *Songlines*, in addition to the book *World Music: The Rough Guide* (London: Rough Guides, 1994). Discographies have also appeared in the *Journal of the Gypsy Lore Society* and *Études Tsiganes* (1994, no. 1).

About the Author

Donald Kenrick is retired from a career as an organizer of adult education during which he pioneered basic education courses for Gypsies and training for those working with them. He was at one time honorary secretary of the UK Gypsy Council and has been an official interpreter for the Romani language at many international meetings. He has written extensively on the history, languages, and social situation of the Gypsies/Romanies.

Honors include the Premio Hidalgo and awards from the Hiroshima Foundation and Bulgarian Romani Baxt. His publications include *Gypsies under the Swastika* (1995), *Moving On: The Gypsies and Travellers of Britain* (1998), and *Gypsies: From the Ganges to the Thames* (2004).